Statman's Racing "Bibles"- Using Statistics To Increase Your Chance Of Backing A Winner

Book One – UK National Hunt

Sean Trivass AKA "The Statman"

Index

BOOK ONE – UK NATIONAL HUNT RACING ONLY

Introduction.

No-one wants to read about me, and I don't need to tell you my life story either, but a little background may at least let you know where I come from, what I know – and why the following pages may well prove well worth reading if you want to increase your chances of making a profit from the horses.

I have been involved in the sport for over 40 years now, starting on the local paper with a weekly article where I was paid the grand sum of a fiver, in the days when I had to write in block capitals with a pen and paper – and cycle to the offices to stick it through their letterbox every Sunday – and no, those weren't the good old days!

Since then I have been to college where I got a Distinction in Quantitative Studies (or Stats to you and I), and for the last 20 years or so I have been a full-time freelance racing journalist writing for all sorts – including The Independent, BetDaq, Alan Brazil Racing Club, What Really Wins, Australian Thoroughbred News, The Daily Sport, Press Association, Post Racing, Worldofsport, Timeform, and numerous others in a rich and varied career.

Like most (all?) punters, I have spent my lifetime searching for the Holy Grail – the system or the tipster who provides you with winner after winner, with all the associated dreams of wealth and happiness, but I have finally drawn the same conclusion that you should – it simply does not exist. If you are reading this thinking "Eureka" turn away now – the stats I have put together will not make you rich overnight – in fact they will undoubtedly find more losers than winners – but what they will do is narrow down the field to the likelier winners on any given racing day, if we assume past history can and does repeat itself – something nobody can ever guarantee – but what I can tell you is that this is my living – and if you stick rigidly to the rules suggested here and bet accordingly, putting in the necessary hard work to go with it – you won't go far wrong IN THE LONG TERM – overnight success belongs in fairy tales I am sorry to say.

What is this all about?

"Lies, damned lies, and statistics" is a much-used quote attributed to Mark Twain, and the truth is, anyone good with figures can make the statistics tell whatever story they want them to tell – but that is not my remit, you will be delighted to know. In my years working as the anonymous "Statman" I produced a monthly racing/betting article looking to find profitable ways to bet on horse racing in the United Kingdom and Ireland with great success – but I was never stupid enough to put them all down in one place and lose the gig – stupid, maybe, but that stupid – no.

When the publication (or my part of it) came to an end, someone suggested to me I produce a compendium – but that would have included a lot of out-of-date information and would be potentially conning the paying public, something I would never knowingly do. So, a new idea was born – how about a list of preferred statistics by racecourse, all accurate at the time of writing, and all easy to refer to on a daily basis.

For early clarity, race statistics are based over the last 20 years (1st January 2002 to the 7th September 2022 when I turned off the wifi to ensure no more updates) , sire, trainer and jockey statistics over the last 10 (1st January 2012 to the 7th September 2022) – the reason for this is simple enough, jockeys and trainers come and go as do the actual horses – but the results remain the same, so if the top weight is profitable to follow at Track A that could or even should continue – but there is no point in telling you that A P McCoy was profitable to follow at Course B when he is (sadly) long retired or that Busted was a top-sire when he passed away in 1988.

How To Make The Most Of This book.

Let me start with one sad but very simple fact – you will almost always make more money backing at Betfair SP than you will with the starting price from the bookmakers – fact. For that reason, ALL my profits and losses are declared to Betfair SP and NOT bookmaker SP as we are looking to make money, end of, and I have taken into account the standard Betfair commission of 2% (correct at the time of writing) in all of my figures.

I have listed every National Hunt racecourse in the United Kingdom in alphabetical order (there will be separate books in the long-term for Irish National Hunt, UK Flat, Irish Flat, and All-Weather to make your research that much easier) – you simply go the course or courses you are interested in on any given day and look at the stats laid out for you.

Included at each and every course you will find the following information:

Backing To Win

Top Jockeys by strike rate

Top Jockeys by profit to £1 level stake at BSP (Betfair Starting Price)

Top Trainers by strike rate

Top Trainers by profit to £1 level stake BSP (Betfair Starting Price)

Most successful trainer jockey combos

Profit or loss by backing favourites

Profit or loss by backing second favourites

Profit or Loss by backing Top-Weights in handicaps

Top Five Profitable Sires to follow

Profit or Loss by backing last time out winners

And all listed by Chase or Hurdles, non-handicaps and handicaps!

Rules:

- All profits and losses are declared to BSP (Betfair Starting Price) to a nominal £1 stake and after an assumed deduction of 2% from all winning bets (Betfair commission at the time of writing).
- Figures declared for top-weights, favourites, and second favourites assume backing all horses if there were joint top weights, Co or Joint favourites and Co or Joint second favourites
- If any sector listed by profitability has less than five results in the black (profitable), only the profitable options will be listed.
- All figures have been based on sensible numbers – a minimum or 10 to qualify – the temptation was there to "interfere" but these are statistics (facts) so 10 will be the minimum for ALL categories come what may. A smaller number would not tell an accurate story, and a larger number would have seen numerous categories left completely unpopulated.
- I saw no point over-cluttering with empty sections. If there are less than five listed, there were less than five who qualified, or if the section is missing, there were no qualifiers.
- Do note - there is a new trend of "shared" training - for example horses that were trained by John Gosden are now trained by Thady and John Gosden – I cannot make allowances for this on historical data, so you need to look for yourselves as this appears to be an ever changing fact. Other examples would include William Muir and Chris Grassic, Charlie and Mark Johnston etc – I'm afraid you will have to spot those for yourself, but the yards remain the same, so if the stats say John Gosden – you can look for horses trained by Thady and John Gosden, and so on. Admittedly this is yet to take off in the National Hunt sphere but if it does you will need to look accordingly. For example, Joe Tizzard has taken over from Colin Tizzard but the yard may well continue as it has for many years – Colin is still there but his name is no longer on the licence – and I have included his statistics as well as Joe's where applicable for that reason.
- You may note that I did NOT include "most winners" in any category – it was seriously considered, but it would be overloaded with trainers/jockeys who have been in the game the longest time with the biggest strings and thus not necessarily of any relevance.
- Bumpers have been deliberately ignored -there are simply not enough of them per track to make any data worthwhile or relevant.
- For those who think I dumped this directly from a database – I wish! Every line was painstakingly typed in by hand and although I can vouch for the accuracy of all the numbers, if there are any typos please forgive me - paying to have this edited was beyond my budget.
- Other books will follow so please look out for future publications with the plans so far including Irish jumps, All-Weather, UKs Flat (turf) and Irish Flat turf.

Gambling Harm

As I write the Gambling review is coming, and centre stage in many people's minds – but that is a discussion for elsewhere. This book is not meant to encourage anyone to gamble, and I urge you all to think twice before placing any bets to make sure you can afford your hobby. For me, racing is exciting and fun – it's not about the gambling, it's about pitting my wits against those who compile the odds – and trying to find a way to beat the bookmakers – I can do that with small **affordable** bets and suggest you do the same. Do NOT let gambling overcome you, do NOT bet more than you can afford to lose – and DO make the most of all the tools available with your bookmaker such as time outs and deposit limits if needed. Please please control your gambling (do not let it control you) and remember that help is available via the National Gambling Helpline (0808 8020 133), and online at Gamcare.org.uk with other services freely available.

How To Use This Book

I have listed all the UK courses in Alphabetical order, so on any given day:

1) Go to your publication of choice (I prefer the Racing Post www.racingpost.com) and look to see what meetings are on that day
2) Look for the course or courses mentioned and go to their pages
3) Refer to the statistics produced and look for any horses that "qualify"
4) Favourites – note the statistics are based on the Returned favourites – i.e., the horse or horses sent off favourite at the off and NOT the horses predicted favourite or at the head of the market some time before the off
5) Sires - you may need to look deeper or adjust your on-line settings to find the sires but it isn't difficult to do
6) Jockeys and trainers are clearly annotated to the right of the horse's name
7) Top-weights in handicaps – look for the word handicap in the race title – the top-weight will be horse number one though remember to look at the weight the horse carries – if horse two three etc has/have the same weight (we ignore any jockey claims) they are joint-top-weights and should all be thought of accordingly.
8) Chases or Hurdles – the word chase (or steeplechase) will appear in the race title, or the word hurdle - simple as that
9) Don't panic – I will put plenty of actual examples and screenshots on the following pages to make life as easy as possible for everyone.
10) Dutching is an option I do employ when more than one horse qualifies for the same race. This involves splitting the bet according to the odds to achieve the same profit if any of them win. There are plenty available via your search engine of choice, but I use the one at oddschecker here https://www.oddschecker.com/betting-tools/dutching-calculator
11) Enjoy – and good luck on your journey to profit, using historical data as your guide.

So How Do I Find A Bet?

That my friend, is down to you! Have you ever seen the TV programme Ready Steady Cook? Contestants bring a bag of assorted unknown goodies, and the chefs then make a delicious meal from whatever they are given. This book is the bag of ingredients, and you are the chef! Some will try to use all the ingredients, others will want to leave some parts out, the choice is yours. By definition, if you find a highly profitable jockey at a particular track that may be a sorely tempting angle – but if you see a 5% strike rate then you know in advance that you may be waiting some time before he or she fires in the next winner with your money on it. That may be fine for some, while others will look for the best strike rates where the winners are more likely to flow – though with lower profit margins. Personally (and this is me, not you talking), I find a race I like the look of first, then head off to the statistics to see what comes out in the wash. I'll give you an example below of how I work – so wish me luck – but please note, these are statistics, they are facts from the past – I cannot guarantee they will repeat themselves, but they do imply a pattern for whatever reason, and have served me well enough over the years.

Examples

I Cannot make it clear enough to everyone that how you use these statistics is entirely up to you! Everyone will have their own preferred way to bet (or not to bet), some will be looking for one horse a week, some one a day – others may fancy a 10p Lucky 15 (four horses), the choice is entirely yours. Below is an example of how they can be used, it is not definitive, and nor is there a right and a wrong – it's your money you are risking after all.

Being brave I have not cherry picked a race or meeting that worked – these are the first National Hunt meetings I could use after finishing the rest of the book – fingers crossed it works or at least gives you a positive impression of how the stats can be used to your advantage.

Newton Abbott, Wednesday 16th September 2022.

The first thing I do (and it is a choice) is look for any statistics from the list that catch my eye as worthy of a second glance. In **Chases** at Newton Abbot they would include:

Jockey Sam Twiston-Davies 48.72% strike rate non-handicaps
Jockey Jonathan Burke 40% strike rage handicaps
Jockey Daryl Jacob 43.75% strike rate and top of the list for profit non-handicaps
Trainer Paul Nicholls 45.9% strike rate non-handicaps
Trainer Joe Tizzard 50% strike rate handicaps
Paul Nicholls/Sam Twiston-Davies combo – 53.33% strike rates non-handicaps
Joe Tizzard/Brendan Powell combo 45.45% strike rate handicaps
Jeremy Scott/Nick Scholfield combo 38.84% strike rate and top of the profit table handicaps

Horses who won last time out +£55.22 in handicaps
Top weights in handicaps +£192.38

Over **hurdles** at Newton Abbot they would include:

Jockey Nico de Boinville 40% strike rate non-handicaps
Jockey William Kennedy +£258.96 non-handicaps
Trainer Olly Murphy 42.86% strike rate non-handicaps
Trainer Paul Nicholls 42.55% strike rate non-handicaps
Trainer Gail Haywood +£445.80 non-handicaps (*but a low strike rate)
Trainer Gail Haywood +£284.97 handicaps (*but a low strike rate)
Paul Nicholls/Harry Cobden combo 42.31% strike rate non-handicaps
Colin Tizzard (read Joe Tizzard)/Harry Cobden 37.50% strike rate handicaps
Jonjo O'Neill/Richie McLernon combo 33.33% strike rate handicaps
Horses who won last time out £56.36 handicaps
Sire - Mahler +£266.73 non-handicaps

Those would be **MY** figures of choice for this particular track and they are very arbitrary, but that is how I like to roll – not how you have to of course, the facts are facts and you can do with them as you wish.

Two additions I then add

An RTF figure for the trainer of at least 40%

The horse must not be out of the weights i.e., carrying more than his or her allotted mark because of race conditions – you will see this (for example) in the 3.55pm where Canal Rocks could have been a bet (third 3/1 by the way) but wasn't – rules are rules and whatever you set for yourself, I suggest you stick with them!

Anyway, using the above statistics via the racecards below (all copied from the Racing Post online at www.racingpost.com).

Possible bets:

Chases:

Joe Tizzard trains L'Air Du Vent in the 4.30pm
Joe Tizzard/Brendan Powell team up with L'Air Du Vent 4.30pm
Top weight in handicaps – L'Air Du Vent 4.30pm
Winner last time out in handicaps – Minella Voucher 4.30pm

Conclusion – two horses in the same race but three pointers to L'Air du Vent, one to Minella Voucher

Bets 3/4pt win L'Air Du Vent, 1/4pt win Minella Voucher

Result: Minella Voucher Won 2/1 (BSP 3.13), L'Air Du Vent pulled up (saddle slipped when beaten) 4/1.

1pt risked 0.752 returned, -0.248pt on the race.

Hurdles:

Horse who won last time out (in handicaps) Mr Yeats 1.35pm

Bet 1pt win Mr Yeats BSP

Result Mr Yeats Won 5/4 (BSP 2.46)

Profit 1.43pts after commission

Horse who won last time out (in handicaps) Canal Rocks 3.55pm NO BET, racing from 1lb out of the handicap.

Total on the day:

2pts bet

3.182 returned after 2% commission

RACING PARTNERSHIP TRP CONDITIONAL JOCKEYS' HANDICAP HURDLE (Class 4) (4yo+ 0-110) Winner £4,302 7 runners
3m2f105y Good To Soft SKY

RACE CONDITIONS £8,600 guaranteed **For** 4yo+ Rated 0-110 (also open to such horses rated 111 and 112 - see Standard Conditions) **Weight raised** 3 **Minimum weights:** 10-2; **Penalties** after September 3rd, each hurdle won 7lb **Allowances** riders who, prior to September 13th, 2022, have not ridden more than 20 winners under any Rules of Racing 3lb; 10 such winners 5lb; 5 such winners 7lb; riders riding for their own stable allowed, in addition 3lb **Art Of Illusion's Handicap Mark** 107 **Entries** 12 pay £29 **Penalty value 1st** £4,302.34 **2nd** £1,982.11 **3rd** £990.66 **4th** £496.12 **5th** £350.00 **6th** £350.00

NO. FORM	HORSE		AGE	WGT OR	JOCKEY ALLOWANCE TRAINER RTF%	TS	RPR	ODDS
1 23-232	Art Of Illusion > p	24	5	12-0 107	J: Caoilin Quinn >⁶ T: Warren Greatrex >	96	109	
2 223231	Mr Yeats > p CD 11		5	12-0 ⁷ᵉˣ 107	J: Bradley Harris >⁸ T: Milton Harris >⁵⁰	95	111	
3 9-3224	Ben Lilly > b	81	5	11-13 106	J: Fergus Gillard >³ T: David Pipe >⁵⁸	93	108	
4 -22124	Jony Max > t C D 18		7	11-13 106	J: Ellis Collier >⁸ T: Christian Williams >⁶⁰	74	90	
5 11-397	Espinator > CD 49		8	11-8 101	J: Kevin Brogan > T: Adrian Wintle >³³	105	114	
6 0-1172	Ballymilan > p 1 tip 24		7	11-7 100	J: Thomas Doggrell >⁶ T: Neil Mulholland >⁷³	81	110	
7 2F2PP-	Ho Que.Oui >	220	5	11-2 95	J: Philip Armson > T: Alexandra Dunn >⁵⁰	-	-	

FUTURE OR Mr Yeats (+5)

2:10 DEVONDALE ELECTRICAL NOVICES' HURDLE (GBB RACE) (Class 4) (4yo+) Winner £4,085 9 runners 2m5f122y Good To Soft SKY

RACE CONDITIONS £7,500 guaranteed **For** 4yo+ which have not won more than two hurdles **Weights** 4yo 10st 11lb; 5yo+ 11st **Penalties** a winner of a hurdle 7lb; of 2 hurdles 12lb **Weight for age** 4yo from 6yo+ 3lb **Allowances** fillies & mares 7lb **Entries** 11 pay £27 **Penalty value** **1st** £4,084.50 **2nd** £1,881.75 **3rd** £940.50 **4th** £471.00

NO. FORM		HORSE	AGE	WGT OR	JOCKEY ALLOWANCE TRAINER RTF%	TS	RPR	ODDS
1 2-2132		Tiger Orchid > 29	7	11-7 112	J: Charlie Hammond > T: Dr Richard Newland >[11]	85	120	
2 321		Bagheera Ginge > 25	4	11-4 115	J: Sam Twiston-Davies > T: Nigel Twiston-Davies >[75]	77	121	
3 5412-U		Harlem Soul > 13	4	11-4 122	J: James Best > T: [2] Syd Hosie >[50]	108	118	
4 PP51-P		Come On Paddy Mac > p[1] 128	6	11-0 ·	J: Mitchell Bastyan > T: [2] Laura Young >	·	·	
5 665/4-		Lunchable Bob > 461	7	11-0 ·	J: Tom O'Brien > T: [1] Paul Henderson >	·	·	
6 F2 F34		Separate Ways > 74	6	11-0 ·	J: Connor Brace > T: [2] David Brace >	52	104	
7 /292/F		Time Flies By > 49	7	11-0 125	J: Jonjo O'Neill Jr > T: Nicky Henderson >[40]	·	·	
8 F3-		Dan Daly > (180P)	4	10-11 ·	J: Jack Tudor > T: [1] Christian Williams >[60]	·	·	
9 5-P		Sans Of Gold > (137P)	4	10-11 ·	J: Angus Cheleda >[5] T: [1] Jimmy Frost >[50]	·	·	

2:45 TORBAY MEDIA NOVICES' CHASE (GBB RACE) (Class 3) (4yo+) Winner £6,535 4 runners 2m75y Good To Soft SKY

RACE CONDITIONS £13,400 guaranteed **For** 4yo+ **Weights** 4yo 10st 8lb; 5yo+ 11st 4lb **Penalties** a winner of a chase 6lb; of 2 chases or of a Class 1 or Class 2 chase 10lb; Excluding the winner, the Official BHA Rating of any horse taking part in this race will not be increased due to performance in this race provided the horse has had at least four prior completed run over chases or hurdles combined **Allowances** fillies & mares 7lb **Entries** 7 pay £45 **Penalty value** **1st** £6,535.20 **2nd** £3,010.80 **3rd** £1,504.80 **4th** £753.60

NO. FORM		HORSE	AGE	WGT OR	JOCKEY ALLOWANCE TRAINER RTF%	TS	RPR	ODDS
1 33-112		Byzantine Empire > t D BF 17	5	12-0 131	J: Jack Hogan >[7] T: Fergal O'Brien >[41]	104	130	
2 3FF14-		Geni De La Cour > 153	6	11-4 127	J: James Best > T: [1] Syd Hosie >[50]	·	·	
3 138-12		Mascat > tp[1] C D BF 53 (18F)	5	11-4 120	J: Brendan Powell > T: Joe Tizzard >[50]	·	·	
4 -31117		Noahthirtytwored > t D 34 (22F)	6	11-4 109	J: Lee Edwards > T: Adam West >[25]	·	·	

9

3:20 DEVONDALE ELECTRICAL MARES' NOVICES' HURDLE (GBB RACE) (Class 4) (4yo+) Winner £4,085 8 runners 2m167y Good To Soft SKY

RACE CONDITIONS £7,500 guaranteed **For** 4yo+ fillies & mares which have not won more than two hurdles **Weights** 4yo 10st 12lb; 5yo+ 11st **Penalties** a winner of a hurdle 7lb; of 2 hurdles 12lb **Entries** 10 pay £29 **Penalty value** **1st** £4,084.50 **2nd** £1,881.75 **3rd** £940.50 **4th** £471.00

NO. FORM	HORSE	AGE	WGT OR	JOCKEY ALLOWANCE TRAINER RTF%	TS	RPR	ODDS
1 6240-3	Div Ine Tara > 16	7	11-0 -	J: Connor Brace > T: Fergal O'Brien >[41]	52	101	
2 F-	Kay's Light > 175	5	11-0 -	J: Tom O'Brien > T: Paul Henderson >	-	-	
3 0/223-	Lady Jane P > C D 245	6	11-0 -	J: Ben Poste > T: [1] Adrian Wintle >[33]	91	115	
4 34	Maire's Dream > 24	5	11-0 -	J: Sean Bowen > T: Olly Murphy >[50]	-	-	
5 P6	Martha Burell > 98	7	11-0 -	J: Harry Kimber >[5] T: Jackie Du Plessis >[100]	-	57	
6 /F319-	Nifty Getaway > D 188	6	11-0 -	J: Gavin Sheehan > T: Archie Watson >[56]	-	-	
7 036	Wrap Your Wings > 27	7	11-0 -	J: James Best > T: [2] Jimmy Frost >[50]	-	82	
8 1-	Ya Know Yaseff > (180P)	5	11-0 -	J: Tom Scudamore > T: [1] David Pipe >[58]	-	-	

3:55 TALK TIDY HANDICAP HURDLE (Class 5) (4yo+ 0-105) Winner £2,941 10 runners 2m167y Good To Soft SKY

RACE CONDITIONS £6,110 guaranteed **For** 4yo+ Rated 0-105 (also open to such horses rated 106 and 107 - see Standard Conditions) **Minimum weights:** 10-2; **Penalties** after September 3rd, each hurdle won 7lb **Weight for age** 4yo from 5yo+ 2lb **Opening Bid's Handicap Mark** 107 **Entries** 22 pay £25 **Penalty value 1st** £2,940.84 **2nd** £1,354.86 **3rd** £677.16 **4th** £350.00 **5th** £350.00 **6th** £350.00

NO. FORM	HORSE	AGE	WGT OR	JOCKEY ALLOWANCE / TRAINER RTF%	TS	RPR	ODDS
1 7P636-	**Opening Bid** › w¹ h CD 148	7	12-2 107	J: James Davies › T: Chris Down ›	99	114	
2 8324-2	**Benandgone** › 134	5	12-0 105	J: Thomas Doggrell ›⁷ T: Brian Barr ›³³	81	107	
3 422438	**Kolisi** › tv D 1 tip 24	4	11-11 104	J: Tom Scudamore › T: David Pipe ›⁵⁸	95	103	
4 111122	**Appreciate** › t CD BF 61 (34F)	4	11-11 104	J: Mitchell Bastyan › T: Milton Harris ›⁵⁰	93	105	
5 5126-F	**Gavin** › h D 107 (45F)	4	11-8 101	J: Danny Burton ›⁵ T: Joe Ponting ›	· 73	98	
6 534P-6	**Begin The Luck** › h D 116	6	11-4 95	J: Angus Cheleda ›⁵ T:¹ Brian Barr ›³³	89	114	
7 43-BP3	**Millies Mite** › t 29	6	10-12 89	J: Tom Cannon › T: John Best & Karen Jewell ›⁵⁰	94	115	
8 116F5-	**Good Impression** › D 162 (22F)	7	10-8 85	J: Ben Jones › T: Bernard Llewellyn ›²⁵	94	110	
9 398-31	**Canal Rocks** › tp D 89 (45F)	6	10-2 79	J: Charlie Price ›³ T: Bernard Llewellyn ›²⁵	99	104	
10 9-P796	**Tiffany Rose** › h D 13	6	10-2 79	J: Sean Houlihan › T: Robert Stephens ›⁵⁷	77	103	

LONG HANDICAP Canal Rocks 10-1, Tiffany Rose 9-9

FUTURE OR Canal Rocks (-1), Tiffany Rose (-7)

4:30 WATCH FREE RACE REPLAYS ON ATTHERACES.COM HANDICAP CHASE (Class 4) (4yo+ 0-110) Winner £4,357 7 runners 3m1f170y
Good To Soft SKY

RACE CONDITIONS £9,400 guaranteed For 4yo+ Rated 0-110 (also open to such horses rated 111 and 112 - see Standard Conditions) **Minimum weights:** 10-2; **Penalties** after September 3rd, each chase won 7lb L'Air Du Vent's Handicap Mark 112 **Entries** 10 pay £33 **Penalty value 1st** £4,356.80 **2nd** £2,007.20 **3rd** £1,003.20 **4th** £502.40 **5th** £350.00 **6th** £350.00 **7th** £350.00

NO. FORM	HORSE	AGE	WGT OR	JOCKEY ALLOWANCE TRAINER RTF%	TS	RPR	ODDS
1 P3P-22	L'Air Du Vent > tp 29	8	12-2 112	J: Brendan Powell > T: Joe Tizzard >50	88	114	
2 4-5143	Aye Aye Charlie > C D 23	10	11-13 109	J: Ellis Collier >7 T: Christian Williams >60	104	116	
3 116663	D'Jango > tb 17	9	11-12 108	J: Tom Scudamore > T: David Pipe >58	107	120	
4 F4FP5-	The Composeur > D 230	7	11-11 107	J: Jonjo O'Neill Jr > T: Jonjo O'Neill >33	55	108	
5 522-23	Miss Jeanne Moon > P BF 1 tip 29	8	11-11 107	J: Sam Twiston-Davies > T: Neil Mulholland >73	106	117	
6 -22241	Minella Voucher > tp CD 11	11	10-7 89	J: Toby Wynne >7 T: Alexandra Dunn >50	109	121	
7 6-38P2	Joey Steel > CD 1 tip 11	9	10-7 89	J: Jack Tudor > T: Christian Williams >60	109	121	

FUTURE OR Minella Voucher (+4), Joey Steel (+3)

Warwick 20th September 2022

Notes:

Chases

Jockey Harry Skelton has a 40% strike rate in non-handicaps
Jockey Jonathan Burke has a profit of £54.15 on non-handicaps
Trainer Alan King has a 50% strike rate non-handicaps
Trainer Paul Nicholls has a 44.83% strike rate non-handicaps
Trainer Nicky Henderson has a 43.75% strike rate handicaps
Trainer Gary Hanmer has a 38.46% strike rate handicaps
Trainer Tom George has a +£76.26 profit in handicaps
Dan Skelton/Harry Skelton combo have a 40% strike rate non-handicaps
Tom George/Jonathan Burke combo have a 45.45% strike rate and a £66.51 profit in handicaps
Backing unnamed favs in all races has shown some profit
Backing horses who won last time out in non-handicaps shows a profit of £107.23
Backing top-weights in handicaps shows a profit of +£125.02
The sire Mahler shows a profit of £48.14 with a strike rate of 37.50% in non-handicaps

The sire Milan shows a profit of +£94.47 and a strike rate of 23.94% in handicaps

Hurdles

Jockey Bryony Frost has a 33.33% strike rate and a profit of +£26.83 from just 12 rides in handicaps
Jockey Jamie Moore has a profit of +£304.22 in non-handicaps but only a strike rate of 14.29%
Jockey Tom Scudamore has a profit of +£179.27 in non-handicaps but a strike rate of 20.00%
Trainer Mrs Jane Williams has a 40% strike rate in handicaps
Trainer Paul Nicholls has a 33% strike rate in handicaps
Trainer Ian Williams has a profit of +£201.55 in non-handicaps but a strike rate of 3.33%
Trainer Jonjo O'Neill has a profit of +£103.13 in handicaps
Trainer Nikki Evans has a profit of +£101.11 in handicaps
Nicky Henderson/Nico de Boinville combo have a 34.38% strike rate in non-handicaps
David Pipe/Tom Scudamore combo have a 33.33% strike rates in non-handicaps
Last time out winners show a profit of £79.99
Sire Yeats shows a profit of +£366.32 and a strike rate of 28.57% in non-handicaps

Possible bets

2.25pm - El Barracho would be considered as top-weight if he is also sent of favourite

3.35pm – Leapaway is **NOT** considered as top-weight if he is also sent off favourite because of the trainer RTF figure

4.10pm – Irish Prophecy is **NOT** considered as top-weight if he is also sent off favourite because of the trainer RTF figure

4.45pm – Joly Maker would be considered as top-weight if he is also sent off favourite (Late non-runner)

Hurdles:

1.50pm – Sophosc (trainer Ian Williams) comes under consideration, but the strike rate worries me

Bets placed:

1.50pm Sophosc 1/2pt to win (because if the low strike rate)

Result Won 15/8 BSP 3.05 profit of 1pt exactly

2.25pm El Barracho won but was not sent off favourite so no bet

1/2pt risked, 1.5 points returned after 2% commission at BSP, 1.25pt profit.

1:50 HAZELTON MOUNTFORD INSURANCE BROKERS NOVICES' HURDLE (GBB RACE) (Class 4) (4yo+) Winner £3,540 11 runners 2m
Good RTV

RACE CONDITIONS £6,500 guaranteed **For** 4yo+ which have not won more than two hurdles **Weights** 4yo 10st 12lb; 5yo+ 11st **Penalties** winner of a hurdle 7lb; of 2 hurdles 12lb **Weight for age** 4yo from 5yo+ 2lb **Allowances** fillies & mares 7lb **Entries** 18 pay £32 **Penalty value 1st** £3,539.90 **2nd** £1,630.85 **3rd** £815.10 **4th** £408.20

NO. FORM	HORSE	AGE	WGT OR	JOCKEY TRAINER RTF%	TS	RPR	ODDS
1 -42321	Larusso > D 1 tip 27	5	11-7 106	J: Ciaran Gethings > T: Stuart Edmunds >67	106	115	SP PLACE BET
2 1	Sophosc > D 135 (12F)	6	11-7 -	J: Charlie Todd > T: Ian Williams >42	84	109	SP PLACE BET
3 24853F	Allbetsoff > 24	6	11-0 110	J: Jamie Hamilton > T: 2 Mark Walford >41	102	123	SP PLACE BET
4 007-49	Charlie My Boy > t 7	5	11-0 -	J: Kevin Brogan > T: J R Jenkins >	39	85	SP PLACE BET
5 2682	Gone In Sixty > 20	5	11-0 -	J: Kielan Woods > T: Alex Hales >67	62	110	SP PLACE BET
6 88	Horse Power > 29	5	11-0 -	J: Jack Hogan >7 T: Fergal O'Brien >31	-	-	SP PLACE BET
7 532174	Ince > D 15	5	11-0 87	J: Connor Brace > T: Fergal O'Brien >31	97	102	SP PLACE BET
8 3-1424	Son Of Aliciaslady > w1 h 36	6	11-0 -	J: Theo Gillard >3 T: Donald McCain >56	44	115	SP PLACE BET
9 3243F-	Cornicello > 180	4	10-12 104	J: Gavin Sheehan > T: Jamie Snowden >100	94	111	SP PLACE BET
10 9	Great Ridley > h1 29	4	10-12 -	J: Conor Ring >3 T: 2 Sarah-Jayne Davies >	-	-	SP PLACE BET
11 49	Robber's Bridge > h 1 tip 56	4	10-12 -	J: David Noonan > T: Simon Earle >	-	-	SP PLACE BET

2:25 PAUL FERGUSONS JUMPERS TO FOLLOW HANDICAP CHASE (Class 3) (4yo+ 0-125) Winner £5,882 3 runners 2m54y Good RTV

RACE CONDITIONS £12,200 guaranteed **For** 4yo+ Rated 0-125 (also open to such horses rated 126 and 127 - see Standard Conditions) **Minimum weights:** 10-2; **Penalties** after September 10th, each chase won 7lb El Borracho's Handicap Mark 127 **Entries** 6 pay £54 **Penalty value 1st** £5,881.68 **2nd** £2,709.72 **3rd** £1,354.32

NO. FORM	HORSE	AGE	WGT OR	JOCKEY TRAINER RTF%	TS	RPR	ODDS
1 -61281	El Borracho > t D 1 tip 19	7	11-12 127	J: Toby Wynne >7 T: Oliver Greenall & Josh Guerriero >60	123	131	SP PLACE BET
2 35P3-P	Fanzio > t D 122	7	11-8 123	J: Philip Armson >5 T: Richard Hobson >100	112	145	SP PLACE BET
3 122121	Ragamuffin > t D 1 tip 21	7	11-2 117	J: Sam Twiston-Davies > T: Neil Mulholland >50	116	130	SP PLACE BET

14

3:00 POUNDLAND FOUNDATION PROUDLY SUPPORTS MAKE-A-WISH UK MARES' HANDICAP HURDLE (Class 4) (3yo+ 0-110) Winner £4,030 9 runners 2m3f Good RTV

RACE CONDITIONS £8,100 guaranteed **For** 3yo+ fillies & mares Rated 0-110 (also open to such horses rated 111 and 112 - see Standard Conditions) **Minimum weights:** 10-2; **Penalties** after September 10th, each hurdle won 7lb **Une De La Seniere's Handicap Mark** 112 **Entries** 17 pay £35 **Penalty value** **1st** £4,030.04 **2nd** £1,856.66 **3rd** £927.96 **4th** £464.72 **5th** £350.00 **6th** £350.00

NO. FORM	HORSE	AGE	WGT OR	JOCKEY ALLOWANCE / TRAINER RTF%	TS	RPR	ODDS
1 -22643	Une De La Seniere > t / 38	7	12-2 / 112	J: Jack Hogan >7 / T: Fergal O'Brien >31	98	117	SP PLACE BET
2 2122-5	Choral Work > / 141	5	11-12 / 108	J: Sean Bowen > / T: Olly Murphy >75	87	112	SP PLACE BET
3 6-2233	Maria Magdalena > / 31	6	11-11 / 107	J: Harriet Tucker >7 / T: Alex Hales >67	100	114	SP PLACE BET
4 7787-4	Solstalla > p / CD 1 tip 93	10	11-5 / 101	J: Page Fuller > / T: David Weston >	110	116	SP PLACE BET
5 83-013	We'llgowats > / 20	7	11-4 / 100	J: Conor McNamara > / T: Liam G O'Brien >	78	109	SP PLACE BET
6 -16372	Blue Collar Glory > ht / D 1 tip 19	5	11-2 / 98	J: Henry Brooke > / T: Oliver Greenall & Josh Guerriero >60	84	110	SP PLACE BET
7 -P2309	Eaton Lady > / 46	6	11-0 / 96	J: Richie McLernon > / T:1 Gary Brown >50	90	108	SP PLACE BET
8 -137F2	Persuer > tb / C 17	6	10-4 / 86	J: Lee Edwards > / T: Tom Gretton >	101	118	SP PLACE BET
9 7515/7	Emmas Dilemma > tv / 34	10	10-2 / 84	J: Marc Goldstein > / T: Hannah James >	-	46	SP PLACE BET

LONG HANDICAP Emmas Dilemma 9-8

FUTURE OR Emmas Dilemma (-8)

3:35 POUNDLAND FOUNDATION PROUDLY SUPPORTS TOMMYS HANDICAP CHASE (Class 3) (4yo+ 0-140) Winner £8,169 5 runners 2m4f Good RTV

RACE CONDITIONS £16,400 guaranteed **For** 4yo+ Rated 0-140 (also open to such horses rated 141 and 142 - see Standard Conditions) **Minimum weights:** 10-2; **Penalties** after September 10th, each chase won 7lb **Leapaway's Handicap Mark** 137 **Entries** 8 pay £75 **Penalty value** **1st** £8,169.00 **2nd** £3,763.50 **3rd** £1,881.00 **4th** £942.00 **5th** £350.00

NO. FORM	HORSE	AGE	WGT OR	JOCKEY ALLOWANCE / TRAINER RTF%	TS	RPR	ODDS
1 2-134U	Leapaway > p / C 1 tip 31	10	12-0 / 137	J: Tom O'Brien > / T: Philip Hobbs >	130	143	SP PLACE BET
2 4-2117	Golden Taipan > t / C D 1 tip 53	8	11-9 / 132	J: Paddy Brennan > / T: Fergal O'Brien >31	118	141	SP PLACE BET
3 512142	Fat Sam > h / CD 28	8	11-6 / 129	J: James Davies > / T: Chris Down >	125	139	SP PLACE BET
4 PP-3F2	Vision Des Flos > t / CD 31	9	11-4 / 127	J: Brendan Powell > / T: Joe Tizzard >25	130	140	SP PLACE BET
5 2P67P5	Al Roc > tb / D 28	11	11-2 / 125	J: Tom Scudamore > / T: David Pipe >46	125	146	SP PLACE BET

15

4:10 — WEATHERBYS NHSTALLIONS.CO.UK HANDICAP CHASE (Class 3) (4yo+ 0-135) Winner £8,169 7 runners 3m1f100y Good RTV

RACE CONDITIONS £16,400 guaranteed **For** 4yo+ Rated 0-135 (also open to such horses rated 136 and 137 - see Standard Conditions) **Minimum weights:** 10-2; **Penalties** after September 10th, each chase won 7lb **Irish Prophecy's Handicap Mark** 135 **Entries** 10 pay £75 **Penalty value 1st** £8,169.00 **2nd** £3,763.50 **3rd** £1,881.00 **4th** £942.00 **5th** £350.00 **6th** £350.00 **7th** £350.00

NO. FORM	HORSE	AGE	WGT OR	JOCKEY ALLOWANCE / TRAINER RTF%	TS	RPR	ODDS
1 1P-4P5	Irish Prophecy > tp[1] 34	9	11-10 135	J: Tom Bellamy > / T: Emma Lavelle >	126	150	SP PLACE BET
2 U2P-12	Soldier Of Love > p D90	9	11-7 132	J: Jack Hogan >[7] / T: Fergal O'Brien >[31]	104	144	SP PLACE BET
3 34-U63	Organdi > 34	10	11-7 132	J: Sam Twiston-Davies > / T: Richard Phillips >	107	145	SP PLACE BET
4 /28P-2	Little Bruce > tp 58	10	11-5 130	J: Lilly Pinchin >[3] / T: Charlie Longsdon >[86]	105	144	SP PLACE BET
5 6-1P95	Sizing Cusimano > tb D15	9	11-4 129	J: Brendan Powell > / T: Joe Tizzard >[25]	121	141	SP PLACE BET
6 562211	El Paso Wood > tb D 2 tips 13	8	11-3 128	J: Tom Scudamore > / T: David Pipe >[46]	129	147	SP PLACE BET
7 215-14	Bbold > b C D34	8	11-2 127	J: Charlie Hammond > / T: Dr Richard Newland >[14]	121	144	SP PLACE BET

4:45 — POUNDLAND FOUNDATION PROUDLY SUPPORTS WHIZZ KIDZ CONDITIONAL JOCKEYS' HANDICAP CHASE (Class 5) (4yo+ 0-105) Winner £3,268 6 runners 2m4f Good RTV

RACE CONDITIONS £7,400 guaranteed **For** 4yo+ Rated 0-105 (also open to such horses rated 106 and 107 - see Standard Conditions) **Minimum weights:** 10-2; **Penalties** after September 10th, each chase won 7lb **Allowances** riders who, prior to September 17th, 2022, have not ridden more than 20 winners under any Rules of Racing 3lb; 10 such winners 5lb; 5 such winners 7lb; riders riding for their own stables allowed, in addition 3lb **Joly Maker's Handicap Mark** 106 **Entries** 16 pay £30 **Penalty value 1st** £3,267.60 **2nd** £1,505.40 **3rd** £752.40 **4th** £376.80 **5th** £350.00 **6th** £350.00

NO. FORM	HORSE	AGE	WGT OR	JOCKEY ALLOWANCE / TRAINER RTF%	TS	RPR	ODDS
1 124-14	Joly Maker > D24	8	12-1 106	J: Jamie Brace >[8] / T: Jonjo O'Neill >[50]	98	109	SP PLACE BET
2 52545-	Calidad > w[2] t 152	6	11-13 104	J: Lilly Pinchin >[3] / T:[1] Charlie Longsdon >[86]	69	96	SP PLACE BET
3 -P4723	Eureu Du Boulay > tp D51	8	11-12 103	J: Toby Wynne >[3] / T: Richard Hobson >[100]	105	120	SP PLACE BET
4 -31112	Serjeant Painter > D 1 tip 38	7	11-9 100	J: Luca Morgan >[3] / T: Ben Pauling >[75]	86	114	
5 4F23P4	Dindin > tb D21	9	11-9 100	J: Philip Armson >[3] / T: David Pipe >[46]	99	119	SP PLACE BET
6 PP-15P	Troed Y Melin > C D81	10	11-2 93	J: Bryan Carver > / T: Chris Honour >[50]	87	112	SP PLACE BET

Perth 21st September 2022.

Notes:

Chases

Jockey Sam Twiston-Davies has a strike rate of 60% in non-handicaps
Jockey Brian Hughes has a profit of £47.64 in handicaps and a 21.72% strike rate
Trainer Nigel Twiston-Davies has a strike rate of 54.55% in non-handicaps
Trainer Fergal O'Brien has a strike rate of 38.46% in non-handicaps
Trainer Paul Nicolls has a strike rate of 50% in non-handicaps
Trainer Fergal O'Brien has a strike rate of 36.36% in non-handicaps
Trainer David Pipe has a strike rate of 33.33% in non-handicaps
Trainer Tim Vaughan Pipe has a strike rate of 33.33% in non-handicaps
Donald McCain/Brian Hughes combo have a strike rate of 41.67% in handicaps
Peter Bowen/James Bowen combo have a strike rate of 38.46% in handicaps
David Pipe/Tom Scudamore combo have a strike rate of 38.46% in handicaps
Gordon Elliott/Sean Bowen combo have a strike rate of 36.84% in handicaps
Tim Reed/Harry Reed combo have a strike rate of 36.36% in handicaps
Horse who won last time out show a loss of +£158.03 in handicaps

Hurdles

Jockey Sean Bowen has a 61.90% strike rate in non-handicaps
Jockey A P Heskin has a 54.55% strike rate in non-handicaps
Jockey Daryl Jacob has a 41.18% strike rate in non-handicaps
Jockey Tom O'Brien has a 35.71% strike rate in non-handicaps
Jockey Harry Skelton has a 40.00% strike rate in handicaps
Jockey Sam Coltherd has a profit of +£149.32 in handicaps but a strike rate of 9.52%
Trainer Gordon Elliott has a strike rate of 45.95% in non-handicaps
Trainer John C McConnell Elliott has a strike rate of 45.95% in non-handicaps
Trainer Tom George has a strike rate of 45.95% in non-handicaps
Trainer Tim Vaughan has a strike rate of 45.95% in non-handicaps
Trainer Nigel Twiston-Davies has a strike rate of 45.95% in non-handicaps
Trainer Dan Skelton has a strike rate of 50.00% in handicaps
Trainer William Young Jr has a profit of +£98.40 from only 28 runners but a strike rate of 7.14% in handicaps
Gordon Elliott/Sean Bowen combo have a strike rate of 66.67% in non-handicaps
Jim Goldie/Brian Hughes combo have a 40% strike rate in handicaps
Backing top weights in handicaps sees a loss of £233.97
Sire Shantou has a profit of +£134.03 from a 21.43% strike rate over hurdles from only 18 runners in handicaps

This time I will look at things race by race (in case that makes life easier for you).

1.00pm – Sean Bowen rides and Gordon Elliott trains Happy D'Ex BUT the trainer has an RTF figure below 40% - no bet for me. Result – Won 1/7

1.35pm – No qualifiers of any kind

2.10pm – No qualifiers of any kind

2.45pm – Brian Hughes rides Bovington Bob BUT the trainer does not have a high enough RTF figure. Gordon Elliott/ Sean Bowen are responsible for Quantum Realm but again the RTF figure is not high enough. Result – both finished unplaced.

3.20pm – No qualifiers of any kind.

3.55pm – Brian Hughes rides Monsieur Code BUT the trainer RTF figure just misses out. Nothing else came closed to qualifying. Result – Monsieur Code unplaced

4.30pm – No qualifiers of any kind.

So, you may be asking – why did we bother with Perth – good question! Firstly, as mentioned, I did not cherry-pick so I had no idea it would be such a fruitless meeting – BUT we also learned that we also need to know when not to bet – two losing bets would have been struck had we failed to adhere to the RTF figure rule.

Standard	At-a-Glance

1:00 PAUL FERGUSON'S JUMPERS TO FOLLOW EBF MARES' NATIONAL HUNT NOVICES' HURDLE (EBF QUAL') (GBB RACE) (Class 4) (4yo+) Winner £3,812 4 runners 2m4f35y Good To Soft RTV

RACE CONDITIONS £7,000 guaranteed For 4yo+ fillies & mares, which are EBF eligible, which have not run in a flat race and which have not won more than one hurdle **Weights** 4yo 10st 11lb; 5yo+ 11st **Penalties** a winner of a hurdle 7lb **Entries** 9 pay £19 **Penalty value 1st** £3,812.20 **2nd** £1,756.30 **3rd** £877.80 **4th** £439.60

NO. FORM		HORSE	AGE	WGT OR	JOCKEY ALLOWANCE TRAINER RTF%		TS	RPR	ODDS
1 468-S1		Happy D'ex >	5	11-7 -	J: Sean Bowen > T: Gordon Elliott >35		111	126	
		45							
2 1P-01		Lady Stanwix > t	5	11-0 -	J: Callum Bewley > T: 2 Justin Landy >100		-	-	
		52							
3 2107-		Solway Molly >	7	11-0 -	J: Thomas Dowson > T: Lisa Harrison >100		-	-	
		319							
4 6/		Solway Primrose >	8	11-0 -	J: Ross Chapman > T: Lisa Harrison >100		-	-	
		665							

1:35   **JOIN RACING TV NOW HANDICAP CHASE (GO NORTH ONE MAN SERIES QUALIFIER)** (Class 4) (4yo+ 0-110) Winner £4,684 5 runners 2m Good To Soft RTV

RACE CONDITIONS £10,000 guaranteed **For** 4yo+ Rated 0-110 (also open to such horses rated 111 and 112 - see Standard Conditions) **Minimum weights:** 10-2; **Penalties** after September 10th, each chase won 7lb **City Derby's Handicap Mark** 111 **Entries** 11 **pay** £30 **Penalty value 1st** £4,683.56 **2nd** £2,157.74 **3rd** £1,078.44 **4th** £540.08 **5th** £350.00

NO. FORM		HORSE	AGE	WGT OR	JOCKEY ALLOWANCE TRAINER RTF%	TS	RPR	ODDS
1 87731-		City Derby > tp **C** **D** 161	6	12-1 111	J: Jack Hogan >[7] T: Fergal O'Brien >[43]	.	.	
2 220532		Sword Of Fate > **CD** 7	9	11-11 107	J: Derek Fox > T: Leonard Kerr >[100]	110	119	
3 1645-1		Spark Of Madness > t **CD** 133	6	11-8 104	J: Stephen Mulqueen > T: Lucinda Russell >[50]	86	113	
4 361312		Tico Times > p **BF** 7	9	11-6 102	J: Danny McMenamin > T: Dianne Sayer >[67]	105	114	.
5 4-38U4		Check My Pulse > p **D** 25	6	10-9 91	J: Henry Brooke > T: Rebecca Menzies >[56]	104	125	

FUTURE OR Sword Of Fate (+2), Tico Times (+2)

2:10   **PKAVS IMPROVING WELLBEING EMPOWERING COMMUNITIES HANDICAP HURDLE** (Class 3) (4yo+ 0-140) Winner £10,511 7 runners 2m7f207y Good To Soft RTV

RACE CONDITIONS £20,000 guaranteed **For** 4yo+ Rated 0-140 (also open to such horses rated 141 and 142 - see Standard Conditions) **Minimum weights:** 10-2; **Penalties** after September 10th, each hurdle won 7lb **Dallas Des Pictons's Handicap Mark** 142 **Entries** 11 **pay** £35 **Penalty value 1st** £10,510.78 **2nd** £4,842.37 **3rd** £2,420.22 **4th** £1,212.04 **5th** £350.00 **6th** £350.00

NO. FORM		HORSE	AGE	WGT OR	JOCKEY ALLOWANCE TRAINER RTF%	TS	RPR	ODDS
1 004-21		Dallas Des Pictons > b **D** 51	9	12-2 142	J: Henry Brooke > T: [1] Dianne Sayer >[67]	128	139	
2 63243-		Teescomponents Lad > p **D** 153	9	11-6 132	J: Tom Midgley >[5] T: Gillian Boanas >[67]	123	145	
3 22124-		Poppa Poutine > **D** 152	6	11-4 130	J: Sam Twiston-Davies > T: Nigel Twiston-Davies >[67]	.	.	
4 P-4P31		Giovanni Change > **D** 39	7	11-1 127	J: Jamie Hamilton > T: Mark Walford >[57]	123	143	
5 /822/6		Jack Devine > v **CD** 141	10	10-8 120	J: Craig Nichol > T: Rose Dobbin >	68	134	
6 4-6073		Native Fighter > w[2] p[1] **C** 23	8	10-2 114	J: Charlotte Jones >[3] T: James Moffatt >	119	150	
7 P-5145		Catchmeifyoucan > tp[1] **D** 25	8	10-2 114	J: Sean Quinlan > T: Jennie Candlish >[60]	124	146	

LONG HANDICAP Native Fighter 10-1, Catchmeifyoucan 10-0

FUTURE OR Giovanni Change (-1), Native Fighter (-1), Catchmeifyoucan (-2)

2:45 WEATHERBYS NHSTALLIONS.CO.UK DAVID WHITAKER HANDICAP CHASE (GBB RACE) (Class 2) (4yo+) Winner £13,203 8 runners 2m7f180y Good To Soft RTV

RACE CONDITIONS £25,000 guaranteed For 4yo+ Minimum weights: 10-2; Penalties after September 10th, each chase won 7lb Jerrysback's Handicap Mark 142 Entries 12 pay £50 Penalty value 1st £13,202.50 2nd £6,075.00 3rd £3,037.50 4th £1,520.00 5th £757.50

NO. FORM		HORSE	AGE	WGT OR	JOCKEY ALLOWANCE TRAINER RTF%	TS	RPR	ODDS
1 P4-611		Jerrysback > 87	10	12-0 142	J: Richie McLernon > T: Ben Haslam >	124	147	
2 11113-		Bavington Bob > D BF 158	7	11-11 139	J: Brian Hughes > T: Ann Hamilton >	104	150	
3 52110-		Ballyandy > C D 188	11	11-11 139	J: Sam Twiston-Davies > T: Nigel Twiston-Davies >67	-	-	
4 421-P7		Gevrey > 33	6	11-5 133	J: James Bowen > T: Gordon Elliott >35	118	144	
5 4-2117		Golden Taipan > t CD 54	8	11-4 132	J: Paddy Brennan > T: Fergal O'Brien >43	123	146	
6 2-0112		Quantum Realm > C D BF 39	6	11-2 130	J: Sean Bowen > T: Gordon Elliott >35	131	144	
7 -22144		Charlie Uberalles > CD BF 37	6	10-7 121	J: Conor O'Farrell > T: Dianne Sayer >67	103	146	
8 8/3P-3		Lord Napier > t C D 14	9	10-3 117	J: Jamie Moore > T: Peter Bowen >67	116	146	

DECLARED OVERNIGHT Golden Taipan: Engaged 3:35 Warwick 20-sep

---

3:20 LORD MANSFIELD MEMORIAL HANDICAP HURDLE (GO NORTH CAB ON TARGET SERIES QUALIFIER) (Class 4) (4yo+ 0-120) Winner £4,520 6 runners 2m4f35y Good To Soft RTV

RACE CONDITIONS £9,000 guaranteed For 4yo+ Rated 0-120 (also open to such horses rated 121 and 122 - see Standard Conditions) Minimum weights: 10-2; Penalties after September 10th, each hurdle won 7lb Big Bad Bear's Handicap Mark 120 Entries 15 pay £25 Penalty value 1st £4,520.18 2nd £2,082.47 3rd £1,040.82 4th £521.24 5th £350.00 6th £350.00

NO. FORM		HORSE	AGE	WGT OR	JOCKEY ALLOWANCE TRAINER RTF%	TS	RPR	ODDS
1 811-43		Big Bad Bear > CD 102	8	12-0 120	J: Sean Quinlan > T: Nicky Richards >100	108	123	
2 57-8P3		Curious Times > t 83	9	11-11 117	J: James Bowen > T: S R B Crawford >	72	122	
3 812632		Battle Of Toro > v 25	6	11-7 113	J: Charlotte Jones >3 T: James Moffatt >	99	122	
4 480-7U		Excelcior > b 118	8	11-1 107	J: Sean Bowen > T: Gordon Elliott >35	69	116	
5 53-351		Idilico > CD 39 (28F)	7	10-11 103	J: Conor O'Farrell > T: Dianne Sayer >67	103	123	
6 5154U3		Malangen > CD 15	7	10-11 103	J: Thomas Dowson > T: Lisa Harrison >100	99	122	

3:55 CELEBRATING JOHN AND SUSAN BRADBURNE HANDICAP CHASE (Class 5) (4yo+ 0-100) Winner £3,594 8 runners 2m4f20y
Good To Soft RTV

RACE CONDITIONS £8,000 guaranteed **For** 4yo+ Rated 0-100 (also open to such horses rated 101 and 102 - see Standard Conditions) **Weight raised** 5 **Minimum weights:** 10-2; **Penalties** after September 10th, each chase won 7lb **Tommydan's Handicap Mark** 95 **Entries** 13 pay £15 **Penalty value 1st** £3,594.36 **2nd** £1,655.94 **3rd** £827.64 **4th** £414.48 **5th** £350.00 **6th** £350.00 **7th** £350.00 **8th** £350.00

NO. FORM	HORSE	AGE	WGT OR	JOCKEY ALLOWANCE TRAINER RTF%	TS	RPR	ODDS
1 982-98	Tommydan > p 37	7	12-0 95	J: Sean Quinlan > T: Jennie Candlish >60	58	93	
2 334-56	Monsieur Co > tp 109 (22F)	9	11-12 93	J: Brian Hughes > T: Keith Dalgleish >39	99	111	
3 531731	Going Mobile > tb D 15	7	11-7 88	J: Jonathan England > T: Sam England >60	87	101	
4 P5-39U	Darius Des Sources > tv D 56	9	11-2 83	J: Alan Doyle >7 T: Chris Grant >	80	103	
5 34-85F	Budarri > tp 102	9	10-13 80	J: Danny McMenamin > T: Stuart Coltherd >	73	109	
6 17-855	Izzy's Champion > tp D 1 tip 56	8	10-10 77	J: Derek Fox > T: Lucinda Russell >50	99	109	
7 P52383	Golden Chancer > tv C 20	8	10-9 76	J: Ross Chapman > T: Daragh Bourke >	78	86	
8 5426-P	Shanbally Rose > 133	8	10-7 74	J: Dylan Johnston >10 T: Rose Dobbin >	95	103	

4:30 **STAY AND DINE AT PERTHLODGE.CO.UK HANDICAP HURDLE** (Class 5) (3yo+ 0-100) Winner £3,431 12 runners 2m4f35y Good To Soft RTV

RACE CONDITIONS £7,000 guaranteed **For** 3yo+ Rated 0-100 (also open to such horses rated 101 and 102 - see Standard Conditions) **Minimum weights:** 10-2; **Penalties** after September 10th, each hurdle won 7lb **Weight for age** 4yo from 5yo+ 3lb **Navegaon Gate's Handicap Mark** 101 **Entries** 18 pay £20 **Penalty value** 1st £3,430.98 2nd £1,580.67 **3rd** £790.02 **4th** £395.64 **5th** £350.00 **6th** £350.00

NO. FORM		HORSE	AGE	WGT OR	JOCKEY ALLOWANCE TRAINER RTF%		TS	RPR	ODDS
1 1-2223		Petite Rhapsody › CD BF 56	7	12-0 99	J: Patrick Wadge ›10 T: Lucinda Russell ›50		79	98	
2 3437-		Navegaon Gate › 174	4	11-13 101	J: Sam Twiston-Davies › T: Nigel Twiston-Davies ›67		61	92	
3 33624-		Rubytwo › b D 154	10	11-10 95	J: Danny McMenamin › T: Nicky Richards ›100		98	105	
4 064-PP		Filou Des Issards › t 23	7	11-10 95	J: Aaron Anderson ›5 T: Jessica Bedi ›		68	105	
5 -64442		Lough Carra › BF 16	5	11-8 93	J: Sean Quinlan › T: Jennie Candlish ›60		86	100	
6 4-2535		Nechako › t1 25	6	11-8 93	J: Charlotte Jones ›3 T: James Moffatt ›		66	101	
7 07-008		Near Kettering › t 34	8	11-7 92	J: Jonathan England › T: Sam England ›60		98	117	
8 5P184-		Coral Blue › D 158	7	11-4 89	J: Ross Chapman › T: Daragh Bourke ›		89	101	
9 333543		Calliope › tb C 7	9	10-12 83	J: Brian Hughes › T: Dianne Sayer ›67		87	117	
10 63-396		Old Jewry › D 109	8	10-6 77	J: Kevin Brogan › T: Daragh Bourke ›		102	110	
11 3-4138		Dan Gun › D 65	8	10-5 76	J: Thomas Willmott ›3 T: Simon Waugh ›		91	110	
12 -9P670		Hattaab › p 23	9	10-2 73	J: Stephen Mulqueen › T: Lisa Harrison ›100		83	118	

LONG HANDICAP Hattaab 10-0

FUTURE OR Calliope (-1), Hattaab (-2)

One final meeting and one last run through to round the workings off for you all.

Fontwell 30th September

Notes:

Chases

Jockey David Maxwell has a 61.54% strike rate in non-handicaps
Jockey Sam Twiston-Davies has a strike rate of 467.62% in non-handicaps
Jockey Daryl Jacob has a strike rate of 38.89% in non-handicaps

Jockey Charlie Deutsch has a strike rate of 38.89% in handicaps
Jockey Harry Skelton has a strike rate of 38.46% in handicaps
Jockey Tom Bellamy has a strike rate of 33.33% in handicaps
Jockey Harry Cobden has a strike rate of 33.33% in handicaps
Jockey Aidan Coleman has a profit of £39.95 and a strike rate of 31.48% in handicaps
Trainer Paul Nicholls has a strike rate of 58.33% in non-handicaps
Trainer Nicky Henderson has a strike rate of 54.55% in non-handicaps
Trainer Neil Mulholland has a strike rate of 33.33% in non-handicaps
Trainer Lucy Wadham has a strike rate of 33.33% in handicaps
Trainer Dan Skelton has a strike rate of 33.33% in handicaps
Trainer Dr Richard Newland has a strike rate of 33.33% in handicaps
The Lawney Hill/Aidan Coleman combo has a 50% strike rate in handicaps
The Venetia Williams/Charlie Deutsch combo has a 50% strike rate in handicaps
The Dan Skelton/Harry Skelton combo has a 40.91% strike rate in handicaps
The David Bridgwater/Tom Scudamore combo has a 38.46% strike rate in handicaps
The Neil King/Trevor Whelan combo has a 35.71% strike rate in handicaps
The Paul Nicholls/Daryl Jacobs combo has a 50% strike rate and a profit in non-handicaps
The Paul Nicholls/Sam Twiston-Davies combo has a 69.23% strike rate and a profit in non-handicaps
The Lawney Hill/Aidan Coleman combo has a 50% strike rate and a profit in handicaps
Favourites show a 33.12% strike rate and a £38.73 profit in handicaps
Top weights show a 20.48% and a profit of £54.40 in handicaps
Dr Massini, Flemensfirth, and King's Theatre all show a better than 25% strike rate as sires and a profit.
Martaline shows a 28% strike rate and a profit of £45.78 as a sire in handicaps

Hurdles

Jockey James Bowen has a 30.77% strike rate in non-handicaps
Jockey Harry Kimber has a 30.77% strike rate in handicaps
Jockey Brendan Powell has a profit of £221.89 in non-handicaps but a strike rate of 11.11%
Jockey Trevor Whelan has a profit of £109.83 and a strike rate of 21.05% in non-handicaps
Trainer Charlie Longsdon has a strike rate of 34.48% in non-handicaps
Trainer Alan King has a strike rate of 33.90% in non-handicaps
Trainer Charlie Longsdon has a strike rate of 33.90% in non-handicaps
Trainer Nicky Henderson has a strike rate of 33.33% in non-handicaps
Trainer Ian Williams has a strike rate of 35.71% in handicaps
Trainer Victor Dartnall has a strike rate of 33.33% in handicaps
Trainer Harry Fry has a strike rate of 32.00% in handicaps
Trainer Neil King has a profit of £107.43 and an 18.52% strike rate in non-handicaps
Trainer Chris Gordon has a profit of +£120.03 and a strike rate of 16.10% in handicaps
The Anthony Honeyball/Rex Dingle combo have a strike rate of 37.50% in non-handicaps
The Warren Greatrex/Gavin Sheehan combo have a strike rate of 35.71% in non-handicaps

The Paul Nicholls/Harry Cobden combo have a strike rate of 33.33% in non-handicaps
The Warren Greatrex/Gavin Sheehan combo have a strike rate of 38.46% in handicaps
The Anthony Honeyball/Aidan Coleman combo have a strike rate of 36.36% in handicaps
The Neil King/Trevor Whelan combo have a profit of £112.83 and a strike rate of 25.00% in non-handicaps
The Chris Gordon/Tom Cannon combo have profit of £101.68 and a strike rate of 17.73% in handicaps
Second favourites show a profit in both handicaps and non-handicaps
Backing top-weights shows a loss in handicaps
Sire Flemensfirth shows a profit of £233.24 but a low strike rate of just 8.33% in non-handicaps

1.40pm

No jockey stats are relevant
No trainer stats are relevant
Favourites and top-weights show a profit
Minella Voucher is a son of profitable to follow sire Kings Theatre

Conclusion:

Top-weight Deben Bank would be a bet if he is also sent off favourite (late non-runner)
In his absence, Minella Voucher is worth a small bet as a son of Kings Theatre

Result: Minella Voucher Won 15/8

Bets: 1/2pt win Minella Voucher Won BSP 3.00 Return 1.48 after commission – Profit 0.98pts

2.15pm

Notes:

Jockey Harry Kimber has a good strike rate in handicap hurdles
Second favourites are profitable to follow in handicaps

Conclusion: Both Soul Icon and Buckos Boy qualify so I would consider "dutching" them both to a total of 1pt, meaning split stakes via a dutching calculator, but with the winner Soul Icon at odds on (1.74 on Betfair) I didn't have a bet though we still found the winner.

2.50pm

Notes:

No relevant jockey or trainer stats to apply.
Second favourites show a profit
Dusky Days is a son of profitable sire Flemensfirth

Conclusion: 1pt win Dusky Days IF he is second favourite – if not 1/2pt win Dusky Days and 1/2pt win second favourite

Result: First Fascinating Lips (15/8 second favourite, 2.86 BSP), third Dusky Days 9/4

Bet 1pt total, return 1.41pts after commission, profit 0.41pts.

3.25pm

Notes:

Jockey James Bowen has as strike rate of 30.77% in non-handicaps and he rides Inspiratrice BUT his trainer does not hit the 40% RTF figure (No Bet)

Second favourites show a profit

Conclusion: a small 1/2pt win bet on the second favourite (Miss Fedora)

Result Mr Freedom Won 5/4f

1/2pt staked nil return, loss on the race of 1/2pt.

4.00pm

Notes:

The only stat of any relevance was profitable top-weights but with Annual Invictus a non-runner that meant joint-top weight Kap Auteuil whose trainer does not fit the 40% RTF criteria

4.35pm

Notes:

Chris Gordon has a profit of over £100 and a strike rate of 16.10% in handicaps
Second favourites show a profit in handicaps BUT top-weights show a loss

Conclusion: Top-weight Baddesley is of some small interest as he is also the second favourite BUT he is also top-weight.

Result Baddesley 4th 85/40 2nd favourite

Bet 1/2pt win Baddesley, returns nil – minus 1/2pt on the race

5.10pm

Notes:

Jockey Tom Bellamy has a 33.33% strike rate in handicaps
Favourites and top-weights both show a profit in handicaps

Conclusion: Tom Bellamy's mount Getaman was a non-runner. That leaves top-weight Blaze A Trail and favourite Braveheart equally qualified, so I dutched the pair at odds of 3/1 and 6/4 meaning 0.38 points on Blaze A Trail and 0.62pts on Braveheart (using a dutching calculator) – result BSP of 4.40 less 2% commission means a return of 1.2662 and a profit of 0.2662 points

1:40 Fontwell
30 SEP 2022 SKY

3m2f (3m1f210y) Follow @attheraces On Twitter Conditional Jockeys' Handicap Chase (Class 4) (4yo+ 0-115)

		Runners:	6 (MAX 16)
		Going:	Good
		No. of fences:	19
		EW Terms:	1/4 1-2

Card   Pro Card   At-a-glance   Odds Comparison

Predictor   Settings

Select Bookmaker   **CORAL***

NO. FORM	HORSE	AGE	WGT OR	JOCKEY ALLOWANCE / TRAINER RTF%	TS	RPR	ODDS↓
1 -P3844	Debden Bank > tp 📋 ⊗ 18	8	12-0 110	J: Finn Lambert >3 T: Martin Keighley >80	100	117	SP PLACE BET
2 166632	D'Jango > tb 📋 ⊗ 1 tip 14	9	12-0 110	J: Philip Armson >3 T: David Pipe >39	105	118	SP PLACE BET
3 3-1141	My Lady Grey > p 📋 ⊗ CD 38	8	11-1 97	J: Harry Kimber >3 T: Joe Tizzard >50	94	118	SP PLACE BET
4 222411	Minella Voucher > tp 📋 ⊗ C D 1 tip 14	11	10-12 94	J: Bradley Harris >3 T: Alexandra Dunn >43	104	116	SP PLACE BET
5 POP-21	Toad Of Toad Hall > 📋 ⊗ CD 114	6	10-3 85	J: Toby Wynne >3 T: Alexandra Dunn >43	95	117	SP PLACE BET
6 413233	Belle Jour > v 📋 ⊗ CD BF 1 tip 38	7	10-2 84	J: Niall Houlihan > T: Chris Gordon >100	92	118	SP PLACE BET

Show all racecards for this meeting on one page >

LONG HANDICAP Belle Jour 10-1

FUTURE OR Belle Jour (-1)

2:15 Fontwell
30 SEP 2022 SKY

2m1½f (2m1f162y) At The Races App Market Movers Handicap Hurdle (Class 3) (3yo+ 0-135)

Runners:	7 (MAX 13)		
Going:	**Good**		
No. of hurdles:	**9**		
EW Terms:	**1/4 1-2**		

Card	Pro Card	At-a-glance	Odds Comparison	❓

⌂ **Predictor** ⚙ **Settings** Select Bookmaker **CORAL** ⌄

NO. FORM	HORSE	AGE	WGT OR	JOCKEY ALLOWANCE / TRAINER RTF%	TS	RPR	ODDS↓
1 41/21-	**Swaffham Bulbeck** › ♀ 🗎 ⊗ **C D** 381 (30F)	8	12-0 / 130	J: Ciaran Gethings › / T: Stuart Edmunds ›75	-	-	**SP** PLACE BET
2 /2510-	**Kannapolis** › ♀ 🗎 ⊗ 167	7	11-9 / 125	J: Tom Cannon › / T: Toby Lawes ›	104	133	**SP** PLACE BET
3 1U-01U	**Peltwell** › P ♀ 🗎 ⊗ **D** 76	9	11-8 / 124	J: Sam Twiston-Davies › / T: Neil Mulholland ›53	111	129	**SP** PLACE BET
4 -23413	**Bucko's Boy** › P ♀ 🗎 ⊗ **D** 31	7	11-0 / 116	J: Page Fuller › / T: Jamie Snowden ›63	113	133	**SP** PLACE BET
5 12-111	**Soul Icon** › ht ♀ 🗎 ⊗ **CD** 2 tips 38	5	10-6 / 108	J: Harry Kimber ›5 / T: Keiran Burke ›100	124	136	**SP** PLACE BET
6 -42351	**Thahab Ifraj** › ♀ 🗎 ⊗ **CD** 43	9	10-5 / 107	J: Philip Armson ›3 / T: Alexandra Dunn ›43	127	133	**SP** PLACE BET
7 668-11	**Denable** › ♀ 🗎 ⊗ 17	6	10-2 / 104	J: Brendan Powell › / T: Anthony Carson ›	113	130	**SP** PLACE BET

Show all racecards for this meeting on one page ›

LONG HANDICAP Denable 9-13

FUTURE OR Denable (-3)

2:50 Fontwell
30 SEP 2022 SKY

2m1½f (2m1f162y) Cazoo Novices' Hurdle (GBB Race) (Class 4) (4yo+)

Going:	**Good**
No. of hurdles:	**9**
EW Terms:	**1/5 1-3**

Card   Pro Card   At-a-glance   Odds Comparison   ❓

⌂ Predictor   ⚙ Settings   Select Bookmaker **CORAL** ⌄

NO. FORM	HORSE	AGE	WGT OR	JOCKEY ALLOWANCE / TRAINER RTF%	TS	RPR	ODDS↓
1 672-1	Mothill › 📄⊗ CD 141	4	11-5 113	J: Tom Scudamore › T: Neil Mulholland ›53	83	113	SP PLACE BET
2 22-1	Bobby Socks › 📄⊗ D 25	5	11-0 ·	J: Aidan Coleman › T: Olly Murphy ›67	·	·	SP PLACE BET
3 14022-	Dusky Days › 📄⊗ BF 166	5	11-0 108	J: Gavin Sheehan › T: Jamie Snowden ›63	99	119	SP PLACE BET
4	Fascinating Lips › 📄⊗ 1 tip (24F)	5	11-0 ·	J: Jamie Moore › T: Gary Moore ›14	·	·	SP PLACE BET
5	Stopnsearch › 📄⊗ (31F)	5	11-0 ·	J: Tom Cannon › T: Brett Johnson ›33	·	·	SP PLACE BET
6 P/5-	Stormbomber › 📄⊗ 390 (9F)	6	11-0 ·	J: Marc Goldstein › T: Michael Madgwick ›50	50	83	SP PLACE BET
7 073-3	Bahtiyar › 📄⊗ 18	4	10-12 108	J: Daryl Jacob › T: 2 Harry Whittington ›100	86	118	SP PLACE BET
8 4-	Unstoppable › h 📄⊗ 259	4	10-12 ·	J: Page Fuller › T: Jo Davis ›	·	·	SP PLACE BET

3:25 Fontwell
30 SEP 2022 SKY

2m1½f (2m1f162y) At The Races App Form Study Juvenile Hurdle (GBB Race) (Class 4) (3yo)

Going:	Good
No. of hurdles:	9
EW Terms:	1/5 1-3

Card | Pro Card | At-a-glance | Odds Comparison ?

Predictor | Settings | Select Bookmaker | CORAL ⌄

NO. FORM	HORSE	AGE	WGT OR	JOCKEY ALLOWANCE / TRAINER RTF%	TS	RPR	ODDS↓
1 311	**Mr Freedom** > CD 1 tip 12	3	11-12 102	J: Marc Goldstein > T: Sheena West >100	95	102	SP PLACE BET
2 3	**Borntobealeader** > h1 BF 12	3	11-0 -	J: Tom Scudamore > T: 2 David Pipe >39	74	83	SP PLACE BET
3	**Briar Bank** > (111F)	3	11-0 -	J: Tom Cannon > T: Toby Lawes >	-	-	SP PLACE BET
4 F3	**Hill Station** > 75	3	11-0 -	J: Jamie Moore > T: Gary Moore >14	36	106	SP PLACE BET
5	**Lightening Gesture** > t (24F)	3	11-0 -	J: Fergus Gregory > T: Jack Jones >100	-	-	SP PLACE BET
6	**Ellencarne** > (43F)	3	10-7 -	J: David Noonan > T: 2 Mark Gillard >50	-	-	SP PLACE BET
7	**Inspiratrice** > h1 (100F)	3	10-7 -	J: James Bowen > T: 1 Nicky Martin >	-	-	SP PLACE BET
8 2	**Miss Fedora** > 1 tip 26	3	10-7 -	J: Micheal Nolan > T: Seamus Mullins >50	28	103	SP PLACE BET

4:00 Fontwell
30 SEP 2022 SKY

2m5½f (2m5f135y) Cazoo Handicap Chase (GBB Race) (Class 2) (4yo+ 0-145)

	Runners:	6 (MAX 16)
	Going:	Good
	No. of fences:	16
	EW Terms:	1/4 1-2

Card | Pro Card | At-a-glance | Odds Comparison

Predictor | Settings

Select Bookmaker **CORAL***

NO. FORM	HORSE	AGE	WGT OR	JOCKEY ALLOWANCE / TRAINER RTF%	TS	RPR	ODDS↓
1 P33V-P	Annual Invictus > p 145	7	12-0 140	J: Tom Cannon > T: Chris Gordon >100	107	146	SP PLACE BET
2 14716-	Kap Auteuil > CD 167	7	12-0 140	J: Tom O'Brien > T: Toby Lawes >	115	144	SP PLACE BET
3 03P31-	Up The Straight > D 1 tip 160	8	11-6 132	J: James Davies > T: Richard Rowe >	122	150	SP PLACE BET
4 F4-834	The Golden Rebel > D 2 tips 17	8	11-4 130	J: Harry Bannister > T: Ben Case >	114	147	SP PLACE BET
5 /FP-P3	Fakir > t 128	7	10-11 123	J: Kevin Jones > T: 1 Milton Harris >56	-	-	SP PLACE BET
6 2P1PP-	Pilbara > CD 315	7	10-11 123	J: Charlie Hammond > T: Suzy Smith >	113	145	SP PLACE BET

Going: **Good**

No. of hurdles: **10**

EW Terms: **1/5 1-3**

2m3f (2m3f49y) Sky Sports Racing HD Virgin 535 Handicap Hurdle (Class 5) (3yo+ 0-105)

| Card | Pro Card | At-a-glance | Odds Comparison | ? |

| Predictor | Settings | | Select Bookmaker | *CORAL* ⌄ |

NO. FORM	HORSE	AGE	WGT OR	JOCKEY ALLOWANCE TRAINER RTF%	TS	RPR	ODDS↓
1 /3236-	Baddesley › t ♡ ▤ ⊗ C BF 214	7	12-2 107	J: Mr Freddie Gordon ›[7] T: Chris Gordon ›[100]	98	107	SP PLACE BET
2 5363-1	Princess T › tp ♡ ▤ ⊗ 1 tip 7	7	11-13 104	J: Thomas Doggrell ›[7] T: Neil Mulholland ›[53]	81	117	SP PLACE BET
3 /63P-P	Albert Van Ornum › ♡ ▤ ⊗ 136	5	11-9 100	J: Jamie Moore › T: Gary Moore ›[14]	96	106	SP PLACE BET
4 31-422	Cluain Aodha › ♡ ▤ ⊗ 44	5	11-9 100	J: Jack Quinlan › T: Neil King ›	51	109	SP PLACE BET
5 7P006-	Dev Of Tara › ♡ ▤ ⊗ 218	6	11-4 95	J: Fergus Gregory › T: [1] Olly Murphy ›[67]	82	93	SP PLACE BET
6 4-3713	Beat The Heat › p ♡ ▤ ⊗ C BF 103 (15F)	5	11-2 93	J: Sean Houlihan › T: Jim Boyle ›[41]	89	106	SP PLACE BET
7 F-6580	Mise Raftaire › p ♡ ▤ ⊗ 17	7	10-7 84	J: Harry Bannister › T: Warren Greatrex ›	80	116	SP PLACE BET
8 536643	Stigwood › p ♡ ▤ ⊗ 1 tip 27	4	10-2 82	J: Connor Brace › T: [1] John Flint ›[83]	97	109	SP PLACE BET
9 5046-5	Iconic Mover › ♡ ▤ ⊗ 114 (37F)	4	10-2 82	J: Niall Houlihan ›[3] T: Pat Phelan ›[25]	58	94	SP PLACE BET
10 6P598-	Shesupincourt › ♡ ▤ ⊗ 170	5	10-2 79	J: Ben Poste › T: Ryan Potter ›[40]	66	103	SP PLACE BET
11 075-26	What's My Line › ♡ ▤ ⊗ 124	5	10-2 79	J: Marc Goldstein › T: Michael Madgwick ›[50]	75	98	SP PLACE BET

Show all racecards for this meeting on one page ›

LONG HANDICAP Iconic Mover 9-12, Shesupincourt 9-11, What's My Line 9-10

FUTURE OR Princess T (+6), Iconic Mover (-4), Shesupincourt (-5), What's My Line (-6)

5:10 Fontwell
30 SEP 2022 SKY

2m2f (2m1f165y) Free Tips Daily On attheraces.com Handicap Chase (Class 5) (4yo+ 0-100)

Going: **Good**
No. of fences: **13**
EW Terms: **1/4 1-2**

| Card | Pro Card | At-a-glance | Odds Comparison | ? |

| ⌂ Predictor | ⚙ Settings | | Select Bookmaker | **CORAL** ⌄ |

NO. FORM		HORSE	AGE	WGT OR	JOCKEY ALLOWANCE TRAINER RTF%	TS	RPR	ODDS↓
1 P76111		**Blaze A Trail** > h ⎙ ⊗ D 27	8	12-0 99	J: Connor Brace > T: John Flint >[83]	86	105	SP PLACE BET
2 /2205-		**Braveheart** > w² t ⎙ ⊗ 225	6	11-7 92	J: Gavin Sheehan > T: Jamie Snowden >[63]	-	-	SP PLACE BET
3 B21241		**Getaman** > b ⎙ ⊗ D 16	9	11-7 92	J: Tom Bellamy > T: D J Jeffreys >[80]	88	103	SP PLACE BET
4 5U134F		**Trumps Benefit** > tp ⎙ ⊗ D [1 tip] 12	9	11-6 91	J: Caoilin Quinn >[7] T: Ryan Potter >[40]	99	112	SP PLACE BET
5 -24252		**Touchthesoul** > tp ⎙ ⊗ 43	7	11-3 88	J: Page Fuller > T: Jo Davis >	77	110	SP PLACE BET
6 P-6518		**The Garrison** > t ⎙ ⊗ D 32	8	10-13 84	J: James Davies > T: Alexandra Dunn >[43]	82	105	SP PLACE BET

National Hunt Racecourses (UK only in alphabetical order):

Aintree - Chases

Top jockeys by Strike Rate – non-handicaps

Name Of Jockey	Rides	Winners	Strike Rate	Profit/Loss to BSP
Nico de Boinville	13	5	38.46%	-£4.39
Paddy Brennan	12	4	33.33%	+£21.50
Bryan Cooper	12	3	25.00%	+£36.12
Harry Cobden	15	3	20.00%	+£4.10
Sam Twiston-Davies	18	3	16.67%	+£3.67

Top jockeys by Strike Rate – handicaps

Name Of Jockey	Rides	Winners	Strike Rate	Profit/Loss to BSP
Ben Poste	11	3	27.27%	+£12.83
Danny McMenamin	11	3	27.27%	+£49.11
Rachael Blackmore	10	2	20.00%	+£10.05
James Best	12	2	16.67%	+£16.69
Derek Fox	18	3	16.67%	+£38.09

Top jockeys by Profit – non-handicaps

Name Of Jockey	Rides	Winners	Strike Rate	Profit/Loss to BSP
Bryan Cooper	12	3	25.00%	+£36.12
Paddy Brennan	12	4	33.33%	+£21.50
Brian Hughes	12	1	8.33%	+£10.56
Harry Cobden	15	3	20.00%	+£4.10
Sam Twiston-Davies	18	3	16.67%	+£3.67

Top jockeys by Profit – handicaps

Name Of Jockey	Rides	Winners	Strike Rate	Profit/Loss to BSP
Ryan Mania	24	1	4.17%	+£100.61
Harry Cobden	18	2	11.11%	+£93.02
Danny McMenamin	11	3	27.27%	+£49.11
Derek Fox	18	3	16.67%	+£38.09
Brian Hughes	87	7	8.05%	+£33.21

Top trainers by Strike Rate – non-handicaps

Name Of Trainer	Runners	Winners	Strike Rate	Profit/Loss to BSP
W P Mullins	20	6	30.00%	+£1.64
Nicky Henderson	39	11	28.21%	-£12.82
Colin Tizzard	25	6	24.00%	-£0.10
Tom George	14	3	21.43%	+£17.33
Nigel Twiston-Davies	15	3	20.00%	+£8.98

Top trainers by Strike Rate – handicaps

Name Of Trainer	Runners	Winners	Strike Rate	Profit/Loss to BSP
Katy Price	10	3	30.00%	+£13.83
James Moffatt	10	2	20.00%	+£26.80
Henry Oliver	11	2	18.18%	+£1.38
Ian Williams	12	2	16.67%	+£0.56
Neil Mulholland	14	2	14.29%	+£7.10

Top trainers by Profit – non-handicaps

Name Of Trainer	Runners	Winners	Strike Rate	Profit/Loss to BSP
Henry De Bromhead	18	3	16.67%	+£32.27
Tom George	14	3	21.43%	+£17.33
Nigel Twiston-Davies	15	3	20.00%	+£8.98
Dan Skelton	18	3	16.67%	+£3.17

W P Mullins	20	6	24.00%	+£1.64

Top trainers by Profit – handicaps

Name Of Trainer	Runners	Winners	Strike Rate	Profit/Loss to BSP
Colin Tizzard	56	6	10.71%	+£111.89
Patrick Griffin	12	1	8.33%	+£95.82
Sue Smith	45	2	4.44%	+£85.60
Dr Richard Newland	33	3	9.09%	+£32.00
James Moffatt	10	2	20.00%	+£26.80

Top trainer/jockey combos by Strike Rate – non-handicaps

Name of Trainer/Jockey	Qualifiers	Winners	Strike Rate	Profit/Loss to BSP
Nicky Henderson/Nico de Boinville	13	5	38.46%	-£4.39
Paul Nicholls/Harry Cobden	13	3	23.08%	+£6.10
Paul Nicholls/Sam Twiston-Davies	14	3	21.43%	+£7.67
Dan Skelton/Harry Skelton	16	2	12.50%	-£1.12

Top trainer/jockey combos by Strike Rate – handicaps

Name of Trainer/Jockey	Qualifiers	Winners	Strike Rate	Profit/Loss to BSP
Katy Price/Ben Poste	10	3	30.00%	+£13.83
Peter Bowen/Sean Bowen	18	4	22.22%	+£12.16
Colin Tizzard/Brendan Powell	10	2	20.00%	+£24.42
Lucinda	10	2	20.00%	+£11.36

Russell/Derek Fox				
Paul Nicholls/Sean Bowen	13	2	15.38%	+£3.75

Top trainer/jockey combos by Profit – non-handicaps

Name of Trainer/Jockey	Qualifiers	Winners	Strike Rate	Profit/Loss to BSP
Paul Nicholls/Sam Twiston-Davies	14	3	21.43%	+£7.67
Paul Nicholls/Harry Cobden	13	3	23.08%	+£6.10

Top trainer/jockey combos by Profit – handicaps

Name of Trainer/Jockey	Qualifiers	Winners	Strike Rate	Profit/Loss to BSP
Sue Smith/Ryan Mania	18	1	5.56%	+£106.61
Colin Tizzard/Brendan Powell	10	2	20.00%	+£24.42
Tom George/Paddy Brennan	28	4	14.29%	+£18.03
Philip Hobbs/Tom O'Brien	20	3	15.00%	+£13.97
Katy Price/ Ben Poste	10	3	30.00%	+£13.83

Profit or Loss backing the unnamed favourite – non-handicaps

Runners	Winners	Strike Rate	Profit/Loss to BSP
186	68	36.56%	-£2.40

Profit or Loss backing the unnamed favourite – handicaps

Runners	Winners	Strike Rate	Profit/Loss to BSP
351	73	20.80%	+£3.39

Profit or loss backing the unnamed second favourite - non-handicaps

Runners	Winners	Strike Rate	Profit/Loss to BSP
175	49	28.00%	+£58.08

Profit or loss backing the unnamed second favourite - handicaps

Runners	Winners	Strike Rate	Profit/Loss to BSP
323	40	12.38%	-£61.17

Profit or Loss backing horses who won last time out - non-handicaps

Runners	Winners	Strike Rate	Profit/Loss to BSP
345	45	13.04%	-£51.91

Profit or Loss backing horses who won last time out - handicaps

Runners	Winners	Strike Rate	Profit/Loss to BSP
641	53	8.27%	-£208.85

Profit or loss backing Top-Weights in handicaps

Runners	Winners	Strike Rate	Profit/Loss to BSP
328	27	8.23%	-£159.21

Most profitable sires – non-handicaps

Sire	Runners	Winners	Strike Rate	Profit/Loss to BSP
Oscar	19	5	26.32%	+£42.15
Kayf Tara	17	3	17.65%	+£40.26
Saint Des Saints	11	3	27.27%	+£10.34
Dom Alco	12	6	50.00%	+£5.68
Poliglote	13	2	15.38%	+£4.48

Most profitable sires – handicaps

Kapgarde	28	5	17.86%	+£101.57
Trempolino	10	1	10.00%	+£97.82
Beneficial	89	9	10.11%	+£71.36
Midnight Legend	40	5	12.50%	+£38.52
Dom Alco	17	2	11.76%	+£29.76

Aintree – Hurdles

Top jockeys by Strike Rate – non-handicaps

Name Of Jockey	Rides	Winners	Strike Rate	Profit/Loss to BSP
Nico de Boinville	34	8	23.53%	+£8.24
Harry Skelton	46	9	19.57%	+£156.19
Paul Townend	16	3	18.75%	-£10.72
Harry Cobden	17	3	17.65%	-£7.00
Aidan Coleman	47	7	14.89%	-£20.77

Top jockeys by Strike Rate – handicaps

Name Of Jockey	Rides	Winners	Strike Rate	Profit/Loss to BSP
David Bass	15	3	20.00%	+£65.78
Harry Skelton	42	8	19.05%	+£25.20
Aidan Coleman	41	7	17.07%	+£32.42
Ciaran Gethings	12	2	16.67%	£-0.49
Sean Quinlan	17	2	11.76%	+£25.91

Top jockeys by Profit – non-handicaps

Name Of Jockey	Rides	Winners	Strike Rate	Profit/Loss to BSP
Harry Skelton	46	9	19.57%	+£156.19
Jamie Moore	13	1	7.69%	+£24.26
A P Heskin	14	2	14.29%	+£9.75
Nico de Boinville	34	8	23.53%	+£8.24
Brian Hughes	40	4	10.00%	+£7.42

Top jockeys by Profit – handicaps

Name Of Jockey	Rides	Winners	Strike Rate	Profit/Loss to BSP
Jonathan Moore	14	1	7.14%	+£109.29
David Bass	15	3	20.00%	+£65.78
Aidan Coleman	41	7	17.07%	+£32.42
Sean Quinlan	17	2	11.76%	+£25.91
Harry Skelton	42	8	19.05%	+£25.20

Top trainers by Strike Rate – non-handicaps

Name Of Trainer	Runners	Winners	Strike Rate	Profit/Loss to BSP
Alan King	42	11	26.19%	+£23.65
Nicky Henderson	94	23	24.47%	+£5.09
Philip Hobbs	21	5	23.81%	+£4.02
Rebecca Curtis	24	5	20.83%	-£13.25
Colin Tizzard	26	5	19.23%	+£69.16

Top trainers by Strike Rate – handicaps

Name Of Trainer	Runners	Winners	Strike Rate	Profit/Loss to BSP
Ruth Jefferson	11	3	27.27%	+£29.63
Olly Murphy	17	4	23.53%	+£5.44
Gordon Elliott	14	3	21.43%	+£15.60
Stuart Edmunds	10	2	20.00%	+£11.90
Neil Mulholland	11	2	18.18%	+£0.75

Top trainers by Profit – non-handicaps

Name Of Trainer	Runners	Winners	Strike Rate	Profit/Loss to BSP
Dan Skelton	53	9	16.98%	+£149.21
Colin Tizzard	26	5	19.23%	+£69.16
Gary Moore	12	1	8.33%	+£25.26
Alan King	42	11	26.19%	+£23.65
Henry De Bromhead	11	1	9.09%	+£11.89

Top trainers by Profit – handicaps

Name Of Trainer	Runners	Winners	Strike Rate	Profit/Loss to BSP
Nicky Henderson	83	12	14.46%	+£59.52
James Moffatt	10	1	10.00%	+£53.72
Ian Williams	24	4	16.67%	+£50.72
Ruth Jefferson	11	3	27.27%	+£29.63
Philip Kirby	18	3	16.67%	+£28.83

Top trainer/jockey combos by Strike Rate – non-handicaps

Name of Trainer/Jockey	Qualifiers	Winners	Strike Rate	Profit/Loss to BSP
Nicky Henderson/ Nico de Boinville	30	8	26.67%	+£12.24
Paul Nicholls/Harry Cobden	15	3	20.00%	-£5.00
Dan Skelton/Harry Skelton	46	9	19.57%	+£156.19
Fergal O'Brien/Paddy Brennan	11	2	18.18%	-£6.54
W P Mullins/Paul Townend	11	2	18.18%	-£7.35

Top trainer/jockey combos by Strike Rate – handicaps

Name of Trainer/Jockey	Qualifiers	Winners	Strike Rate	Profit/Loss to BSP
Dan Skelton/Harry Skelton	40	8	20.00%	+£27.20
Jennie Candlish/Sean Quinlan	12	2	16.67%	+£30.91
Nicky Henderson/Daryl Jacob	10	1	10.00%	-£3.78
Donald	10	1	10.00%	-£4.44

McCain/Brian Hughes				
Tim Vaughan/Alan Johns	12	1	8.33%	+£16.15

Top trainer/jockey combos by Profit – non-handicaps

Name of Trainer/Jockey	Qualifiers	Winners	Strike Rate	Profit/Loss to BSP
Dan Skelton/Harry Skelton	46	9	19.57%	+£158.19
Paul Nicholls/Sam Twiston-Davies	14	2	14.29%	+£13.80
Nicky Henderson/Nico de Boinville	30	8	26.67%	+£12.24

Top trainer/jockey combos by Profit – handicaps

Name of Trainer/Jockey	Qualifiers	Winners	Strike Rate	Profit/Loss to BSP
Jennie Candlish/Sean Quinlan	12	2	16.67%	+£30.91
Dan Skelton/Harry Skelton	40	8	20.00%	+£27.20
Tim Vaughan/Alan Johns	12	1	8.33%	+£16.15

Profit or Loss backing the unnamed favourite – non-handicaps

Runners	Winners	Strike Rate	Profit/Loss to BSP
274	110	40.15%	-£4.72

Profit or Loss backing the unnamed favourite – handicaps

Runners	Winners	Strike Rate	Profit/Loss to

			BSP
297	72	24.24%	+£27.40

Profit or loss backing the unnamed second favourite - non-handicaps

Runners	Winners	Strike Rate	Profit/Loss to BSP
263	52	19.77%	-£34.33

Profit or loss backing the unnamed second favourite - handicaps

Runners	Winners	Strike Rate	Profit/Loss to BSP
253	42	16.60%	+£9.85

Profit or Loss backing horses who won last time out- non-handicaps

Runners	Winners	Strike Rate	Profit/Loss to BSP
546	83	15.20%	+£54.60

Profit or Loss backing horses who won last time out- handicaps

Runners	Winners	Strike Rate	Profit/Loss to BSP
605	74	12.23%	-£59.90

Profit or loss backing Top-Weights in handicaps

Runners	Winners	Strike Rate	Profit/Loss to BSP
282	30	10.64%	+£112.35

Most profitable sires – non-handicaps

Sire	Runners	Winners	Strike Rate	Profit/Loss to BSP
Flemensfirth	20	2	10.00%	+£67.93
Presenting	18	3	16.67%	+£44.97
Kayf Tara	32	6	18.75%	+£40.95
Shirocco	11	4	36.36%	+£29.25
Milan	24	8	33.33%	+£15.71

Most profitable sires – handicaps

Vinnie Roe	20	4	20.00%	+£34.55
Presenting	46	3	6.52%	+£32.00
Old Vic	17	2	11.76%	+£24.48
Definite Article	10	2	20.00%	+£22.62
Passing Glance	13	2	15.38%	+£18.27

Ascot - Chases

Top jockeys by Strike Rate – non-handicaps

Name Of Jockey	Rides	Winners	Strike Rate	Profit/Loss to BSP
Nico de Boinville	16	8	50.00%	+£1.20
David Bass	13	5	38.46%	+£16.34
Sam Twiston-Davies	25	8	32.00%	-£0.24
Daryl Jacob	18	5	27.78%	-£4.24
Harry Cobden	22	6	27.27%	-£4.50

Top jockeys by Strike Rate – handicaps

Name Of Jockey	Rides	Winners	Strike Rate	Profit/Loss to BSP
Jonathan Burke	11	3	27.27%	+£24.03
Jonjo O'Neill Jr	12	3	25.00%	+£17.27
Charlie Deutsch	29	7	24.14%	+£12.27
Jamie Moore	42	9	21.43%	+£37.58
James Best	21	4	19.05%	+£30.77

Top jockeys by Profit – non-handicaps

Name Of Jockey	Rides	Winners	Strike Rate	Profit/Loss to BSP
David Bass	13	5	38.46%	+£16.34
Tom Scudamore	11	2	18.18%	+£3.15
Tom O'Brien	11	1	9.09%	+£1.78
Nico de Boinville	16	8	50.00%	+£1.20

Top jockeys by Profit – handicaps

Name Of Jockey	Rides	Winners	Strike Rate	Profit/Loss to BSP
Aidan Coleman	52	9	17.31%	+£65.11
Jamie Moore	42	9	21.43%	+£37.58
James Best	21	4	19.05%	+£30.77
Harry Cobden	37	7	18.92%	+£25.57
Richie McLernon	29	4	13.79%	+£25.14

Top trainers by Strike Rate – non-handicaps

Name Of Trainer	Runners	Winners	Strike Rate	Profit/Loss to BSP
Kim Bailey	12	6	50.00%	+£19.25
Nicky Henderson	48	16	33.33%	-£9.39
Paul Nicholls	73	21	28.77%	-£14.26
Philip Hobbs	24	5	20.83%	+£8.62
Alan King	10	2	20.00%	+£3.99

Top trainers by Strike Rate – handicaps

Name Of Trainer	Runners	Winners	Strike Rate	Profit/Loss to BSP
Robert Walford	10	3	30.00%	+£36.06
Kim Bailey	19	5	26.32%	+£27.10
Fergal O'Brien	10	2	20.00%	-£0.04
Anthony Honeyball	26	5	19.23%	+£71.28
Venetia Williams	101	18	17.82%	+£66.66

Top trainers by Profit – non-handicaps

Name Of Trainer	Runners	Winners	Strike Rate	Profit/Loss to BSP
Kim Bailey	12	6	50.00%	+£19.25
Philip Hobbs	24	5	20.83%	+£8.62
Alan King	10	2	20.00%	+£3.99

Top trainers by Profit – handicaps

Name Of Trainer	Runners	Winners	Strike Rate	Profit/Loss to BSP
Anthony Honeyball	26	5	19.23%	+£71.28
Venetia Williams	101	18	17.82%	+£66.66
Nicky Henderson	51	9	17.65%	+£66.15
Robert Walford	10	3	30.00%	+£36.06
Colin Tizzard	51	6	11.76%	+£30.96

Top trainer/jockey combos by Strike Rate – non-handicaps

Name of Trainer/Jockey	Qualifiers	Winners	Strike Rate	Profit/Loss to BSP
Nicky Henderson/Nico de Boinville	14	8	57.14%	+£3.20
Kim Bailey/David Bass	10	4	40.00%	+£17.34
Paul Nicholls/Sam Twiston-Davies	16	5	31.25%	-£3.53
Paul Nicholls/Harry Cobden	21	6	28.57%	-£3.50

Top trainer/jockey combos by Strike Rate – handicaps

Name of Trainer/Jockey	Qualifiers	Winners	Strike Rate	Profit/Loss to BSP
Gary Moore/Jamie Moore	34	8	23.53%	+£35.96
Anthony Honeyball/Richie McLernon	17	4	23.53%	+£37.14
Nicky Henderson/Nico de Boinville	19	4	21.05%	+£3.86
Venetia Williams/Aidan Coleman	35	7	20.00%	+£40.78
David Pipe/Tom Scudamore	16	3	18.75%	+£9.25

Top trainer/jockey combos by Profit – non-handicaps

Name of Trainer/Jockey	Qualifiers	Winners	Strike Rate	Profit/Loss to BSP
Kim Bailey/David Bass	10	4	40.00%	+£17.34

Nicky Henderson/Nico de Boinville	14	8	57.14%	+£3.20

Top trainer/jockey combos by Profit – handicaps

Name of Trainer/Jockey	Qualifiers	Winners	Strike Rate	Profit/Loss to BSP
Venetia Williams/Aidan Coleman	36	7	20.00%	+£40.78
Anthony Honeyball/Richie McLernon	17	4	23.53%	+£37.14
Gary Moore/Jamie Moore	34	8	23.53%	+£35.96
Colin Tizzard/Brendan Powell	10	1	10.00%	+£21.38
Dr Richard Newland/Sam Twiston-Davies	11	2	18.18%	+£20.22

Profit or Loss backing the unnamed favourite – non-handicaps

Runners	Winners	Strike Rate	Profit/Loss to BSP
181	87	48.07%	+£9.85

Profit or Loss backing the unnamed favourite – handicaps

Runners	Winners	Strike Rate	Profit/Loss to BSP
291	63	21.65%	-£52.28

Profit or loss backing the unnamed second favourite - non-handicaps

Runners	Winners	Strike Rate	Profit/Loss to BSP
159	34	21.38%	-£40.35

Profit or loss backing the unnamed second favourite - handicaps

Runners	Winners	Strike Rate	Profit/Loss to BSP
282	48	17.02%	-£23.32

Profit or Loss backing horses who won last time out- non-handicaps

Runners	Winners	Strike Rate	Profit/Loss to BSP
225	63	28.00%	-£20.51

Profit or Loss backing horses who won last time out- handicaps

Runners	Winners	Strike Rate	Profit/Loss to BSP
413	68	16.46%	+£54.33

Profit or loss backing Top-Weights in handicaps

Runners	Winners	Strike Rate	Profit/Loss to BSP
297	45	15.15%	+£55.34

Most profitable sires – non-handicaps

Sire	Runners	Winners	Strike Rate	Profit/Loss to BSP
King's Theatre	26	8	30.77%	+£14.61
Flemensfirth	16	4	25.00%	+£3.20
Oscar	11	2	18.18%	+£3.13
Poliglote	12	5	41.67%	+£2.58

Most profitable sires – handicaps

King's Theatre	67	9	13.43%	+£48.54
Dr Massini	14	4	28.57%	+£46.39
Kayf Tara	39	2	5.13%	+£39.33
Martaline	15	1	6.67%	+£18.34
Dubai Destination	11	2	18.18%	+£11.69

Ascot – Hurdles

Top jockeys by Strike Rate – non-handicaps

Name Of Jockey	Rides	Winners	Strike Rate	Profit/Loss to BSP
Nico de Boinville	38	13	34.21%	+£2.26
Harry Skelton	20	5	25.00%	+£2.83
Nick Scholfield	16	4	25.00%	-£3.13
Sean Bowen	13	3	23.08%	-£2.97
Aidan Coleman	32	6	18.75%	-£8.76

Top jockeys by Strike Rate – handicaps

Name Of Jockey	Rides	Winners	Strike Rate	Profit/Loss to BSP
Aidan Coleman	34	8	23.53%	+£36.60
Harry Skelton	26	6	23.08%	+£58.20
Nico de Boinville	27	6	22.22%	+£6.73
Paddy Brennan	17	3	17.65%	+£14.14
Adam Wedge	14	2	14.29%	-£4.93

Top jockeys by Profit – non-handicaps

Name Of Jockey	Rides	Winners	Strike Rate	Profit/Loss to BSP
Jamie Moore	29	5	17.24%	+£40.80
David Bass	23	2	8.70%	+£35.63
Paddy Brennan	15	12	6.87%	+£6.92
Harry Skelton	20	5	25.00%	+£2.83
Nico de Boinville	38	13	34.21%	+£2.26

Top jockeys by Profit – handicaps

Name Of Jockey	Rides	Winners	Strike Rate	Profit/Loss to BSP
Harry Skelton	26	6	23.08%	+£58.20
Aidan Coleman	34	8	23.53%	+£36.60
Bryony Frost	12	1	8.33%	+£29.18
Tom O'Brien	22	2	9.09%	+£20.94
Harry Cobden	34	3	8.82%	+£17.41

Top trainers by Strike Rate – non-handicaps

Name Of Trainer	Runners	Winners	Strike Rate	Profit/Loss to BSP
Harry Fry	25	12	48.00%	+£16.21
Nicky Henderson	106	28	26.42%	-£23.85
Nick Williams	14	3	21.43%	+£3.24
Paul Nicholls	66	14	21.21%	+£13.67
Philip Hobbs	30	6	20.00%	-£11.63

Top trainers by Strike Rate – handicaps

Name Of Trainer	Runners	Winners	Strike Rate	Profit/Loss to BSP
Dr Richard Newland	26	5	19.23%	+£13.66
Fergal O'Brien	17	3	17.65%	+£2.47
Dan Skelton	41	7	17.07%	+£48.42
Philip Hobbs	50	8	16.00%	+£8.51
Harry Fry	26	4	15.38%	+£15.57

Top trainers by Profit – non-handicaps

Name Of Trainer	Runners	Winners	Strike Rate	Profit/Loss to BSP
Alan King	56	11	19.54%	+£56.98
Ben Pauling	12	2	16.67%	+£47.74
Rebecca Curtis	11	1	9.09%	+£22.34
Ian Williams	14	1	7.14%	+£17.14
Harry Fry	25	12	48.00%	+£16.21

Top trainers by Profit – handicaps

Name Of Trainer	Runners	Winners	Strike Rate	Profit/Loss to BSP
Nick Gifford	18	2	11.11%	+£62.85
Dan Skelton	41	7	17.07%	+£48.42
Tom Symonds	14	2	14.29%	+£34.55
Paul Nicholls	84	9	10.71%	+£25.80
Stuart Edmunds	13	1	7.69%	+£19.32

Top trainer/jockey combos by Strike Rate – non-handicaps

Name of	Qualifiers	Winners	Strike Rate	Profit/Loss to

Trainer/Jockey				BSP
Nicky Henderson/Nico de Boinville	36	12	33.33%	+£0.32
Dan Skelton/Harry Skelton	20	5	25.00%	+£2.83
Gary Moore/Jamie Moore	19	4	21.05%	+£17.46
Paul Nicholls/Sam Twiston-Davies	17	3	17.65%	+£2.42
Paul Nicholls/Harry Cobden	18	2	11.11%	-£10.90

Top trainer/jockey combos by Strike Rate – handicaps

Dan Skelton/Harry Skelton	24	6	25.00%	+£60.20
Nicky Henderson/Nico de Boinville	21	5	23.81%	+£3.52
Venetia Williams/Aidan Coleman	12	2	16.67%	+£1.62
David Pipe/Tom Scudamore	23	3	13.04%	+£0.14
Jonjo O'Neill/Jonjo O'Neill Jr	12	1	8.33%	-£6.13

Top trainer/jockey combos by Profit – non-handicaps

Name of Trainer/Jockey	Qualifiers	Winners	Strike Rate	Profit/Loss to BSP
Gary Moore/Jamie Moore	19	4	21.05%	+£17.46
Fergal O'Brien/Paddy	10	1	10.00%	+£11.92

Brennan				
Dan Skelton/Harry Skelton	20	5	25.00%	+£2.83
Paul Nicholls/Sam Twiston-Davies	17	3	17.65%	+£2.42
Nicky Henderson/Nico de Boinville	36	12	33.33%	+£0.32

Top trainer/jockey combos by Profit – handicaps

Name of Trainer/Jockey	Qualifiers	Winners	Strike Rate	Profit/Loss to BSP
Dan Skelton/Harry Skelton	24	6	25.00%	+£60.20
Paul Nicholls/Harry Cobden	29	2	6.90%	+£5.73
Nicky Henderson/Nico de Boinville	21	5	23.81%	+£3.52
Venetia Williams/Aidan Coleman	12	2	16.67%	+£1.62
David Pipe/Tom Scudamore	23	3	13.04%	+£0.14

Profit or Loss backing the unnamed favourite – non-handicaps

Runners	Winners	Strike Rate	Profit/Loss to BSP
261	113	43.30%	-£0.03

Profit or Loss backing the unnamed favourite – handicaps

Runners	Winners	Strike Rate	Profit/Loss to BSP
240	59	24.58%	+£21.69

Profit or loss backing the unnamed second favourite - non-handicaps

Runners	Winners	Strike Rate	Profit/Loss to BSP
245	54	22.04%	-£21.52

Profit or loss backing the unnamed second favourite - handicaps

Runners	Winners	Strike Rate	Profit/Loss to BSP
210	27	12.86%	-£27.48

Profit or Loss backing horses who won last time out- non-handicaps

Runners	Winners	Strike Rate	Profit/Loss to BSP
410	91	22.20%	-£76.03

Profit or Loss backing horses who won last time out- handicaps

Runners	Winners	Strike Rate	Profit/Loss to BSP
462	49	10.61%	-£51.13

Profit or loss backing Top-Weights in handicaps

Runners	Winners	Strike Rate	Profit/Loss to BSP
244	22	9.02%	-£35.60

Most profitable sires – non-handicaps

Sire	Runners	Winners	Strike Rate	Profit/Loss to BSP
Shantou	13	5	38.46%	+£88.55
Westerner	23	3	13.04%	+£28.82
Presenting	31	4	12.90%	+£14.72
Midnight Legend	16	3	18.75%	+£11.62
Flemensfirth	24	5	20.83%	+£9.08

Most profitable sires – handicaps

Beat Hollow	13	4	30.77%	+£74.00
Flemensfirth	20	5	25.00%	+£51.60

Cape Cross	11	1	9.09%	+£43.83
Yeats	21	3	14.29%	+£23.05
Presenting	37	3	8.11%	+£17.52

Ayr - Chases

Top jockeys by Strike Rate – non-handicaps

Name Of Jockey	Rides	Winners	Strike Rate	Profit/Loss to BSP
Brian Hughes	18	6	33.33%	+£14.67

Top jockeys by Strike Rate – handicaps

Name Of Jockey	Rides	Winners	Strike Rate	Profit/Loss to BSP
Tom Scudamore	23	7	30.43%	+£26.05
Harry Skelton	26	7	26.92%	+£6.58
Nico de Boinville	10	2	20.00%	+£0.72
Brian Hughes	175	35	20.00%	+£7.00
Daryl Jacob	10	2	20.00%	+£8.01

Top jockeys by Profit – non-handicaps

Name Of Jockey	Rides	Winners	Strike Rate	Profit/Loss to BSP
Brian Hughes	18	6	33.33%	+£14.67

Top jockeys by Profit – handicaps

Name Of Jockey	Rides	Winners	Strike Rate	Profit/Loss to BSP
Harry Reed	17	3	17.65%	+£109.61
Craig Nichol	72	11	15.28%	+£31.29
Sean Quinlan	56	8	14.29%	+£30.64
Tom Scudamore	23	7	30.43%	+£26.05
Brian Harding	58	10	17.24%	+£15.95

Top trainers by Strike Rate – non-handicaps

Name Of Trainer	Runners	Winners	Strike Rate	Profit/Loss to BSP
Nicky Richards	10	5	50.00%	+£1.57
Donald McCain	15	5	33.33%	-£1.47

| Lucinda Russell | 18 | 4 | 22.22% | -£3.49 |

Top trainers by Strike Rate – handicaps

Name Of Trainer	Runners	Winners	Strike Rate	Profit/Loss to BSP
Dan Skelton	26	8	30.77%	+£10.93
Alison Hamilton	12	3	25.00%	+£10.23
William Young Jnr	27	7	25.00%	+£34.75
Lisa Harrison	17	4	23.53%	+£11.70
Chris Grant	17	4	23.53%	+£4.43

Top trainers by Profit – non-handicaps

Name Of Trainer	Runners	Winners	Strike Rate	Profit/Loss to BSP
Nicky Richards	10	5	50.00%	+1.57

Top trainers by Profit – handicaps

Name Of Trainer	Runners	Winners	Strike Rate	Profit/Loss to BSP
Peter Bowen	15	1	6.67%	+£44.99
William Young Jnr	28	7	25.00%	+£34.75
Nicky Richards	84	18	21.43%	+£21.31
N W Alexander	119	21	17.65%	+£17.34
Paul Nicholls	33	5	15.15%	+£16.04

Top trainer/jockey combos by Strike Rate – handicaps

Name of Trainer/Jockey	Qualifiers	Winners	Strike Rate	Profit/Loss to BSP
Dan Skelton/Harry Skelton	21	7	33.33%	+£11.58
Nicky Richards/Brian Hughes	18	6	33.33%	-£0.02
Nicky Richards/Craig Nichol	15	4	26.67%	+£2.71

Donald McCain/Brian Hughes	23	6	26.09%	-£0.37
Sandy Thomson/Ryan Mania	29	7	24.14%	+£9.07

Top trainer/jockey combos by Profit – handicaps

Name of Trainer/Jockey	Qualifiers	Winners	Strike Rate	Profit/Loss to BSP
Paul Nicholls/Sam Twiston-Davies	13	2	15.38%	+£20.36
Dan Skelton/Harry Skelton	21	7	33.33%	+£11.58
James Ewart/Brian Hughes	17	4	23.53%	+£10.92
N W Alexander/Brian Hughes	12	5	41.67%	+£9.73
Sandy Thomson/Ryan Mania	29	7	24.14%	+£9.07

Profit or Loss backing the unnamed favourite – non-handicaps

Runners	Winners	Strike Rate	Profit/Loss to BSP
151	74	49.01%	+£12.49

Profit or Loss backing the unnamed favourite – handicaps

Runners	Winners	Strike Rate	Profit/Loss to BSP
518	171	33.01%	+£69.46

Profit or loss backing the unnamed second favourite - non-handicaps

Runners	Winners	Strike Rate	Profit/Loss to BSP

147	31	21.09%	-£22.96

Profit or loss backing the unnamed second favourite - handicaps

Runners	Winners	Strike Rate	Profit/Loss to BSP
502	91	18.13%	-£49.40

Profit or Loss backing horses who won last time out - non-handicaps

Runners	Winners	Strike Rate	Profit/Loss to BSP
112	37	33.04%	-£3.39

Profit or Loss backing horses who won last time out - handicaps

Runners	Winners	Strike Rate	Profit/Loss to BSP
595	105	17.65%	+£56.56

Profit or loss backing Top-Weights in handicaps

Runners	Winners	Strike Rate	Profit/Loss to BSP
524	80	15.27%	-£82.53

Most profitable sires – handicaps

Fair Maid Marion	16	6	37.50%	+£43.02
Dr Alice	10	4	40.00%	+£26.57
Odd Decision	14	3	21.43%	+£9.91

Ayr – Hurdles

Top jockeys by Strike Rate – non-handicaps

Name Of Jockey	Rides	Winners	Strike Rate	Profit/Loss to BSP
Aidan Coleman	10	3	30.00%	-£5.33
Brian Hughes	103	25	24.27%	+£15.59
Ross Chapman	13	3	23.08%	+£2.74

| Brian Harding | 39 | 5 | 12.82% | -£28.36 |
| Craig Nichol | 59 | 7 | 11.86% | -£1.36 |

Top jockeys by Strike Rate – handicaps

Name Of Jockey	Rides	Winners	Strike Rate	Profit/Loss to BSP
Sean Bowen	26	6	23.08%	+£29.96
Alan Doyle	14	3	21.43%	+£11.22
Paddy Brennan	10	2	20.00%	-£1.36
Dale Irving	26	5	19.23%	+£22.33
Henry Brooke	73	14	19.18%	+£122.37

Top jockeys by Profit – non-handicaps

Name Of Jockey	Rides	Winners	Strike Rate	Profit/Loss to BSP
Brian Hughes	103	25	24.27%	+£15.59
Derek Fox	71	7	9.86%	+£11.86
Conor O'Farrell	41	4	9.76%	+£10.34
Ross Chapman	13	3	23.08%	+£2.74

Top jockeys by Profit – handicaps

Name Of Jockey	Rides	Winners	Strike Rate	Profit/Loss to BSP
Henry Brooke	73	14	19.18%	+£122.37
Derek Fox	64	5	7.81%	+£67.80
Sean Quinlan	54	7	12.96%	+£41.70
Sean Bowen	26	6	23.08%	+£29.96
Sam Coltherd	36	6	16.67%	+£25.24

Top trainers by Strike Rate – non-handicaps

Name Of Trainer	Runners	Winners	Strike Rate	Profit/Loss to BSP
Donald McCain	48	18	37.50%	+£3.40
Olly Murphy	14	5	35.71%	+£3.49
Gordon Elliott	34	9	26.47%	-£6.06
Nicky Richards	89	19	21.35%	-£38.78
Ruth Jefferson	10	2	20.00%	-£3.99

Top trainers by Strike Rate – handicaps

Name Of Trainer	Runners	Winners	Strike Rate	Profit/Loss to BSP
Harriet Graham	16	4	25.00%	+£11.77
Donald Whillans	57	12	21.05%	+£188.01
Sandy Thomson	44	9	20.45%	-£0.35
Ruth Jefferson	10	2	20.00%	+£14.43
David Pipe	15	3	20.00%	+£6.15

Top trainers by Profit – non-handicaps

Name Of Trainer	Runners	Winners	Strike Rate	Profit/Loss to BSP
Ian Duncan	52	4	7.69%	+£23.41
Donald Whillans	13	2	15.38%	+£22.37
Rose Dobbin	34	5	14.71%	+£13.03
Olly Murphy	14	5	35.71%	+£3.49
Donald McCain	48	18	37.50%	+£3.40

Top trainers by Profit – handicaps

Name Of Trainer	Runners	Winners	Strike Rate	Profit/Loss to BSP
Donald Whillans	57	12	21.05%	+£188.01
Chris Grant	26	3	11.54%	+£48.23
N W Alexander	174	22	12.64%	+£44.94
Rebecca Menzies	18	3	16.67%	+£38.34
James Ewart	48	9	18.75%	+£26.61

Top trainer/jockey combos by Strike Rate – non-handicaps

Name of Trainer/Jockey	Qualifiers	Winners	Strike Rate	Profit/Loss to BSP
Donald McCain/Brian Hughes	10	4	40.00%	+£6.01
S R B Crawford/Brian Hughes	13	4	30.77%	-£1.10
Rose Dobbin/Craig Nichol	21	4	19.05%	+£21.95

James Ewart/Brian Hughes	17	2	11.76%	-£6.43
Lucinda Russell/Derek Fox	51	6	11.76%	+£12.24

Top trainer/jockey combos by Strike Rate – handicaps

Name of Trainer/Jockey	Qualifiers	Winners	Strike Rate	Profit/Loss to BSP
Jim Goldie/Henry Brooke	20	7	35.00%	+£48.29
Donald McCain/Brian Hughes	12	4	33.33%	+£2.24
Tristan Davidson/Harry Reed	15	4	26.67%	+£15.84
Sandy Thomson/Ryan Mania	19	5	26.32%	-£3.94
Stuart Coltherd/Sam Coltherd	24	6	25.00%	+£37.24

Top trainer/jockey combos by Profit – non-handicaps

Name of Trainer/Jockey	Qualifiers	Winners	Strike Rate	Profit/Loss to BSP
Rose Dobbin/Craig Nichol	21	4	19.05%	+£21.95
Lucinda Russell/Derek Fox	51	6	11.76%	+£12.24
Ian Duncan/Derek Fox	13	1	7.69%	+£6.62
Donald McCain/Brian Hughes	10	4	40.00%	+£6.01
Nicky Richards/Brian	17	8	47.06%	+£4.22

Hughes				

Top trainer/jockey combos by Profit – handicaps

Name of Trainer/Jockey	Qualifiers	Winners	Strike Rate	Profit/Loss to BSP
Jim Goldie/Henry Brooke	20	7	35.00%	+£48.29
Stuart Coltherd/Sam Coltherd	24	6	25.00%	+£37.24
N W Alexander/Bruce Lynn	16	2	12.50%	+£18.33
Paul Nicholls/Sam Twiston-Davies	12	3	25.00%	+£15.90
Tristan Davidson/Harry Reed	15	4	26.67%	+£15.84

Profit or Loss backing the unnamed favourite – non-handicaps

Runners	Winners	Strike Rate	Profit/Loss to BSP
307	155	50.49%	+£1.60

Profit or Loss backing the unnamed favourite – handicaps

Runners	Winners	Strike Rate	Profit/Loss to BSP
542	163	30.07%	+£61.08

Profit or loss backing the unnamed second favourite - non-handicaps

Runners	Winners	Strike Rate	Profit/Loss to BSP
301	60	19.93%	-£36.52

Profit or loss backing the unnamed second favourite - handicaps

Runners	Winners	Strike Rate	Profit/Loss to

			BSP
483	68	14.08%	-£141.07

Profit or Loss backing horses who won last time out- non-handicaps

Runners	Winners	Strike Rate	Profit/Loss to BSP
220	75	34.09%	-£2.35

Profit or Loss backing horses who won last time out - handicaps

Runners	Winners	Strike Rate	Profit/Loss to BSP
558	97	17.38%	+£144.08

Profit or loss backing Top-Weights in handicaps

Runners	Winners	Strike Rate	Profit/Loss to BSP
554	76	13.72%	-£28.59

Most profitable sires – non-handicaps

Sire	Runners	Winners	Strike Rate	Profit/Loss to BSP
Dylan Thomas	11	2	18.18%	+£24.81
Beneficial	19	2	10.53%	+£16.84
Zagreb	14	1	7.14%	+£15.14
Midnight Legend	12	5	41.67%	+£9.10
Jeremy	15	4	26.67%	+£8.51

Most profitable sires – handicaps

Gamut	10	2	20.00%	+£95.51
Gold Well	52	11	21.15%	+£84.79
Midnight Legend	37	7	18.92%	+£41.29
Presenting	41	4	9.76%	+£32.79
Old Vic	23	5	21.74%	+£31.30

Bangor-On-Dee - Chases

Top jockeys by Strike Rate – handicaps

Name Of Jockey	Rides	Winners	Strike Rate	Profit/Loss to BSP
Tom Scudamore	37	11	29.73%	+£11.51
Gavin Sheehan	27	7	25.93%	+£15.07
Craig Nichol	12	3	25.00%	+£13.77
Jonjo O'Neill Jr	12	3	25.00%	-£3.94
Paddy Brennan	40	10	25.00%	+£12.00
Derek Fox	17	4	23.53%	+£10.48

Top jockeys by Profit – handicaps

Name Of Jockey	Rides	Winners	Strike Rate	Profit/Loss to BSP
Brendan Powell	20	4	20.00%	+£168.46
Charlie Deutsch	34	7	20.59%	+£45.18
Adam Wedge	35	8	22.86%	+£40.26
Brian Hughes	80	12	15.00%	+£35.01
Richie McLernon	29	6	20.69%	+£34.33

Top trainers by Strike Rate – non-handicaps

Name Of Trainer	Runners	Winners	Strike Rate	Profit/Loss to BSP
Dan Skelton	13	4	30.77%	-£1.38
Donald McCain	26	8	30.77%	-£1.70
Rebecca Curtis	14	4	28.57%	-£4.48
Charlie Longsdon	11	3	27.27%	+£2.42
Paul Nicholls	15	4	26.67%	-£6.28

Top trainers by Strike Rate – handicaps

Name Of Trainer	Runners	Winners	Strike Rate	Profit/Loss to BSP
Nicky Richards	11	5	45.45%	+£20.95
David Pipe	15	5	33.33%	+£11.98
Mark Walford	10	3	30.00%	+£1.40
Brian Ellison	14	4	28.57%	+£28.71

David Rees	18	5	27.78%	+£64.46

Top trainers by Profit – non-handicaps

Name Of Trainer	Runners	Winners	Strike Rate	Profit/Loss to BSP
Charlie Longsdon	11	3	27.27%	+£2.42

Top trainers by Profit – handicaps

Name Of Trainer	Runners	Winners	Strike Rate	Profit/Loss to BSP
David Rees	18	5	27.78%	+£64.46
Venetia Williams	85	17	20.00%	+£56.99
Alan King	26	6	23.08%	+£43.83
Brian Ellison	14	4	28.57%	+£28.71
Jennie Candlish	50	12	24.00%	+£28.53

Top trainer/jockey combos by Strike Rate – handicaps

Name of Trainer/Jockey	Qualifiers	Winners	Strike Rate	Profit/Loss to BSP
Fergal O'Brien/Paddy Brennan	19	6	31.58%	+£5.82
Jonjo O'Neill/Richie McLernon	17	5	29.41%	+£23.53
Lucina Russell/Derek Fox	16	4	25.00%	+£11.48
Venetia Williams/Aidan Coleman	17	4	23.53%	+£16.46
Jennie Candlish/Sean Quinlan	39	9	23.08%	+£19.69

Top trainer/jockey combos by Profit – handicaps

Name of Trainer/Jockey	Qualifiers	Winners	Strike Rate	Profit/Loss to BSP

Venetia Williams/Charlie Deutsch	30	6	20.00%	+£38.38
Jonjo O'Neill/Richie McLernon	17	5	29.41%	+£23.53
Jennie Candlish/Sean Quinlan	39	9	23.08%	+£19.69
Venetia Williams/Aidan Coleman	17	4	23.53%	+£16.46
Dan Skelton/Harry Skelton	33	7	21.21%	+£12.62

Profit or Loss backing the unnamed favourite – non-handicaps

Runners	Winners	Strike Rate	Profit/Loss to BSP
236	116	49.15%	+£24.02

Profit or Loss backing the unnamed favourite – handicaps

Runners	Winners	Strike Rate	Profit/Loss to BSP
582	153	26.29%	-£33.26

Profit or loss backing the unnamed second favourite - non-handicaps

Runners	Winners	Strike Rate	Profit/Loss to BSP
213	47	22.07%	-£18.64

Profit or loss backing the unnamed second favourite - handicaps

Runners	Winners	Strike Rate	Profit/Loss to BSP
526	99	18.82%	-£52.80

Profit or Loss backing horses who won last time out - non-handicaps

Runners	Winners	Strike Rate	Profit/Loss to

			BSP
178	56	31.46%	+£3.87

Profit or Loss backing horses who won last time out - handicaps

Runners	Winners	Strike Rate	Profit/Loss to BSP
491	95	19.35%	-£10.30

Profit or loss backing Top-Weights in handicaps

Runners	Winners	Strike Rate	Profit/Loss to BSP
595	85	14.29%	-£79.46

Most profitable sires – non-handicaps

Sire	Runners	Winners	Strike Rate	Profit/Loss to BSP
King's Theatre	12	6	50.00%	+£21.65
Presenting	14	2	14.29%	+£13.81

Most profitable sires – handicaps

Gold Well	32	7	21.88%	+£168.77
Alflora	31	7	22.58%	+£86.44
Midnight Legend	35	6	17.14%	+£38.85
Shantou	23	3	13.04%	+£33.77
Passing Glance	12	2	16.67%	+£27.09

Bangor-On-Dee – Hurdles

Top jockeys by Strike Rate – non-handicaps

Name Of Jockey	Rides	Winners	Strike Rate	Profit/Loss to BSP
Brian Hughes	72	28	38.89%	+£25.72
Nico de Boinville	13	5	38.46%	+£2.45
Brendan Powell	14	4	28.57%	+£17.90
Aidan Coleman	42	12	28.57%	-£0.56
Gavin Sheehan	25	6	24.00%	+£32.67

Top jockeys by Strike Rate – handicaps

Name Of Jockey	Rides	Winners	Strike Rate	Profit/Loss to BSP
Bridget Andrews	10	3	30.00%	-£0.47
Tom Bellamy	10	3	30.00%	+£0.32
Paddy Brennan	24	7	29.17%	+£6.53
Luca Morgan	12	3	25.00%	+£31.72
Lorcan Murtagh	25	6	24.00%	+£37.49

Top jockeys by Profit – non-handicaps

Name Of Jockey	Rides	Winners	Strike Rate	Profit/Loss to BSP
Kielan Woods	15	3	20.00%	+£52.41
William Kennedy	57	10	17.54%	+£36.05
Gavin Sheehan	25	6	24.00%	+£32.67
Brian Hughes	72	28	38.89%	+£25.72
Fergus Gregory	13	2	15.38%	+£24.14

Top jockeys by Profit – handicaps

Name Of Jockey	Rides	Winners	Strike Rate	Profit/Loss to BSP
Kielan Woods	37	6	16.22%	+£83.60
Robert Dunne	27	3	11.11%	+£51.66
Lorcan Murtagh	25	6	24.00%	+£37.49
William Kennedy	54	9	16.67%	+£35.73
Luca Morgan	12	3	25.00%	+£31.72

Top trainers by Strike Rate – non-handicaps

Name Of Trainer	Runners	Winners	Strike Rate	Profit/Loss to BSP
Rebecca Curtis	34	15	44.12%	+£30.71
Nicky Henderson	39	12	30.77%	-£10.16
Donald McCain	212	61	28.77%	+£112.28
Alan King	44	12	27.27%	-£15.27
Nigel Twiston-Davies	36	9	25.00%	+£8.60

Top trainers by Strike Rate – handicaps

Name Of Trainer	Runners	Winners	Strike Rate	Profit/Loss to BSP
Henry Daly	22	8	36.36%	+£35.65
Fergal O'Brien	26	8	30.77%	+£11.11
Oliver Sherwood	10	3	30.00%	+£20.44
Alan King	25	6	24.00%	-£0.75
Sue Smith	13	3	23.08%	+£1.66

Top trainers by Profit – non-handicaps

Name Of Trainer	Runners	Winners	Strike Rate	Profit/Loss to BSP
Donald McCain	212	61	28.77%	+£112.28
Rebecca Curtis	34	15	44.12%	+£30.71
Warren Greatrex	29	6	20.69%	+£28.34
Henry Daly	30	4	13.33%	+£28.12
Oliver Sherwood	13	3	23.08%	+£19.40

Top trainers by Profit – handicaps

Name Of Trainer	Runners	Winners	Strike Rate	Profit/Loss to BSP
Donald McCain	241	53	21.99%	+£149.25
Michael Mullineaux	39	2	5.13%	+£70.48
Tony Carroll	24	5	20.83%	+£57.31
Gary Hanmer	32	3	9.38%	+£47.17
Adrian Wintle	23	3	13.04%	+£37.67

Top trainer/jockey combos by Strike Rate – non-handicaps

Name of Trainer/Jockey	Qualifiers	Winners	Strike Rate	Profit/Loss to BSP
Donald McCain/Brian Hughes	51	24	47.06%	+£29.30
Warren Greatrex/Gavin Sheehan	12	5	41.67%	+£43.98
Donald McCain/William Kennedy	32	9	28.13%	+£57.33

Nigel Twiston-Davies/Sam Twiston-Davies	22	6	27.27%	+£12.80
Jennie Candlish/Sean Quinlan	18	4	22.22%	-£3.98

Top trainer/jockey combos by Strike Rate – handicaps

Name of Trainer/Jockey	Qualifiers	Winners	Strike Rate	Profit/Loss to BSP
Fergal O'Brien/Paddy Brennan	10	5	50.00%	+£9.77
Donald McCain/Lorcan Murtagh	20	6	30.00%	+£42.49
Donald McCain/Brian Hughes	47	14	29.79%	+£33.48
Peter Bowen/Sean Bowen	11	3	27.27%	+£18.82
Donald McCain/William Kennedy	33	9	27.27%	+£56.73

Top trainer/jockey combos by Profit – non-handicaps

Name of Trainer/Jockey	Qualifiers	Winners	Strike Rate	Profit/Loss to BSP
Donald McCain/William Kennedy	32	9	28.13%	+£57.33
Warren Greatrex/Gavin Sheehan	12	5	41.67%	+£43.98
Donald McCain/Brian Hughes	51	24	47.06%	+£29.30
Nigel Twiston-Davies/Sam Twiston-Davies	22	6	27.27%	+£12.80

Nicky Henderson/Nico de Boinville	10	5	50.00%	+£5.45

Top trainer/jockey combos by Profit – handicaps

Name of Trainer/Jockey	Qualifiers	Winners	Strike Rate	Profit/Loss to BSP
Donald McCain/William Kennedy	33	9	27.27%	+£56.73
Donald McCain/Lorcan Murtagh	20	6	30.00%	+£42.49
Donald McCain/Brian Hughes	47	14	29.79%	+£33.48
Donald McCain/Henry Brooke	13	2	15.38%	+£25.91
Peter Bowen/Sean Bowen	11	3	27.27%	+£18.82

Profit or Loss backing the unnamed favourite – non-handicaps

Runners	Winners	Strike Rate	Profit/Loss to BSP
513	237	46.20%	+£5.06

Profit or Loss backing the unnamed favourite – handicaps

Runners	Winners	Strike Rate	Profit/Loss to BSP
543	142	26.15%	-£40.03

Profit or loss backing the unnamed second favourite - non-handicaps

Runners	Winners	Strike Rate	Profit/Loss to BSP
499	130	26.05%	+£32.41

Profit or loss backing the unnamed second favourite - handicaps

Runners	Winners	Strike Rate	Profit/Loss to BSP
526	111	21.10%	+£41.21

Profit or Loss backing horses who won last time out- non-handicaps

Runners	Winners	Strike Rate	Profit/Loss to BSP
345	116	33.62%	-£12.45

Profit or Loss backing horses who won last time out - handicaps

Runners	Winners	Strike Rate	Profit/Loss to BSP
544	102	18.75%	-£12.74

Profit or loss backing Top-Weights in handicaps

Runners	Winners	Strike Rate	Profit/Loss to BSP
590	87	14.75%	+£42.45

Most profitable sires – non-handicaps

Sire	Runners	Winners	Strike Rate	Profit/Loss to BSP
Westerner	30	9	30.00%	+£35.04
Sulamani	18	4	22.22%	+£23.43
Vinnie Roe	15	3	20.00%	+£21.11
Shantou	22	6	27.27%	+£14.03
Yeats	16	4	25.00%	+£9.12

Most profitable sires – handicaps

Grape Tree Road	14	2	14.29%	+£59.04
Old Vic	18	4	22.22%	+£56.33
Nayef	16	5	31.25%	+£47.12
Champs Elysees	11	2	18.18%	+£15.95
Multiplex	19	3	15.79%	+£15.61

Carlisle - Chases

Top jockeys by Strike Rate – non-handicaps

Name Of Jockey	Rides	Winners	Strike Rate	Profit/Loss to BSP
Brian Hughes	40	9	22.50%	-£11.01
Henry Brooke	12	1	8.33%	-£4.82
Ryan Mania	18	1	5.56%	-£9.77

Top jockeys by Strike Rate – handicaps

Name Of Jockey	Rides	Winners	Strike Rate	Profit/Loss to BSP
Charlie Deutsch	17	5	29.41%	+£15.95
Jonathan England	21	6	28.57%	+£19.74
Sam Twiston-Davies	28	6	21.43%	+£9.73
Conor O'Farrell	42	9	21.43%	+£29.54
Jonjo O'Neill Jr	15	3	20.00%	+£4.70
William Kennedy	28	5	17.86%	-£0.81

Top jockeys by Profit – handicaps

Name Of Jockey	Rides	Winners	Strike Rate	Profit/Loss to BSP
John Kington	14	1	7.14%	+£49.72
Conor O'Farrell	42	9	21.43%	+£29.54
Paddy Brennan	17	3	17.65%	+£25.45
Jonathan England	21	6	28.57%	+£19.74
Derek Fox	58	7	12.07%	+£19.10

Top trainers by Strike Rate – non-handicaps

Name Of Trainer	Runners	Winners	Strike Rate	Profit/Loss to BSP
Brian Ellison	10	4	40.00%	+£1.70
Lucinda Russell	14	4	28.57%	+£3.45
Donald McCain	27	5	18.52%	-£13.88
Nicky Richards	18	3	16.67%	-£6.28
Sue Smith	30	5	16.67%	-£2.53

Top trainers by Strike Rate – handicaps

Name Of Trainer	Runners	Winners	Strike Rate	Profit/Loss to BSP
Evan Williams	10	4	40.00%	+£10.06
Peter Bowen	12	4	33.33%	+£33.41
Mark Walford	13	4	30.77%	+£16.71
Maurice Barnes	37	10	27.03%	+£52.90
Sam England	15	4	26.67%	+£6.10

Top trainers by Profit – non-handicaps

Name Of Trainer	Runners	Winners	Strike Rate	Profit/Loss to BSP
Lucinda Russell	14	4	28.57%	+£3.45
Brian Ellison	10	4	40.00%	+£1.70

Top trainers by Profit – handicaps

Name Of Trainer	Runners	Winners	Strike Rate	Profit/Loss to BSP
Maurice Barnes	37	10	27.03%	+£52.90
Stuart Coltherd	64	13	20.31%	+£38.27
Venetia Williams	41	10	24.39%	+£33.76
Peter Bowen	12	4	33.33%	+£33.41
Malcolm Jefferson	31	8	25.81%	+£31.54

Top trainer/jockey combos by Strike Rate – non-handicaps

Name of Trainer/Jockey	Qualifiers	Winners	Strike Rate	Profit/Loss to BSP
Sue Smith/Ryan Mania	13	1	7.69%	-£4.77

Top trainer/jockey combos by Strike Rate – handicaps

Name of Trainer/Jockey	Qualifiers	Winners	Strike Rate	Profit/Loss to BSP
Venetia Williams/Charlie	17	5	29.41%	+£15.95

Deutsch				
Sam England/Jonathan England	12	3	25.00%	+£4.98
Jonjo O'Neill/Jonjo O'Neill Jr	12	3	25.00%	+£7.70
James Ewart/Brian Hughes	18	4	22.22%	-£6.22
Stuart Coltherd/Sam Coltherd	36	8	22.22%	+£16.87

Top trainer/jockey combos by Profit – handicaps

Name of Trainer/Jockey	Qualifiers	Winners	Strike Rate	Profit/Loss to BSP
Stuart Coltherd/Sam Coltherd	36	8	22.22%	+£16.87
Venetia Williams/Charlie Deutsch	17	5	29.41%	+£15.95
Jennie Candlish/Sean Quinlan	27	5	18.52%	+£14.85
Lucinda Russell/Derek Fox	41	5	12.20%	+£13.64
Nigel Twiston-Davies/Sam Twiston-Davies	21	4	19.05%	+£7.96

Profit or Loss backing the unnamed favourite – non-handicaps

Runners	Winners	Strike Rate	Profit/Loss to BSP
224	101	45.09%	-£5.95

Profit or Loss backing the unnamed favourite – handicaps

Runners	Winners	Strike Rate	Profit/Loss to

			BSP
528	141	26.70%	+£2.81

Profit or loss backing the unnamed second favourite - non-handicaps

Runners	Winners	Strike Rate	Profit/Loss to BSP
215	65	30.23%	+£58.67

Profit or loss backing the unnamed second favourite - handicaps

Runners	Winners	Strike Rate	Profit/Loss to BSP
498	94	18.88%	-£24.52

Profit or Loss backing horses who won last time out - non-handicaps

Runners	Winners	Strike Rate	Profit/Loss to BSP
199	56	28.14%	+£4.91

Profit or Loss backing horses who won last time out - handicaps

Runners	Winners	Strike Rate	Profit/Loss to BSP
491	90	18.33%	+£16.25

Profit or loss backing Top-Weights in handicaps

Runners	Winners	Strike Rate	Profit/Loss to BSP
535	86	16.07%	+£85.12

Most profitable sires – non-handicaps

Sire	Runners	Winners	Strike Rate	Profit/Loss to BSP
Presenting	12	3	25.00%	+£2.83

Most profitable sires – handicaps

Goldmark	11	4	36.36%	+£45.30
Sir Harry Lewis	25	4	16.00%	+£36.42

Generous	16	4	25.00%	+£33.57
Gold Well	46	8	17.39%	+£26.43
Flemensfirth	68	11	16.18%	+£19.40

Carlisle – Hurdles

Top jockeys by Strike Rate – non-handicaps

Name Of Jockey	Rides	Winners	Strike Rate	Profit/Loss to BSP
Tom Scudamore	12	5	41.67%	+£3.84
Sam Twiston-Davies	16	6	37.50%	-£1.32
Harry Skelton	15	5	33.33%	+£0.58
Aidan Coleman	13	4	30.77%	-£4.17
William Kennedy	24	7	29.17%	+£7.92

Top jockeys by Strike Rate – handicaps

Name Of Jockey	Rides	Winners	Strike Rate	Profit/Loss to BSP
Harry Skelton	11	5	45.45%	+£32.76
Aidan Coleman	16	7	43.75%	+£46.01
William Kennedy	20	4	20.00%	+£43.19
Theo Gillard	10	2	20.00%	+£17.50
Danny McMenamin	42	8	19.05%	+£12.21

Top jockeys by Profit – non-handicaps

Name Of Jockey	Rides	Winners	Strike Rate	Profit/Loss to BSP
Jamie Hamilton	20	3	15.00%	+£97.86
Derek Fox	24	3	12.50%	+£76.88
Jonjo O'Neill Jr	12	3	25.00%	+£12.17
William Kennedy	24	7	29.17%	+£7.92
Tom Scudamore	12	5	41.67%	+£3.84

Top jockeys by Profit – handicaps

Name Of Jockey	Rides	Winners	Strike Rate	Profit/Loss to BSP

Ryan Mania	30	4	13.33%	+£76.30
Aidan Coleman	16	7	43.75%	+£46.01
William Kennedy	20	4	20.00%	+£43.19
Harry Skelton	11	5	45.45%	+£32.76
Conor O'Farrell	26	3	11.54%	+£29.98

Top trainers by Strike Rate – non-handicaps

Name Of Trainer	Runners	Winners	Strike Rate	Profit/Loss to BSP
Nigel Twiston-Davies	12	6	50.00%	+£3.89
James Moffatt	13	6	46.15%	+£15.03
Dan Skelton	15	5	33.33%	+£0.58
Venetia Williams	10	3	30.00%	-£4.29
Jonjo O'Neill	25	7	28.00%	+£11.25

Top trainers by Strike Rate – handicaps

Name Of Trainer	Runners	Winners	Strike Rate	Profit/Loss to BSP
Dan Skelton	11	4	36.36%	+£26.31
Nigel Hawke	14	5	35.71%	+£50.83
Keith Dalgleish	13	4	30.77%	+£7.97
Harriet Graham	10	3	30.00%	+£106.00
Nicky Richards	62	18	29.03%	+£84.99

Top trainers by Profit – non-handicaps

Name Of Trainer	Runners	Winners	Strike Rate	Profit/Loss to BSP
Lucinda Russell	46	7	15.22%	+£79.59
Chris Grant	24	2	8.33%	+£39.05
Tim Easterby	16	3	18.75%	+£31.68
James Moffatt	13	6	46.15%	+£15.03
Philip Kirby	22	2	9.09%	+£11.89

Top trainers by Profit – handicaps

Name Of Trainer	Runners	Winners	Strike Rate	Profit/Loss to BSP
Harriet Graham	10	3	30.00%	+£106.00
Nicky Richards	62	18	29.03%	+£84.99

Tim Easterby	18	4	22.22%	+£53.96
Nigel Hawke	14	5	35.71%	+£50.83
Dianne Sayer	55	6	10.91%	+£49.33

Top trainer/jockey combos by Strike Rate – non-handicaps

Name of Trainer/Jockey	Qualifiers	Winners	Strike Rate	Profit/Loss to BSP
Dan Skelton/Harry Skelton	15	5	33.33%	+£0.58
Donald McCain/Brian Hughes	36	12	33.33%	+£0.97
Jonjo O'Neill/Jonjo O'Neill Jr	12	3	25.00%	+£12.17
Donald McCain/William Kennedy	21	5	23.81%	+£6.23
Sandy Thomson/Ryan Mania	10	2	20.00%	-£1.38

Top trainer/jockey combos by Strike Rate – handicaps

Name of Trainer/Jockey	Qualifiers	Winners	Strike Rate	Profit/Loss to BSP
Dan Skelton/Harry Skelton	10	4	40.00%	+£27.31
Nicky Richards/Danny McMenamin	12	4	33.33%	+£10.95
Donald McCain/William Kennedy	17	4	23.53%	+£46.19
Dianne Sayer/Danny McMenamin	10	2	20.00%	+£11.50
Sandy Thomson/Ryan Mania	10	2	20.00%	+£2.44

Top trainer/jockey combos by Profit – non-handicaps

Name of Trainer/Jockey	Qualifiers	Winners	Strike Rate	Profit/Loss to BSP
Lucinda Russell/Derek Fox	16	3	18.75%	+£84.88
Jonjo O'Neill/Jonjo O'Neill Jr	12	3	25.00%	+£12.17
Donald McCain/William Kennedy	21	5	23.81%	+£6.23
Donald McCain/Brian Hughes	36	12	33.33%	+£0.97
Dan Skelton/Harry Skelton	15	5	33.33%	+£0.58

Top trainer/jockey combos by Profit – handicaps

Name of Trainer/Jockey	Qualifiers	Winners	Strike Rate	Profit/Loss to BSP
Donald McCain/William Kennedy	17	4	23.53%	+£46.19
Dan Skelton/Harry Skelton	10	4	40.00%	+£27.31
James Moffatt/Charlotte Jones	10	2	20.00%	+£25.22
Stuart Coltherd/Sam Coltherd	27	4	14.81%	+£23.67
John Dixon/John Dixon	39	5	12.82%	+£13.95

Profit or Loss backing the unnamed favourite – non-handicaps

Runners	Winners	Strike Rate	Profit/Loss to BSP

281	133	47.33%	-£0.27

Profit or Loss backing the unnamed favourite – handicaps

Runners	Winners	Strike Rate	Profit/Loss to BSP
408	110	26.96%	-£44.91

Profit or loss backing the unnamed second favourite - non-handicaps

Runners	Winners	Strike Rate	Profit/Loss to BSP
265	55	20.75%	-£41.52

Profit or loss backing the unnamed second favourite - handicaps

Runners	Winners	Strike Rate	Profit/Loss to BSP
392	60	15.31%	-£80.58

Profit or Loss backing horses who won last time out- non-handicaps

Runners	Winners	Strike Rate	Profit/Loss to BSP
191	75	39.27%	+£43.86

Profit or Loss backing horses who won last time out - handicaps

Runners	Winners	Strike Rate	Profit/Loss to BSP
370	77	20.81%	+£15.36

Profit or loss backing Top-Weights in handicaps

Runners	Winners	Strike Rate	Profit/Loss to BSP
441	54	12.24%	-£48.91

Most profitable sires – non-handicaps

Sire	Runners	Winners	Strike Rate	Profit/Loss to BSP
Gold Well	18	5	27.78%	+£98.59

Court Cave	26	3	11.54%	+£61.59
Tikkanen	16	2	12.50%	+£47.05
Multiplex	14	2	14.29%	+£25.44
Kayf Tara	30	7	23.33%	+£18.90

Most profitable sires – handicaps

Shirocco	10	1	10.00%	+£76.70
Galileo	13	4	30.77%	+£47.22
Westerner	30	5	16.67%	+£46.83
Alderbrook	12	3	25.00%	+£34.97
Generous	15	4	26.67%	+£30.57

Cartmel - Chases

Top jockeys by Strike Rate – non-handicaps

Name Of Jockey	Rides	Winners	Strike Rate	Profit/Loss to BSP
Brian Hughes	28	7	25.00%	-£10.49
Thomas Greenwood	12	1	8.33%	+£3.21

Top jockeys by Strike Rate – handicaps

Name Of Jockey	Rides	Winners	Strike Rate	Profit/Loss to BSP
Charlotte Jones	11	8	72.73%	+£15.35
Aidan Coleman	13	4	30.77%	+£9.87
Jonathon Bewley	11	3	27.27%	+£9.05
Sean Bowen	42	11	26.19%	+£13.94
Richie McLernon	31	7	22.58%	+£47.06
Sam Coltherd	20	4	20.00%	+£17.63

Top jockeys by Profit – non-handicaps

Name Of Jockey	Rides	Winners	Strike Rate	Profit/Loss to BSP
Thomas Greenwood	12	1	8.33%	+£3.21

Top jockeys by Profit – handicaps

Name Of Jockey	Rides	Winners	Strike Rate	Profit/Loss to BSP
Henry Brooke	81	14	17.28%	+£50.91
Richie McLernon	31	7	22.58%	+£47.06
Derek Fox	49	5	10.20%	+£46.18
Jamie Hamilton	17	2	11.76%	+£44.65
Nathan Moscrop	13	2	15.38%	+£24.77

Top trainers by Strike Rate – non-handicaps

Name Of Trainer	Runners	Winners	Strike Rate	Profit/Loss to BSP
Peter Bowen	11	4	36.36%	-£1.78
Donald McCain	26	8	30.77%	-£6.78
Sophie Leech	10	3	30.00%	+£19.54

Top trainers by Strike Rate – handicaps

Name Of Trainer	Runners	Winners	Strike Rate	Profit/Loss to BSP
George Bewley	16	5	31.25%	+£27.54
James Ewart	10	3	30.00%	+£6.47
Ben Haslam	26	7	26.92%	+£36.08
Oliver Greenall	12	3	25.00%	+£32.70
Maurice Barnes	21	5	23.81%	+£18.63

Top trainers by Profit – non-handicaps

Name Of Trainer	Runners	Winners	Strike Rate	Profit/Loss to BSP
Sophie Leech	10	3	30.00%	+£19.54

Top trainers by Profit – handicaps

Name Of Trainer	Runners	Winners	Strike Rate	Profit/Loss to BSP
Michael Chapman	36	3	8.33%	+£67.03
Henry Hogarth	21	3	14.29%	+£54.13
Ben Haslam	26	7	26.92%	+£36.08
Oliver Greenall	12	3	25.00%	+£32.70
George Bewley	16	5	31.25%	+£27.54

Top trainer/jockey combos by Strike Rate – handicaps

Name of Trainer/Jockey	Qualifiers	Winners	Strike Rate	Profit/Loss to BSP
James Moffatt/Charlotte Jones	11	8	72.73%	+£15.35
Laura	10	3	30.00%	+£4.06

Morgan/Adam Wedge				
Donald McCain/Brian Hughes	21	6	28.57%	+£6.74
Martin Todhunter/Henry Brooke	11	3	27.27%	+£0.17
George Bewley/Jonathon Bewley	11	3	27.27%	+£9.05

Top trainer/jockey combos by Profit – handicaps (10 to qualify)

Name of Trainer/Jockey	Qualifiers	Winners	Strike Rate	Profit/Loss to BSP
Ben Haslam/Richie McLernon	19	5	26.32%	+£32.29
James Moffatt/Henry Brooke	10	2	20.00%	+£25.52
James Moffatt/Charlotte Jones	11	8	72.73%	+£15.35
George Bewley/Jonathon Bewley	11	3	27.27%	+£9.05
Peter Bowen/Sean Bowen	35	8	22.86%	+£8.38

Profit or Loss backing the unnamed favourite – non-handicaps

Runners	Winners	Strike Rate	Profit/Loss to BSP
126	44	34.92%	-£31.28

Profit or Loss backing the unnamed favourite – handicaps

Runners	Winners	Strike Rate	Profit/Loss to BSP
343	94	27.41%	+£1.60

Profit or loss backing the unnamed second favourite - non-handicaps

Runners	Winners	Strike Rate	Profit/Loss to BSP
128	35	27.34%	+£34.41

Profit or loss backing the unnamed second favourite - handicaps

Runners	Winners	Strike Rate	Profit/Loss to BSP
290	46	15.86%	-£72.74

Profit or Loss backing horses who won last time out - non-handicaps

Runners	Winners	Strike Rate	Profit/Loss to BSP
44	13	29.55%	+£2.00

Profit or Loss backing horses who won last time out - handicaps

Runners	Winners	Strike Rate	Profit/Loss to BSP
313	56	17.89%	-£57.48

Profit or loss backing Top-Weights in handicaps

Runners	Winners	Strike Rate	Profit/Loss to BSP
335	46	13.73%	-£31.93

Most profitable sires – handicaps

Presenting	59	13	22.03%	+£80.72
Oscar	28	3	10.71%	+£37.82
Midnight Legend	23	10	43.48%	+£31.89
Overbury	14	4	28.57%	+£30.64
Key of Luck	11	3	27.27%	+£22.67

Cartmel – Hurdles

Top jockeys by Strike Rate – non-handicaps

Name Of Jockey	Rides	Winners	Strike Rate	Profit/Loss to BSP
Charlotte Jones	15	5	33.33%	+£8.57
Brian Hughes	72	18	25.00%	+£36.78
Sam Twiston-Davies	13	3	23.08%	-£5.49
Derek Fox	16	3	18.75%	+£13.79
William Kennedy	13	2	15.38%	-£6.95

Top jockeys by Strike Rate – handicaps

Name Of Jockey	Rides	Winners	Strike Rate	Profit/Loss to BSP
James Bowen	17	5	29.41%	+£58.57
Jonathan England	35	10	28.57%	+£45.58
Harry Reed	16	4	25.00%	+£18.92
Charlotte Jones	61	12	19.67%	+£28.19
Theo Gillard	11	2	18.18%	-£2.00

Top jockeys by Profit – non-handicaps

Name Of Jockey	Rides	Winners	Strike Rate	Profit/Loss to BSP
Brian Hughes	72	18	25.00%	+£36.78
Henry Brooke	47	5	10.64%	+£16.56
Derek Fox	16	3	18.75%	+£13.79
Charlotte Jones	15	5	33.33%	+£8.57

Top jockeys by Profit – handicaps

Name Of Jockey	Rides	Winners	Strike Rate	Profit/Loss to BSP
James Bowen	17	5	29.41%	+£58.57
Jonathan England	35	10	28.57%	+£45.58
Callum Bewley	41	3	7.32%	+£34.73
Charlotte Jones	61	12	19.67%	+£28.19
Sean Quinlan	69	11	15.94%	+£27.15

Top trainers by Strike Rate – non-handicaps

Name Of Trainer	Runners	Winners	Strike Rate	Profit/Loss to BSP
Gordon Elliott	14	7	50.00%	+£7.80
John Quinn	11	5	45.45%	+£17.84
Donald McCain	72	22	30.56%	-£8.56
James Moffatt	66	13	19.70%	+£87.44
Brian Ellison	19	3	15.79%	-£2.54

Top trainers by Strike Rate – handicaps

Name Of Trainer	Runners	Winners	Strike Rate	Profit/Loss to BSP
Tim Easterby	10	3	30.00%	+£11.74
Tristan Davidson	11	3	27.27%	+£19.49
Sam England	31	8	25.81%	+£27.66
Gary Hanmer	16	4	25.00%	+£30.40
Nicky Richards	20	5	25.00%	+£5.22

Top trainers by Profit – non-handicaps

Name Of Trainer	Runners	Winners	Strike Rate	Profit/Loss to BSP
James Moffatt	66	13	19.70%	+£87.44
John Quinn	11	5	45.45%	+£17.84
Michael Chapman	10	1	10.00%	+£14.54
Gordon Elliott	14	7	50.00%	+£7.80
Micky Hammond	16	1	6.25%	+£0.95

Top trainers by Profit – handicaps

Name Of Trainer	Runners	Winners	Strike Rate	Profit/Loss to BSP
Peter Bowen	51	11	21.57%	+£58.69
Barry Murtagh	41	3	7.32%	+£49.11
Philip Kirby	36	5	13.89%	+£43.59
Gary Hanmer	16	4	25.00%	+£30.40
Sam England	31	8	25.81%	+£27.66

Top trainer/jockey combos by Strike Rate – non-handicaps

Name of	Qualifiers	Winners	Strike Rate	Profit/Loss to

Trainer/Jockey				BSP
Donald McCain/Brian Hughes	27	11	40.74%	+£8.19
James Moffatt/Charlotte Jones	15	5	33.33%	+£8.57
James Moffatt/Brian Hughes	15	3	20.00%	+£7.45

Top trainer/jockey combos by Strike Rate – handicaps

Name of Trainer/Jockey	Qualifiers	Winners	Strike Rate	Profit/Loss to BSP
Peter Bowen/James Bowen	10	4	40.00%	+£54.77
Tristan Davidson/Harry Reed	10	3	30.00%	+£20.49
Sam England/Jonathan England	27	8	29.63%	+£31.66
Dianne Sayer/Danny McMenamin	16	4	25.00%	+£7.33
James Moffatt/Charlotte Jones	59	12	20.34%	+£30.19

Top trainer/jockey combos by Profit – non-handicaps

Name of Trainer/Jockey	Qualifiers	Winners	Strike Rate	Profit/Loss to BSP
James Moffatt/Charlotte Jones	15	5	33.33%	+£8.57
Donald McCain/Brian Hughes	27	11	40.74%	+£8.19
James Moffatt/Brian	15	3	20.00%	+£7.45

Hughes				

Top trainer/jockey combos by Profit – handicaps

Name of Trainer/Jockey	Qualifiers	Winners	Strike Rate	Profit/Loss to BSP
Peter Bowen/James Bowen	10	4	40.00%	+£54.77
James Moffatt/Callum Bewley	11	1	9.09%	+£53.77
Sam England/Jonathan England	27	8	29.63%	+£31.66
James Moffatt/Charlotte Jones	59	12	20.34%	+£30.19
Donald McCain/Lorcan Murtagh	18	2	11.11%	+£28.10

Profit or Loss backing the unnamed favourite – non-handicaps

Runners	Winners	Strike Rate	Profit/Loss to BSP
243	101	41.56%	+£2.53

Profit or Loss backing the unnamed favourite – handicaps

Runners	Winners	Strike Rate	Profit/Loss to BSP
374	97	25.94%	+£14.06

Profit or loss backing the unnamed second favourite - non-handicaps

Runners	Winners	Strike Rate	Profit/Loss to BSP
238	56	23.53%	+£8.42

Profit or loss backing the unnamed second favourite - handicaps

Runners	Winners	Strike Rate	Profit/Loss to

			BSP
365	74	20.27%	+£47.28

Profit or Loss backing horses who won last time out- non-handicaps

Runners	Winners	Strike Rate	Profit/Loss to BSP
116	49	42.24%	+£38.32

Profit or Loss backing horses who won last time out - handicaps

Runners	Winners	Strike Rate	Profit/Loss to BSP
380	58	15.26%	-£50.46

Profit or loss backing Top-Weights in handicaps

Runners	Winners	Strike Rate	Profit/Loss to BSP
406	46	11.33%	-£126.79

Most profitable sires – non-handicaps

Sire	Runners	Winners	Strike Rate	Profit/Loss to BSP
Authorized	12	4	33.33%	+£52.42

Most profitable sires – handicaps

Galileo	19	2	10.53%	+£58.43
Barathea	22	5	22.73%	+£50.86
Golan	16	5	31.25%	+£48.86
Robin Des Pres	16	4	25.00%	+£31.26
Born To Sea	13	3	23.08%	+£30.11

Catterick - Chases

Top jockeys by Strike Rate – non-handicaps

Name Of Jockey	Rides	Winners	Strike Rate	Profit/Loss to BSP
Brian Hughes	27	6	22.22%	+£11.10

Top jockeys by Strike Rate – handicaps

Name Of Jockey	Rides	Winners	Strike Rate	Profit/Loss to BSP
Harry Skelton	10	3	30.00%	+£4.43
Ross Chapman	15	4	26.67%	+£4.30
Nathan Moscrop	12	3	25.00%	+£3.36
Adam Wedge	12	3	25.00%	+£8.12
Jonathan England	50	12	24.00%	+£18.89

Top jockeys by Profit – non-handicaps

Name Of Jockey	Rides	Winners	Strike Rate	Profit/Loss to BSP
Brian Hughes	27	6	22.22%	+£11.10

Top jockeys by Profit – handicaps

Name Of Jockey	Rides	Winners	Strike Rate	Profit/Loss to BSP
Jonathan England	50	12	24.00%	+£18.89
Adam Wedge	12	3	25.00%	+£8.12
William Kennedy	27	5	18.52%	+£7.54
Harry Skelton	10	3	30.00%	+£4.43
Ross Chapman	15	4	26.67%	+£4.30

Top trainers by Strike Rate – non-handicaps

Name Of Trainer	Runners	Winners	Strike Rate	Profit/Loss to BSP
Sue Smith	11	7	63.64%	+£38.46

| Donald McCain | 14 | 4 | 28.57% | -£5.84 |
| Micky Hammond | 13 | 1 | 7.69% | -£2.20 |

Top trainers by Strike Rate – handicaps

Name Of Trainer	Runners	Winners	Strike Rate	Profit/Loss to BSP
Malcolm Jefferson	13	4	30.77%	+£9.34
Dan Skelton	13	4	30.77%	+£2.97
Peter Niven	11	3	27.27%	+£24.44
Sue Smith	71	18	25.35%	+£17.61
Martin Keighley	17	4	23.53%	+£1.86

Top trainers by Profit – non-handicaps

Name Of Trainer	Runners	Winners	Strike Rate	Profit/Loss to BSP
Sue Smith	11	7	63.64%	+£38.46

Top trainers by Profit – handicaps

Name Of Trainer	Runners	Winners	Strike Rate	Profit/Loss to BSP
Micky Hammond	89	10	11.24%	+£57.08
Peter Niven	11	3	27.27%	+£24.44
Sue Smith	71	18	25.35%	+£17.61
Donald McCain	73	15	20.55%	+£17.48
Chris Grant	24	1	4.17%	+£13.53

Top trainer/jockey combos by Strike Rate – handicaps

Name of Trainer/Jockey	Qualifiers	Winners	Strike Rate	Profit/Loss to BSP
Sam England/Jonathan England	34	7	20.59%	+£0.14
Donald McCain/William Kennedy	14	2	14.29%	+£2.17
Sue Smith/Ryan	15	2	13.33%	-£5.61

Mania				
Donald McCain/Brian Hughes	18	2	11.11%	-£12.61
Jennie Candlish/Sean Quinlan	18	1	5.56%	-£10.14

Top trainer/jockey combos by Profit – handicaps

Name of Trainer/Jockey	Qualifiers	Winners	Strike Rate	Profit/Loss to BSP
Donald McCain/William Kennedy	14	2	14.29%	+£2.17
Sam England/Jonathan England	34	7	20.59%	+£0.14

Profit or Loss backing the unnamed favourite – non-handicaps

Runners	Winners	Strike Rate	Profit/Loss to BSP
137	50	36.50%	-£17.22

Profit or Loss backing the unnamed favourite – handicaps

Runners	Winners	Strike Rate	Profit/Loss to BSP
324	101	31.17%	+£20.19

Profit or loss backing the unnamed second favourite - non-handicaps

Runners	Winners	Strike Rate	Profit/Loss to BSP
130	32	24.62%	+£5.81

Profit or loss backing the unnamed second favourite - handicaps

Runners	Winners	Strike Rate	Profit/Loss to BSP
277	57	20.58%	+£27.86

Profit or Loss backing horses who won last time out- non-handicaps

Runners	Winners	Strike Rate	Profit/Loss to BSP
49	15	30.61%	-£3.50

Profit or Loss backing horses who won last time out - handicaps

Runners	Winners	Strike Rate	Profit/Loss to BSP
265	52	19.62%	-£60.09

Profit or loss backing Top-Weights in handicaps

Runners	Winners	Strike Rate	Profit/Loss to BSP
328	53	16.16%	-£61.26

Most profitable sires – non-handicaps

Sire	Runners	Winners	Strike Rate	Profit/Loss to BSP
Presenting	11	3	27.27%	+£9.90
Flemensfirth	12	4	33.33%	+£6.45

Most profitable sires – handicaps

Getaway	14	3	21.43%	+£79.72
Cloudings	18	7	38.89%	+£21.47
Bollin Eric	11	3	27.27%	+£10.27
Generous	14	4	28.57%	+£9.25
Overbury	21	2	9.52%	+£7.61

Catterick – Hurdles

Top jockeys by Strike Rate – non-handicaps

Name Of Jockey	Rides	Winners	Strike Rate	Profit/Loss to BSP
Aidan Coleman	18	7	38.89%	+£11.77
Harry Skelton	18	6	33.33%	+£67.33
Kielan Woods	14	4	28.57%	+£9.54

	12	3	25.00%	-£3.04
Jack Quinlan				
William Kennedy	21	5	23.81%	-£11.07
Alan Johns	11	2	18.18%	+£11.59

Top jockeys by Strike Rate – handicaps

Name Of Jockey	Rides	Winners	Strike Rate	Profit/Loss to BSP
Conor O'Farrell	19	6	31.58%	+£69.11
Ryan Mania	11	3	27.27%	+£21.37
Ross Chapman	20	5	25.00%	+£3.44
Brian Hughes	70	16	22.86%	+£33.24
William Kennedy	15	3	20.00%	+£1.17

Top jockeys by Profit – non-handicaps

Name Of Jockey	Rides	Winners	Strike Rate	Profit/Loss to BSP
Harry Skelton	18	6	33.33%	+£67.33
Richie McLernon	15	2	13.33%	+£25.33
Aidan Coleman	18	7	38.89%	+£11.77
Alan Johns	11	2	18.18%	+£11.59
Kielan Woods	14	4	28.57%	+£9.54

Top jockeys by Profit – handicaps

Name Of Jockey	Rides	Winners	Strike Rate	Profit/Loss to BSP
Thomas Willmott	10	2	20.00%	+£77.71
Conor O'Farrell	19	6	31.58%	+£69.11
Brian Hughes	70	16	22.86%	+£33.24
Ryan Mania	11	3	27.27%	+£21.37
Craig Nichol	28	3	10.71%	+£5.50

Top trainers by Strike Rate – non-handicaps

Name Of Trainer	Runners	Winners	Strike Rate	Profit/Loss to BSP
Jonjo O'Neill	20	7	35.00%	+£79.35
Dan Skelton	21	7	33.33%	-£5.58
John Quinn	29	8	27.59%	-£4.78

Olly Murphy	12	3	25.00%	-£2.85
Brian Ellison	44	10	22.73%	-£12.61

Top trainers by Strike Rate – handicaps

Name Of Trainer	Runners	Winners	Strike Rate	Profit/Loss to BSP
Rebecca Menzies	22	6	27.27%	+£53.74
Jennie Candlish	14	3	21.43%	+£2.26
Iain Jardine	16	3	18.75%	+£4.22
Brian Ellison	22	4	18.18%	-£3.02
Dianne Sayer	34	6	17.65%	+£33.74

Top trainers by Profit – non-handicaps

Name Of Trainer	Runners	Winners	Strike Rate	Profit/Loss to BSP
Dianne Sayer	16	1	6.25%	+£152.62
Jonjo O'Neill	20	7	35.00%	+£79.35
Oliver Greenall	19	2	10.53%	+£60.62
David Thompson	12	1	8.33%	+£46.82
Sue Smith	34	6	17.65%	+£39.11

Top trainers by Profit – handicaps

Name Of Trainer	Runners	Winners	Strike Rate	Profit/Loss to BSP
Joanne Foster	19	1	5.26%	+£137.82
Micky Hammond	133	12	9.02%	+£73.45
Sue Smith	55	7	12.73%	+£60.34
Rebecca Menzies	22	6	27.27%	+£53.74
Dianne Sayer	34	6	17.65%	+£33.74

Top trainer/jockey combos by Strike Rate – non-handicaps

Name Of Jockey	Rides	Winners	Strike Rate	Profit/Loss to BSP
Dan Skelton/Harry Skelton	16	5	31.25%	-£4.19

Donald McCain/Brian Hughes	29	7	24.14%	-£0.68
Donald McCain/William Kennedy	13	3	23.08%	-£5.84
John Quinn/Dougie Costello	11	2	18.18%	-£7.23
Philip Kirby/Thomas Dowson	19	3	15.79%	+£8.81

Top trainer/jockey combos by Strike Rate – handicaps

Name of Trainer/Jockey	Qualifiers	Winners	Strike Rate	Profit/Loss to BSP
Barbara Butterworth/Sean Quinlan	10	3	30.00%	+£14.85
Donald McCain/Abbie McCain	16	3	18.75%	+£5.19
Sam England/Jonathan England	17	2	11.76%	-£2.33
Micky Hammond/Becky Smith	19	2	10.53%	+£4.19
George Bewley/Jonathon Bewley	16	1	6.25%	-£11.67

Top trainer/jockey combos by Profit – non-handicaps

Name Of Jockey	Rides	Winners	Strike Rate	Profit/Loss to BSP
Philip Kirby/Thomas Dowson	19	3	15.79%	+£8.81

Top trainer/jockey combos by Profit – handicaps

Name of Trainer/Jockey	Qualifiers	Winners	Strike Rate	Profit/Loss to BSP
Barbara Butterworth/Sean Quinlan	10	3	30.00%	+£14.85
Donald McCain/Abbie McCain	16	3	18.75%	+£5.19
Micky Hammond/Becky Smith	19	2	10.53%	+£4.19

Profit or Loss backing the unnamed favourite – non-handicaps

Runners	Winners	Strike Rate	Profit/Loss to BSP
308	139	45.13%	+£7.10

Profit or Loss backing the unnamed favourite – handicaps

Runners	Winners	Strike Rate	Profit/Loss to BSP
321	80	24.92%	-£22.97

Profit or loss backing the unnamed second favourite - non-handicaps

Runners	Winners	Strike Rate	Profit/Loss to BSP
297	68	22.90%	-£0.69

Profit or loss backing the unnamed second favourite - handicaps

Runners	Winners	Strike Rate	Profit/Loss to BSP
296	56	18.92%	+£37.59

Profit or Loss backing horses who won last time out - non-handicaps

Runners	Winners	Strike Rate	Profit/Loss to BSP
184	60	32.61%	-£6.43

Profit or Loss backing horses who won last time out - handicaps

Runners	Winners	Strike Rate	Profit/Loss to BSP
255	48	18.82%	-£22.26

Profit or loss backing Top-Weights in handicaps

Runners	Winners	Strike Rate	Profit/Loss to BSP
337	38	11.28%	-£83.65

Most profitable sires – non-handicaps

Sire	Runners	Winners	Strike Rate	Profit/Loss to BSP
Tobougg	10	1	10.00%	+£158.60
Medicean	10	2	20.00%	+£32.37
Fame And Glory	15	4	26.67%	+£19.47
High Chaparral	12	2	16.67%	+£10.92
Jeremy	13	1	7.69%	+£3.29

Most profitable sires – handicaps

Court Cave	16	1	6.25%	+£140.82
Oscar	18	3	16.67%	+£82.95
Alflora	20	4	20.00%	+£55.45
Turtle Island	14	3	21.43%	+£38.43
Selkirk	11	2	18.18%	+£20.70

Cheltenham - Chases

Top jockeys by Strike Rate – non-handicaps

Bryony Frost	15	6	40.00%	+£27.54
Nico de Boinville	48	15	31.25%	+£19.19
Jack Kennedy	13	4	30.77%	+£11.88
Harry Skelton	31	8	25.81%	-£5.70
Tommie M O'Brien	12	3	25.00%	-£2.02

Top jockeys by Strike Rate – handicaps

Name Of Jockey	Rides	Winners	Strike Rate	Profit/Loss to BSP
Bryony Frost	17	4	23.53%	+£11.27
Derek Fox	10	2	20.00%	+£6.54
Richard Patrick	20	4	20.00%	+£16.03
Alan Johns	10	2	20.00%	+£32.99
Davy Russell	29	5	17.24%	+£40.43

Top jockeys by Profit – non-handicaps

Name Of Jockey	Rides	Winners	Strike Rate	Profit/Loss to BSP
Charlie Deutsch	20	3	15.00%	+£286.36
Martin McIntyre	10	2	20.00%	+£69.85
Bryony Frost	15	6	40.00%	+£27.54
Jamie Codd	23	4	17.39%	+£26.51
Davy Russell	53	9	16.98%	+£24.33

Top jockeys by Profit – handicaps

Name Of Jockey	Rides	Winners	Strike Rate	Profit/Loss to BSP
Kielan Woods	18	3	16.67%	+£192.77
Robert Dunne	21	2	9.52%	+£74.46
Adam Wedge	43	5	11.63%	+£59.69
Jamie Moore	43	6	13.95%	+£49.96

| Gina Andrews | 12 | 1 | 8.33% | +£43.49 |

Top trainers by Strike Rate – non-handicaps

Name Of Trainer	Runners	Winners	Strike Rate	Profit/Loss to BSP
Nicky Henderson	116	31	26.72%	+£0.81
Neil Mulholland	16	4	25.00%	+£6.25
Jonjo O'Neill	31	7	22.58%	+£18.84
Dan Skelton	33	7	21.21%	-£15.17
Gordon Elliott	65	13	20.00%	+£40.60

Top trainers by Strike Rate – handicaps

Name Of Trainer	Runners	Winners	Strike Rate	Profit/Loss to BSP
Michael Scudamore	34	8	23.53%	+£101.13
Nigel Hawke	15	3	20.00%	+£25.32
Mick Channon	21	4	19.05%	+£8.31
David Bridgwater	16	3	18.75%	+£14.42
Gary Moore	44	7	15.91%	+£30.87

Top trainers by Profit – non-handicaps

Name Of Trainer	Runners	Winners	Strike Rate	Profit/Loss to BSP
Richard Bandey	11	2	18.18%	+£68.85
Henry De Bromhead	77	11	14.29%	+£40.70
Gordon Elliott	65	13	20.00%	+£40.60
David Pipe	44	7	15.91%	+£28.94
Jonjo O'Neill	31	7	22.58%	+£18.84

Top trainers by Profit – handicaps

Name Of Trainer	Runners	Winners	Strike Rate	Profit/Loss to BSP
Ben Case	15	2	13.33%	+£172.40
Michael Scudamore	34	8	23.53%	+£101.13

Venetia Williams	156	11	7.05%	+£71.75
Fergal O'Brien	86	11	12.79%	+£49.79
Evan Williams	62	7	11.29%	+£45.54

Top trainer/jockey combos by Strike Rate – non-handicaps

Name of Trainer/Jockey	Qualifiers	Winners	Strike Rate	Profit/Loss to BSP
Nicky Henderson/Nico de Boinville	41	14	34.15%	+£17.35
Dan Skelton/Harry Skelton	30	7	23.33%	-£12.17
Philip Rowley/Alex Edwards	18	4	22.22%	-£8.73
Gordon Elliott/Jamie Codd	14	3	21.43%	+£19.32
W P Mullins/Paul Townend	39	8	20.51%	-£1.19

Top trainer/jockey combos by Strike Rate – handicaps

Name of Trainer/Jockey	Qualifiers	Winners	Strike Rate	Profit/Loss to BSP
Michael Scudamore/Tom Scudamore	11	4	36.36%	+£60.01
Paul Nicholls/Bryony Frost	15	4	26.67%	+£13.27
Gordon Elliott/Davy Russell	12	3	25.00%	+£13.14
Kerry Lee/Richard Patrick	14	3	21.43%	+£19.19
Gary Moore/Jamie Moore	22	4	18.18%	+£34.31

Top trainer/jockey combos by Profit – non-handicaps

Name of Trainer/Jockey	Qualifiers	Winners	Strike Rate	Profit/Loss to BSP
David Pipe/Tom Scudamore	33	6	18.18%	+£36.13
Gordon Elliott/Jamie Codd	14	3	21.43%	+£19.32
Nicky Henderson/Nico de Boinville	41	14	34.15%	+£17.35

Top trainer/jockey combos by Profit – handicaps

Name of Trainer/Jockey	Qualifiers	Winners	Strike Rate	Profit/Loss to BSP
Michael Scudamore/Tom Scudamore	11	4	36.36%	+£60.01
Evan Williams/Adam Wedge	28	4	14.29%	+£49.04
Kim Bailey/David Bass	21	3	14.29%	+£44.77
Paul Nicholls/Sam Twiston-Davies	41	4	9.76%	+£34.98
Gary Moore/Jamie Moore	22	4	18.18%	+£34.31

Profit or Loss backing the unnamed favourite – non-handicaps

Runners	Winners	Strike Rate	Profit/Loss to BSP
586	214	36.52%	-£14.80

Profit or Loss backing the unnamed favourite – handicaps

Runners	Winners	Strike Rate	Profit/Loss to

			BSP
627	117	18.66%	-£78.41

Profit or loss backing the unnamed second favourite - non-handicaps

Runners	Winners	Strike Rate	Profit/Loss to BSP
574	123	21.43%	+£25.56

Profit or loss backing the unnamed second favourite - handicaps

Runners	Winners	Strike Rate	Profit/Loss to BSP
551	85	15.43%	+£8.38

Profit or Loss backing horses who won last time out - non-handicaps

Runners	Winners	Strike Rate	Profit/Loss to BSP
1448	237	16.37%	-£40.87

Profit or Loss backing horses who won last time out - handicaps

Runners	Winners	Strike Rate	Profit/Loss to BSP
1322	131	9.91%	-£109.74

Profit or loss backing Top-Weights in handicaps

Runners	Winners	Strike Rate	Profit/Loss to BSP
607	61	10.05%	-£122.64

Most profitable sires – non-handicaps

Sire	Runners	Winners	Strike Rate	Profit/Loss to BSP
Brian Boru	22	2	9.09%	+£216.13
Buck's Boum	11	4	36.36%	+£209.78
Kayf Tara	68	10	14.71%	+£37.83
Muhtathir	14	3	21.43%	+£37.16
Heron Island	15	5	33.33%	+£32.77

Most profitable sires – handicaps

Croco Rouge	10	1	10.00%	+£166.42
Robin Des Champs	17	3	17.65%	+£93.78
Silver Patriarch	12	1	8.33%	+£52.93
Dubai Destination	19	4	21.05%	+£51.94
Alflora	25	3	12.00%	+£45.14

Cheltenham – Hurdles

Top jockeys by Strike Rate – non-handicaps

Name Of Jockey	Rides	Winners	Strike Rate	Profit/Loss to BSP
Rachael Blackmore	30	7	23.33%	+£129.31
Joshua Moore	15	3	20.00%	+£9.96
Nico de Boinville	51	10	19.61%	+£58.95
Jack Kennedy	25	4	16.00%	+£41.04
Tom Scudamore	79	12	15.19%	-£37.48

Top jockeys by Strike Rate – handicaps

Name Of Jockey	Rides	Winners	Strike Rate	Profit/Loss to BSP
Kieron Edgar	17	4	23.53%	+£49.96
David Noonan	11	2	18.18%	+£6.68
Richard Patrick	17	3	17.65%	+£11.50
Davy Russell	30	5	16.67%	+£30.90
Jack Tudor	13	2	15.38%	+£18.01

Top jockeys by Profit – non-handicaps

Name Of Jockey	Rides	Winners	Strike Rate	Profit/Loss to BSP
Rachael Blackmore	30	7	23.33%	+£129.31
Adam Wedge	21	2	9.52%	+£104.86
Nico de Boinville	51	10	19.61%	+£58.95
Jack Kennedy	25	4	16.00%	+£41.04

Danny Mullins	35	4	11.43%	+£38.67

Top jockeys by Profit – handicaps

Name Of Jockey	Rides	Winners	Strike Rate	Profit/Loss to BSP
James Best	28	3	10.71%	+£69.67
Nico de Boinville	67	10	14.93%	+£69.34
Brian Hughes	34	2	5.88%	+£55.53
Kieron Edgar	17	4	23.53%	+£49.96
Bridget Andrews	26	2	7.69%	+£48.72

Top trainers by Strike Rate – non-handicaps

Name Of Trainer	Runners	Winners	Strike Rate	Profit/Loss to BSP
John C McConnell	14	4	28.57%	+£16.71
Emma Lavelle	23	6	26.09%	+£8.82
Nick Williams	34	8	23.53%	+£35.10
Harry Fry	35	7	20.00%	+£5.09
Jeremy Scott	10	2	20.00%	-£1.72

Top trainers by Strike Rate – handicaps

Name Of Trainer	Runners	Winners	Strike Rate	Profit/Loss to BSP
Kerry Lee	11	2	18.18%	+£0.08
Nigel Hawke	15	2	13.33%	+£16.95
Fergal O'Brien	79	9	11.39%	+£8.23
Lucy Wadham	18	2	11.11%	-£8.79
Ian Williams	49	5	10.20%	-£12.75

Top trainers by Profit – non-handicaps

Name Of Trainer	Runners	Winners	Strike Rate	Profit/Loss to BSP
Henry De Bromhead	43	8	18.60%	+£119.72
Rebecca Curtis	41	3	7.32%	+£88.47
Noel Meade	12	1	8.33%	+£48.57
W P Mullins	236	31	13.14%	+£39.90
John Quinn	12	1	8.33%	+£33.10

Top trainers by Profit – handicaps

Name Of Trainer	Runners	Winners	Strike Rate	Profit/Loss to BSP
Gordon Elliott	130	11	8.46%	+£109.57
Noel Meade	21	1	4.76%	+£96.95
Philip Hobbs	152	12	7.89%	+£43.25
Dan Skelton	119	11	9.24%	+£32.99
Jonjo O'Neill	105	8	7.62%	+£31.72

Top trainer/jockey combos by Strike Rate – non-handicaps

Name of Trainer/Jockey	Qualifiers	Winners	Strike Rate	Profit/Loss to BSP
Nigel Twiston-Davies/Daryl Jacob	13	5	38.46%	+£2.14
Henry De Bromhead/Rachael Blackmore	21	7	33.33%	+£138.31
Colin Tizzard/Harry Cobden	20	5	25.00%	+£42.19
Colin Tizzard / Tom Scudamore	13	3	23.08%	-£2.09
Nicky Henderson/Nico de Boinville	45	10	22.22%	+£64.95

Top trainer/jockey combos by Strike Rate – handicaps

Name of Trainer/Jockey	Qualifiers	Winners	Strike Rate	Profit/Loss to BSP
Ian Williams/Tom O'Brien	10	3	30.00%	+£15.57
Philip Hobbs/James Best	10	2	20.00%	+£79.22
Nicky Henderson/James Bowen	10	2	20.00%	+£17.08
Tom George/Paddy Brennan	17	3	17.65%	+£9.85

Jonjo O'Neill/Aidan Coleman	12	2	16.67%	+£23.35

Top trainer/jockey combos by Profit – non-handicaps

Name of Trainer/Jockey	Qualifiers	Winners	Strike Rate	Profit/Loss to BSP
Henry De Bromhead/Rachael Blackmore	21	7	33.33%	+£138.31
Nicky Henderson/Nico de Boinville	45	10	22.22%	+£64.95
Colin Tizzard/Harry Cobden	20	5	25.00%	+£42.19
Gordon Elliott/Jack Kennedy	19	3	15.79%	+£35.26
Warren Greatrex/Gavin Sheehan	18	2	11.11%	+£6.37

Top trainer/jockey combos by Profit – handicaps

Name of Trainer/Jockey	Qualifiers	Winners	Strike Rate	Profit/Loss to BSP
Philip Hobbs/James Best	10	2	20.00%	+£79.22
Nicky Henderson/Nico de Boinville	55	6	10.91%	+£51.69
Dan Skelton/Bridget Andrews	25	2	8.00%	+£49.72
W P Mullins/Paul Townend	23	3	13.04%	+£35.41
Gordon Elliott/Jack Kennedy	16	1	6.25%	+£33.02

Profit or Loss backing the unnamed favourite – non-handicaps

Runners	Winners	Strike Rate	Profit/Loss to BSP
543	213	39.23%	-£16.73

Profit or Loss backing the unnamed favourite – handicaps

Runners	Winners	Strike Rate	Profit/Loss to BSP
512	106	20.70%	-£15.02

Profit or loss backing the unnamed second favourite - non-handicaps

Runners	Winners	Strike Rate	Profit/Loss to BSP
519	91	17.53%	-£87.70

Profit or loss backing the unnamed second favourite - handicaps

Runners	Winners	Strike Rate	Profit/Loss to BSP
445	59	13.26%	-£45.42

Profit or Loss backing horses who won last time out- non-handicaps

Runners	Winners	Strike Rate	Profit/Loss to BSP
1824	285	15.63%	-£184.06

Profit or Loss backing horses who won last time out - handicaps

Runners	Winners	Strike Rate	Profit/Loss to BSP
1533	148	9.65%	+£137.00

Profit or loss backing Top-Weights in handicaps

Runners	Winners	Strike Rate	Profit/Loss to BSP
517	51	9.86%	+£69.23

Most profitable sires – non-handicaps

Sire	Runners	Winners	Strike Rate	Profit/Loss to BSP
Oscar	74	16	21.62%	+£156.60
Beat Hollow	14	2	14.29%	+£135.85
Saddler Maker	15	5	33.33%	+£88.65
Martaline	39	8	20.51%	+£87.38
Yeats	33	6	18.18%	+£49.68

Most profitable sires – handicaps

Fame And Glory	15	4	26.67%	+£61.17
High Chaparral	17	1	5.88%	+£58.93
King's Theatre	98	11	11.22%	+£57.59
Intikhab	12	1	8.33%	+£56.62
Definite Article	19	3	15.79%	+£53.87

Chepstow - Chases

Top jockeys by Strike Rate – non-handicaps

Name Of Jockey	Rides	Winners	Strike Rate	Profit/Loss to BSP
Tom Scudamore	13	4	30.77%	-£3.89
Harry Cobden	11	2	18.18%	-£5.02
Sam Twiston-Davies	11	2	18.18%	-£5.35
Bradley Gibbs	10	1	10.00%	-£6.62

Top jockeys by Strike Rate – handicaps

Name of Trainer/Jockey	Qualifiers	Winners	Strike Rate	Profit/Loss to BSP
Ben Jones	21	7	33.33%	+£38.31
Stan Sheppard	35	11	31.43%	+£43.99
Connor Brace	15	4	26.67%	+£16.04
Jonjo O'Neill Jr	24	6	25.00%	+£4.41
James Bowen	36	8	22.22%	+£22.45

Top jockeys by Profit – handicaps

Name Of Jockey	Rides	Winners	Strike Rate	Profit/Loss to BSP
Sean Bowen	69	14	20.29%	+£84.75
Conor Ring	45	7	15.56%	+£53.14
Stan Sheppard	35	11	31.43%	+£43.99
Ben Jones	21	7	33.33%	+£38.31
Robert Dunne	53	9	16.98%	+£37.95

Top trainers by Strike Rate – non-handicaps

Name Of Trainer	Runners	Winners	Strike Rate	Profit/Loss to BSP
Colin Tizzard	14	5	35.71%	+£16.93
Philip Hobbs	17	6	35.29%	+£3.83
Paul Nicholls	28	7	25.00%	-£11.45
Rebecca Curtis	14	3	21.43%	-£4.45

David Brace	11	2	18.18%	-£5.05

Top trainers by Strike Rate – handicaps

Name Of Trainer	Runners	Winners	Strike Rate	Profit/Loss to BSP
Harry Whittington	13	4	30.77%	+£9.17
Tom Lacey	14	4	28.57%	-£0.28
Katy Price	12	3	25.00%	+£4.49
Sam Thomas	13	3	23.08%	+£14.94
Matt Sheppard	41	9	21.95%	+£52.62

Top trainers by Profit – non-handicaps

Name Of Trainer	Runners	Winners	Strike Rate	Profit/Loss to BSP
Colin Tizzard	14	5	35.71%	+£16.93
Philip Hobbs	17	6	35.29%	+£3.83

Top trainers by Profit – handicaps

Name Of Trainer	Runners	Winners	Strike Rate	Profit/Loss to BSP
Alan Jones	10	2	20.00%	+£63.09
Matt Sheppard	41	9	21.95%	+£52.62
Neil Mulholland	50	7	14.00%	+£42.71
David Pipe	67	12	17.91%	+£36.90
Jamie Snowden	11	2	18.18%	+£25.39

Top trainer/jockey combos by Strike Rate – non-handicaps

Name Of Jockey	Rides	Winners	Strike Rate	Profit/Loss to BSP
Paul Nicholls/Harry Cobden	11	2	18.18%	-£5.02

Top trainer/jockey combos by Strike Rate – handicaps

Name of Trainer/Jockey	Qualifiers	Winners	Strike Rate	Profit/Loss to BSP
Jonjo	13	4	30.77%	+£5.48

O'Neill/Jonjo O'Neill Jr				
Philip Hobbs/James best	15	4	26.67%	+£9.25
Venetia Williams/Charlie Deutsch	52	11	21.15%	-£5.83
Colin Tizzard/Tom Scudamore	10	2	20.00&	-£2.29
Evan Williams/Isabel Williams	10	2	20.00%	-£2.66

Top trainer/jockey combos by Profit – handicaps

Name of Trainer/Jockey	Qualifiers	Winners	Strike Rate	Profit/Loss to BSP
David Pipe/Tom Scudamore	26	4	15.38%	+£37.25
Christian Williams/Jack Tudor	13	2	15.38%	+£30.03
Dan Skelton/Bridget Andrews	13	2	15.38%	+£17.62
Philip Hobbs/James Best	15	4	26.67%	+£9.25
Colin Tizzard/Harry Cobden	25	4	16.00%	+£6.51

Profit or Loss backing the unnamed favourite – non-handicaps

Runners	Winners	Strike Rate	Profit/Loss to BSP
191	86	45.03%	+£9.56

Profit or Loss backing the unnamed favourite – handicaps

Runners	Winners	Strike Rate	Profit/Loss to

			BSP
656	180	27.44%	+£21.69

Profit or loss backing the unnamed second favourite - non-handicaps

Runners	Winners	Strike Rate	Profit/Loss to BSP
166	44	26.51%	+£3.07

Profit or loss backing the unnamed second favourite - handicaps

Runners	Winners	Strike Rate	Profit/Loss to BSP
575	98	17.04%	-£70.92

Profit or Loss backing horses who won last time out - non-handicaps

Runners	Winners	Strike Rate	Profit/Loss to BSP
123	38	30.89%	+£25.46

Profit or Loss backing horses who won last time out - handicaps

Runners	Winners	Strike Rate	Profit/Loss to BSP
607	100	16.47%	-£36.35

Profit or loss backing Top-Weights in handicaps

Runners	Winners	Strike Rate	Profit/Loss to BSP
674	84	12.46%	-£128.25

Most profitable sires – non-handicaps

Sire	Runners	Winners	Strike Rate	Profit/Loss to BSP
King's Theatre	12	4	33.33%	+£9.61

Most profitable sires – handicaps

Flemensfirth	106	16	15.09%	+£80.67
Oscar	78	14	17.95%	+£60.86

Craigsteel	31	4	12.90%	+£60.00
Turgeon	32	6	18.75%	+£52.89
Exit To Nowhere	19	4	21.05%	+£37.20

Chepstow – Hurdles

Top jockeys by Strike Rate – non-handicaps

Name Of Jockey	Rides	Winners	Strike Rate	Profit/Loss to BSP
Harry Cobden	63	19	30.16%	-£15.52
Bridget Andrews	11	3	27.27%	+£3.87
Rex Dingle	12	3	25.00%	-£1.51
Nico de Boinville	21	5	23.81%	+£41.94
Daryl Jacob	44	9	20.45%	-£11.79

Top jockeys by Strike Rate – handicaps

Name Of Jockey	Rides	Winners	Strike Rate	Profit/Loss to BSP
Rex Dingle	14	4	28.57%	+£16.62
Charlie Price	11	3	27.27%	+£31.86
Lorcan Williams	11	3	27.27%	-£0.12
Nico de Boinville	16	4	25.00%	+£9.51
Sean Bowen	40	8	20.00%	+£23.66

Top jockeys by Profit – non-handicaps

Name Of Jockey	Rides	Winners	Strike Rate	Profit/Loss to BSP
Adam Wedge	76	14	18.42%	+£207.99
Robert Dunne	44	3	6.82%	+£94.71
Nico de Boinville	21	5	23.81%	+£41.94
Lee Edwards	17	3	17.65%	+£17.31
Lorcan Williams	20	1	5.00%	+£9.42

Top jockeys by Profit – handicaps

Name Of Jockey	Rides	Winners	Strike Rate	Profit/Loss to BSP
James Davies	48	5	10.42%	+£104.99
Sean Quinlan	10	1	10.00%	+£50.25

Aidan Coleman	37	5	13.51%	+£34.13
Charlie Price	11	3	27.27%	+£31.86
Harry Skelton	32	5	15.63%	+£31.84

Top trainers by Strike Rate – non-handicaps

Name Of Trainer	Runners	Winners	Strike Rate	Profit/Loss to BSP
Alastair Ralph	11	4	36.36%	+£24.92
Paul Nicholls	139	39	28.06%	+£6.87
Nicky Henderson	33	9	27.27%	-£2.63
Emma Lavelle	38	9	23.68%	+£7.72
Rebecca Curtis	48	11	22.92%	+£21.21

Top trainers by Strike Rate – handicaps

Name Of Trainer	Runners	Winners	Strike Rate	Profit/Loss to BSP
Tom Lacey	17	5	29.41%	+£12.95
Debra Hamer	17	4	23.53%	+£24.66
Anthony Honeyball	17	4	23.53%	+£2.77
Mark Gillard	22	5	22.73%	+£9.22
Henry Oliver	31	7	22.58%	+£9.05

Top trainers by Profit – non-handicaps

Name Of Trainer	Runners	Winners	Strike Rate	Profit/Loss to BSP
Evan Williams	101	17	16.83%	+£202.27
Seamus Mullins	16	2	12.50%	+£184.00
David Dennis	13	1	7.69%	+£166.76
Tom Lacey	28	4	14.29%	+£56.28
Philip Hobbs	90	20	22.22%	+£39.84

Top trainers by Profit – handicaps

Name Of Trainer	Runners	Winners	Strike Rate	Profit/Loss to BSP
Chris Down	37	7	18.92%	+£130.85
Evan Williams	140	14	10.00%	+£96.68
Robert Walford	22	3	13.64%	+£57.49

Richard Phillips	18	2	11.11%	+£51.11
Victor Dartnall	34	6	17.65%	+£46.15

Top trainer/jockey combos by Strike Rate – non-handicaps

Name of Trainer/Jockey	Qualifiers	Winners	Strike Rate	Profit/Loss to BSP
Nicky Henderson/Nico de Boinville	10	4	40.00%	+£1.60
Paul Nicholls/Harry Cobden	52	18	34.62%	-£8.22
Paul Nicholls/Sam Twiston-Davies	28	9	32.14%	-£2.41
Dan Skelton/Bridget Andrews	11	3	27.27%	+£3.87
Tom George/Paddy Brennan	12	3	25.00%	-£0.39

Top trainer/jockey combos by Strike Rate – handicaps

Name of Trainer/Jockey	Qualifiers	Winners	Strike Rate	Profit/Loss to BSP
Neil Mulholland/Tom Scudamore	10	3	30.00%	+£8.79
Peter Bowen/Sean Bowen	17	5	29.41%	+£31.95
Paul Nicholls/Harry Cobden	19	5	26.32%	+£11.18
Philip Hobbs/Tom O'Brien	13	3	23.08%	+£12.74
Chris Down/James Davies	18	4	22.22%	+£130.56

Top trainer/jockey combos by Profit – non-handicaps

Name of Trainer/Jockey	Qualifiers	Winners	Strike Rate	Profit/Loss to BSP
Evan Williams/Adam Wedge	53	12	22.64%	+£218.65
Paul Nicholls/Lorcan Williams	12	1	8.33%	+£17.42
Dan Skelton/Bridget Andrews	11	3	27.27%	+£3.87
Nicky Henderson/Nico de Boinville	10	4	40.00%	+£1.60

Top trainer/jockey combos by Profit – handicaps

Name of Trainer/Jockey	Qualifiers	Winners	Strike Rate	Profit/Loss to BSP
Chris Down/James Davies	18	4	22.22%	+£130.56
Dan Skelton/Harry Skelton	25	4	16.00%	+£32.74
Peter Bowen/Sean Bowen	17	5	29.41%	+£31.95
Venetia Williams/Charlie Deutsch	14	2	14.29%	+£25.72
Evan Williams/Adam Wedge	47	5	10.64%	+£23.80

Profit or Loss backing the unnamed favourite – non-handicaps

Runners	Winners	Strike Rate	Profit/Loss to BSP
552	235	42.57%	+£2.58

Profit or Loss backing the unnamed favourite – handicaps

Runners	Winners	Strike Rate	Profit/Loss to BSP
523	142	27.15%	+£0.98

Profit or loss backing the unnamed second favourite - non-handicaps

Runners	Winners	Strike Rate	Profit/Loss to BSP
547	128	23.40%	+£2.17

Profit or loss backing the unnamed second favourite - handicaps

Runners	Winners	Strike Rate	Profit/Loss to BSP
488	75	15.37%	-£54.20

Profit or Loss backing horses who won last time out- non-handicaps

Runners	Winners	Strike Rate	Profit/Loss to BSP
441	97	22.00%	-£73.21

Profit or Loss backing horses who won last time out - handicaps

Runners	Winners	Strike Rate	Profit/Loss to BSP
549	94	17.12%	+£84.76144

Profit or loss backing Top-Weights in handicaps

Runners	Winners	Strike Rate	Profit/Loss to BSP
549	67	12.20%	+£8.08

Most profitable sires – non-handicaps

Sire	Runners	Winners	Strike Rate	Profit/Loss to BSP
Robin Des Champs	25	4	16.00%	+£208.49
Flemensfirth	90	9	10.00%	+£167.11

Sulamani	23	2	8.70%	+£159.40
Alflora	23	2	8.70%	+£133.68
Kapgarde	20	6	30.00%	+£17.76

Most profitable sires – handicaps

Craigsteel	24	6	25.00%	+£96.00
Court Cave	24	2	8.33%	+£90.73
Flemensfirth	75	9	12.00%	+£44.64
Whipper	13	3	23.08%	+£26.90
Old Vic	38	7	18.42%	+£22.01

Doncaster - Chases

Top jockeys by Strike Rate – non-handicaps

Name Of Jockey	Rides	Winners	Strike Rate	Profit/Loss to BSP
Nico de Boinville	12	6	50.00%	+£3.53
Aidan Coleman	10	2	20.00%	-£3.07
Sam Twiston-Davies	11	2	18.28%	-£3.48
Brian Hughes	21	3	14.29%	-£13.29

Top jockeys by Strike Rate – handicaps

Name Of Jockey	Rides	Winners	Strike Rate	Profit/Loss to BSP
Charlie Todd	11	4	36.36%	+£23.37
Robert Dunne	15	4	26.67%	+£31.37
Paddy Brennan	34	8	23.53%	+£47.39
Henry Brooke	26	6	23.08%	+£28.27
Charlie Deutsch	13	3	23.08%	+£0.38
Tom Scudamore	22	5	22.73%	+£28.27

Top jockeys by Profit – non-handicaps

Name Of Jockey	Rides	Winners	Strike Rate	Profit/Loss to BSP
Nico de Boinville	12	6	50.00%	+£3.53

Top jockeys by Profit – handicaps

Name Of Jockey	Rides	Winners	Strike Rate	Profit/Loss to BSP
Sean Quinlan	31	6	19.35%	+£99.49
Nick Scholfield	22	4	18.18%	+£71.41
Paddy Brennan	34	8	23.53%	+£47.39
Robert Dunne	15	4	26.67%	+£31.37
Henry Brooke	26	6	23.08%	+£28.27

Top trainers by Strike Rate – non-handicaps

Name Of Trainer	Runners	Winners	Strike Rate	Profit/Loss to BSP
Nicky Henderson	30	12	40.00%	-£2.74
Paul Nicholls	35	13	37.14%	+£5.08
Warren Greatrex	12	4	33.33%	-£4.01
Alan King	16	4	25.00%	-£8.21

Top trainers by Strike Rate – handicaps

Name Of Trainer	Runners	Winners	Strike Rate	Profit/Loss to BSP
Oliver Greenall	11	4	36.36%	+£27.05
Ian Williams	27	7	25.93%	+£20.69
Nicky Richards	27	7	25.93%	+£89.87
Ben Case	12	3	25.00%	+£17.17
Emma Lavelle	28	6	21.43%	-£4.18

Top trainers by Profit – non-handicaps

Name Of Trainer	Runners	Winners	Strike Rate	Profit/Loss to BSP
Paul Nicholls	35	13	37.14%	+£5.08

Top trainers by Profit – handicaps

Name Of Trainer	Runners	Winners	Strike Rate	Profit/Loss to BSP
Nicky Richards	27	7	25.93%	+£89.87
Peter Winks	11	2	18.18%	+£82.23
Kim Bailey	21	4	19.05%	+£50.16
Brian Ellison	20	3	15.00%	+£40.55
Oliver Greenall	11	4	36.36%	+£27.05

Top trainer/jockey combos by Strike Rate – non-handicaps

Name Of Jockey	Rides	Winners	Strike Rate	Profit/Loss to BSP
Nicky Henderson/Nico de Boinville	10	5	50.00%	-£0.28

Top trainer/jockey combos by Strike Rate – handicaps

Name of Trainer/Jockey	Qualifiers	Winners	Strike Rate	Profit/Loss to BSP
Alan King/Tom Bellamy	10	3	30.00%	+£15.44
Venetia Williams/Charlie Deutsch	13	3	23.08%	+£0.38
Kim Bailey/David Bass	14	3	21.43%	+£4.89
Tom George/Paddy Brennan	19	4	21.05%	+£21.32
Dan Skelton/Bridget Andrews	10	2	20.00%	+£1.51

Top trainer/jockey combos by Profit – handicaps

Name of Trainer/Jockey	Qualifiers	Winners	Strike Rate	Profit/Loss to BSP
Tom George/Paddy Brennan	19	4	21.05%	+£21.32
Alan King/Tom Bellamy	10	3	30.00%	+£15.44
Jonjo O'Neill/Richie McLernon	14	2	14.29%	+£11.27
Kim Bailey/David Bass	14	3	21.43%	+£4.89
Dan Skelton/Bridget Andrews	10	2	20.00%	+£1.51

Profit or Loss backing the unnamed favourite – non-handicaps

Favourite	Runners	Winners	Strike Rate	Profit/Loss to BSP
	149	73	48.99%	-£1.97

Profit or Loss backing the unnamed favourite – handicaps

Favourite	Runners	Winners	Strike Rate	Profit/Loss to BSP
	361	91	25.21%	-£15.89

Profit or loss backing the unnamed second favourite - non-handicaps

Second Favourite	Runners	Winners	Strike Rate	Profit/Loss to BSP
	151	44	29.14%	+£15.43

Profit or loss backing the unnamed second favourite - handicaps

Second Favourite	Runners	Winners	Strike Rate	Profit/Loss to BSP
	331	65	19.64%	+£1.46

Profit or Loss backing horses who won last time out - non-handicaps

Won Last Time out	Runners	Winners	Strike Rate	Profit/Loss to BSP
	144	43	29.86%	-£32.57

Profit or Loss backing horses who won last time out - handicaps

Won Last Time Out	Runners	Winners	Strike Rate	Profit/Loss to BSP
	372	63	16.94%	+£21.31

Profit or loss backing Top-Weights in handicaps

Top Weight	Runners	Winners	Strike Rate	Profit/Loss to BSP
	365	58	15.89%	-£38.38

Most profitable sires – non-handicaps

Sire	Runners	Winners	Strike Rate	Profit/Loss to BSP
Midnight Legend	12	1	8.33%	+£25.96
Beneficial	10	5	50.00%	+£6.24

Presenting	16	6	37.50%	+£6.09

Most profitable sires – handicaps

Winged Love	15	3	20.00%	+£109.52
Brian Boru	16	4	25.00%	+£95.01
Robin Des Pres	16	3	18.75%	+£25.04
Gold Well	42	9	21.43%	+£24.63
Alflora	14	2	14.29%	+£21.45

Doncaster – Hurdles

Top jockeys by Strike Rate – non-handicaps

Name Of Jockey	Rides	Winners	Strike Rate	Profit/Loss to BSP
Nico de Boinville	40	13	32.50%	+£9.85
Nick Scholfield	17	4	23.53%	+£0.88
Max Kendrick	13	3	23.08%	+£8.18
James Bowen	13	3	23.08%	-£1.56
David Bass	41	9	21.95%	+£67.04

Top jockeys by Strike Rate – handicaps

Name Of Jockey	Rides	Winners	Strike Rate	Profit/Loss to BSP
Theo Gillard	10	5	50.00%	+£85.18
Harry Skelton	17	4	23.53%	+£8.64
Jonjo O'Neill Jr	13	3	23.08%	+£12.05
David Bass	23	5	21.74%	-£1.61
Lee Edwards	15	3	20.00%	+£23.73

Top jockeys by Profit – non-handicaps

Name Of Jockey	Rides	Winners	Strike Rate	Profit/Loss to BSP
Paddy Brennan	33	7	21.21%	+£93.89
David Bass	41	9	21.95%	+£67.04
Robert Dunne	21	2	9.52%	+£45.87
David Noonan	13	1	7.69%	+£22.86
Dougie Costello	23	5	21.74%	+£13.26

Top jockeys by Profit – handicaps

Name Of Jockey	Rides	Winners	Strike Rate	Profit/Loss to BSP
Theo Gillard	10	5	50.00%	+£85.18
Ben Poste	16	1	6.25%	+£48.69
Sean Quinlan	36	4	11.11%	+£31.55
William Kennedy	28	5	17.86%	+£26.95
Harry Bannister	11	1	9.09%	+£26.48

Top trainers by Strike Rate – non-handicaps

Name Of Trainer	Runners	Winners	Strike Rate	Profit/Loss to BSP
Nicky Henderson	93	36	38.71%	+£21.81
John Quinn	20	7	35.00%	+£31.51
Amy Murphy	10	3	30.00%	-£2.37
Ben Pauling	42	11	26.19%	+£129.12
Brian Ellison	13	3	23.08%	+£8.68

Top trainers by Strike Rate – handicaps

Name Of Trainer	Runners	Winners	Strike Rate	Profit/Loss to BSP
Gillian Boanas	14	5	35.71%	+£67.49
Emma Lavelle	17	5	29.41%	+£11.31
Oliver Greenall	15	4	26.67%	+£19.93
Fergal O'Brien	16	4	25.00%	+£31.83
Sue Smith	17	4	23.53%	+£25.00

Top trainers by Profit – non-handicaps

Name Of Trainer	Runners	Winners	Strike Rate	Profit/Loss to BSP
Ben Pauling	42	11	26.19%	+£129.12
Tom George	27	4	14.81%	+£75.50
Ben Case	22	4	18.18%	+£48.90
David Pipe	23	4	17.39%	+£33.72
Ian Williams	57	4	7.02%	+£31.74

Top trainers by Profit – handicaps

Name Of Trainer	Runners	Winners	Strike Rate	Profit/Loss to BSP
Gillian Boanas	14	5	35.71%	+£67.49
Jennie Candlish	25	5	20.00%	+£54.66
Tony Carroll	20	3	15.00%	+£33.85
Fergal O'Brien	16	4	25.00%	+£31.83
Philip Hobbs	24	5	20.83%	+£29.91

Top trainer/jockey combos by Strike Rate – non-handicaps

Name of Trainer/Jockey	Qualifiers	Winners	Strike Rate	Profit/Loss to BSP
Ben Pauling/David Bass	11	4	36.36%	+£85.71
Nicky Henderson/Nico de Boinville	29	10	34.48%	-£1.26
Ben Pauling/Nico de Boinville	10	3	30.00%	+£12.11
David Pipe/Tom Scudamore	13	3	23.08%	+£7.87
Donald McCain/Brian Hughes	15	3	20.00%	+£18.82

Top trainer/jockey combos by Strike Rate – handicaps

Name of Trainer/Jockey	Qualifiers	Winners	Strike Rate	Profit/Loss to BSP
Dan Skelton/Harry Skelton	13	4	30.77%	+£12.64
Kim Bailey/David Bass	14	3	21.43%	+£0.65
Jennie Candlish/Sean Quinlan	15	3	20.00%	+£47.93
Donald McCain/Brian Hughes	10	2	20.00%	+£8.29

Dan Skelton/Bridget Andrews	11	2	18.18%	+£0.11

Top trainer/jockey combos by Profit – non-handicaps

Name of Trainer/Jockey	Qualifiers	Winners	Strike Rate	Profit/Loss to BSP
Ben Pauling/David Bass	11	4	36.36%	+£85.71
Tom George/Paddy Brennan	14	2	14.29%	+£84.22
Donald McCain/Brian Hughes	15	3	20.00%	+£18.82
Ben Pauling/Nico de Boinville	10	3	30.00%	+£12.11
David Pipe/Tom Scudamore	13	3	23.08%	+£7.87

Top trainer/jockey combos by Profit – handicaps

Name of Trainer/Jockey	Qualifiers	Winners	Strike Rate	Profit/Loss to BSP
Jennie Candlish/Sean Quinlan	15	3	20.00%	+£47.93
Dan Skelton/Harry Skelton	13	4	30.77%	+£12.64
Alan King/Tom Cannon	15	2	13.33%	+£11.04
Donald McCain/Brian Hughes	10	2	20.00%	+£8.29
Richard Phillips/Daniel Hiskett	14	1	7.14%	+£6.05

Profit or Loss backing the unnamed favourite – non-handicaps

Runners	Winners	Strike Rate	Profit/Loss to BSP
378	154	40.74%	-£28.12

Profit or Loss backing the unnamed favourite – handicaps

Runners	Winners	Strike Rate	Profit/Loss to BSP
341	96	28.15%	+£30.53

Profit or loss backing the unnamed second favourite - non-handicaps

Runners	Winners	Strike Rate	Profit/Loss to BSP
360	81	22.50%	-£4.78

Profit or loss backing the unnamed second favourite - handicaps

Runners	Winners	Strike Rate	Profit/Loss to BSP
317	55	17.35%	-£20.58

Profit or Loss backing horses who won last time out- non-handicaps

Runners	Winners	Strike Rate	Profit/Loss to BSP
409	94	22.98%	+£105.19

Profit or Loss backing horses who won last time out - handicaps

Runners	Winners	Strike Rate	Profit/Loss to BSP
326	52	15.95%	-£59.07

Profit or loss backing Top-Weights in handicaps

Runners	Winners	Strike Rate	Profit/Loss to BSP
372	52	13.98%	-£3.49

Most profitable sires – non-handicaps

Sire	Runners	Winners	Strike Rate	Profit/Loss to

				BSP
Milan	32	6	18.75%	+£108.09
Shirocco	39	6	15.38%	+£60.91
Passing Glance	19	4	21.05%	+£59.66
Gold Well	16	3	18.75%	+£46.52
King's Theatre	41	10	24.39%	+£18.30

Most profitable sires – handicaps

Sulamani	26	7	26.92%	+£80.84
Alflora	15	1	6.67%	+£49.69
Milan	53	8	15.09%	+£32.15
Overbury	12	2	16.67%	+£28.17
Presenting	49	9	18.37%	+£22.49

Exeter - Chases

Top jockeys by Strike Rate – non-handicaps

Name Of Jockey	Rides	Winners	Strike Rate	Profit/Loss to BSP
Sam Twiston-Davies	17	6	35.29%	-£3.42
Darren Edwards	12	4	33.33%	+£17.26
Aidan Coleman	15	5	33.33%	+£14.86
Tom O'Brien	16	5	31.25%	+£1.26
Harry Cobden	10	3	30.00%	-£4.87

Top jockeys by Strike Rate – handicaps

Name Of Jockey	Rides	Winners	Strike Rate	Profit/Loss to BSP
Bryan Carver	10	3	30.00%	+£22.11
Alan Johns	25	7	28.00%	+£30.98
Stan Sheppard	14	3	21.43%	+£0.89
Aidan Coleman	49	10	20.41%	+£10.45
Robert Dunne	15	3	20.00%	+£23.33

Top jockeys by Profit – non-handicaps

Name Of Jockey	Rides	Winners	Strike Rate	Profit/Loss to BSP
William Biddick	12	3	25.00%	+£43.52
Darren Edwards	12	4	33.33%	+£17.26
Aidan Coleman	15	5	33.33%	+£14.86
Sean Bowen	10	3	30.00%	+£4.26
Tom O'Brien	16	5	31.25%	+£1.26

Top jockeys by Profit – handicaps

Name Of Jockey	Rides	Winners	Strike Rate	Profit/Loss to BSP
James Best	92	17	18.48%	+£62.05
Alan Johns	25	7	28.00%	+£30.98
Matt Griffiths	16	3	18.75%	+£29.94

Paddy Brennan	51	10	19.61%	+£26.83
Michael Nolan	36	7	19.44%	+£24.92

Top trainers by Strike Rate – non-handicaps

Name Of Trainer	Runners	Winners	Strike Rate	Profit/Loss to BSP
Paul Nicholls	42	18	42.86%	-£0.87
Harry Fry	21	8	38.10%	+£9.75
Colin Tizzard	43	16	37.21%	+£20.81
Alan King	17	5	29.41%	-£3.45
Evan Williams	22	5	22.73%	+£14.49

Top trainers by Strike Rate – handicaps

Name Of Trainer	Runners	Winners	Strike Rate	Profit/Loss to BSP
Harry Fry	13	5	38.46%	+£28.16
Dr Richard Newland	12	4	33.33%	+£3.87
Robert Stephens	11	3	27.27%	+£2.29
Jamie Snowden	12	3	25.00%	+£1.44
Sue Gardner	40	9	22.50%	+£17.68

Top trainers by Profit – non-handicaps

Name Of Trainer	Runners	Winners	Strike Rate	Profit/Loss to BSP
Colin Tizzard	43	16	37.21%	+£20.81
Evan Williams	22	5	22.73%	+£!4.49
Harry Fry	21	8	38.10%	+£9.75
Philip Hobbs	42	9	21.43%	+£0.70

Top trainers by Profit – handicaps

Name Of Trainer	Runners	Winners	Strike Rate	Profit/Loss to BSP
Jackie Du Plessis	35	6	17.14%	+£67.72
Christian Williams	21	4	19.05%	+£47.71
Jimmy Frost	45	3	6.67%	+£30.19
Harry Fry	13	5	38.46%	+£28.16
Jeremy Scott	43	5	11.63%	+£23.75

Top trainer/jockey combos by Strike Rate – non-handicaps

Name Of Trainer/Jockey	Rides	Winners	Strike Rate	Profit/Loss to BSP
Paul Nicholls/Sam Twiston-Davies	12	4	33.33%	-£4.05
Evan Williams/Adam Wedge	12	1	8.33%	-£8.60

Top trainer/jockey combos by Strike Rate – handicaps

Name Of Trainer/Jockey	Rides	Winners	Strike Rate	Profit/Loss to BSP
Emma Lavelle/Aidan Coleman	10	5	50.00%	+£14.23
Paul Nicholls/Harry Cobden	15	4	26.67%	-£2.14
Jackie Du Plessis/James Best	15	4	26.67%	+£47.18
Tim Vaughan/Alan Johns	17	4	23.53%	+£24.50
Tom George/Paddy Brennan	17	4	23.53%	+£13.81

Top trainer/jockey combos by Profit – handicaps

Name of Trainer/Jockey	Qualifiers	Winners	Strike Rate	Profit/Loss to BSP
Jackie Du Plessis/James Best	15	4	26.67%	+£47.18
Tim Vaughan/Alan Johns	17	4	23.53%	+£24.50
Emma	10	5	50.00%	+£14.23

Lavelle/Aidan Coleman				
Tom George Paddy Brennan	17	4	23.53%	+£13.81
Fergal O'Brien/Paddy Brennan	20	3	15.00%	+£13.04

Profit or Loss backing the unnamed favourite – non-handicaps

Runners	Winners	Strike Rate	Profit/Loss to BSP
359	161	44.85%	+£2.53

Profit or Loss backing the unnamed favourite – handicaps

Runners	Winners	Strike Rate	Profit/Loss to BSP
501	120	23.95%	-£41.16

Profit or loss backing the unnamed second favourite - non-handicaps

Runners	Winners	Strike Rate	Profit/Loss to BSP
343	86	25.07%	+£16.25

Profit or loss backing the unnamed second favourite - handicaps

Runners	Winners	Strike Rate	Profit/Loss to BSP
481	84	17.46%	-£64.97

Profit or Loss backing horses who won last time out - non-handicaps

Runners	Winners	Strike Rate	Profit/Loss to BSP
254	63	24.80%	-£19.44

Profit or Loss backing horses who won last time out - handicaps

Runners	Winners	Strike Rate	Profit/Loss to BSP
506	77	15.22%	+£66.98

Profit or loss backing Top-Weights in handicaps

Runners	Winners	Strike Rate	Profit/Loss to BSP
544	85	15.63%	-£32.67

Most profitable sires – non-handicaps

Sire	Runners	Winners	Strike Rate	Profit/Loss to BSP
Flemensfirth	15	5	33.33%	+£24.52
Alflora	13	4	30.77%	+£12.70
King's Theatre	28	8	28.57%	+£10.85
Beneficial	16	5	31.25%	+£9.07
Milan	18	3	16.67%	+£3.32

Most profitable sires – handicaps

Midnight Legend	77	13	16.88%	+£149.92
Black Sam Bellamy	17	4	23.53%	+£35.11
Silver Patriarch	12	2	16.67%	+£33.67
Alflora	44	8	18.18%	+£30.23
Gold Well	20	3	15.00%	+£28.31

Exeter – Hurdles

Top jockeys by Strike Rate – non-handicaps

Name Of Jockey	Rides	Winners	Strike Rate	Profit/Loss to BSP
Harry Skelton	20	6	30.00%	+£19.40
Aidan Coleman	51	12	23.53%	-£8.35
Nico de Boinville	19	4	21.05%	-£8.57
Sam Twiston-Davies	63	13	20.63%	-£16.31
Paddy Brennan	40	8	20.00%	-£8.18

Top jockeys by Strike Rate – handicaps

Name Of Jockey	Rides	Winners	Strike Rate	Profit/Loss to

				BSP
Mitchell Bastyan	20	7	35.00%	+£18.07
Isabel Williams	15	5	33.33%	+£17.19
Gavin Sheehan	31	8	25.81%	+£20.57
Max Kendrick	13	3	23.08%	+£19.55
Joshua Newman	13	3	23.08%	+£2.85

Top jockeys by Profit – non-handicaps

Name Of Jockey	Rides	Winners	Strike Rate	Profit/Loss to BSP
Matt Griffiths	38	1	2.63%	+£64.31
David Bass	31	5	16.13%	+£24.11
Page Fuller	11	2	18.18%	+£19.89
Harry Skelton	20	6	30.00%	+£19.40
Brendan Powell	43	8	18.60%	+£11.98

Top jockeys by Profit – handicaps

Name Of Jockey	Rides	Winners	Strike Rate	Profit/Loss to BSP
Tom Bellamy	42	8	19.05%	+£129.72
James Best	89	8	8.99%	+£89.27
Conor O'Farrell	28	5	17.86%	+£59.98
Jamie Moore	21	1	4.76%	+£37.09
Sean Bowen	34	5	14.71%	+£31.25

Top trainers by Strike Rate – non-handicaps

Name Of Trainer	Runners	Winners	Strike Rate	Profit/Loss to BSP
Harry Fry	60	23	38.33%	+£64.39
Paul Nicholls	119	38	31.93%	+£17.98
Dan Skelton	21	6	28.57%	+£18.40
Venetia Williams	36	10	27.78%	+£10.65
Nicky Henderson	24	6	25.00%	-£11.01

Top trainers by Strike Rate – handicaps

Name Of Trainer	Runners	Winners	Strike Rate	Profit/Loss to BSP
Katy Price	14	5	35.71%	+£15.13

Anthony Honeyball	29	8	27.59%	+£50.88
Warren Greatrex	22	6	27.27%	+£12.14
Evan Williams	49	13	26.53%	+£63.58
Gary Moore	15	3	20.00%	+£24.57

Top trainers by Profit – non-handicaps

Name Of Trainer	Runners	Winners	Strike Rate	Profit/Loss to BSP
Sue Gardner	70	3	4.29%	+£101.97
Harry Fry	60	23	38.33%	+£64.39
Dan Skelton	21	6	28.57%	+£18.40
Paul Nicholls	119	38	31.93%	+£17.98
Kim Bailey	42	5	11.90%	+£13.13

Top trainers by Profit – handicaps

Name Of Trainer	Runners	Winners	Strike Rate	Profit/Loss to BSP
Richard Mitchell	22	4	18.18%	+£140.44
Evan Williams	49	13	26.53%	+£63.58
Anthony Honeyball	29	8	27.59%	+£50.88
Fiona Shaw	12	1	8.33%	+£48.20
Polly Gundry	21	2	9.52%	+£48.04

Top trainer/jockey combos by Strike Rate – non-handicaps

Name of Trainer/Jockey	Qualifiers	Winners	Strike Rate	Profit/Loss to BSP
Venetia Williams/Aidan Coleman	14	7	50.00%	+£15.95
Paul Nicholls/Sam Twiston-Davies	32	12	37.50%	+£6.08
Harry Fry/Sean Bowen	11	4	36.36%	-£1.87
Nicky Henderson/Nico de Boinville	12	4	33.33%	-£1.57
Dan	18	6	33.33%	+£21.40

Skelton/Harry Skelton				

Top trainer/jockey combos by Strike Rate – handicaps

Name of Trainer/Jockey	Qualifiers	Winners	Strike Rate	Profit/Loss to BSP
Evan Williams/Isabel Williams	12	5	41.67%	+£20.19
David Pipe/Conor O'Farrell	12	4	33.33%	+£22.06
Warren Greatrex/Gavin Sheehan	13	4	30.77%	+£13.40
Fergal O'Brien/Paddy Brennan	17	5	29.41%	-£0.98
Jeremy Scott/Matt Griffiths	27	7	25.93%	+£17.58

Top trainer/jockey combos by Profit – non-handicaps

Name of Trainer/Jockey	Qualifiers	Winners	Strike Rate	Profit/Loss to BSP
Sue Gardner/Sean Houlihan	14	1	7.14%	+£35.02
Colin Tizzard/Brendan Powell	19	6	31.58%	+£31.64
Kim Bailey/David Bass	24	5	20.83%	+£31.11
Dan Skelton/Harry Skelton	18	6	33.33%	+£21.40
Venetia Williams/Aidan Coleman	14	7	50.00%	+£15.95

Top trainer/jockey combos by Profit – handicaps

Name of Trainer/Jockey	Qualifiers	Winners	Strike Rate	Profit/Loss to BSP
Evan Williams/Adam Wedge	15	3	20.00%	+£27.98
David Pipe/Conor O'Farrell	12	4	33.33%	+£22.06
Evan Williams/Isabel Williams	12	5	41.67%	+£20.19
Jeremy Scott/Matt Griffiths	27	7	25.93%	+£17.58
Chris Down/James Davies	43	5	11.63%	+£15.94

Profit or Loss backing the unnamed favourite – non-handicaps

Runners	Winners	Strike Rate	Profit/Loss to BSP
512	245	47.85%	+£1.63

Profit or Loss backing the unnamed favourite – handicaps

Runners	Winners	Strike Rate	Profit/Loss to BSP
681	192	28.19%	-£8.62

Profit or loss backing the unnamed second favourite - non-handicaps

Runners	Winners	Strike Rate	Profit/Loss to BSP
517	103	19.92%	-£54.85

Profit or loss backing the unnamed second favourite - handicaps

Runners	Winners	Strike Rate	Profit/Loss to BSP
644	130	20.19%	+£79.59

Profit or Loss backing horses who won last time out- non-handicaps

Runners	Winners	Strike Rate	Profit/Loss to BSP
335	95	28.36%	-£57.63

Profit or Loss backing horses who won last time out - handicaps

Runners	Winners	Strike Rate	Profit/Loss to BSP
628	125	19.90%	+£18.76

Profit or loss backing Top-Weights in handicaps

Runners	Winners	Strike Rate	Profit/Loss to BSP
726	85	11.71%	-£95.30

Most profitable sires – non-handicaps

Sire	Runners	Winners	Strike Rate	Profit/Loss to BSP
King's Theatre	42	8	19.05%	+£24.63
Act One	10	1	10.00%	+£19.45
Shantou	32	4	12.50%	+£16.71
Stowaway	30	9	30.00%	+£15.44
Geordieland	11	2	18.18%	+£15.44

Most profitable sires – handicaps

Baryshnikov	10	1	10.00%	+£97.82
Kapgarde	20	4	20.00%	+£89.78
Storming Home	17	4	23.53%	+£63.51
Westerner	39	6	15.38%	+£54.69
Kayf Tara	90	9	10.00%	+£49.20

Fakenham - Chases

Top jockeys by Strike Rate – handicaps

Name Of Jockey	Rides	Winners	Strike Rate	Profit/Loss to BSP
Tom Cannon	13	5	38.46%	+£18.73
James Bowen	25	7	28.00%	+£2.46
Joshua Moore	11	3	27.27%	+£7.49
Kielan Woods	31	8	25.81%	+£13.91
Brian Hughes	12	3	25.00%	+£16.34

Top jockeys by Profit – handicaps

Name Of Jockey	Rides	Winners	Strike Rate	Profit/Loss to BSP
Tom Cannon	13	5	38.46%	+£18.73
Brian Hughes	12	3	25.00%	+£16.34
Lee Edwards	14	2	14.29%	+£14.50
Kielan Woods	31	8	25.81%	+£13.91
Ben Poste	16	4	25.00%	+£10.63

Top trainers by Strike Rate – non-handicaps

Name Of Trainer	Runners	Winners	Strike Rate	Profit/Loss to BSP
Dan Skelton	11	8	72.73%	+£10.04
Paul Nicholls	22	7	31.82%	-£3.99
Nicky Henderson	10	3	30.00%	-£5.61

Top trainers by Strike Rate – handicaps

Name Of Trainer	Runners	Winners	Strike Rate	Profit/Loss to BSP
Michael Gates	13	6	46.15%	+£21.50
Oliver Sherwood	14	5	35.71%	+£17.20
Dr Richard Newland	15	5	33.33%	+£6.86
Lucy Wadham	39	12	30.77%	+£18.33
Henry Daly	10	3	30.00%	-£0.06

Top trainers by Profit – non-handicaps

Name Of Trainer	Runners	Winners	Strike Rate	Profit/Loss to BSP
Dan Skelton	11	8	72.73%	+£10.04

Top trainers by Profit – handicaps

Name Of Trainer	Runners	Winners	Strike Rate	Profit/Loss to BSP
Laura Morgan	22	5	22.73%	+£26.70
Michael Gates	13	6	46.15%	+£21.50
Lucy Wadham	39	12	30.77%	+£18.33
Oliver Sherwood	14	5	35.71%	+£17.20
Christian Williams	40	12	30.00%	+£11.42

Top trainer/jockey combos by Strike Rate – handicaps

Name of Trainer/Jockey	Qualifiers	Winners	Strike Rate	Profit/Loss to BSP
Christian Williams/James Bowen	10	3	30.00%	-£1.36
Alex Hales/Kielan Woods	11	3	27.27%	+£7.83
Christian Williams/Jack Tudor	17	4	23.53%	-£0.01
Dan Skelton/Harry Skelton	13	2	15.38%	-£2.49
Evan Williams/Adam Wedge	14	2	14.29%	-£1.16

Top trainer/jockey combos by Profit – handicaps

Name of Trainer/Jockey	Qualifiers	Winners	Strike Rate	Profit/Loss to BSP
Alex	11	3	27.27%	+£7.83

Hales/Kielan Woods				
Paul Henderson/Tom O'Brien	13	1	7.69%	+£2.58

Profit or Loss backing the unnamed favourite – non-handicaps

Runners	Winners	Strike Rate	Profit/Loss to BSP
222	108	48.65%	-£2.61

Profit or Loss backing the unnamed favourite – handicaps

Runners	Winners	Strike Rate	Profit/Loss to BSP
394	118	29.95%	-£15.78

Profit or loss backing the unnamed second favourite - non-handicaps

Runners	Winners	Strike Rate	Profit/Loss to BSP
222	66	29.73%	+£40.20

Profit or loss backing the unnamed second favourite - handicaps

Runners	Winners	Strike Rate	Profit/Loss to BSP
350	86	24.57%	+£17.93

Profit or Loss backing horses who won last time out - non-handicaps

Runners	Winners	Strike Rate	Profit/Loss to BSP
127	40	31.50%	-£18.45

Profit or Loss backing horses who won last time out - handicaps

Runners	Winners	Strike Rate	Profit/Loss to BSP
308	64	20.78%	-£13.13

Profit or loss backing Top-Weights in handicaps

Runners	Winners	Strike Rate	Profit/Loss to BSP
397	85	21.41%	+£45.92

Most profitable sires – non-handicaps

Sire	Runners	Winners	Strike Rate	Profit/Loss to BSP
Posidonas	10	3	30.00%	+£4.32

Most profitable sires – handicaps

Midnight Legend	78	21	26.92%	+£37.31
King's Theatre	22	6	27.27%	+£36.83
Turtle Island	36	6	16.67%	+£23.37
Beneficial	51	8	15.69%	+£10.69
Sir Harry Lewis	13	2	15.38%	+£7.63

Fakenham – Hurdles

Top jockeys by Strike Rate – non-handicaps

Name Of Jockey	Rides	Winners	Strike Rate	Profit/Loss to BSP
Tom Scudamore	18	9	50.00%	+£6.88
Nico de Boinville	16	7	43.75%	+£271.23
Ciaran Gethings	17	7	41.18%	+£53.22
Joshua Moore	10	3	30.00%	+£9.98
Aidan Coleman	19	5	26.32%	-£7.47

Top jockeys by Strike Rate – handicaps

Name Of Jockey	Rides	Winners	Strike Rate	Profit/Loss to BSP
Harry Skelton	18	6	33.33%	+£4.89
Brian Hughes	18	5	27.78%	+£63.09
Harry Bannister	18	5	27.78%	+£7.73
David England	11	3	27.27%	+£7.54
Jack Tudor	11	3	27.27%	+£4.48

Top jockeys by Profit – non-handicaps

Name Of Jockey	Rides	Winners	Strike Rate	Profit/Loss to BSP
Nico de Boinville	16	7	43.75%	+£271.23
James Davies	13	1	7.69%	+£114.42
Ciaran Gethings	17	7	41.18%	+£53.22
Fergus Gregory	12	3	25.00%	+£18.60
Joshua Moore	10	3	30.00%	+£9.98

Top jockeys by Profit – handicaps

Name Of Jockey	Rides	Winners	Strike Rate	Profit/Loss to BSP
Robert Dunne	15	4	26.67%	+£77.27
Brian Hughes	18	5	27.78%	+£63.09
Adam Wedge	25	4	16.00%	+£19.93
Tom Scudamore	26	7	26.92%	+£17.78
Trevor Whelan	36	4	11.11%	+£11.49

Top trainers by Strike Rate – non-handicaps

Name Of Trainer	Runners	Winners	Strike Rate	Profit/Loss to BSP
David Pipe	13	7	53.85%	+£18.42
Stuart Edmunds	14	7	50.00%	+£56.22
Nicky Henderson	36	15	41.67%	-£1.19
Dr Richard Newland	26	9	34.62%	+£14.22
Ben Case	12	4	33.33%	+£0.41

Top trainers by Strike Rate – handicaps

Name Of Trainer	Runners	Winners	Strike Rate	Profit/Loss to BSP
Christian Williams	17	6	35.29%	+£7.01
Neil Mulholland	44	14	31.82%	+£18.94
David Pipe	10	3	30.00%	-£0.07
Peter Bowen	12	3	25.00%	+£3.84
Olly Murphy	54	13	24.07%	-£7.62

Top trainers by Profit – non-handicaps

Name Of Trainer	Runners	Winners	Strike Rate	Profit/Loss to BSP
Pam Sly	16	2	12.50%	+£71.13
Stuart Edmunds	14	7	50.00%	+£56.22
David Pipe	13	7	53.85%	+£18.42
Olly Murphy	60	15	25.00%	+£15.54
Dr Richard Newland	26	9	34.62%	+£14.22

Top trainers by Profit – handicaps

Name Of Trainer	Runners	Winners	Strike Rate	Profit/Loss to BSP
David Thompson	27	4	14.81%	+£63.68
Sarah Humphrey	41	6	14.63%	+£24.54
Neil King	53	10	18.87%	+£23.56
Neil Mulholland	44	14	31.82%	+£18.94
Ali Stronge	18	3	16.67%	+£18.09

Top trainer/jockey combos by Strike Rate – non-handicaps

Name of Trainer/Jockey	Qualifiers	Winners	Strike Rate	Profit/Loss to BSP
Stuart Edmunds/Ciaran Gethings	12	7	58.33	+£58.22
David Pipe/Tom Scudamore	10	5	50.00%	+£1.50
Nicky Henderson/Nico de Boinville	14	6	42.86%	-£1.19
Dan Skelton/Harry Skelton	16	5	31.25%	+£1.07
Neil King/Trevor Whelan	14	1	7.14%	-£5.45

Top trainer/jockey combos by Strike Rate – handicaps

Name of Trainer/Jockey	Qualifiers	Winners	Strike Rate	Profit/Loss to BSP
Dan	11	3	27.27%	-£1.46

Skelton/Harry Skelton				
Stuart Edmunds/Ciaran Gethings	11	2	18.18%	-£2.13
Neil King/Trevor Whelan	24	4	16.67%	+£23.49
Tim Vaughan/Alan Johns	26	4	15.38%	+£2.04
Pam Sly/Paul O'Brien	10	1	10.00%	-£1.23

Top trainer/jockey combos by Profit – non-handicaps

Name of Trainer/Jockey	Qualifiers	Winners	Strike Rate	Profit/Loss to BSP
Stuart Edmunds/Ciaran Gethings	12	7	58.33	+£58.22
David Pipe/Tom Scudamore	10	5	50.00%	+£1.50
Dan Skelton/Harry Skelton	16	5	31.25%	+£1.07

Top trainer/jockey combos by Profit – handicaps

Name of Trainer/Jockey	Qualifiers	Winners	Strike Rate	Profit/Loss to BSP
Neil King/Trevor Whelan	24	4	16.67%	+£23.49
Tim Vaughan/Alan Johns	26	4	15.38%	+£2.04

Profit or Loss backing the unnamed favourite – non-handicaps

Runners	Winners	Strike Rate	Profit/Loss to BSP
313	130	41.53%	-£15.46

Profit or Loss backing the unnamed favourite – handicaps

Runners	Winners	Strike Rate	Profit/Loss to BSP
439	135	30.75%	+£3.41

Profit or loss backing the unnamed second favourite - non-handicaps

Runners	Winners	Strike Rate	Profit/Loss to BSP
302	82	27.15%	+£53.33

Profit or loss backing the unnamed second favourite - handicaps

Runners	Winners	Strike Rate	Profit/Loss to BSP
390	78	20.00%	-£7.62

Profit or Loss backing horses who won last time out- non-handicaps

Runners	Winners	Strike Rate	Profit/Loss to BSP
153	47	30.72%	+£7.59

Profit or Loss backing horses who won last time out - handicaps

Runners	Winners	Strike Rate	Profit/Loss to BSP
299	82	27.42%	+£16.78

Profit or loss backing Top-Weights in handicaps

Runners	Winners	Strike Rate	Profit/Loss to BSP
447	71	15.88%	-£34.11

Most profitable sires – non-handicaps

Sire	Runners	Winners	Strike Rate	Profit/Loss to BSP
Midnight Legend	23	7	30.43%	+£5.57
Flemensfirth	15	3	20.00%	+£4.83
Gold Well	10	2	20.00%	+£1.54
Westerner	18	6	33.33%	+£0.35

Most profitable sires – handicaps

Kayf Tara	31	6	19.35%	+£39.62
Passing Glance	15	6	40.00%	+£32.87
Oscar	16	4	25.00%	+£26.02
Halling	16	1	6.25%	+£16.53
Morozov	11	4	36.36%	+£5.45

Ffos Las - Chases

Top jockeys by Strike Rate – non-handicaps

Name Of Jockey	Rides	Winners	Strike Rate	Profit/Loss to BSP
Sam Twiston-Davies	10	6	60.00%	+£15.35
Sean Bowen	11	3	27.27%	+£2.50
Adam Wedge	11	1	9.09%	-£9.49

Top jockeys by Strike Rate – handicaps

Name Of Jockey	Rides	Winners	Strike Rate	Profit/Loss to BSP
Jonathan Moore	11	4	36.36%	+£4.04
Sean Bowen	111	34	30.63%	+£73.98
Harry Cobden	18	5	27.78%	+£17.78
Connor Brace	18	5	27.78%	+£22.78
Harry Skelton	11	3	27.27%	+£11.77

Top jockeys by Profit – non-handicaps

Name Of Jockey	Rides	Winners	Strike Rate	Profit/Loss to BSP
Sam Twiston-Davies	10	6	60.00%	+£15.35
Sean Bowen	11	3	27.27%	+£2.50

Top jockeys by Profit – handicaps

Name Of Jockey	Rides	Winners	Strike Rate	Profit/Loss to BSP
Sean Bowen	111	34	30.63%	+£73.98
Paddy Brennan	30	8	26.67%	+£47.76
Tom Scudamore	81	18	22.22%	+£31.15
Gavin Sheehan	30	6	20.00%	+£26.47
James Bowen	59	9	15.25%	+£24.70

Top trainers by Strike Rate – non-handicaps

Name Of Trainer	Runners	Winners	Strike Rate	Profit/Loss to BSP
Nigel Twiston-Davies	10	4	40.00%	+£11.80
Paul Nicholls	10	3	30.00%	-£1.89
Peter Bowen	22	6	27.27%	+£9.92
Rebecca Curtis	11	2	18.18%	-£5.26
Evan Williams	20	2	10.00%	-£13.50

Top trainers by Strike Rate – handicaps

Name Of Trainer	Runners	Winners	Strike Rate	Profit/Loss to BSP
Jamie Snowden	14	4	28.57%	+£13.10
Rebecca Curtis	59	16	27.12%	+£35.01
Anthony Honeyball	23	6	26.09%	+£5.77
Debra Hamer	47	12	25.53%	+£56.10
Tom George	29	7	24.14%	+£11.26

Top trainers by Profit – non-handicaps

Name Of Trainer	Runners	Winners	Strike Rate	Profit/Loss to BSP
Nigel Twiston-Davies	10	4	40.00%	+£11.80
Peter Bowen	22	6	27.27%	+£9.92

Top trainers by Profit – handicaps

Name Of Trainer	Runners	Winners	Strike Rate	Profit/Loss to BSP
Debra Hamer	47	12	25.53%	+£56.10
Matt Sheppard	10	2	20.00%	+£53.20
Peter Bowen	206	43	20.87%	+£52.77
Rebecca Curtis	59	16	27.12%	+£35.01
Neil Mulholland	51	6	11.76%	+£33.47

Top trainer/jockey combos by Strike Rate – handicaps

Name of Trainer/Jockey	Qualifiers	Winners	Strike Rate	Profit/Loss to BSP
Rebecca	11	4	36.36%	+£4.04

Curtis/Jonathan Moore				
Peter Bowen/Sean Bowen	76	24	31.58%	+£39.98
David Rees/Sean Bowen	16	5	31.25%	+£16.38
Dan Skelton/Harry Skelton	11	3	27.27%	+£11.77
Debra Hamer/Trevor Whelan	15	4	26.67%	+£5.43

Top trainer/jockey combos by Profit – handicaps

Name of Trainer/Jockey	Qualifiers	Winners	Strike Rate	Profit/Loss to BSP
Peter Bowen/Sean Bowen	76	24	31.58%	+£39.98
Peter Bowen/James Bowen	44	7	15.91%	+£34.63
David Pipe-Tom Scudamore	31	8	25.81%	+£22.85
Philip Hobbs/Tom O'Brien	10	2	20.00%	+£17.93
David Rees/Sean Bowen	16	5	31.25%	+£16.38

Profit or Loss backing the unnamed favourite – non-handicaps

Runners	Winners	Strike Rate	Profit/Loss to BSP
93	44	47.31%	+£6.40

Profit or Loss backing the unnamed favourite – handicaps

Runners	Winners	Strike Rate	Profit/Loss to BSP
450	129	28.67%	-£2.98

Profit or loss backing the unnamed second favourite - non-handicaps

Runners	Winners	Strike Rate	Profit/Loss to BSP
92	21	22.83%	-£7.33

Profit or loss backing the unnamed second favourite - handicaps

Runners	Winners	Strike Rate	Profit/Loss to BSP
416	97	23.32%	+£31.58

Profit or Loss backing horses who won last time out - non-handicaps

Runners	Winners	Strike Rate	Profit/Loss to BSP
58	15	25.86%	-£11.96

Profit or Loss backing horses who won last time out - handicaps

Runners	Winners	Strike Rate	Profit/Loss to BSP
364	83	22.80%	+£32.73

Profit or loss backing Top-Weights in handicaps

Runners	Winners	Strike Rate	Profit/Loss to BSP
479	78	16.28%	-£10.57

Most profitable sires – non-handicaps

Sire	Runners	Winners	Strike Rate	Profit/Loss to BSP
Milan	13	4	30.77%	+£1.01

Most profitable sires – handicaps

Sire	Runners	Winners	Strike Rate	Profit/Loss to BSP
Court Cave	32	6	18.75%	+£38.46
Beat All	18	4	22.22%	+£35.90
Vinnie Roe	10	4	40.00%	+£32.67
Black Sam	12	3	25.00%	+£28.82

Bellamy				
Brian Boru	20	8	40.00%	+£25.74

Ffos Las – Hurdles

Top jockeys by Strike Rate – non-handicaps

Name Of Jockey	Rides	Winners	Strike Rate	Profit/Loss to BSP
Kielan Woods	10	4	40.00%	+£49.28
David Bass	18	7	38.89%	+£15.91
Daryl Jacob	28	7	25.00%	-£7.54
Gavin Sheehan	42	10	23.81%	-£17.09
Richie McLernon	18	4	22.22%	+£1.77

Top jockeys by Strike Rate – handicaps

Name Of Jockey	Rides	Winners	Strike Rate	Profit/Loss to BSP
Charlie Deutsch	11	4	36.36%	+£28.49
Lorcan Williams	16	5	31.25%	+£28.79
Nico de Boinville	17	5	29.41%	+£28.43
Fergus Gillard	14	4	28.57%	+£6.27
Kielan Woods	12	3	25.00%	+£8.94

Top jockeys by Profit – non-handicaps

Name Of Jockey	Rides	Winners	Strike Rate	Profit/Loss to BSP
Nick Scholfield	42	4	11.90%	+£51.53
Kielan Woods	10	4	40.00%	+£49.28
Tom Bellamy	26	5	19.23%	+£27.43
Tom Scudamore	63	10	15.87%	+£22.28
Richard Patrick	22	2	9.09%	+£17.39

Top jockeys by Profit – handicaps

Name Of Jockey	Rides	Winners	Strike Rate	Profit/Loss to BSP
Adam Wedge	122	24	19.67%	+£72.71
Michael Nolan	24	4	16.67%	+£51.43
Charlie	10	1	10.00%	+£44.21

Hammond				
David Bass	25	5	20.00%	+£30.24
Lorcan Williams	16	5	31.25%	+£28.79

Top trainers by Strike Rate – non-handicaps

Name Of Trainer	Runners	Winners	Strike Rate	Profit/Loss to BSP
Nicky Henderson	31	17	54.84%	+£2.86
Ben Pauling	11	6	54.55%	+£67.83
Paul Nicholls	16	6	37.50%	+£4.94
Jamie Snowden	21	6	28.57%	-£3.71
Harry Whittington	11	3	27.27%	-£1.21

Top trainers by Strike Rate – handicaps

Name Of Trainer	Runners	Winners	Strike Rate	Profit/Loss to BSP
Tom Lacey	10	3	30.00%	+£10.15
Dr Richard Newland	29	8	27.59%	+£3.27
Warren Greatrex	17	4	23.53%	+£7.97
Venetia Williams	17	4	23.53%	+£23.30
Brian Eckley	13	3	23.08%	+£5.99

Top trainers by Profit – non-handicaps

Name Of Trainer	Runners	Winners	Strike Rate	Profit/Loss to BSP
Jeremy Scott	12	1	8.33%	+£94.49
Evan Williams	153	22	14.38%	+£76.49
Ben Pauling	11	6	54.55%	+£67.83
David Rees	43	4	9.30%	+£53.27
Nigel Twiston-Davies	64	17	26.56%	+£48.30

Top trainers by Profit – handicaps

Name Of Trainer	Runners	Winners	Strike Rate	Profit/Loss to BSP
Bernard	100	12	12.00%	+£172.38

Llewellyn				
David Rees	71	9	12.68%	+£108.02
Evan Williams	251	35	13.94%	+£43.95
Kim Bailey	27	6	22.22%	+£32.48
Oliver Sherwood	14	3	21.43%	+£29.48

Top trainer/jockey combos by Strike Rate – non-handicaps

Name of Trainer/Jockey	Qualifiers	Winners	Strike Rate	Profit/Loss to BSP
Jonjo O'Neill/Richie McLernon	12	4	33.33%	+£7.77
Kim Bailey/David Bass	10	3	30.00%	-£0.52
Warren Greatrex/Gavin Sheehan	16	4	25.00%	-£3.83
Peter Bowen/Sean Bowen	35	8	22.86%	+£7.79
David Pipe/Tom Scudamore	23	5	21.74%	-£2.08

Top trainer/jockey combos by Strike Rate – handicaps

Name of Trainer/Jockey	Qualifiers	Winners	Strike Rate	Profit/Loss to BSP
Dr Richard Newland/Sam Twiston-Davies	11	4	36.36%	+£2.62
Kim Bailey/David Bass	16	5	31.25%	+£39.24
Peter Bowen/Tom O'Brien	18	5	27.78%	+£12.15
David Pipe/Fergus Gillard	11	3	27.27%	+£4.64
Evan Williams/Adam	97	21	21.65%	+£70.60

Wedge				

Top trainer/jockey combos by Profit – non-handicaps

Name of Trainer/Jockey	Qualifiers	Winners	Strike Rate	Profit/Loss to BSP
Peter Bowen/Sean Bowen	35	8	22.86%	+£7.79
Jonjo O'Neill/Richie McLernon	12	4	33.33%	+£7.77
Nigel Twiston-Davies/Sam Twiston-Davies	39	8	20.51%	+£7.55
Evan Williams/Conor Ring	26	1	3.85%	+£0.48

Top trainer/jockey combos by Profit – handicaps

Name of Trainer/Jockey	Qualifiers	Winners	Strike Rate	Profit/Loss to BSP
Evan Williams/Adam Wedge	97	21	21.65%	+£70.60
Kim Bailey/David Bass	16	5	31.25%	+£39.24
Peter Bowen/Tom O'Brien	18	5	27.78%	+£12.15
David Pipe/Tom Scudamore	44	7	15.91%	+£6.46
Peter Bowen/James Bowen	23	3	13.04%	+£5.24

Profit or Loss backing the unnamed favourite – non-handicaps

Runners	Winners	Strike Rate	Profit/Loss to BSP
313	139	44.41%	-£17.31

Profit or Loss backing the unnamed favourite – handicaps

Runners	Winners	Strike Rate	Profit/Loss to BSP
402	107	26.62%	-£38.95

Profit or loss backing the unnamed second favourite - non-handicaps

Runners	Winners	Strike Rate	Profit/Loss to BSP
305	66	21.64%	-£31.65

Profit or loss backing the unnamed second favourite - handicaps

Runners	Winners	Strike Rate	Profit/Loss to BSP
380	67	17.63%	-£39.86

Profit or Loss backing horses who won last time out- non-handicaps

Runners	Winners	Strike Rate	Profit/Loss to BSP
203	62	30.54%	-£15.02

Profit or Loss backing horses who won last time out - handicaps

Runners	Winners	Strike Rate	Profit/Loss to BSP
385	66	17.14%	+£11.57

Profit or loss backing Top-Weights in handicaps

Runners	Winners	Strike Rate	Profit/Loss to BSP
438	58	13.24%	-£29.39

Most profitable sires – non-handicaps

Sire	Runners	Winners	Strike Rate	Profit/Loss to BSP
Brian Boru	13	4	30.77%	+£35.37
Westerner	33	6	18.18%	+£27.36

Old Vic	17	5	29.41%	+£24.14
Mahler	19	5	26.32%	+£23.12
Gold Well	12	3	25.00%	+£13.54

Most profitable sires – handicaps

Karinga Bay	16	2	12.50%	+£138.49
Kapgarde	24	8	33.33%	+£72.90
Moscow Society	10	3	30.00%	+£66.91
Kayf Tara	54	10	18.52%	+£54.61
Craigsteel	28	3	10.71%	+£44.58

Fontwell - Chases

Top jockeys by Strike Rate – non-handicaps

Name Of Jockey	Rides	Winners	Strike Rate	Profit/Loss to BSP
David Maxwell	13	8	61.54%	+£1.38
Sam Twiston-Davies	21	10	47.62%	+£22.37
Daryl Jacob	18	7	38.89%	+£2.21
Bryony Frost	10	3	30.00%	-£1.95
Aidan Coleman	17	3	17.65%	-£5.56

Top jockeys by Strike Rate – handicaps

Name Of Jockey	Rides	Winners	Strike Rate	Profit/Loss to BSP
Charlie Deutsch	18	7	38.89%	+£13.23
Harry Skelton	26	10	38.46%	+£12.74
Tom Bellamy	12	4	33.33%	+£12.66
Harry Cobden	45	15	33.33%	+£5.91
Aidan Coleman	54	17	31.48%	+£39.95

Top jockeys by Profit – non-handicaps

Name Of Jockey	Rides	Winners	Strike Rate	Profit/Loss to BSP
Sam Twiston-Davies	21	10	47.62%	+£22.37
Daryl Jacob	18	7	38.89%	+£2.21
David Maxwell	13	8	61.54%	+£1.38

Top jockeys by Profit – handicaps

Name Of Jockey	Rides	Winners	Strike Rate	Profit/Loss to BSP
Nick Scholfield	80	17	21.25%	+£54.03
Tom Cannon	152	26	17.11%	+£40.76
Aidan Coleman	54	17	31.48%	+£39.95
Marc Goldstein	100	17	17.00%	+£25.20
Brendan Powell	85	16	18.82%	+£23.75

Top trainers by Strike Rate – non-handicaps

Name Of Trainer	Runners	Winners	Strike Rate	Profit/Loss to BSP
Paul Nicholls	60	35	58.33%	+£16.02
Nicky Henderson	11	6	54.55%	+£2.31
Neil Mulholland	15	5	33.33%	+£18.91
Gary Moore	22	6	27.27%	-£3.94
Colin Tizzard	10	2	20.00%	+£0.65

Top trainers by Strike Rate – handicaps

Name Of Trainer	Runners	Winners	Strike Rate	Profit/Loss to BSP
Lucy Wadham	12	4	33.33%	+£23.08
Dan Skelton	39	13	33.33%	+£6.54
Dr Richard Newland	24	8	33.33%	+£3.87
Anthony Honeyball	32	10	31.25%	+£18.27
Pat Murphy	13	4	30.77%	+£6.83

Top trainers by Profit – non-handicaps

Name Of Trainer	Runners	Winners	Strike Rate	Profit/Loss to BSP
Neil Mulholland	15	5	33.33%	+£18.91
Paul Nicholls	60	35	58.33%	+£16.02
Nicky Henderson	11	6	54.55%	+£2.31
Colin Tizzard	10	2	20.00%	+£0.65

Top trainers by Profit – handicaps

Name Of Trainer	Runners	Winners	Strike Rate	Profit/Loss to BSP
David Bridgwater	68	17	25.00%	+£23.97
Lucy Wadham	12	4	33.33%	+£23.08
Michael Madgwick	11	2	18.18%	+£18.72

Anthony Honeyball	32	10	31.25%	+£18.27
Venetia Williams	45	11	24.44%	+£17.82

Top trainer/jockey combos by Strike Rate – non-handicaps

Name Of Trainer/Jockey	Rides	Winners	Strike Rate	Profit/Loss to BSP
Paul Nicholls/Sam Twiston-Davies	13	9	69.23%	+£3.23
Paul Nicholls/Daryl Jacob	14	7	50.00%	+£6.21
Gary Moore/Joshua Moore	11	2	18.18%	-£0.03

Top trainer/jockey combos by Strike Rate – handicaps

Name of Trainer/Jockey	Qualifiers	Winners	Strike Rate	Profit/Loss to BSP
Lawney Hill/Aidan Coleman	12	6	50.00%	+£18.19
Venetia Williams/Charlie Deutsch	11	5	45.45%	+£10.95
Dan Skelton/Harry Skelton	22	9	40.91%	+£7.53
David Bridgwater/Tom Scudamore	13	5	38.46%	+£7.21
Neil King/Trevor Whelan	14	5	35.71%	+£6.81

Top trainer/jockey combos by Profit – non-handicaps

Name Of Trainer/Jockey	Rides	Winners	Strike Rate	Profit/Loss to BSP
Paul Nicholls/Daryl	14	7	50.00%	+£6.21

Jacob				
Paul Nicholls/Sam Twiston-Davies	13	9	69.23%	+£3.23

Top trainer/jockey combos by Profit – handicaps

Name of Trainer/Jockey	Qualifiers	Winners	Strike Rate	Profit/Loss to BSP
Lawney Hill/Aidan Coleman	12	6	50.00%	+£18.19
Gary Moore/Joshua Moore	59	13	22.03%	+£15.02
Lydia Richards/Marc Goldstein	37	8	21.62%	+£13.85
Diana Grissell/Marc Goldstein	19	3	15.79%	+£12.37
Seamus Mullins/Kevin Jones	18	2	11.11%	+£11.93

Profit or Loss backing the unnamed favourite – non-handicaps

Favourite	Runners	Winners	Strike Rate	Profit/Loss to BSP
	322	165	51.24%	+£0.81

Profit or Loss backing the unnamed favourite – handicaps

Favourite	Runners	Winners	Strike Rate	Profit/Loss to BSP
	927	307	33.12%	+£38.73

Profit or loss backing the unnamed second favourite - non-handicaps

Second Favourite	Runners	Winners	Strike Rate	Profit/Loss to BSP
	312	75	24.04%	-£41.17

Profit or loss backing the unnamed second favourite - handicaps

Second Favourite	Runners	Winners	Strike Rate	Profit/Loss to BSP
	883	180	20.39	-£68.10

Profit or Loss backing horses who won last time out - non-handicaps

Won Last Time out	Runners	Winners	Strike Rate	Profit/Loss to BSP
	165	59	35.76%	-£17.83

Profit or Loss backing horses who won last time out - handicaps

Won Last Time Out	Runners	Winners	Strike Rate	Profit/Loss to BSP
	688	174	25.29%	-£5.79

Profit or loss backing Top-Weights in handicaps

Top Weight	Runners	Winners	Strike Rate	Profit/Loss to BSP
	957	196	20.48%	+£54.40

Most profitable sires – non-handicaps

Sire	Runners	Winners	Strike Rate	Profit/Loss to BSP
Dr Massini	11	3	27.27%	+£75.96
Flemensfirth	18	5	27.78%	+£18.62
King's Theatre	19	6	31.58%	+£0.41

Most profitable sires – handicaps

Martaline	25	7	28.00%	+£45.78
Midnight Legend	99	21	21.21%	+£35.28
Shirocco	13	4	30.77%	+£30.78
Sulamani	12	3	25.00%	+£27.23
Norse Dancer	10	1	10.00%	+£24.63

Fontwell – Hurdles

Top jockeys by Strike Rate – non-handicaps

Name Of Jockey	Rides	Winners	Strike Rate	Profit/Loss to BSP
James Bowen	13	4	30.77%	+£5.81
Aidan Coleman	51	15	29.41%	+£9.79
Sean Bowen	11	3	27.27%	-£1.89
Gavin Sheehan	57	15	26.32%	+£31.98
Paddy Brennan	19	5	26.32%	-£4.40

Top jockeys by Strike Rate – handicaps

Name Of Jockey	Rides	Winners	Strike Rate	Profit/Loss to BSP
Harry Kimber	13	4	30.77%	+£18.65
Rex Dingle	34	8	23.53%	+£13.11
Daryl Jacob	30	7	23.33%	+£3.17
Harry Skelton	36	8	22.22%	-£4.37
Gavin Sheehan	73	16	21.92%	+£27.80

Top jockeys by Profit – non-handicaps

Name Of Jockey	Rides	Winners	Strike Rate	Profit/Loss to BSP
Brendan Powell	54	6	11.11%	+£221.89
Marc Goldstein	100	4	4.00%	+£109.93
Trevor Whelan	19	4	21.05%	+£109.83
Nick Scholfield	54	6	11.11%	+£53.79
Gavin Sheehan	57	15	26.32%	+£31.98

Top jockeys by Profit – handicaps

Name Of Jockey	Rides	Winners	Strike Rate	Profit/Loss to BSP
Jamie Moore	177	22	12.43%	+£82.04
Tom Cannon	222	34	15.32%	+£80.55
Marc Goldstein	137	11	8.03%	+£75.80
Joshua Moore	114	20	17.54%	+£73.60
Sam Twiston-Davies	46	6	13.04%	+£40.66

Top trainers by Strike Rate – non-handicaps

Name Of Trainer	Runners	Winners	Strike Rate	Profit/Loss to BSP
Charlie Longsdon	29	10	34.48%	+£8.53
Alan King	59	20	33.90%	+£21.48
Nicky Henderson	30	10	33.33%	+£15.87
Fergal O'Brien	10	3	30.00%	-£0.88
Anthony Honeyball	40	12	30.00%	-£0.13

Top trainers by Strike Rate – handicaps

Name Of Trainer	Runners	Winners	Strike Rate	Profit/Loss to BSP
Ian Williams	14	5	35.71%	+£7.76
Victor Dartnall	12	4	33.33%	+£4.99
Harry Fry	25	8	32.00%	+£17.20
Anthony Honeyball	53	16	30.19%	+£14.16
Alex Hales	10	3	30.00%	+£12.81

Top trainers by Profit – non-handicaps

Name Of Trainer	Runners	Winners	Strike Rate	Profit/Loss to BSP
Michael Madgwick	42	2	4.76%	+£151.92
Neil King	27	5	18.52%	+£107.43
Jeremy Scott	14	1	7.14%	+£77.97
Gary Moore	178	36	20.22%	+£66.38
Warren Greatrex	38	7	18.42%	+£44.58

Top trainers by Profit – handicaps

Name Of Trainer	Runners	Winners	Strike Rate	Profit/Loss to BSP
Chris Gordon	236	38	16.10%	+£120.03
Neil Mulholland	139	28	20.14%	+£90.42
Lydia Richards	29	5	17.24%	+£67.57
Gary Moore	285	44	15.44%	+£61.59
Mark Gillard	13	1	7.69%	+£54.57

Top trainer/jockey combos by Strike Rate – non-handicaps

Name of Trainer/Jockey	Qualifiers	Winners	Strike Rate	Profit/Loss to BSP
Anthony Honeyball/Rex Dingle	16	6	37.50%	+£12.20
Warren Greatrex/Gavin Sheehan	14	5	35.71%	+£1.31
Paul Nicholls/Harry Cobden	15	5	33.33%	-£5.21
Gary Moore/Jamie Moore	89	24	26.97%	+£50.70
Neil King/Trevor Whelan	16	4	25.00%	+£112.83

Top trainer/jockey combos by Strike Rate – handicaps

Name of Trainer/Jockey	Qualifiers	Winners	Strike Rate	Profit/Loss to BSP
Warren Greatrex/Gavin Sheehan	13	5	38.46%	+£3.90
Anthony Honeyball/Aidan Coleman	11	4	36.36%	+£9.02
Alan King/Tom Cannon	10	3	30.00%	+£3.89
Jeremy Scott/Matt Griffiths	11	3	27.27%	+£1.87
Anthony Honeyball/Rex Dingle	15	4	26.67%	+£4.82

Top trainer/jockey combos by Profit – non-handicaps

Name of Trainer/Jockey	Qualifiers	Winners	Strike Rate	Profit/Loss to BSP
Michael	32	2	6.25%	+£161.92

Madgwick/Marc Goldstein				
Neil King/Trevor Whelan	16	4	25.00%	+£112.83
Gary Moore/Jamie Moore	89	24	26.97%	+£50.70
Gary Moore/Joshua Moore	67	11	16.42%	+£33.99
Anthony Honeyball/Rex Dingle	16	6	37.50%	+£12.20

Top trainer/jockey combos by Profit – handicaps

Name of Trainer/Jockey	Qualifiers	Winners	Strike Rate	Profit/Loss to BSP
Chris Gordon/Tom Cannon	141	25	17.73%	+£101.68
Lydia Richards/Marc Goldstein	12	2	16.67%	+£65.46
Gary Moore/Joshua Moore	95	17	17.89%	+£48.84
Gary Moore/George Gorman	15	2	13.33%	+£31.75
Chris Gordon/Marc Goldstein	12	2	16.67%	+£29.79

Profit or Loss backing the unnamed favourite – non-handicaps

Runners	Winners	Strike Rate	Profit/Loss to BSP
722	284	39.34%	-£89.96

Profit or Loss backing the unnamed favourite – handicaps

Runners	Winners	Strike Rate	Profit/Loss to

			BSP
897	249	27.76%	-£70.90

Profit or loss backing the unnamed second favourite - non-handicaps

Runners	Winners	Strike Rate	Profit/Loss to BSP
688	187	27.18%	+£95.59

Profit or loss backing the unnamed second favourite - handicaps

Runners	Winners	Strike Rate	Profit/Loss to BSP
868	192	22.12%	+£141.61

Profit or Loss backing horses who won last time out- non-handicaps

Runners	Winners	Strike Rate	Profit/Loss to BSP
473	131	27.70%	-£48.04

Profit or Loss backing horses who won last time out - handicaps

Runners	Winners	Strike Rate	Profit/Loss to BSP
715	143	20.00%	-£64.95

Profit or loss backing Top-Weights in handicaps

Runners	Winners	Strike Rate	Profit/Loss to BSP
986	138	14.00%	-£28.67

Most profitable sires – non-handicaps

Sire	Runners	Winners	Strike Rate	Profit/Loss to BSP
Flemensfirth	36	3	8.33%	+£233.24
Shirocco	39	9	23.08%	+£44.91
Schiaparelli	14	2	14.29%	+£33.57
Champs Elysees	17	1	5.88%	+£22.22
Sixties Icon	26	5	19.23%	+£13.81

Most profitable sires – handicaps

Yeats	48	9	18.75%	+£46.21
Black Sam Bellamy	21	3	14.29%	+£45.99
Danehill Dancer	17	3	17.65%	+£36.63
Midnight Legend	91	15	16.48%	+£35.29
Whitmore's Conn	11	3	27.27%	+£34.04

Haydock – Chases

Top jockeys by Strike Rate – non-handicaps

Name Of Jockey	Rides	Winners	Strike Rate	Profit/Loss to BSP
Daryl Jacob	18	8	44.44%	+£13.49
Sam Twiston-Davies	17	4	23.53%	-£6.84
Brian Hughes	19	4	21.05%	-£8.02
Tom Scudamore	13	2	15.38%	+£14.70
Harry Skelton	10	1	10.00%	-£6.99

Top jockeys by Strike Rate – handicaps

Name Of Jockey	Rides	Winners	Strike Rate	Profit/Loss to BSP
Daryl Jacob	17	7	41.18%	+£41.79
Sean Bowen	16	6	37.50%	+£28.86
Tom Cannon	10	3	30.00%	+£42.74
Harry Bannister	10	3	30.00%	+£65.70
Jamie Moore	11	3	27.27%	+£6.29

Top jockeys by Profit – non-handicaps

Name Of Jockey	Rides	Winners	Strike Rate	Profit/Loss to BSP
Tom Scudamore	13	2	15.38%	+£14.70
Daryl Jacob	18	8	44.44%	+£13.49

Top jockeys by Profit – handicaps

Name Of Jockey	Rides	Winners	Strike Rate	Profit/Loss to BSP
Harry Bannister	10	3	30.00%	+£65.70
Tom Cannon	10	3	30.00%	+£42.74
Daryl Jacob	17	7	41.18%	+£41.79
Sean Bowen	16	6	37.50%	+£28.86
Paddy Brennan	35	7	20.00%	+£26.55

Top trainers by Strike Rate – non-handicaps

Name Of Trainer	Runners	Winners	Strike Rate	Profit/Loss to BSP
Paul Nicholls	32	17	53.13%	+£24.92
Donald McCain	17	5	29.41%	-£2.74
Colin Tizzard	17	5	29.41%	+£8.98
Nigel Twiston-Davies	14	4	28.57%	+£2.34
Venetia Williams	11	3	27.27%	+£8.29

Top trainers by Strike Rate – handicaps

Name Of Trainer	Runners	Winners	Strike Rate	Profit/Loss to BSP
Jamie Snowden	11	4	36.36%	+£7.67
Ian Williams	18	5	27.78%	+£9.65
Peter Bowen	22	6	27.27%	+£15.60
Fergal O'Brien	15	4	26.67%	+£12.89
Sam England	10	2	20.00%	+£5.76

Top trainers by Profit – non-handicaps

Name Of Trainer	Runners	Winners	Strike Rate	Profit/Loss to BSP
Paul Nicholls	32	17	53.13%	+£24.92
Sue Smith	14	3	21.43%	+£11.81
Colin Tizzard	17	5	29.41%	+£8.98
Venetia Williams	11	3	27.27%	+£8.29
Nigel Twiston-Davies	14	4	28.57%	+£2.34

Top trainers by Profit – handicaps

Name Of Trainer	Runners	Winners	Strike Rate	Profit/Loss to BSP
Alex Hales	11	1	9.09%	+£43.41
Alan King	29	3	10.34%	+£32.43
Nicky Richards	10	1	10.00%	+£17.46
Peter Bowen	22	6	27.27%	+£15.60
Fergal O'Brien	15	4	26.67%	+£12.89

Top trainer/jockey combos by Strike Rate – handicaps

Name of Trainer/Jockey	Qualifiers	Winners	Strike Rate	Profit/Loss to BSP
Tom George/Paddy Brennan	13	4	30.77%	+£24.46
Fergal O'Brien/Paddy Brennan	11	3	27.27%	+£13.09
Donald McCain/William Kennedy	15	4	26.67%	+£12.53
Philip Hobbs/Tom O'Brien	16	4	25.00%	+£7.66
Venetia Williams/Charlie Deutsch	25	6	24.00%	+£10.24

Top trainer/jockey combos by Profit – handicaps

Name of Trainer/Jockey	Qualifiers	Winners	Strike Rate	Profit/Loss to BSP
Tom George/Paddy Brennan	13	4	30.77%	+£24.46
Sue Smith/Ryan Mania	26	3	11.54%	+£14.50
Fergal O'Brien/Paddy Brennan	11	3	27.27%	+£13.09
Donald McCain/William Kennedy	15	4	26.67%	+£12.53
Stuart Coltherd/Sam Coltherd	10	2	20.00%	+£11.77

Profit or Loss backing the unnamed favourite – non-handicaps

Runners	Winners	Strike Rate	Profit/Loss to BSP
154	68	44.16%	+£11.76

Profit or Loss backing the unnamed favourite – handicaps

Runners	Winners	Strike Rate	Profit/Loss to BSP
387	81	20.93%	-£63.39

Profit or loss backing the unnamed second favourite - non-handicaps

Runners	Winners	Strike Rate	Profit/Loss to BSP
148	39	26.35%	+£5.02

Profit or loss backing the unnamed second favourite - handicaps

Runners	Winners	Strike Rate	Profit/Loss to BSP
343	68	19.83%	+£40.90

Profit or Loss backing horses who won last time out - non-handicaps

Runners	Winners	Strike Rate	Profit/Loss to BSP
207	49	23.67%	-£16.57

Profit or Loss backing horses who won last time out - handicaps

Runners	Winners	Strike Rate	Profit/Loss to BSP
527	77	14.61%	+£43.72

Profit or loss backing Top-Weights in handicaps

Runners	Winners	Strike Rate	Profit/Loss to BSP
392	63	16.07%	+£93.86

Most profitable sires – non-handicaps

Sire	Runners	Winners	Strike Rate	Profit/Loss to BSP
Westerner	10	4	40.00%	+£46.04
Oscar	13	2	15.38%	+£3.39
King's Theatre	16	3	18.75%	+£2.57

Flemensfirth	16	5	31.25%	+£0.61

Most profitable sires – handicaps

Alflora	18	2	11.11%	+£43.68
Cloudings	31	5	16.13%	+£39.09
Midnight Legend	47	9	19.15%	+£37.56
King's Theatre	42	3	7.14%	+£22.26
Yeats	12	3	25.00%	+£17.23

Haydock – Hurdles

Top jockeys by Strike Rate – non-handicaps

Name Of Jockey	Rides	Winners	Strike Rate	Profit/Loss to BSP
Sean Bowen	12	5	41.67%	+£7.33
David Bass	11	4	36.36%	+£0.08
Paddy Brennan	17	6	35.29%	+£2.17
Sam Twiston-Davies	29	10	34.48%	+£27.37
Daryl Jacob	17	5	29.41%	+£8.68

Top jockeys by Strike Rate – handicaps

Name Of Jockey	Rides	Winners	Strike Rate	Profit/Loss to BSP
Jonjo O'Neill Jr	15	5	33.33%	+£7.51
Tom O'Brien	35	8	22.86%	+£28.29
Jack Quinlan	11	2	18.18%	+£53.50
Richie McLernon	12	2	16.67%	-£1.69
James Bowen	13	2	15.38%	-£5.88

Top jockeys by Profit – non-handicaps

Name Of Jockey	Rides	Winners	Strike Rate	Profit/Loss to BSP
Aidan Coleman	23	5	21.74%	+£101.15
Sam Twiston-Davies	29	10	34.48%	+£27.37
Daryl Jacob	17	5	29.41%	+£8.68
Sean Bowen	12	5	41.67%	+£7.33

| Henry Brooke | 13 | 2 | 15.38% | +£6.64 |

Top jockeys by Profit – handicaps

Name Of Jockey	Rides	Winners	Strike Rate	Profit/Loss to BSP
Jack Quinlan	11	2	18.18%	+£53.50
Tom O'Brien	35	8	22.86%	+£28.29
Conor O'Farrell	13	2	15.38%	+£22.31
Gavin Sheehan	26	2	7.69%	+£13.73
Harry Cobden	12	1	8.33%	+£9.79

Top trainers by Strike Rate – non-handicaps

Name Of Trainer	Runners	Winners	Strike Rate	Profit/Loss to BSP
Nigel Twiston-Davies	31	10	32.26%	+£18.51
Nicky Henderson	31	10	32.26%	-£1.51
Lucinda Russell	18	5	27.78%	+£53.31
Donald McCain	55	15	27.27%	+£0.07
Venetia Williams	20	5	25.00%	+£105.21

Top trainers by Strike Rate – handicaps

Name Of Trainer	Runners	Winners	Strike Rate	Profit/Loss to BSP
Neil King	10	3	30.00%	+£55.87
Olly Murphy	13	3	23.08%	+£1.76
Evan Williams	51	11	21.57%	+£95.00
Rebecca Menzies	14	3	21.43%	+£29.77
Philip Kirby	24	5	20.83%	+£23.55

Top trainers by Profit – non-handicaps

Name Of Trainer	Runners	Winners	Strike Rate	Profit/Loss to BSP
Venetia Williams	20	5	25.00%	+£105.21
Lucinda Russell	18	5	27.78%	+£53.31
Philip Kirby	10	1	10.00%	+£21.86
Nigel Twiston-	31	10	32.26%	+£18.51

Davies				
Donald McCain	55	15	27.27%	+£0.07

Top trainers by Profit – handicaps

Name Of Trainer	Runners	Winners	Strike Rate	Profit/Loss to BSP
Evan Williams	51	11	21.57%	+£95.00
Sue Smith	58	8	13.79%	+£73.52
David Pipe	68	11	16.18%	+£56.27
Neil King	10	3	30.00%	+£55.87
Rebecca Menzies	14	3	21.43%	+£29.77

Top trainer/jockey combos by Strike Rate – non-handicaps

Name of Trainer/Jockey	Qualifiers	Winners	Strike Rate	Profit/Loss to BSP
Nigel Twiston-Davies/Sam Twiston-Davies	16	9	56.25%	+£30.98
Donald McCain/Brian Hughes	11	3	27.27%	-£1.64
Dan Skelton/Harry Skelton	21	3	14.29%	-£7.20

Top trainer/jockey combos by Strike Rate – handicaps

Name of Trainer/Jockey	Qualifiers	Winners	Strike Rate	Profit/Loss to BSP
Jonjo O'Neill/Jonjo O'Neill Jr	12	5	41.67%	+£10.51
Philip Hobbs/Tom O'Brien	14	5	35.71%	+£16.74
Nigel Twiston-Davies/Jamie Bargary	13	2	15.38%	+£7.55
Evan Williams/Adam Wedge	21	3	14.29%	+£2.88

James Moffatt/Charlotte Jones	15	2	13.33%	+£3.17

Top trainer/jockey combos by Profit – non-handicaps

Name of Trainer/Jockey	Qualifiers	Winners	Strike Rate	Profit/Loss to BSP
Nigel Twiston-Davies/Sam Twiston-Davies	16	9	56.25%	+£30.98

Top trainer/jockey combos by Profit – handicaps

Name of Trainer/Jockey	Qualifiers	Winners	Strike Rate	Profit/Loss to BSP
David Pipe/Conor O'Farrell	11	1	9.09%	+£17.82
Philip Hobbs/Tom O'Brien	14	5	35.71%	+£16.74
Jonjo O'Neill/Jonjo O'Neill Jr	12	5	41.67%	+£10.51
Nigel Twiston-Davies/Jamie Bargary	13	2	15.38%	+£7.55
James Moffatt/Charlotte Jones	15	2	13.33%	+£3.17

Profit or Loss backing the unnamed favourite – non-handicaps

Runners	Winners	Strike Rate	Profit/Loss to BSP
298	141	47.32%	+£25.42

Profit or Loss backing the unnamed favourite – handicaps

Runners	Winners	Strike Rate	Profit/Loss to BSP
359	93	25.91%	+£33.22

Profit or loss backing the unnamed second favourite - non-handicaps

Runners	Winners	Strike Rate	Profit/Loss to BSP
294	63	21.43%	-£26.52

Profit or loss backing the unnamed second favourite - handicaps

Runners	Winners	Strike Rate	Profit/Loss to BSP
351	55	15.67%	-£26.44

Profit or Loss backing horses who won last time out- non-handicaps

Runners	Winners	Strike Rate	Profit/Loss to BSP
481	119	24.74%	-£49.00

Profit or Loss backing horses who won last time out - handicaps

Runners	Winners	Strike Rate	Profit/Loss to BSP
708	84	11.86%	-£27.63

Profit or loss backing Top-Weights in handicaps

Runners	Winners	Strike Rate	Profit/Loss to BSP
377	45	11.94%	+£37.69

Most profitable sires – non-handicaps

Sire	Runners	Winners	Strike Rate	Profit/Loss to BSP
Kapgarde	11	3	27.27%	+£108.77
King's Theatre	16	7	43.75%	+£1.26
Cloudings	10	2	20.00%	+£0.56

Most profitable sires – handicaps

Galileo	12	3	25.00%	+£70.98
Beneficial	32	6	18.75%	+£44.87
Midnight Legend	34	3	8.82%	+£32.04
Cloudings	10	2	20.00%	+£23.96

| Old Vic | 14 | 4 | 28.57% | +£18.88 |

Hereford – Chases

Top jockeys by Strike Rate – handicaps

Name Of Jockey	Rides	Winners	Strike Rate	Profit/Loss to BSP
Jonjo O'Neill Jr	10	6	60.00%	+£11.43
Sean Bowen	10	5	50.00%	+£23.68
Aidan Coleman	14	6	42.86%	+£27.70
Paddy Brennan	21	6	28.57%	+£4.01
Richard Patrick	19	4	21.05%	-£1.81
Ben Jones	10	2	20.00%	+£1.27

Top jockeys by Profit – non-handicaps

Name Of Jockey	Rides	Winners	Strike Rate	Profit/Loss to BSP
Aidan Coleman	14	6	42.86%	+£27.70
Sean Bowen	10	5	50.00%	+£23.68
Jonjo O'Neill Jr	10	6	60.00%	+£11.43
Jonathan Burke	16	3	18.75%	+£11.40
Tom O'Brien	25	3	12.00%	+£10.11

Top trainers by Strike Rate – non-handicaps

Name Of Trainer	Runners	Winners	Strike Rate	Profit/Loss to BSP
Dan Skelton	10	2	20.00%	-£0.22

Top trainers by Strike Rate – handicaps

Name Of Trainer	Runners	Winners	Strike Rate	Profit/Loss to BSP
Jonjo O'Neill	15	8	53.33%	+£23.04
Jamie Snowden	11	5	45.45%	+£24.20
Rebecca Curtis	12	4	33.33%	+£11.12
Venetia Williams	49	14	28.57%	+£27.07
Martin Keighley	11	3	27.27%	+£12.57

Top trainers by Profit – handicaps

Name Of Trainer	Runners	Winners	Strike Rate	Profit/Loss to

				BSP
Venetia Williams	49	14	28.57%	+£27.07
Jamie Snowden	11	5	45.45%	+£24.20
Jonjo O'Neill	15	8	53.33%	+£23.04
Tim Vaughan	16	3	18.75%	+£21.59
Henry Oliver	21	5	23.81%	+£18.51

Top trainer/jockey combos by Strike Rate – handicaps

Name of Trainer/Jockey	Qualifiers	Winners	Strike Rate	Profit/Loss to BSP
Kerry Lee/Richard Patrick	14	3	21.43%	+£0.37
Venetia Williams/Charlie Deutsch	25	5	20.00%	+£9.35
Nigel Twiston-Davies/Sam Twiston-Davies	10	2	20.00%	-£2.02
Evan Williams/Conor Ring	13	1	7.69%	+£8.58

Top trainer/jockey combos by Profit – handicaps

Name of Trainer/Jockey	Qualifiers	Winners	Strike Rate	Profit/Loss to BSP
Venetia Williams/Charlie Deutsch	25	5	20.00%	+£9.35
Evan Williams/Conor Ring	13	1	7.69%	+£8.58
Kerry Lee/Richard Patrick	14	3	21.43%	+£0.37

Profit or Loss backing the unnamed favourite – non-handicaps

Runners	Winners	Strike Rate	Profit/Loss to BSP
186	84	45.16%	+£5.01

Profit or Loss backing the unnamed favourite – handicaps

Runners	Winners	Strike Rate	Profit/Loss to BSP
429	129	30.07%	+£14.14

Profit or loss backing the unnamed second favourite - non-handicaps

Runners	Winners	Strike Rate	Profit/Loss to BSP
170	37	21.76%	-£12.80

Profit or loss backing the unnamed second favourite - handicaps

Runners	Winners	Strike Rate	Profit/Loss to BSP
399	84	21.05%	+£50.81

Profit or Loss backing horses who won last time out - non-handicaps

Runners	Winners	Strike Rate	Profit/Loss to BSP
82	21	25.61%	+£18.54

Profit or Loss backing horses who won last time out - handicaps

Runners	Winners	Strike Rate	Profit/Loss to BSP
296	63	21.28%	-£6.26

Profit or loss backing Top-Weights in handicaps

Runners	Winners	Strike Rate	Profit/Loss to BSP
468	72	15.38%	+£26.09

Most profitable sires – handicaps

Gold Well	13	2	15.38%	+£13.86
Flemensfirth	25	4	16.00%	+£10.82
Stowaway	19	5	26.32%	+£10.38
Blueprint	10	2	20.00%	+£9.74

Kayf Tara	30	4	13.33%	+£9.37

Hereford – Hurdles

Top jockeys by Strike Rate – non-handicaps

Name Of Jockey	Rides	Winners	Strike Rate	Profit/Loss to BSP
Harry Skelton	24	9	37.50%	-£4.34
Aidan Coleman	25	8	32.00%	+£24.60
David Bass	19	6	31.58%	+£94.79
Harry Bannister	10	3	30.00%	-£2.46
Jamie Moore	11	3	27.27%	+£49.42

Top jockeys by Strike Rate – handicaps

Name Of Jockey	Rides	Winners	Strike Rate	Profit/Loss to BSP
Sam Twiston-Davies	29	9	31.03%	+£74.56
Harry Skelton	16	4	25.00%	+£2.98
Charlie Deutsch	16	4	25.00%	+£14.10
Aidan Coleman	23	5	21.74%	+£34.53
Tom Scudamore	28	6	21.43%	+£3.70

Top jockeys by Profit – non-handicaps

Name Of Jockey	Rides	Winners	Strike Rate	Profit/Loss to BSP
David Bass	19	6	31.58%	+£94.79
Richie McLernon	12	2	16.67%	+£72.68
Sean Houlihan	14	2	14.29%	+£53.80
Jamie Moore	11	3	27.27%	+£49.42
Aidan Coleman	25	8	32.00%	+£24.60

Top jockeys by Profit – handicaps

Name Of Jockey	Rides	Winners	Strike Rate	Profit/Loss to BSP
Sam Twiston-Davies	29	9	31.03%	+£74.56
Aidan Coleman	23	5	21.74%	+£34.53

Tom Bellamy	10	2	20.00%	+£33.30
Robert Dunne	24	3	12.50%	+£29.25
Jack Tudor	15	1	6.67%	+£28.66

Top trainers by Strike Rate – non-handicaps

Name Of Trainer	Runners	Winners	Strike Rate	Profit/Loss to BSP
Nicky Henderson	19	10	52.63%	+£1.11
Dan Skelton	28	10	35.71%	-£5.10
Alan King	20	7	35.00%	+£18.63
Paul Nicholls	24	7	29.17%	-£7.04
Jonjo O'Neill	19	5	26.32%	+£76.95

Top trainers by Strike Rate – handicaps

Name Of Trainer	Runners	Winners	Strike Rate	Profit/Loss to BSP
Tom George	11	4	36.36%	+£12.99
Tom Lacey	15	5	33.33%	+£18.63
Henry Daley	10	3	30.00%	+£8.11
Kerry Lee	16	4	25.00%	+£2.67
Neil Mulholland	28	7	25.00%	+£11.28

Top trainers by Profit – non-handicaps

Name Of Trainer	Runners	Winners	Strike Rate	Profit/Loss to BSP
Jonjo O'Neill	19	5	26.32%	+£76.95
Ben Pauling	17	2	11.76%	+£74.73
Sheila Lewis	14	2	14.29%	+£53.80
Alastair Ralph	21	4	19.05%	+£24.20
Tom Symonds	21	3	14.29%	+£22.63

Top trainers by Profit – handicaps

Name Of Trainer	Runners	Winners	Strike Rate	Profit/Loss to BSP
Matt Sheppard	28	2	7.14%	+£41.87
Richard Price	10	1	10.00%	+£32.83
Nigel Hawke	14	2	14.29%	+£31.27
Olly Murphy	17	2	11.76%	+£22.10

David Pipe	25	4	16.00%	+£18.64

Top trainer/jockey combos by Strike Rate – non-handicaps

Name of Trainer/Jockey	Qualifiers	Winners	Strike Rate	Profit/Loss to BSP
Dan Skelton/Harry Skelton	19	8	42.11%	-£3.79
Kim Bailey/David Bass	10	3	30.00%	+£11.26
Nigel Twiston-Davies/Sam Twiston-Davies	10	3	30.00%	+£2.74
Paul Nicholls/Harry Cobden	11	3	27.27%	-£3.35
Venetia Williams/Charlie Deutsch	13	2	15.38%	+£1.73

Top trainer/jockey combos by Strike Rate – handicaps

Name of Trainer/Jockey	Qualifiers	Winners	Strike Rate	Profit/Loss to BSP
Tom Symonds/Ben Poste	12	4	33.33%	+£22.16
Dan Skelton/Harry Skelton	13	4	30.77%	+£5.98
Venetia Williams/Charlie Deutsch	14	4	28.57%	+£16.10
David Pipe/Tom Scudamore	11	3	27.27%	+£3.32
John O'Shea/Brodie Hampson	14	2	14.29%	+£10.93

Top trainer/jockey combos by Profit – non-handicaps

Name of Trainer/Jockey	Qualifiers	Winners	Strike Rate	Profit/Loss to BSP
Kim Bailey/David Bass	10	3	30.00%	+£11.26
Nigel Twiston-Davies/Sam Twiston-Davies	10	3	30.00%	+£2.74
Venetia Williams/Charlie Deutsch	13	2	15.38%	+£1.73

Top trainer/jockey combos by Profit – handicaps

Name of Trainer/Jockey	Qualifiers	Winners	Strike Rate	Profit/Loss to BSP
Tom Symonds/Ben Poste	12	4	33.33%	+£22.16
Venetia Williams/Charlie Deutsch	14	4	28.57%	+£16.10
John O'Shea/Brodie Hampson	14	2	14.29%	+£10.93
Dan Skelton/Harry Skelton	13	4	30.77%	+£5.98
David Pipe/Tom Scudamore	11	3	27.27%	+£3.32

Profit or Loss backing the unnamed favourite – non-handicaps

Runners	Winners	Strike Rate	Profit/Loss to BSP
453	185	40.84%	-£12.62

Profit or Loss backing the unnamed favourite – handicaps

Runners	Winners	Strike Rate	Profit/Loss to BSP
467	124	26.55%	+£2.73

Profit or loss backing the unnamed second favourite - non-handicaps

Runners	Winners	Strike Rate	Profit/Loss to BSP
425	105	24.71%	+£38.38

Profit or loss backing the unnamed second favourite - handicaps

Runners	Winners	Strike Rate	Profit/Loss to BSP
422	83	19.67%	+£29.54

Profit or Loss backing horses who won last time out- non-handicaps

Runners	Winners	Strike Rate	Profit/Loss to BSP
241	68	28.22%	+£1.93

Profit or Loss backing horses who won last time out - handicaps

Runners	Winners	Strike Rate	Profit/Loss to BSP
390	63	16.15%	-£68.49

Profit or loss backing Top-Weights in handicaps

Runners	Winners	Strike Rate	Profit/Loss to BSP
515	59	11.46%	-£78.77

Most profitable sires – non-handicaps

Sire	Runners	Winners	Strike Rate	Profit/Loss to BSP
Shantou	14	3	21.43%	+£85.27
Flemensfirth	28	6	21.43%	+£16.53
Oscar	24	5	20.83%	+£6.56
Presenting	15	1	6.67%	+£3.64
Yeats	24	2	8.33%	+£0.97

Most profitable sires – handicaps

Kayf Tara	39	8	20.51%	+£49.15
Shirocco	12	3	25.00%	+£43.24

Midnight Legend	34	10	29.41%	+£41.82
Kalanisi	10	1	10.00%	+£19.32
Yeats	49	8	16.33%	+£15.83

Hexham – Chases

Top jockeys by Strike Rate – non-handicaps

Name Of Jockey	Rides	Winners	Strike Rate	Profit/Loss to BSP
Ryan Mania	10	3	30.00%	+£8.92
Brian Hughes	27	8	29.63%	-£4.67
Thomas Dowson	12	1	8.33%	-£5.71

Top jockeys by Strike Rate – handicaps

Name Of Jockey	Rides	Winners	Strike Rate	Profit/Loss to BSP
Emma Smith-Chaston	14	4	28.57%	+£14.15
Thomas Willmott	31	7	22.58%	+£35.19
Amie Waugh	18	4	22.22%	+£36.54
Jonathon Bewley	63	13	20.63%	+£55.76
Paddy Brennan	11	2	18.18%	-£6.88
Sean Quinlan	95	16	16.84%	-£14.82

Top jockeys by Profit – non-handicaps

Name Of Jockey	Rides	Winners	Strike Rate	Profit/Loss to BSP
Ryan Mania	10	3	30.00%	+£8.92

Top jockeys by Profit – handicaps

Name Of Jockey	Rides	Winners	Strike Rate	Profit/Loss to BSP
Jonathon Bewley	63	13	20.63%	+£55.76
Derek Fox	111	17	15.32%	+£41.19
Amie Waugh	18	4	22.22%	+£36.54
Thomas Willmott	31	7	22.58%	+£35.19
Ross Chapman	61	10	16.39%	+£34.92

Top trainers by Strike Rate – non-handicaps

Name Of Trainer	Runners	Winners	Strike Rate	Profit/Loss to BSP
Lucinda Russell	14	6	42.86%	+£109.08
Maurice Barnes	20	1	5.00%	-£17.09

Top trainers by Strike Rate – handicaps

Name Of Trainer	Runners	Winners	Strike Rate	Profit/Loss to BSP
Sam England	15	5	33.33%	+£4.05
Paul Collins	11	3	27.27%	+£31.01
Jennie Candlish	27	7	25.93%	+£0.62
Stuart Coltherd	90	22	24.44%	+£121.91
Nicky Richards	25	6	24.00%	+£6.03

Top trainers by Profit – non-handicaps

Name Of Trainer	Runners	Winners	Strike Rate	Profit/Loss to BSP
Lucinda Russell	14	6	42.86%	+£109.08

Top trainers by Profit – handicaps

Name Of Trainer	Runners	Winners	Strike Rate	Profit/Loss to BSP
Stuart Coltherd	90	22	24.44%	+£121.91
William Young Jr	22	4	18.18%	+£52.46
Lucinda Russell	229	43	18.78%	+£36.75
Sue Smith	105	13	12.38%	+£34.04
Andrew Crook	14	2	14.29%	+£31.71

Top trainer/jockey combos by Strike Rate – handicaps

Name of Trainer/Jockey	Qualifiers	Winners	Strike Rate	Profit/Loss to BSP
Sam England/Jonathan England	13	5	38.46%	+£6.05
Jane Walton/Ross Chapman	14	5	35.71%	+£21.88

	12	4	33.33%	+£16.15
Micky Hammond/Emma Smith-Chaston				
Lucinda Russell/Craig Nichol	12	4	33.33%	+£20.69
Jennie Candlish/Sean Quinlan	22	7	31.82%	+£5.62

Top trainer/jockey combos by Profit – handicaps

Name of Trainer/Jockey	Qualifiers	Winners	Strike Rate	Profit/Loss to BSP
Stuart Coltherd/Sam Coltherd	57	11	19.30%	+£43.27
Ben Haslam/Richie McLernon	23	4	17.39%	+£24.38
Jane Walton/Ross Chapman	14	5	35.71%	+£21.88
Lucinda Russell/Craig Nichol	12	4	33.33%	+£20.69
Sue Smith/Ryan Mania	27	6	22.22%	+£18.94

Profit or Loss backing the unnamed favourite – non-handicaps

Runners	Winners	Strike Rate	Profit/Loss to BSP
226	93	41.15%	-£10.62

Profit or Loss backing the unnamed favourite – handicaps

Runners	Winners	Strike Rate	Profit/Loss to BSP
603	150	24.88%	-£62.69

Profit or loss backing the unnamed second favourite - non-handicaps

Runners	Winners	Strike Rate	Profit/Loss to BSP
219	52	23.74%	-£11.40

Profit or loss backing the unnamed second favourite - handicaps

Runners	Winners	Strike Rate	Profit/Loss to BSP
565	112	19.82%	+£23.69

Profit or Loss backing horses who won last time out - non-handicaps

Runners	Winners	Strike Rate	Profit/Loss to BSP
126	34	26.98%	+£18.49

Profit or Loss backing horses who won last time out - handicaps

Runners	Winners	Strike Rate	Profit/Loss to BSP
427	76	17.80%	-£114.20

Profit or loss backing Top-Weights in handicaps

Runners	Winners	Strike Rate	Profit/Loss to BSP
603	81	13.43%	-£111.83

Most profitable sires – non-handicaps

Sire	Runners	Winners	Strike Rate	Profit/Loss to BSP
Milan	16	3	18.75%	+£79.20

Most profitable sires – handicaps

Old Vic	22	8	36.36%	+£75.67
Yeats	21	5	23.81%	+£55.68
Blueprint	17	8	47.06%	+£51.11
Kapgarde	18	5	27.78%	+£44.58
Getaway	10	3	30.00%	+£39.77

Hexham – Hurdles

Top jockeys by Strike Rate – non-handicaps

Name Of Jockey	Rides	Winners	Strike Rate	Profit/Loss to BSP
William Kennedy	17	5	29.41%	+£1.11
Gavin Sheehan	14	4	28.57%	+£20.46
Brian Hughes	125	31	24.80%	+£5.67
Richie McLernon	13	3	23.08%	+£13.38
Craig Nichol	59	9	15.25%	-£18.36

Top jockeys by Strike Rate – handicaps

Name Of Jockey	Rides	Winners	Strike Rate	Profit/Loss to BSP
Kit Alexander	11	3	27.27%	+£3.74
Harry Reed	21	5	23.81%	+£167.15
Emma Smith-Chaston	18	4	22.22%	+£26.04
Thomas Dowson	70	14	20.00%	+£26.40
Tom Midgley	20	4	20.00%	+£16.74

Top jockeys by Profit – non-handicaps

Name Of Jockey	Rides	Winners	Strike Rate	Profit/Loss to BSP
Ryan Mania	40	5	12.50%	+£228.31
Jamie Hamilton	52	4	7.69%	+£107.83
Gavin Sheehan	14	4	28.57%	+£20.46
Jonathon Bewley	30	3	10.00%	+£20.08
Richie McLernon	13	3	23.08%	+£13.38

Top jockeys by Profit – handicaps

Name Of Jockey	Rides	Winners	Strike Rate	Profit/Loss to BSP
Harry Reed	21	5	23.81%	+£167.15
Philip Armson	10	1	10.00%	+£137.02
Ross Chapman	51	9	17.65%	+£94.96
Ryan Mania	27	4	14.81%	+£30.41

John Kington	21	1	4.76%	+£28.02

Top trainers by Strike Rate – non-handicaps

Name Of Trainer	Runners	Winners	Strike Rate	Profit/Loss to BSP
Jedd O'Keeffe	12	6	50.00%	+£9.34
Dr Richard Newland	13	6	46.15%	+£13.99
Jamie Snowden	10	4	40.00%	-£2.56
Dan Skelton	12	4	33.33%	-£2.69
Nicky Richards	37	10	27.03%	-£5.51

Top trainers by Strike Rate – handicaps

Name Of Trainer	Runners	Winners	Strike Rate	Profit/Loss to BSP
James Walton	24	8	33.33%	+£49.99
Nicky Richards	31	9	29.03%	+£8.14
Tristan Davidson	11	3	27.27%	£0.00
Keith Dalgleish	16	4	25.00%	-£2.62
Mark Walford	38	9	23.68%	+£2.49

Top trainers by Profit – non-handicaps

Name Of Trainer	Runners	Winners	Strike Rate	Profit/Loss to BSP
Sandy Thomson	29	3	10.34%	+£213.37
Ruth Jefferson	16	2	12.50%	+£115.43
Maurice Barnes	71	4	5.63%	+£46.68
Mark Walford	26	4	15.38%	+£39.72
Victor Thompson	22	1	4.55%	+£23.25

Top trainers by Profit – handicaps

Name Of Trainer	Runners	Winners	Strike Rate	Profit/Loss to BSP
Daragh Bourke	16	1	6.25%	+£145.54
Sue Smith	58	8	13.79%	+£111.17
James Walton	24	7	33.33%	+£49.99
Andrew Crook	18	1	5.56%	+£31.02
Sara Ender	18	1	5.56%	+£24.71

Top trainer/jockey combos by Strike Rate – non-handicaps

Name Of Trainer/Jockey	Runners	Winners	Strike Rate	Profit/Loss to BSP
Donald McCain/William Kennedy	11	4	36.36%	+£4.48
Sandy Thomson/Ryan Mania	11	2	18.18%	+£228.83
Sue Smith/Ryan Mania	12	2	16.67%	+£10.58
Mark Walford/Jamie Hamilton	12	2	16.67%	+£16.42
Rose Dobbin/Craig Nichol	13	2	15.38%	+£1.73

Top trainer/jockey combos by Strike Rate – handicaps

Name of Trainer/Jockey	Qualifiers	Winners	Strike Rate	Profit/Loss to BSP
Sue Smith/Jonathan England	10	4	40.00%	+£6.01
Jonathan Haynes/Thomas Dowson	27	7	25.93%	+£29.07
Tim Easterby/Jamie Hamilton	12	3	25.00%	+£5.38
Donald McCain/Brian Hughes	11	2	18.18%	-£5.63
Ben Haslam/Richie McLernon	33	6	18.18%	+£13.19

Top trainer/jockey combos by Profit – non-handicaps

Name of	Qualifiers	Winners	Strike Rate	Profit/Loss to

Trainer/Jockey				BSP
Sandy Thomson/Ryan Mania	11	2	18.18%	+£228.83
George Bewley/Jonathon Bewley	29	3	10.34%	+£21.08
Mark Walford/Jamie Hamilton	12	2	16.67%	+£16.42
Sue Smith/Ryan Mania	12	2	16.67%	+£10.58
Donald McCain/William Kennedy	11	4	36.36%	+£4.48

Top trainer/jockey combos by Profit – handicaps

Name of Trainer/Jockey	Qualifiers	Winners	Strike Rate	Profit/Loss to BSP
Sara Ender/Nathan Moscrop	13	1	7.69%	+£29.71
Jonathan Haynes/Thomas Dowson	27	7	25.93%	+£29.07
Stuart Coltherd/Sam Coltherd	32	5	15.63%	+£18.45
Ben Haslam/Richie McLernon	33	6	18.18%	+£13.19
Sue Smith/Jonathan England	10	4	40.00%	+£6.01

Profit or Loss backing the unnamed favourite – non-handicaps

Runners	Winners	Strike Rate	Profit/Loss to BSP
615	240	46.60%	+£4.21

Profit or Loss backing the unnamed favourite – handicaps

Runners	Winners	Strike Rate	Profit/Loss to BSP
544	150	27.57%	-£24.70

Profit or loss backing the unnamed second favourite - non-handicaps

Runners	Winners	Strike Rate	Profit/Loss to BSP
519	117	22.54%	-£36.78

Profit or loss backing the unnamed second favourite - handicaps

Runners	Winners	Strike Rate	Profit/Loss to BSP
518	112	21.62%	+£105.18

Profit or Loss backing horses who won last time out- non-handicaps

Runners	Winners	Strike Rate	Profit/Loss to BSP
292	104	35.62%	-£23.24

Profit or Loss backing horses who won last time out - handicaps

Runners	Winners	Strike Rate	Profit/Loss to BSP
442	86	19.46%	-£68.61

Profit or loss backing Top-Weights in handicaps

Runners	Winners	Strike Rate	Profit/Loss to BSP
557	66	11.85%	+£20.09

Most profitable sires – non-handicaps

Sire	Runners	Winners	Strike Rate	Profit/Loss to BSP
Midnight Legend	18	4	22.22%	+£226.87
Getaway	19	6	31.58%	+£140.34
Beneficial	39	6	15.38%	+£107.93
Craigsteel	12	5	41.67%	+£16.28

Scorpion	17	4	23.53%	+£14.27

Most profitable sires – handicaps

King's Theatre	34	4	11.76%	+£125.27
Saddler's Hall	30	6	20.00%	+£36.02
Fair Mix	25	2	8.00%	+£34.39
Act One	13	2	15.38%	+£32.57
Hawk Wing	13	4	30.77%	+£30.56

Huntingdon – Chases

Top jockeys by Strike Rate – non-handicaps

Name Of Jockey	Runners	Winners	Strike Rate	Profit/Loss to BSP
Nico de Boinville	10	4	40.00%	+£14.40
Harry Skelton	20	6	30.00%	-£1.37
Sam Twiston-Davies	14	1	7.14%	-£8.10

Top jockeys by Strike Rate – handicaps

Name Of Jockey	Rides	Winners	Strike Rate	Profit/Loss to BSP
James Bowen	12	4	33.33%	+£37.29
Sean Bowen	27	8	29.63%	+£15.88
Alan Johns	12	3	25.00%	+£4.66
Sam Twiston-Davies	49	12	24.49%	+£21.90
Ben Poste	41	10	24.39%	+£70.58

Top jockeys by Profit – non-handicaps

Name Of Jockey	Rides	Winners	Strike Rate	Profit/Loss to BSP
Nico de Boinville	10	4	40.00%	+£14.40

Top jockeys by Profit – handicaps

Name Of Jockey	Rides	Winners	Strike Rate	Profit/Loss to BSP
Ben Poste	41	10	24.39%	+£70.58
Patrick Cowley	13	3	23.08%	+£56.32
James Bowen	12	4	33.33%	+£37.29
Trevor Whelan	29	4	13.79%	+£32.74
Tom Cannon	30	7	23.33%	+£29.78

Top trainers by Strike Rate – non-handicaps

Name Of Trainer	Runners	Winners	Strike Rate	Profit/Loss to

				BSP
Kim Bailey	12	7	58.33%	+£20.23
Ben Pauling	10	5	50.00%	+£12.75
Nicky Henderson	27	13	48.15%	+£3.10
Charlie Longsdon	11	4	36.36%	+£3.03
Paul Nicholls	17	6	35.29%	+£5.85

Top trainers by Strike Rate – handicaps

Name Of Trainer	Runners	Winners	Strike Rate	Profit/Loss to BSP
Dr Richard Newland	13	5	38.46%	+£9.71
Fergal O'Brien	36	12	33.33%	+£15.95
Alan King	28	9	32.14%	+£37.07
Nick Gifford	17	5	29.41%	+£3.15
David Pipe	11	3	27.27%	+£0.44

Top trainers by Profit – non-handicaps

Name Of Trainer	Runners	Winners	Strike Rate	Profit/Loss to BSP
Kim Bailey	12	7	58.33%	+£20.23
Venetia Williams	14	3	21.43%	+£17.46
Ben Pauling	10	5	50.00%	+£12.75
Paul Nicholls	17	6	35.29%	+£5.85
Nicky Henderson	27	13	48.15%	+£3.10

Top trainers by Profit – handicaps

Name Of Trainer	Runners	Winners	Strike Rate	Profit/Loss to BSP
John Cornwall	67	9	13.43%	+£91.99
Caroline Bailey	55	13	23.64%	+£52.85
Alan King	28	9	32.14%	+£37.07
David Bridgwater	19	4	21.05%	+£21.73
Richard Phillips	10	2	20.00%	+£20.65

Top trainer/jockey combos by Strike Rate – non-handicaps

Name Of Trainer/Jockey	Rides	Winners	Strike Rate	Profit/Loss to BSP
Dan Skelton/Harry Skelton	17	5	29.41%	-£1.29

Top trainer/jockey combos by Strike Rate – handicaps

Name of Trainer/Jockey	Qualifiers	Winners	Strike Rate	Profit/Loss to BSP
Fergal O'Brien/Paddy Brennan	16	7	43.75%	+£13.45
John Cornwall/Ben Poste	13	5	38.46%	+£64.10
Charlie Longsdon/Paul O'Brien	14	4	28.57%	+£19.32
Diana Grissell/Marc Goldstein	11	3	27.27%	+£12.57
Chris Gordon/Tom Cannon	11	3	27.27%	+£10.56

Top trainer/jockey combos by Profit – handicaps

Name of Trainer/Jockey	Qualifiers	Winners	Strike Rate	Profit/Loss to BSP
John Cornwall/Ben Poste	13	5	38.46%	+£64.10
Charlie Longsdon/Paul O'Brien	14	4	28.57%	+£19.32
Fergal O'Brien/Paddy Brennan	16	7	43.75%	+£13.45
Diana Grissell/Marc Goldstein	11	3	27.27%	+£12.57

Chris Gordon/Tom Cannon	11	3	27.27%	+£10.56

Profit or Loss backing the unnamed favourite – non-handicaps

Runners	Winners	Strike Rate	Profit/Loss to BSP
304	141	46.38%	+£0.87

Profit or Loss backing the unnamed favourite – handicaps

Runners	Winners	Strike Rate	Profit/Loss to BSP
631	179	28.37%	-£22.46

Profit or loss backing the unnamed second favourite - non-handicaps

Runners	Winners	Strike Rate	Profit/Loss to BSP
298	67	22.48%	-£30.30

Profit or loss backing the unnamed second favourite - handicaps

Runners	Winners	Strike Rate	Profit/Loss to BSP
589	117	19.86%	-£44.65

Profit or Loss backing horses who won last time out - non-handicaps

Runners	Winners	Strike Rate	Profit/Loss to BSP
234	74	31.62%	+£48.33

Profit or Loss backing horses who won last time out - handicaps

Runners	Winners	Strike Rate	Profit/Loss to BSP
471	104	21.44%	+£0.32

Profit or loss backing Top-Weights in handicaps

Runners	Winners	Strike Rate	Profit/Loss to BSP
675	147	21.78%	+£177.62

Most profitable sires – non-handicaps

Sire	Runners	Winners	Strike Rate	Profit/Loss to BSP
Oscar	11	4	36.36%	+£21.90
Milan	10	5	50.00%	+£14.94
King's Theatre	15	6	40.00%	+£8.18
Beneficial	13	3	23.08%	+£1.51

Most profitable sires – handicaps

Oscar	44	9	20.45%	+£76.04
Kayf Tara	57	12	21.05%	+£40.40
Montmartre	13	3	23.08%	+£24.37
Mahler	30	5	16.67%	+£24.28
Getaway	33	7	21.21%	+£24.06

Huntingdon – Hurdles

Top jockeys by Strike Rate – non-handicaps

Name Of Jockey	Rides	Winners	Strike Rate	Profit/Loss to BSP
Nico de Boinville	42	17	40.48%	+£67.46
Jonjo O'Neill Jr	14	4	28.57%	+£91.83
Stan Sheppard	11	3	27.27%	+£35.23
Bridget Andrews	12	3	25.00%	-£5.57
Brian Hughes	17	4	23.53%	+£1.46

Top jockeys by Strike Rate – handicaps

Name Of Jockey	Rides	Winners	Strike Rate	Profit/Loss to BSP
Jonjo O'Neill Jr	20	6	30.00%	+£9.02
Kieron Edgar	10	3	30.00%	+£16.28
Connor Brace	15	4	26.67%	+£5.88
Paddy Brennan	48	12	25.00%	+£50.18

Tom Buckley	12	3	25.00%	+£43.36

Top jockeys by Profit – non-handicaps

Name Of Jockey	Rides	Winners	Strike Rate	Profit/Loss to BSP
Daniel Hiskett	11	2	18.18%	+£107.80
Jonjo O'Neill Jr	14	4	28.57%	+£91.83
Kielan Woods	44	3	6.82%	+£70.63
Nico de Boinville	42	17	40.48%	+£67.46
Jamie Moore	58	8	13.79%	+£66.98

Top jockeys by Profit – handicaps

Name Of Jockey	Rides	Winners	Strike Rate	Profit/Loss to BSP
Tabitha Worsley	24	4	16.67%	+£93.08
Paddy Brennan	48	12	25.00%	+£50.18
Joshua Moore	40	7	17.50%	+£48.44
Aidan Coleman	72	13	18.06%	+£46.85
Tom Buckley	12	3	25.00%	+£43.36

Top trainers by Strike Rate – non-handicaps

Name Of Trainer	Runners	Winners	Strike Rate	Profit/Loss to BSP
Nicky Henderson	89	34	38.20%	+£13.35
Tom Lacey	13	4	30.77%	+£5.53
Dr Richard Newland	21	5	23.81%	+£9.52
Tom George	17	4	23.53%	-£3.15
Stuart Edmunds	34	8	23.53%	+£7.35

Top trainers by Strike Rate – handicaps

Name Of Trainer	Runners	Winners	Strike Rate	Profit/Loss to BSP
Tom Lacey	21	7	33.33%	+£42.73
Denis Quinn	18	5	27.78%	+£32.81
Nicky Richards	15	4	26.67%	-£0.32
Jonjo O'Neill	91	23	25.27%	+£54.14
Oliver Greenall	17	4	23.53%	+£8.81

Top trainers by Profit – non-handicaps

Name Of Trainer	Runners	Winners	Strike Rate	Profit/Loss to BSP
Richard Phillips	22	2	9.09%	+£96.80
Seamus Mullins	10	2	20.00%	+£73.05
Jonjo O'Neill	68	9	13.24%	+£61.63
Ben Pauling	45	6	13.33%	+£61.46
Amy Murphy	14	3	21.43%	+£58.46

Top trainers by Profit – handicaps

Name Of Trainer	Runners	Winners	Strike Rate	Profit/Loss to BSP
Gary Moore	87	16	18.39%	+£91.91
Ben Case	44	7	15.91%	+£69.73
James Evans	25	2	8.00%	+£57.99
Jonjo O'Neill	91	23	25.27%	+£54.14
Tom Lacey	21	7	33.33%	+£42.73

Top trainer/jockey combos by Strike Rate – non-handicaps

Name of Trainer/Jockey	Qualifiers	Winners	Strike Rate	Profit/Loss to BSP
Nicky Henderson/Nico de Boinville	33	13	39.39%	+£2.81
Dr Richard Newland/Sam Twiston-Davies	12	4	33.33%	+£15.85
Jonjo O'Neill/Jonjo O'Neill Jr	14	4	28.57%	+£91.83
Stuart Edmunds/Ciaran Gethings	26	7	26.92%	+£13.13
Dan Skelton/Bridget Andrews	12	3	25.00%	-£5.57

Top trainer/jockey combos by Strike Rate – handicaps

Name of Trainer/Jockey	Qualifiers	Winners	Strike Rate	Profit/Loss to BSP
Fergal O'Brien/Paddy Brennan	18	6	33.33%	+£11.57
Venetia Williams/Aidan Coleman	15	5	33.33%	+£16.48
Stuart Edmunds/Ciaran Gethings	14	4	28.57%	+£14.60
Jonjo O'Neill/Jonjo O'Neill Jr	19	5	26.32%	+£6.96
Gary Moore/Joshua Moore	22	5	22.73%	+£52.87

Top trainer/jockey combos by Profit – non-handicaps

Name of Trainer/Jockey	Qualifiers	Winners	Strike Rate	Profit/Loss to BSP
Jonjo O'Neill/Jonjo O'Neill Jr	14	4	28.57%	+£91.83
Neil King/Trevor Whelan	23	4	17.39%	+£61.10
Amy Murphy/Jack Whelan	10	2	20.00%	+£58.57
Dr Richard Newland/Sam Twiston-Davies	12	4	33.33%	+£!5.85
Stuart Edmunds/Ciaran Gethings	26	7	26.92%	+£13.13

Top trainer/jockey combos by Profit – handicaps

Name of Trainer/Jockey	Qualifiers	Winners	Strike Rate	Profit/Loss to BSP
Gary Moore/Joshua Moore	22	5	22.73%	+£52.87

Gary Moore/Jamie Moore	31	5	16.13%	+£35.83
James Eustace/Jack Quinlan	11	3	27.27%	+£25.91
Kim Bailey/David Bass	26	5	19.23%	+£21.71
David Pipe/Tom Scudamore	20	5	25.00%	+£18.74

Profit or Loss backing the unnamed favourite – non-handicaps

Runners	Winners	Strike Rate	Profit/Loss to BSP
582	245	42.10%	-£41.49

Profit or Loss backing the unnamed favourite – handicaps

Runners	Winners	Strike Rate	Profit/Loss to BSP
736	213	28.98%	+£50.58

Profit or loss backing the unnamed second favourite - non-handicaps

Runners	Winners	Strike Rate	Profit/Loss to BSP
544	125	22.98%	-£29.32

Profit or loss backing the unnamed second favourite - handicaps

Runners	Winners	Strike Rate	Profit/Loss to BSP
687	112	16.30%	-£103.80

Profit or Loss backing horses who won last time out- non-handicaps

Runners	Winners	Strike Rate	Profit/Loss to BSP
367	96	26.16%	-£12.27

Profit or Loss backing horses who won last time out - handicaps

Runners	Winners	Strike Rate	Profit/Loss to BSP
596	106	17.79%	-£78.04

Profit or loss backing Top-Weights in handicaps

Runners	Winners	Strike Rate	Profit/Loss to BSP
803	122	15.19%	+£68.89

Most profitable sires – non-handicaps

Sire	Runners	Winners	Strike Rate	Profit/Loss to BSP
Robin Des Champs	20	4	20.00%	+£126.92
Jeremy	11	2	18.18%	+£79.12
Sakhee	15	3	20.00%	+£58.86
Champs Elysees	22	4	18.18%	+£56.57
Milan	44	4	9.09%	+£23.93

Most profitable sires – handicaps

Flemensfirth	62	10	16.13%	+£41.93
Royal Applause	13	3	23.08%	+£38.37
Moscow Society	16	3	18.75%	+£33.97
Midnight Legend	89	14	15.73%	+£29.41
Jeremy	15	1	6.67%	+£28.87

Kelso – Chases

Top jockeys by Strike Rate – non-handicaps

Name Of Jockey	Rides	Winners	Strike Rate	Profit/Loss to BSP
Ryan Mania	13	4	30.77%	+£7.92
Brian Hughes	27	8	29.63%	+£26.80
Jamie Hamilton	15	3	20.00%	+£6.12
Nick Orpwood	22	4	18.18%	+£51.54
John Dawson	16	2	12.50%	-£6.76

Top jockeys by Strike Rate – handicaps

Name Of Jockey	Rides	Winners	Strike Rate	Profit/Loss to BSP
Sam Twiston-Davies	20	7	35.00%	+£22.11
William Kennedy	17	4	23.53%	+£26.63
Danny McMenamin	27	6	22.22%	+£21.16
Ryan Mania	88	19	21.59%	+£13.24
Richie McLernon	29	6	20.69%	+£6.39

Top jockeys by Profit – non-handicaps

Name Of Jockey	Rides	Winners	Strike Rate	Profit/Loss to BSP
Nick Orpwood	22	4	18.18%	+£51.54
Brian Hughes	27	8	29.63%	+£26.80
Ryan Mania	13	4	30.77%	+£7.92
Jamie Hamilton	15	3	20.00%	+£6.12
Craig Nichol	86	16	18.60%	+£16.53

Top jockeys by Profit – handicaps

Name Of Jockey	Rides	Winners	Strike Rate	Profit/Loss to BSP
Thomas Willmott	23	4	17.39%	+£30.51
William Kennedy	17	4	23.53%	+£26.63

Sam Twiston-Davies	20	7	35.00%	+£22.11
Danny McMenamin	27	6	22.22%	+£21.16

Top trainers by Strike Rate – non-handicaps

Name Of Trainer	Runners	Winners	Strike Rate	Profit/Loss to BSP
Sandy Thomson	17	6	35.29%	+£16.06
Paul Nicholls	13	4	30.77%	-£3.93
Sue Smith	11	3	27.27%	+£3.39
Lucinda Russell	20	5	25.00%	£0.00
Katie Scott	12	3	25.00%	+£16.62

Top trainers by Strike Rate – handicaps

Name Of Trainer	Runners	Winners	Strike Rate	Profit/Loss to BSP
Michael Scudamore	13	6	46.15%	+£23.27
Ann Hamilton	28	8	28.57%	+£18.24
Iain Jardine	29	8	27.59%	+£24.81
Jennie Candlish	15	4	26.67%	-£1.40
Dr Richard Newland	15	4	26.67%	+£4.65

Top trainers by Profit – non-handicaps

Name Of Trainer	Runners	Winners	Strike Rate	Profit/Loss to BSP
Stuart Coltherd	22	4	18.18%	+£17.08
Katie Scott	12	3	25.00%	+£16.62
Sandy Thomson	17	6	35.29%	+£16.06
Victor Thompson	26	2	7.69%	+£9.42

Top trainers by Profit – handicaps

Name Of Trainer	Runners	Winners	Strike Rate	Profit/Loss to BSP
Stuart Coltherd	78	14	17.95%	+£62.95
Donald McCain	79	17	21.52%	+£35.22

Iain Jardine	29	8	27.59%	+£24.81
Chris Grant	35	6	17.14%	+£24.14
Michael Scudamore	13	6	46.15%	+£23.27

Top trainer/jockey combos by Strike Rate – non-handicaps

Name of Trainer/Jockey	Qualifiers	Winners	Strike Rate	Profit/Loss to BSP
N W Alexander/Kit Alexander	15	1	6.67%	-£9.07

Top trainer/jockey combos by Strike Rate – handicaps

Name of Trainer/Jockey	Qualifiers	Winners	Strike Rate	Profit/Loss to BSP
Donald McCain/William Kennedy	12	4	33.33%	+£31.63
Sandy Forster/Jamie Hamilton	14	4	28.57%	+£1.14
Rose Dobbin/Craig Nichol	32	9	28.13%	+£16.70
Dianne Sayer/Brian Hughes	11	3	27.27%	+£4.74
Sandy Thomson/Ryan Mania	35	9	25.71%	-£0.65

Top trainer/jockey combos by Profit – handicaps

Name of Trainer/Jockey	Qualifiers	Winners	Strike Rate	Profit/Loss to BSP
Donald McCain/William Kennedy	12	4	33.33%	+£31.63
Sue Smith/Ryan Mania	21	4	19.05%	+£17.29
Rose	32	9	28.13%	+£16.70

Dobbin/Craig Nichol				
Iain Jardine/Conor O'Farrell	13	3	23.08%	+£12.94
Lucinda Russell/Thomas Willmott	11	2	18.18%	+£11.31

Profit or Loss backing the unnamed favourite – non-handicaps

Runners	Winners	Strike Rate	Profit/Loss to BSP
291	128	43.99%	-£7.05

Profit or Loss backing the unnamed favourite – handicaps

Runners	Winners	Strike Rate	Profit/Loss to BSP
579	166	28.67%	-£12.32

Profit or loss backing the unnamed second favourite - non-handicaps

Runners	Winners	Strike Rate	Profit/Loss to BSP
273	62	22.71%	+£8.29

Profit or loss backing the unnamed second favourite - handicaps

Runners	Winners	Strike Rate	Profit/Loss to BSP
564	100	17.73%	-£66.82

Profit or Loss backing horses who won last time out - non-handicaps

Runners	Winners	Strike Rate	Profit/Loss to BSP
222	60	27.03%	-£10.03

Profit or Loss backing horses who won last time out - handicaps

Runners	Winners	Strike Rate	Profit/Loss to BSP

549	104	18.94%	-£21.25

Profit or loss backing Top-Weights in handicaps

Runners	Winners	Strike Rate	Profit/Loss to BSP
578	93	16.09%	-£44.20

Most profitable sires – non-handicaps

Sire	Runners	Winners	Strike Rate	Profit/Loss to BSP
Flemensfirth	21	5	23.81%	+£60.91
Westerner	16	5	31.25%	+£8.97
Saddler's Hall	10	2	20.00%	+£5.06
Overbury	10	1	10.00%	+£4.86
Oscar	16	3	18.75%	+£31.2

Most profitable sires – handicaps

Overbury	46	13	28.26%	+£68.22
Milan	63	13	20.63%	+£41.42
Alflora	29	5	17.24%	+£32.32
Cloudings	36	6	16.67%	+£31.03
Sir Harry Lewis	17	3	17.65%	+£25.02

Kelso – Hurdles

Top jockeys by Strike Rate – non-handicaps

Name Of Jockey	Rides	Winners	Strike Rate	Profit/Loss to BSP
Brian Hughes	129	31	24.03%	-£26.56
Dougie Costello	11	2	18.18%	+£6.58
Ryan Mania	56	7	12.50%	-£29.00
Danny McMenamin	17	2	11.76%	-£9.28
Craig Nichol	78	9	11.54%	-£18.25

Top jockeys by Strike Rate – handicaps

Name Of Jockey	Rides	Winners	Strike Rate	Profit/Loss to

				BSP
Bruce Lynn	23	5	21.74%	+£25.67
Jonathan England	12	2	16.67%	-£7.93
Jonathon Bewley	44	7	15.91%	+£34.99
Sean Quinlan	65	10	15.38%	+£0.17
William Kennedy	13	2	15.38%	-£3.53

Top jockeys by Profit – non-handicaps

Name Of Jockey	Rides	Winners	Strike Rate	Profit/Loss to BSP
Callum Bewley	53	3	5.66%	+£108.09
Sean Quinlan	45	3	6.67%	+£58.71
Henry Brooke	60	2	3.33%	+£55.91
Derek Fox	56	6	10.71%	+£19.24
Dougie Costello	11	2	18.18%	+£6.58

Top jockeys by Profit – handicaps

Name Of Jockey	Rides	Winners	Strike Rate	Profit/Loss to BSP
Jonathon Bewley	44	7	15.91%	+£34.99
Bruce Lynn	23	5	21.74%	+£25.67
Brian Hughes	154	17	11.04%	+£10.25
Callum Bewley	85	7	8.24%	+£1.71
Sean Quinlan	65	10	15.38%	+£0.17

Top trainers by Strike Rate – non-handicaps

Name Of Trainer	Runners	Winners	Strike Rate	Profit/Loss to BSP
John Quinn	11	3	27.27%	-£2.41
Donald McCain	99	26	26.26%	-£14.64
Nicky Richards	67	17	25.37%	+£16.33
Brian Ellison	21	3	14.29%	-£13.41
Ann Hamilton	15	2	13.33%	-£4.13

Top trainers by Strike Rate – handicaps

Name Of Trainer	Runners	Winners	Strike Rate	Profit/Loss to

217

				BSP
Tim Vaughan	10	3	30.00%	+£2.22
Keith Dalgleish	50	11	22.00%	+£50.42
Harriet Graham	39	8	20.51%	+£6.84
Olly Murphy	10	2	20.00%	-£0.42
Ben Haslam	15	3	20.00%	+£6.27

Top trainers by Profit – non-handicaps

Name Of Trainer	Runners	Winners	Strike Rate	Profit/Loss to BSP
N W Alexander	98	12	12.24%	+£214.02
Sandy Thomson	53	7	13.21%	+£185.88
Chris Grant	47	5	10.64%	+£167.39
R Mike Smith	27	1	3.70%	+£129.82
Maurice Barnes	46	2	4.35%	+£112.80

Top trainers by Profit – handicaps

Name Of Trainer	Runners	Winners	Strike Rate	Profit/Loss to BSP
N W Alexander	135	18	13.33%	+£152.68
Keith Dalgleish	50	11	22.00%	+£50.42
Stuart Coltherd	50	8	16.00%	+£33.24
George Bewley	52	8	15.38%	+£33.20
James Ewart	54	9	16.67%	+£21.22

Top trainer/jockey combos by Strike Rate – non-handicaps

Name of Trainer/Jockey	Qualifiers	Winners	Strike Rate	Profit/Loss to BSP
Donald McCain/Brian Hughes	27	7	25.93%	-£13.84
Sandy Thomson/Ryan Mania	20	5	25.00%	-£0.09
Rose Dobbin/Craig Nichol	35	5	14.29%	+£14.22
Harriet Graham/Callum Bewley	14	2	14.29%	-£9.73

James Ewart/Brian Hughes	17	2	11.76%	-£7.95

Top trainer/jockey combos by Strike Rate – handicaps

Name of Trainer/Jockey	Qualifiers	Winners	Strike Rate	Profit/Loss to BSP
N W Alexander/Bruce Lynn	12	3	25.00%	+£15.66
Keith Dalgleish/Craig Nichol	13	3	23.08%	+£7.17
Dianne Sayer/Brian Hughes	10	2	20.00%	+£10.30
Donald McCain/William Kennedy	11	2	18.18%	-£1.53
George Bewley/Jonathon Bewley	42	7	16.67%	+£36.99

Top trainer/jockey combos by Profit – non-handicaps

Name of Trainer/Jockey	Qualifiers	Winners	Strike Rate	Profit/Loss to BSP
Lucinda Russell/Derek Fox	46	5	10.87%	+£25.88
Rose Dobbin/Craig Nichol	35	5	14.29%	+£14.22

Top trainer/jockey combos by Profit – handicaps

Name of Trainer/Jockey	Qualifiers	Winners	Strike Rate	Profit/Loss to BSP
George Bewley/Jonathon Bewley	42	7	16.67%	+£36.99
James Ewart/Brian	13	1	7.69%	+£15.81

Hughes				
N W Alexander/Bruce Lynn	12	3	25.00%	+£15.66
Dianne Sayer/Brian Hughes	10	2	20.00%	+£10.30
Keith Dalgleish/Craig Nichol	13	3	23.08%	+£7.17

Profit or Loss backing the unnamed favourite – non-handicaps

Runners	Winners	Strike Rate	Profit/Loss to BSP
429	201	46.85%	+£15.14

Profit or Loss backing the unnamed favourite – handicaps

Runners	Winners	Strike Rate	Profit/Loss to BSP
528	133	25.19%	-£31.25

Profit or loss backing the unnamed second favourite - non-handicaps

Runners	Winners	Strike Rate	Profit/Loss to BSP
423	86	20.33%	-£26.74

Profit or loss backing the unnamed second favourite - handicaps

Runners	Winners	Strike Rate	Profit/Loss to BSP
493	94	19.07%	+£23.70

Profit or Loss backing horses who won last time out- non-handicaps

Runners	Winners	Strike Rate	Profit/Loss to BSP
351	105	29.91%	-£21.04

Profit or Loss backing horses who won last time out - handicaps

Runners	Winners	Strike Rate	Profit/Loss to BSP
526	98	18.63%	-£13.09

Profit or loss backing Top-Weights in handicaps

Runners	Winners	Strike Rate	Profit/Loss to BSP
537	78	14.53%	+£14.49

Most profitable sires – non-handicaps

Sire	Runners	Winners	Strike Rate	Profit/Loss to BSP
Craigsteel	12	3	25.00%	+£252.63
Stowaway	20	4	20.00%	+£77.81
Mahler	13	1	7.69%	+£23.21
Getaway	20	3	15.00%	+£14.36
Oscar	25	4	16.00%	+£9.15

Most profitable sires – handicaps

Alflora	21	4	19.05%	+£33.94
Motivator	12	3	25.00%	+£31.37
Intikhab	13	3	23.08%	+£29.64
Martaline	18	3	16.67%	+£28.47
Fame And Glory	15	5	33.33%	+£22.29

Kempton – Chases

Top jockeys by Strike Rate – non-handicaps

Name Of Jockey	Rides	Winners	Strike Rate	Profit/Loss to BSP
Nico de Boinville	27	14	51.85%	+£4.46
Harry Cobden	28	8	28.57%	+£9.65
Daryl Jacob	27	7	25.93%	-£0.65
Sam Twiston-Davies	34	8	23.53%	-£12.16
Harry Skelton	11	2	18.18%	+£17.45
Paddy Brennan	13	2	15.38%	+£46.72

Top jockeys by Strike Rate – handicaps

Name Of Jockey	Rides	Winners	Strike Rate	Profit/Loss to BSP
Jack Quinlan	17	8	47.06%	+£38.03
James Bowen	14	4	28.57%	+£26.97
Adam Wedge	20	5	25.00%	+£12.63
Paddy Brennan	50	11	22.00%	+£33.60
David Bass	20	4	20.00%	+£14.41

Top jockeys by Profit – non-handicaps

Name Of Jockey	Rides	Winners	Strike Rate	Profit/Loss to BSP
Paddy Brennan	13	2	15.38%	+£46.72
Harry Skelton	11	2	18.18%	+£17.45
Harry Cobden	28	8	28.57%	+£9.65
Nico de Boinville	27	14	51.85%	+£4.46
Daryl Jacob	27	7	25.93%	-£0.65

Top jockeys by Profit – handicaps

Name Of Jockey	Rides	Winners	Strike Rate	Profit/Loss to BSP
Tom Cannon	66	11	16.67%	+£52.71
Jack Quinlan	17	8	47.06%	+£38.03

James Davies	15	3	20.00%	+£34.38
Paddy Brennan	50	11	22.00%	+£33.60
James Bowen	14	4	28.57%	+£26.97

Top trainers by Strike Rate – non-handicaps

Name Of Trainer	Runners	Winners	Strike Rate	Profit/Loss to BSP
Nicky Henderson	71	29	40.85%	-£8.34
Paul Nicholls	102	35	34.31%	+£28.28
Gary Moore	15	3	20.00%	-£2.15
Philip Hobbs	21	4	19.05%	-£2.00
Alan King	27	5	18.52%	-£4.07

Top trainers by Strike Rate – handicaps

Name Of Trainer	Runners	Winners	Strike Rate	Profit/Loss to BSP
Oliver Sherwood	21	5	23.81%	+£22.09
Tom George	85	18	21.18%	+£36.66
Emma Lavelle	44	9	20.45%	+£6.43
Fergal O'Brien	20	4	20.00%	+£5.32
Chris Gordon	57	11	19.30%	+£35.31

Top trainers by Profit – non-handicaps

Name Of Trainer	Runners	Winners	Strike Rate	Profit/Loss to BSP
Colin Tizzard	34	6	17.65%	+£46.84
Paul Nicholls	102	35	34.31%	+£28.28
Dan Skelton	17	3	17.65%	+£14.12

Top trainers by Profit – handicaps

Name Of Trainer	Runners	Winners	Strike Rate	Profit/Loss to BSP
Tom George	85	18	21.18%	+£36.66
Chris Gordon	57	11	19.30%	+£35.31
Ben Pauling	19	3	15.79%	+£34.11
Neil Mulholland	30	4	13.33%	+£31.42
Paul Henderson	29	3	10.34%	+£22.55

Top trainer/jockey combos by Strike Rate – non-handicaps

Name Of Trainer/Jockey	Rides	Winners	Strike Rate	Profit/Loss to BSP
Nicky Henderson/Nico de Boinville	23	12	52.17%	-£0.51
Paul Nicholls/Sam Twiston-Davies	25	8	32.00%	-£3.16
Dan Skelton/Harry Skelton	11	2	18.18%	+£17.45

Top trainer/jockey combos by Strike Rate – handicaps

Name of Trainer/Jockey	Qualifiers	Winners	Strike Rate	Profit/Loss to BSP
Tom George/Paddy Brennan	28	8	28.57%	+£29.80
Kim Bailey/David Bass	11	3	27.27%	+£15.35
Tom George/A P Heskin	15	4	26.67%	+£8.84
Emma Lavelle/Aidan Coleman	13	3	23.08%	+£1.75
Colin Tizzard/Brendan Powell	13	3	23.08%	+£1.79

Top trainer/jockey combos by Profit – non-handicaps

Name Of Trainer/Jockey	Rides	Winners	Strike Rate	Profit/Loss to BSP
Dan Skelton/Harry Skelton	11	2	18.18%	+£17.45
Paul Nicholls/Harry Cobden	28	8	28.57%	+£9.65

Top trainer/jockey combos by Profit – handicaps

Name of Trainer/Jockey	Qualifiers	Winners	Strike Rate	Profit/Loss to BSP
Chris Gordon/Tom Cannon	34	7	20.59%	+£41.22
Tom George/Paddy Brennan	28	8	28.57%	+£29.80
Kim Bailey/David Bass	11	3	27.27%	+£15.35
Venetia Williams/Charlie Deutsch	11	2	18.18%	+£10.52
Dan Skelton/Bridget Andrews	11	1	9.09%	+£9.15

Profit or Loss backing the unnamed favourite – non-handicaps

Runners	Winners	Strike Rate	Profit/Loss to BSP
248	123	49.60%	+£1.35

Profit or Loss backing the unnamed favourite – handicaps

Runners	Winners	Strike Rate	Profit/Loss to BSP
441	128	29.02%	+£40.97

Profit or loss backing the unnamed second favourite - non-handicaps

Runners	Winners	Strike Rate	Profit/Loss to BSP
231	50	21.65%	-£40.23

Profit or loss backing the unnamed second favourite - handicaps

Runners	Winners	Strike Rate	Profit/Loss to BSP

378	64	16.93%	-£51.38

Profit or Loss backing horses who won last time out - non-handicaps

Runners	Winners	Strike Rate	Profit/Loss to BSP
341	89	26.10%	-£7.01

Profit or Loss backing horses who won last time out - handicaps

Runners	Winners	Strike Rate	Profit/Loss to BSP
505	79	15.64%	-£16.94

Profit or loss backing Top-Weights in handicaps

Runners	Winners	Strike Rate	Profit/Loss to BSP
455	73	16.04%	+£41.74

Most profitable sires – non-handicaps

Sire	Runners	Winners	Strike Rate	Profit/Loss to BSP
King's Theatre	30	6	20.00%	+£44.36
Nickname	10	6	60.00%	+£22.07
Flemensfirth	15	2	13.33%	+£14.76
Kapgarde	12	3	25.00%	+£13.17
Beneficial	11	1	9.09%	+£4.46

Most profitable sires – handicaps

Midnight Legend	58	11	18.97%	+£44.46
Winged Love	16	4	25.00%	+£29.83
Court Cave	22	3	13.64%	+£12.06
Mahler	14	5	35.71%	+£11.28
Black Sam Bellamy	11	2	18.18%	+£10.89

Kempton – Hurdles

Top jockeys by Strike Rate – non-handicaps

Name Of Jockey	Rides	Winners	Strike Rate	Profit/Loss to BSP
Nico de Boinville	74	23	31.08%	+£3.04
Bridget Andrews	12	3	25.00%	+£5.53
Daryl Jacob	48	11	22.92%	+£55.03
Tom O'Brien	40	8	20.00%	-£4.10
Nick Scholfield	38	7	18.42%	+£14.42

Top jockeys by Strike Rate – handicaps

Name Of Jockey	Rides	Winners	Strike Rate	Profit/Loss to BSP
Bryony Frost	18	5	27.78%	+£50.80
David Noonan	14	3	21.43%	+£15.17
Jack Quinlan	16	3	18.75%	+£504.71
Michael Nolan	11	2	18.18%	-£1.58
Page Fuller	11	2	18.18%	+£1.46

Top jockeys by Profit – non-handicaps

Name Of Jockey	Rides	Winners	Strike Rate	Profit/Loss to BSP
Daryl Jacob	48	11	22.92%	+£55.03
Joshua Moore	43	3	6.98%	+£41.14
Tom Bellamy	16	2	12.50%	+£20.09
Nick Scholfield	38	7	18.42%	+£14.42
Marc Goldstein	33	1	3.03%	+£8.57

Top jockeys by Profit – handicaps

Name Of Jockey	Rides	Winners	Strike Rate	Profit/Loss to BSP
Jack Quinlan	16	3	18.75%	+£504.71
Tom Cannon	49	7	14.29%	+£55.47
Bryony Frost	18	5	27.78%	+£50.80
Jamie Moore	36	5	13.89%	+£36.77
Tom Bellamy	25	2	8.00%	+£29.40

Top trainers by Strike Rate – non-handicaps

Name Of Trainer	Runners	Winners	Strike Rate	Profit/Loss to BSP

Donald McCain	10	3	30.00%	+£11.97
Nicky Henderson	170	48	28.24%	+£16.30
Nigel Twiston-Davies	24	6	25.00%	+£8.93
Harry Fry	28	7	25.00%	-£8.75
Colin Tizzard	26	6	23.08%	+£6.71

Top trainers by Strike Rate – handicaps

Name Of Trainer	Runners	Winners	Strike Rate	Profit/Loss to BSP
Henry Daly	12	4	33.33%	+£27.06
Ian Williams	17	5	29.41%	+£10.48
Harry Fry	26	6	23.08%	-£3.80
Lucy Wadham	22	5	22.73%	+£11.85
Tom George	10	2	20.00%	+£11.67

Top trainers by Profit – non-handicaps

Name Of Trainer	Runners	Winners	Strike Rate	Profit/Loss to BSP
Michael Madgwick	11	1	9.09%	+£30.57
Neil Mulholland	16	2	12.50%	+£24.62
Nicky Henderson	170	48	28.24%	+£16.30
Tim Vaughan	11	2	18.18%	+£12.17
Donald McCain	10	3	30.00%	+£11.97

Top trainers by Profit – handicaps

Name Of Trainer	Runners	Winners	Strike Rate	Profit/Loss to BSP
Nicky Henderson	122	24	19.67%	+£77.00
Emma Lavelle	32	4	12.50%	+£62.57
Seamus Mullins	20	1	5.00%	+£32.26
Nigel Twiston-Davies	34	4	11.76%	+£28.24
Henry Daly	12	4	33.33%	+£27.06

Top trainer/jockey combos by Strike Rate – non-handicaps

Name of Trainer/Jockey	Qualifiers	Winners	Strike Rate	Profit/Loss to BSP
Paul Nicholls/Nick Scholfield	10	4	40.00%	+£14.99
Nicky Henderson/Nico de Boinville	58	18	31.03%	-£6.59
Nigel Twiston-Davies/Sam Twiston-Davies	15	4	26.67%	-£7.69
Dan Skelton/Bridget Andrews	12	3	25.00%	+£5.53
Chris Gordon/Tom Cannon	13	3	23.08%	+£5.18

Top trainer/jockey combos by Strike Rate – handicaps

Name of Trainer/Jockey	Qualifiers	Winners	Strike Rate	Profit/Loss to BSP
Stuart Edmunds/Ciaran Gethings	10	2	20.00%	+£14.05
Jeremy Scott/Nick Scholfield	11	2	18.18%	+£4.72
Nicky Henderson/Nico de Boinville	37	6	16.22%	+£1.38
Chris Gordon/Tom Cannon	19	3	15.79%	+£33.65
Jonjo O'Neill/Jonjo O'Neill Jr	13	2	15.38%	-£7.34

Top trainer/jockey combos by Profit – non-handicaps

Name of Trainer/Jockey	Qualifiers	Winners	Strike Rate	Profit/Loss to BSP

Gary Moore/Joshua Moore	32	3	9.38%	+£52.14
Alan King/Tom Bellamy	10	2	20.00%	+£26.09
Paul Nicholls/Nick Scholfield	10	4	40.00%	+£14.99
Dan Skelton/Bridget Andrews	12	3	25.00%	+£5.53
Chris Gordon/Tom Cannon	13	3	23.08%	+£5.18

Top trainer/jockey combos by Profit – handicaps

Name of Trainer/Jockey	Qualifiers	Winners	Strike Rate	Profit/Loss to BSP
Chris Gordon/Tom Cannon	19	3	15.79%	+£33.65
Stuart Edmunds/Ciaran Gethings	10	2	20.00%	+£14.05
Jeremy Scott/Nick Scholfield	11	2	18.18%	+£4.72
Gary Moore/Jamie Moore	19	2	10.53%	+£4.61
Nicky Henderson/Nico de Boinville	37	6	16.22%	+£1.38

Profit or Loss backing the unnamed favourite – non-handicaps

Runners	Winners	Strike Rate	Profit/Loss to BSP
442	207	46.83%	+£11.91

Profit or Loss backing the unnamed favourite – handicaps

Runners	Winners	Strike Rate	Profit/Loss to

			BSP
358	90	25.14%	-£15.75

Profit or loss backing the unnamed second favourite - non-handicaps

Runners	Winners	Strike Rate	Profit/Loss to BSP
422	94	22.27%	-£12.04

Profit or loss backing the unnamed second favourite - handicaps

Runners	Winners	Strike Rate	Profit/Loss to BSP
342	66	19.30%	+£32.72

Profit or Loss backing horses who won last time out- non-handicaps

Runners	Winners	Strike Rate	Profit/Loss to BSP
544	134	24.63%	-£40.38

Profit or Loss backing horses who won last time out - handicaps

Runners	Winners	Strike Rate	Profit/Loss to BSP
529	89	16.82%	+£117.22

Profit or loss backing Top-Weights in handicaps

Runners	Winners	Strike Rate	Profit/Loss to BSP
375	47	12.53%	+£54.64

Most profitable sires – non-handicaps

Sire	Runners	Winners	Strike Rate	Profit/Loss to BSP
Canford Cliffs	10	2	20.00%	+£56.11
Definite Article	10	2	20.00%	+£53.18
Fame And Glory	10	5	50.00%	+£21.89
High Chaparral	15	3	20.00%	+£10.15
Dark Angel	14	3	21.43%	+£5.86

Most profitable sires – handicaps

Oscar	50	9	18.00%	+£24.81
Beneficial	30	4	13.33%	+£24.51
Kalanisi	19	3	15.79%	+£21.90
Heron Island	14	3	21.43%	+£14.50
Court Cave	10	1	10.00%	+£13.00

Leicester - Chases

Top jockeys by Strike Rate – non-handicaps

Name Of Jockey	Rides	Winners	Strike Rate	Profit/Loss to BSP
Sam Twiston-Davies	14	6	42.86%	-£3.75

Top jockeys by Strike Rate – handicaps

Name Of Jockey	Rides	Winners	Strike Rate	Profit/Loss to BSP
A P Heskin	15	6	40.00%	+£8.69
Bryony Frost	13	4	30.77%	+£50.06
Brian Hughes	11	3	27.27%	-£3.69
Paddy Brennan	73	17	23.29%	+£27.65
James Bowen	13	3	23.08%	+£2.72

Top jockeys by Profit – handicaps

Name Of Jockey	Rides	Winners	Strike Rate	Profit/Loss to BSP
Bryony Frost	13	4	30.77%	+£50.06
Harry Bannister	14	2	14.29%	+£44.54
Lee Edwards	37	6	16.22%	+£27.89
Paddy Brennan	73	17	23.29%	+£27.65
Sam Twiston-Davies	66	13	19.70%	+£23.51

Top trainers by Strike Rate – non-handicaps

Name Of Trainer	Runners	Winners	Strike Rate	Profit/Loss to BSP
Dan Skelton	12	6	50.00%	+£10.41
Paul Nicholls	10	4	40.00%	-£4.57
Nigel Twiston-Davies	13	4	30.77%	-£5.15

Top trainers by Strike Rate – handicaps

Name Of Trainer	Runners	Winners	Strike Rate	Profit/Loss to BSP
Andrew Martin	10	4	40.00%	+£11.25
John Groucott	15	5	33.33%	+£16.57
David Pipe	16	5	31.25%	+£12.87
Laura Morgan	13	4	30.77%	+£1.73
Philip Hobbs	14	4	28.57%	+£1.92

Top trainers by Profit – non-handicaps

Name Of Trainer	Runners	Winners	Strike Rate	Profit/Loss to BSP
Dan Skelton	12	6	50.00%	+£10.41

Top trainers by Profit – handicaps

Name Of Trainer	Runners	Winners	Strike Rate	Profit/Loss to BSP
Tony Carroll	35	5	14.29%	+£76.32
Nigel Twiston-Davies	66	13	19.70%	+£45.19
Fergal O'Brien	47	9	19.15%	+£38.80
Tom George	74	21	28.38%	+£35.88
Dr Richard Newland	12	2	16.67%	+£20.77

Top trainer/jockey combos by Strike Rate – handicaps

Name of Trainer/Jockey	Qualifiers	Winners	Strike Rate	Profit/Loss to BSP
Tom George/A P Heskin	13	5	38.46%	+£7.68
Evan Williams/Adam Wedge	10	3	30.00%	+£6.14
Venetia Williams/Charlie Deutsch	10	3	30.00%	+£5.25
Tom George/Paddy Brennan	37	10	27.03%	+£3.91
Dan Skelton/Harry	12	3	25.00%	+£5.98

Skelton				

Top trainer/jockey combos by Profit – handicaps

Name of Trainer/Jockey	Qualifiers	Winners	Strike Rate	Profit/Loss to BSP
Tony Carroll/Lee Edwards	24	4	16.67%	+£31.84
Fergal O'Brien/Paddy Brennan	26	5	19.23%	+£27.86
Nigel Twiston-Davies/Sam Twiston-Davies	48	9	18.75%	+£25.61
John Cornwall/Ben Poste	14	1	7.14%	+£23.26
Tom George/A P Heskin	13	5	38.46%	+£7.68

Profit or Loss backing the unnamed favourite – non-handicaps

Runners	Winners	Strike Rate	Profit/Loss to BSP
255	122	47.84%	+£21.32

Profit or Loss backing the unnamed favourite – handicaps

Runners	Winners	Strike Rate	Profit/Loss to BSP
457	135	29.54%	-£26.89

Profit or loss backing the unnamed second favourite - non-handicaps

Runners	Winners	Strike Rate	Profit/Loss to BSP
238	51	21.43%	-£34.72

Profit or loss backing the unnamed second favourite - handicaps

Runners	Winners	Strike Rate	Profit/Loss to BSP
428	99	23.13%	+£41.90

Profit or Loss backing horses who won last time out - non-handicaps

Runners	Winners	Strike Rate	Profit/Loss to BSP
119	35	29.41%	+£43.84

Profit or Loss backing horses who won last time out - handicaps

Runners	Winners	Strike Rate	Profit/Loss to BSP
348	86	24.71%	+£40.69

Profit or loss backing Top-Weights in handicaps

Runners	Winners	Strike Rate	Profit/Loss to BSP
480	85	17.71%	-£44.21

Most profitable sires – non-handicaps

Sire	Runners	Winners	Strike Rate	Profit/Loss to BSP
Milan	11	4	36.36%	+£3.25
Court Cave	10	3	30.00%	+£3.13

Most profitable sires – handicaps

Sire	Runners	Winners	Strike Rate	Profit/Loss to BSP
Mahler	18	6	33.33%	+£53.18
Tikkanen	12	4	33.33%	+£28.95
Exit To Nowhere	10	1	10.00%	+£27.26
Westerner	21	5	23.81%	+£24.18
Flemensfirth	25	5	20.00%	+£20.32

Leicester – Hurdles

Top jockeys by Strike Rate – non-handicaps

Name Of Jockey	Rides	Winners	Strike Rate	Profit/Loss to BSP
Tom Scudamore	22	7	31.82%	+£11.21
Aidan Coleman	24	7	29.17%	+£4.09

Harry Skelton	29	8	27.59%	-£4.19
Daryl Jacob	11	3	27.27%	+£35.85
Sam Twiston-Davies	35	7	20.00%	-£16.60

Top jockeys by Strike Rate – handicaps

Name Of Jockey	Rides	Winners	Strike Rate	Profit/Loss to BSP
Sam Twiston-Davies	25	6	24.00%	+£18.74
Harry Skelton	17	4	23.53%	+£12.09
Tom O'Brien	10	2	20.00%	-£4.88
Jamie Moore	12	2	16.67%	-£6.04
Kielan Woods	13	2	15.38%	+£7.13

Top jockeys by Profit – non-handicaps

Name Of Jockey	Rides	Winners	Strike Rate	Profit/Loss to BSP
Daryl Jacob	11	3	27.27%	+£35.85
Tom Scudamore	22	7	31.82%	+£11.21
Aidan Coleman	24	7	29.17%	+£4.09
James Davies	18	1	5.56%	+£1.77

Top jockeys by Profit – handicaps

Name Of Jockey	Rides	Winners	Strike Rate	Profit/Loss to BSP
Ciaran Gethings	17	2	11.76%	+£22.73
Sam Twiston-Davies	25	6	24.00%	+£18.74
Charlie Hammond	13	1	7.69%	+£14.46
Harry Skelton	17	4	23.53%	+£12.09
Daniel Hiskett	10	1	10.00%	+£11.19

Top trainers by Strike Rate – non-handicaps

Name Of Trainer	Runners	Winners	Strike Rate	Profit/Loss to BSP
David Pipe	22	11	50.00%	+£23.29
Olly Murphy	17	8	47.06%	+£57.18

Philip Hobbs	13	4	30.77%	-£0.65
Alan King	11	3	27.27%	+£8.46
Stuart Edmunds	12	3	25.00%	+£5.53

Top trainers by Strike Rate – handicaps

Name Of Trainer	Runners	Winners	Strike Rate	Profit/Loss to BSP
Philip Hobbs	10	5	50.00%	+£9.23%
Ali Stronge	11	4	36.36%	+£19.10
Nigel Twiston-Davies	23	7	30.43%	+£27.00
Olly Murphy	10	3	30.00%	+£7.82
Tom Symonds	10	3	30.00%	+£18.23

Top trainers by Profit – non-handicaps

Name Of Trainer	Runners	Winners	Strike Rate	Profit/Loss to BSP
Olly Murphy	17	8	47.06%	+£57.18
Henry Daly	13	2	15.38%	+£50.29
Paul Webber	19	1	5.26%	+£29.61
Ben Pauling	16	3	18.75%	+£25.80
David Pipe	22	11	50.00%	+£23.29

Top trainers by Profit – handicaps

Name Of Trainer	Runners	Winners	Strike Rate	Profit/Loss to BSP
Sophie Leech	11	2	18.18%	+£28.73
Nigel Twiston-Davies	23	7	30.43%	+£27.00
Ali Stronge	11	4	36.36%	+£19.10
Tom Symonds	10	3	30.00%	+£18.23
Henry Oliver	19	3	15.79%	+£17.80

Top trainer/jockey combos by Strike Rate – non-handicaps

Name of Trainer/Jockey	Qualifiers	Winners	Strike Rate	Profit/Loss to BSP
David Pipe/Tom Scudamore	12	6	50.00%	+£16.74
Dan	26	7	26.92%	-£6.19

Skelton/Harry Skelton				
Kim Bailey/David Bass	10	2	20.00%	+£5.05
Nigel Twiston-Davies/Sam Twiston-Davies	20	4	20.00%	-£11.35
Neil King/Trevor Whelan	11	2	18.18%	-£0.14

Top trainer/jockey combos by Strike Rate – handicaps

Name of Trainer/Jockey	Qualifiers	Winners	Strike Rate	Profit/Loss to BSP
Nigel Twiston-Davies/Sam Twiston-Davies	15	5	33.33%	+£22.36
Dan Skelton/Harry Skelton	14	4	28.57%	+£15.09
David Pipe/Tom Scudamore	12	2	16.67%	-£4.27
Kim Bailey/David Bass	11	1	9.09%	-£5.79
Tony Carroll/Lee Edwards	19	1	5.26%	-£9.77

Top trainer/jockey combos by Profit – non-handicaps

Name of Trainer/Jockey	Qualifiers	Winners	Strike Rate	Profit/Loss to BSP
David Pipe/Tom Scudamore	12	6	50.00%	+£16.74
Kim Bailey/David Bass	10	2	20.00%	+£5.05

Top trainer/jockey combos by Profit – handicaps

Name of Trainer/Jockey	Qualifiers	Winners	Strike Rate	Profit/Loss to BSP
Nigel Twiston-	15	5	33.33%	+£22.36

Davies/Sam Twiston-Davies				
Dan Skelton/Harry Skelton	14	4	28.57%	+£15.09

Profit or Loss backing the unnamed favourite – non-handicaps

Runners	Winners	Strike Rate	Profit/Loss to BSP
282	124	43.97%	+£3.36

Profit or Loss backing the unnamed favourite – handicaps

Runners	Winners	Strike Rate	Profit/Loss to BSP
215	66	30.70%	+£18.38

Profit or loss backing the unnamed second favourite - non-handicaps

Runners	Winners	Strike Rate	Profit/Loss to BSP
288	60	20.83%	-£38.83

Profit or loss backing the unnamed second favourite - handicaps

Runners	Winners	Strike Rate	Profit/Loss to BSP
195	31	15.90%	-£30.72

Profit or Loss backing horses who won last time out- non-handicaps

Runners	Winners	Strike Rate	Profit/Loss to BSP
201	52	25.87%	-£13.75

Profit or Loss backing horses who won last time out - handicaps

Runners	Winners	Strike Rate	Profit/Loss to BSP
183	34	18.58%	-£40.45

Profit or loss backing Top-Weights in handicaps

Runners	Winners	Strike Rate	Profit/Loss to BSP
219	33	15.07%	-£47.25

Most profitable sires – non-handicaps

Sire	Runners	Winners	Strike Rate	Profit/Loss to BSP
Oscar	28	6	21.43%	+£32.42
Kayf Tara	25	4	16.00%	+£32.27
Flemensfirth	21	4	19.05%	+£21.89
Westerner	14	3	21.43%	+£8.28
Black Sam Bellamy	10	1	10.00%	+£5.11

Most profitable sires – handicaps

Kayf Tara	27	7	25.93%	+£24.78
Midnight Legend	17	2	11.76%	+£15.68
Flemensfirth	13	3	23.08%	+£2.53

Lingfield - Chases

Top jockeys by Strike Rate – non-handicaps

Name Of Jockey	Rides	Winners	Strike Rate	Profit/Loss to BSP
Jamie Moore	10	2	20.00%	+£6.44

Top jockeys by Strike Rate – handicaps

Name Of Jockey	Rides	Winners	Strike Rate	Profit/Loss to BSP
Joshua Moore	37	12	32.43%	+£48.75
Charlie Deutsch	31	8	25.81%	+£2.55
Jamie Moore	45	10	22.22%	+£3.31
Tom O'Brien	15	3	20.00%	-£0.91
Sam Twiston-Davies	10	2	20.00%	-£2.61

Top jockeys by Profit – non-handicaps

Name Of Jockey	Rides	Winners	Strike Rate	Profit/Loss to BSP
Jamie Moore	10	2	20.00%	+£6.44

Top jockeys by Profit – handicaps

Name Of Jockey	Rides	Winners	Strike Rate	Profit/Loss to BSP
Joshua Moore	37	12	32.43%	+£48.76
Harry Cobden	11	2	18.18%	+£18.73
Jamie Bargary	11	2	18.18%	+£16.87
James Davies	14	2	14.29%	+£10.43
Rex Dingle	12	2	16.67%	+£6.02

Top trainers by Strike Rate – non-handicaps

Name Of Trainer	Runners	Winners	Strike Rate	Profit/Loss to BSP
Gary Moore	11	2	18.18%	+£5.44

Top trainers by Strike Rate – handicaps

Name Of Trainer	Runners	Winners	Strike Rate	Profit/Loss to BSP
Dan Skelton	13	5	38.46%	+£24.82
Evan Williams	10	3	30.00%	+£4.55
Gary Moore	76	21	27.63%	+£49.77
Venetia Williams	56	12	21.43%	-£5.77
David Pipe	10	2	20.00%	+£1.06

Top trainers by Profit – non-handicaps

Name Of Trainer	Runners	Winners	Strike Rate	Profit/Loss to BSP
Gary Moore	11	2	18.18%	+£5.44

Top trainers by Profit – handicaps

Name Of Trainer	Runners	Winners	Strike Rate	Profit/Loss to BSP
Gary Moore	76	21	27.63%	+£49.77
Seamus Mullins	37	6	16.22%	+£34.39
Mark Gillard	20	3	15.00%	+£32.91
Dan Skelton	13	5	38.46%	+£24.82
Nigel Twiston-Davies	25	4	16.00%	+£19.10

Top trainer/jockey combos by Strike Rate – handicaps

Name of Trainer/Jockey	Qualifiers	Winners	Strike Rate	Profit/Loss to BSP
Venetia Williams/Aidan Coleman	13	4	30.77%	+£3.47
Venetia Williams/Charlie Deutsch	23	7	30.43%	+£6.73
Gary Moore/Jamie Moore	33	10	30.30%	+£15.31
Gary Moore/Joshua Moore	33	10	30.30%	+£32.68

Chris Gordon/Tom Cannon	22	4	18.18%	+£0.18

Top trainer/jockey combos by Profit – handicaps

Name of Trainer/Jockey	Qualifiers	Winners	Strike Rate	Profit/Loss to BSP
Gary Moore/Joshua Moore	33	10	30.30%	+£32.68
Gary Moore/Jamie Moore	33	10	30.30%	+£15.31
Venetia Williams/Charlie Deutsch	23	7	30.43%	+£6.73
Venetia Williams/Aidan Coleman	13	4	30.77%	+£3.47
Chris Gordon/Tom Cannon	22	4	18.18%	+£0.18

Profit or Loss backing the unnamed favourite – non-handicaps

Runners	Winners	Strike Rate	Profit/Loss to BSP
57	29	50.88%	+£3.02

Profit or Loss backing the unnamed favourite – handicaps

Runners	Winners	Strike Rate	Profit/Loss to BSP
262	83	31.68%	-£2.08

Profit or loss backing the unnamed second favourite - non-handicaps

Runners	Winners	Strike Rate	Profit/Loss to BSP
60	13	21.67%	-£4.37

Profit or loss backing the unnamed second favourite - handicaps

Runners	Winners	Strike Rate	Profit/Loss to BSP
246	38	15.45%	-£71.86

Profit or Loss backing horses who won last time out - non-handicaps

Runners	Winners	Strike Rate	Profit/Loss to BSP
41	11	26.83%	+£4.25

Profit or Loss backing horses who won last time out - handicaps

Runners	Winners	Strike Rate	Profit/Loss to BSP
201	36	17.91%	-£38.06

Profit or loss backing Top-Weights in handicaps

Runners	Winners	Strike Rate	Profit/Loss to BSP
277	53	19.13%	+£119.48

Most profitable sires – handicaps

King's Theatre	30	8	26.67%	+£39.30
Dr Massini	11	4	36.36%	+£38.20
Milan	21	3	14.29%	+£35.18
Flemensfirth	30	8	26.67%	+£18.29
Definite Article	15	3	20.00%	+£3.18

Lingfield – Hurdles

Top jockeys by Strike Rate – non-handicaps

Name Of Jockey	Rides	Winners	Strike Rate	Profit/Loss to BSP
Gavin Sheehan	23	10	43.48%	+£14.35
Aidan Coleman	23	8	34.78%	+£162.85
Tom O'Brien	11	3	27.27%	-£0.45
Paddy Brennan	12	3	25.00%	+£25.05
Harry Skelton	12	3	25.00%	-£2.99

Top jockeys by Strike Rate – handicaps

Name Of Jockey	Rides	Winners	Strike Rate	Profit/Loss to BSP
Gavin Sheehan	11	4	36.36%	+£11.95
Paddy Brennan	16	3	18.75%	-£0.92
Sam Twiston-Davies	11	2	18.18%	+£7.54
Tom Scudamore	24	4	16.67%	-£5.57
Jamie Moore	34	5	14.71%	+£22.06

Top jockeys by Profit – non-handicaps

Name Of Jockey	Rides	Winners	Strike Rate	Profit/Loss to BSP
Aidan Coleman	23	8	34.78%	+£162.85
James Davies	12	1	8.33%	+£125.27
Paddy Brennan	12	3	25.00%	+£25.05
Gavin Sheehan	23	10	43.48%	+£14.35
Tom O'Brien	11	3	27.27%	-£0.45

Top jockeys by Profit – handicaps

Name Of Jockey	Rides	Winners	Strike Rate	Profit/Loss to BSP
Jamie Moore	34	5	14.71%	+£22.06
Gavin Sheehan	11	4	36.36%	+£11.95
Sam Twiston-Davies	11	2	18.18%	+£7.54
Tom O'Brien	12	1	8.33%	+£1.40
Adam Wedge	10	1	10.00%	+£1.17

Top trainers by Strike Rate – non-handicaps

Name Of Trainer	Runners	Winners	Strike Rate	Profit/Loss to BSP
Lucy Wadham	14	5	35.71%	+£81.43
Warren Greatrex	24	7	29.17%	+£18.46
Jamie Snowden	21	6	28.57%	+£6.78
Nicky Henderson	11	3	27.27%	-£6.31
Emma Lavelle	13	3	23.08%	+£14.74

Top trainers by Strike Rate – handicaps

Name Of Trainer	Runners	Winners	Strike Rate	Profit/Loss to BSP
Marin Keighley	12	4	33.33%	+£1.18
Dan Skelton	13	3	23.08%	+£6.08
Colin Tizzard	10	2	20.00%	-£1.48
David Pipe	21	4	19.05%	+£1.88
Seamus Mullins	23	4	17.39%	+£10.74

Top trainers by Profit – non-handicaps

Name Of Trainer	Runners	Winners	Strike Rate	Profit/Loss to BSP
Richard Rowe	13	1	7.69%	+£124.27
Venetia Williams	21	3	14.29%	+£120.69
Lucy Wadham	14	5	35.71%	+£81.43
Seamus Mullins	22	3	13.64%	+£38.43
Neil Mulholland	12	1	8.33%	+£30.46

Top trainers by Profit – handicaps

Name Of Trainer	Runners	Winners	Strike Rate	Profit/Loss to BSP
Seamus Mullins	23	4	17.39%	+£10.74
Dan Skelton	13	3	23.08%	+£6.08
Gary Moore	68	8	11.76%	+£3.87
David Pipe	21	4	19.05%	+£1.88
Paul Henderson	12	1	8.33%	+£1.40

Top trainer/jockey combos by Strike Rate – non-handicaps

Name of Trainer/Jockey	Qualifiers	Winners	Strike Rate	Profit/Loss to BSP
Warren Greatrex/Gavin Sheehan	14	5	35.71%	-£0.97
Dan Skelton/Harry Skelton	12	3	25.00%	-£2.99
Chris Gordon/Tom	11	2	18.18%	-£4.37

Cannon				
Gary Moore/Joshua Moore	26	3	11.54%	-£2.26
Gary Moore/Jamie Moore	29	3	10.34%	-£15.24

Top trainer/jockey combos by Strike Rate – handicaps

Name of Trainer/Jockey	Qualifiers	Winners	Strike Rate	Profit/Loss to BSP
Gary Moore/Jamie Moore	26	5	19.23%	+£30.06
Chris Gordon/Tom Cannon	23	4	17.39%	-£4.75
David Pipe/Tom Scudamore	15	2	13.33%	-£5.54
Gary Moore/Joshua Moore	21	2	9.52%	-£11.48

Top trainer/jockey combos by Profit – handicaps

Name of Trainer/Jockey	Qualifiers	Winners	Strike Rate	Profit/Loss to BSP
Gary Moore/Jamie Moore	26	5	19.23%	+£30.06

Profit or Loss backing the unnamed favourite – non-handicaps

Runners	Winners	Strike Rate	Profit/Loss to BSP
175	74	42.29%	-£16.07

Profit or Loss backing the unnamed favourite – handicaps

Runners	Winners	Strike Rate	Profit/Loss to BSP
170	50	29.41%	+£0.33

Profit or loss backing the unnamed second favourite - non-handicaps

Runners	Winners	Strike Rate	Profit/Loss to BSP
165	33	20.00%	-£18.28

Profit or loss backing the unnamed second favourite - handicaps

Runners	Winners	Strike Rate	Profit/Loss to BSP
155	32	20.65%	+£7.83

Profit or Loss backing horses who won last time out- non-handicaps

Runners	Winners	Strike Rate	Profit/Loss to BSP
128	34	26.56%	-£21.39

Profit or Loss backing horses who won last time out - handicaps

Runners	Winners	Strike Rate	Profit/Loss to BSP
132	26	19.70%	+£2.10

Profit or loss backing Top-Weights in handicaps

Runners	Winners	Strike Rate	Profit/Loss to BSP
185	30	16.22%	+£14.12

Most profitable sires – non-handicaps

Sire	Runners	Winners	Strike Rate	Profit/Loss to BSP
Stowaway	13	5	38.46%	+£107.91
Midnight Legend	13	1	7.69%	+£29.46
Kayf Tara	22	4	18.18%	+£10.15
Westerner	22	7	31.82%	+£5.15
Milan	22	7	31.82%	+£1.71

Most profitable sires – handicaps

Oscar	19	5	26.32%	+£6.03
Midnight Legend	15	3	20.00%	+£4.61
Flemensfirth	24	4	16.67%	+£0.59
Presenting	12	2	16.67%	+£0.57

Ludlow - Chases

Top jockeys by Strike Rate – non-handicaps

Name Of Jockey	Rides	Winners	Strike Rate	Profit/Loss to BSP
Tommie M O'Brien	10	3	30.00%	+£24.23
David Maxwell	13	3	23.08%	-£5.09
Alex Edwards	15	3	20.00%	+£16.14
Sam Twiston-Davies	12	2	16.67%	-£8.06

Top jockeys by Strike Rate – handicaps

Name Of Jockey	Rides	Winners	Strike Rate	Profit/Loss to BSP
Alan Johns	15	6	40.00%	+£41.19
Paddy Brennan	76	28	36.84%	+£35.30
James Bowen	18	5	27.78%	+£17.13
Harry Bannister	13	3	23.08%	+£16.17
Stan Sheppard	22	5	22.73%	+£8.06

Top jockeys by Profit – non-handicaps

Name Of Jockey	Rides	Winners	Strike Rate	Profit/Loss to BSP
Tommie M O'Brien	10	3	30.00%	+£24.23
Alex Edwards	15	3	20.00%	+£16.14

Top jockeys by Profit – handicaps

Name Of Jockey	Rides	Winners	Strike Rate	Profit/Loss to BSP
Miss Tabitha Worsley	11	2	18.18%	+£42.35
Alan Johns	15	6	40.00%	+£41.19
Paddy Brennan	76	28	36.84%	+£35.30
Robert Dunne	26	3	11.54%	+£33.53
Kielan Woods	31	6	19.35%	+£27.56

Top trainers by Strike Rate – non-handicaps

Name Of Trainer	Runners	Winners	Strike Rate	Profit/Loss to BSP
Philip Hobbs	22	8	36.36%	+£5.21
Paul Nicholls	15	5	33.33%	-£1.39
Nicky Henderson	15	4	26.67%	-£6.20
Evan Williams	18	4	22.22%	-£5.73
Venetia Williams	10	1	10.00%	-£6.91

Top trainers by Strike Rate – handicaps

Name Of Trainer	Runners	Winners	Strike Rate	Profit/Loss to BSP
Alan King	19	6	31.58%	+£1.94
Martin Keighley	21	6	28.57%	+£37.51
Gary Moore	11	3	27.27%	+£6.76
Martin Bosley	11	3	27.27%	+£10.06
Kerry Lee	24	6	25.00%	+£13.97

Top trainers by Profit – non-handicaps

Name Of Trainer	Runners	Winners	Strike Rate	Profit/Loss to BSP
Philip Hobbs	22	8	36.36%	+£5.21

Top trainers by Profit – handicaps

Name Of Trainer	Runners	Winners	Strike Rate	Profit/Loss to BSP
John Groucott	36	9	25.00%	+£47.57
Tim Vaughan	36	9	25.00%	+£44.95
Martin Keighley	21	6	28.57%	+£37.51
Venetia Williams	114	23	20.18%	+£20.16
Tom George	104	25	24.04%	+£20.08

Top trainer/jockey combos by Strike Rate – handicaps

Name of Trainer/Jockey	Qualifiers	Winners	Strike Rate	Profit/Loss to BSP
Tom	38	16	42.11%	+£31.07

George/Paddy Brennan				
Tim Vaughan/Alan Johns	13	5	38.46%	+£31.89
Fergal O'Brien/Paddy Brennan	27	10	37.04%	+£7.38
Paul Nicholls/Harry Cobden	19	6	31.58%	+£0.19
Philip Hobbs/Michael Nolan	10	3	30.00%	+£11.72

Top trainer/jockey combos by Profit – handicaps

Name of Trainer/Jockey	Qualifiers	Winners	Strike Rate	Profit/Loss to BSP
Tim Vaughan/Alan Johns	13	5	38.46%	+£31.89
Tom George/Paddy Brennan	38	16	42.11%	+£31.07
Dr Richard Newland/Sam Twiston-Davies	10	2	20.00%	+£12.19
Philip Hobbs/Michael Nolan	10	3	30.00%	+£11.72
Alex Hales/Kielan Woods	10	2	20.00%	+£11.37

Profit or Loss backing the unnamed favourite – non-handicaps

Runners	Winners	Strike Rate	Profit/Loss to BSP
285	129	45.26%	+£16.60

Profit or Loss backing the unnamed favourite – handicaps

Runners	Winners	Strike Rate	Profit/Loss to BSP
567	188	33.16%	+£63.81

Profit or loss backing the unnamed second favourite - non-handicaps

Runners	Winners	Strike Rate	Profit/Loss to BSP
279	67	24.01%	+£16.35

Profit or loss backing the unnamed second favourite - handicaps

Runners	Winners	Strike Rate	Profit/Loss to BSP
546	100	18.32%	-£26.51

Profit or Loss backing horses who won last time out - non-handicaps

Runners	Winners	Strike Rate	Profit/Loss to BSP
163	43	26.38%	-£1.96

Profit or Loss backing horses who won last time out - handicaps

Runners	Winners	Strike Rate	Profit/Loss to BSP
490	104	21.22%	+£16.84

Profit or loss backing Top-Weights in handicaps

Runners	Winners	Strike Rate	Profit/Loss to BSP
598	91	15.22%	+£11.07

Most profitable sires – non-handicaps

Sire	Runners	Winners	Strike Rate	Profit/Loss to BSP
Oscar	20	6	30.00%	+£81.09
Westerner	17	6	35.29%	+£13.00
Galileo	10	2	20.00%	+£8.42
Mahler	10	1	10.00%	+£2.72

Most profitable sires – handicaps

Kayf Tara	68	15	22.06%	+£42.13
Bollin Eric	13	2	15.38%	+£34.18
Overbury	20	7	35.00%	+£24.88
Kapgarde	20	7	35.00%	+£24.88
Brier Creek	19	4	21.05%	+£19.70

Ludlow – Hurdles

Top jockeys by Strike Rate – non-handicaps

Name Of Jockey	Rides	Winners	Strike Rate	Profit/Loss to BSP
Nico de Boinville	48	14	29.17%	-£5.01
Tom Cannon	18	5	27.78%	-£8.82
Harry Skelton	72	20	27.78%	+£3.14
David Bass	67	17	25.37%	+£212.49
Harry Cobden	20	4	20.00%	-£10.84

Top jockeys by Strike Rate – handicaps

Name Of Jockey	Rides	Winners	Strike Rate	Profit/Loss to BSP
Robert Dunne	17	6	35.29%	+£40.01
Tom Scudamore	20	7	35.00%	+£55.13
Jonjo O'Neill Jr	23	8	34.78%	+£25.64
Ben Jones	20	6	30.00%	+£17.48
Matt Griffiths	11	3	27.27%	+£13.51

Top jockeys by Profit – non-handicaps

Name Of Jockey	Rides	Winners	Strike Rate	Profit/Loss to BSP
Tom Scudamore	27	4	14.81%	+£8.68
Brendan Powell	36	1	2.78%	+£3.24
Harry Skelton	72	20	27.78%	+£3.14

Top jockeys by Profit – handicaps

Name Of Jockey	Rides	Winners	Strike Rate	Profit/Loss to BSP

Tom Scudamore	20	7	35.00%	+£55.13
Robert Dunne	17	6	35.29%	+£40.01
Tom O'Brien	46	9	19.57%	+£26.03
Jonjo O'Neill Jr	23	8	34.78%	+£25.64
Nico de Boinville	22	3	13.64%	+£19.96

Top trainers by Strike Rate – non-handicaps

Name Of Trainer	Runners	Winners	Strike Rate	Profit/Loss to BSP
Nicky Henderson	99	30	30.30%	-£3.96
Colin Tizzard	10	3	30.00%	-£3.45
Harry Fry	14	4	28.57%	+£1.52
Olly Murphy	22	6	27.27%	-£8.49
Dan Skelton	86	21	24.42%	-£6.86

Top trainers by Strike Rate – handicaps

Name Of Trainer	Runners	Winners	Strike Rate	Profit/Loss to BSP
Tom Lacey	12	5	41.67%	+£9.43
Philip Hobbs	45	13	28.89%	+£12.52
Paul Nicholls	15	4	26.67%	-£0.60
Jeremy Scott	28	7	25.00%	+£16.59
Tom Symonds	20	5	25.00%	+£12.37

Top trainers by Profit – non-handicaps

Name Of Trainer	Runners	Winners	Strike Rate	Profit/Loss to BSP
Alastair Ralph	49	5	10.20%	+£96.51
Neil Mulholland	17	4	23.53%	+£59.32
Nigel Hawke	20	1	5.00%	+£48.62
Kim Bailey	69	16	23.19%	+£35.11
Harry Whittington	16	3	18.75%	+£28.63

Top trainers by Profit – handicaps

Name Of Trainer	Runners	Winners	Strike Rate	Profit/Loss to BSP
David Pipe	33	5	15.15%	+£36.15

Colin Tizzard	14	3	21.43%	+£23.27
John Flint	15	3	20.00%	+£22.85
Alastair Ralph	33	7	21.21%	+£20.45
Alan King	29	6	20.69%	+£19.29

Top trainer/jockey combos by Strike Rate – non-handicaps

Name of Trainer/Jockey	Qualifiers	Winners	Strike Rate	Profit/Loss to BSP
Kim Bailey/David Bass	37	13	35.14%	+£27.07
Nicky Henderson/Nico de Boinville	34	10	29.41%	-£14.11
Dan Skelton/Harry Skelton	65	19	29.23%	+£8.95
David Pipe/Tom Scudamore	11	3	27.27%	-£3.37
Ben Pauling/Nico de Boinville	11	3	27.27%	+£3.27

Top trainer/jockey combos by Strike Rate – handicaps

Name of Trainer/Jockey	Qualifiers	Winners	Strike Rate	Profit/Loss to BSP
David Pipe/Tom Scudamore	12	4	33.33%	+£38.12
Henry Daly/Tom O'Brien	12	4	33.33%	+£21.88
Venetia Williams/Lucy Turner	11	3	27.27%	+£4.05
Jonjo O'Neill/Jonjo O'Neill Jr	15	4	26.67%	+£7.46
Dan Skelton/Harry Skelton	30	8	26.67%	-£3.61

Top trainer/jockey combos by Profit – non-handicaps

Name of Trainer/Jockey	Qualifiers	Winners	Strike Rate	Profit/Loss to BSP
Alastair Ralph/Lee Edwards	16	2	12.50%	+£49.31
Philip Hobbs/Tom O'Brien	16	3	18.75%	+£27.56
Kim Bailey/David Bass	37	13	35.14%	+£27.07
Tom George/ Jonathan Burke	13	2	15.38%	+£20.09
Dan Skelton/Harry Skelton	65	19	29.23%	+£8.95

Top trainer/jockey combos by Profit – handicaps

Name of Trainer/Jockey	Qualifiers	Winners	Strike Rate	Profit/Loss to BSP
David Pipe/Tom Scudamore	12	4	33.33%	+£38.12
Henry Daly/Tom O'Brien	12	4	33.33%	+£21.88
Richard Phillips/Daniel Hiskett	13	3	23.08%	+£14.88
Fergal O'Brien/Paddy Brennan	18	4	22.22%	+£10.74
Jonjo O'Neill/Jonjo O'Neill jr	15	4	26.67%	+£7.46

Profit or Loss backing the unnamed favourite – non-handicaps

Runners	Winners	Strike Rate	Profit/Loss to BSP
626	259	41.37%	-£50.15

Profit or Loss backing the unnamed favourite – handicaps

Runners	Winners	Strike Rate	Profit/Loss to BSP

505	148	29.31%	-£8.65

Profit or loss backing the unnamed second favourite - non-handicaps

Runners	Winners	Strike Rate	Profit/Loss to BSP
601	128	21.30%	-£19.23

Profit or loss backing the unnamed second favourite - handicaps

Runners	Winners	Strike Rate	Profit/Loss to BSP
471	96	20.38%	+£32.19

Profit or Loss backing horses who won last time out- non-handicaps

Runners	Winners	Strike Rate	Profit/Loss to BSP
325	103	31.69%	+£13.54

Profit or Loss backing horses who won last time out - handicaps

Runners	Winners	Strike Rate	Profit/Loss to BSP
467	93	19.91%	-£5.78

Profit or loss backing Top-Weights in handicaps

Runners	Winners	Strike Rate	Profit/Loss to BSP
528	65	12.31%	-£129.85

Most profitable sires – non-handicaps

Sire	Runners	Winners	Strike Rate	Profit/Loss to BSP
Authorized	17	4	23.53%	+£86.38
King's Theatre	35	9	25.71%	+£51.86
Fame And Glory	18	5	27.78%	+£27.57
Sulamani	28	3	10.71%	+£25.73
Definite Article	12	3	25.00%	+£23.13

Most profitable sires – handicaps

Sadler's Wells	10	2	20.00%	+£77.81
Midnight Legend	70	10	14.29%	+£49.55
Mahler	13	5	38.46%	+£49.10
Blueprint	10	3	30.00%	+£16.82
Robin Des Champs	20	2	10.00%	+£15.80

Market Rasen - Chases

Top jockeys by Strike Rate – non-handicaps

Name Of Jockey	Rides	Winners	Strike Rate	Profit/Loss to BSP
Tom Scudamore	10	5	50.00%	+£7.15
Harry Skelton	12	5	41.67%	+£2.71
Brian Hughes	14	3	21.43%	+£10.51
Aidan Coleman	10	2	20.00%	-£2.98
Sam Twiston-Davies	10	2	20.00%	-£3.93

Top jockeys by Strike Rate – handicaps

Name Of Jockey	Rides	Winners	Strike Rate	Profit/Loss to BSP
David Bass	35	11	31.43%	+£28.31
Bridget Andrews	16	5	31.25%	+£19.27
A P Heskin	14	4	28.57%	+£9.03
Sam Twiston-Davies	72	19	26.39%	+£37.83
James Banks	20	5	25.00%	+£46.48

Top jockeys by Profit – non-handicaps

Name Of Jockey	Rides	Winners	Strike Rate	Profit/Loss to BSP
Brian Hughes	14	3	21.43%	+£10.51
Tom Scudamore	10	5	50.00%	+£7.15
Harry Skelton	12	5	41.67%	+£2.71

Top jockeys by Profit – handicaps

Name Of Jockey	Rides	Winners	Strike Rate	Profit/Loss to BSP
Aidan Coleman	91	19	20.88%	+£66.10
James Banks	20	5	25.00%	+£46.48

Tom O'Brien	57	9	15.79%	+£38.05
Sam Twiston-Davies	72	19	26.39%	+£37.83
Jamie Hamilton	40	7	17.50%	+£31.71

Top trainers by Strike Rate – non-handicaps

Name Of Trainer	Runners	Winners	Strike Rate	Profit/Loss to BSP
Dan Skelton	13	4	30.77%	-£2.23
Brian Ellison	10	2	20.00%	-£1.31
Jonjo O'Neill	10	2	20.00%	-£4.57
Nicky Henderson	11	2	18.18%	-£6.59

Top trainers by Strike Rate – handicaps

Name Of Trainer	Runners	Winners	Strike Rate	Profit/Loss to BSP
Martin Keighley	15	5	33.33%	+£2.38
Henry Daly	15	5	33.33%	+£14.76
Andrew Martin	10	3	30.00%	+£22.36
Kim Bailey	30	9	30.00%	+£5.11
Lawney Hill	14	4	28.57%	+£28.05

Top trainers by Profit – handicaps

Name Of Trainer	Runners	Winners	Strike Rate	Profit/Loss to BSP
Michael Chapman	92	3	3.26%	+£124.47
Jennie Candlish	38	6	15.79%	+£44.22
Micky Hammond	72	12	16.67%	+£43.24
Tom George	41	9	21.95%	+£38.86
Fergal O'Brien	67	10	14.93%	+£37.81

Top trainer/jockey combos by Strike Rate – non-handicaps

Name Of Trainer/Jockey	Rides	Winners	Strike Rate	Profit/Loss to BSP
Dan Skelton/Harry	11	4	36.36%	-£0.23

Skelton				

Top trainer/jockey combos by Strike Rate – handicaps

Name of Trainer/Jockey	Qualifiers	Winners	Strike Rate	Profit/Loss to BSP
Nigel Hawke/Tom Scudamore	10	5	50.00%	+£26.42
Dan Skelton/Bridget Andrews	12	5	41.67%	+£23.27
Kim Bailey/David Bass	15	6	40.00%	+£6.61
Dr Richard Newland/Sam Twiston-Davies	26	9	34.62%	+£17.21
Peter Bowen/Sean Bowen	33	7	21.21%	+£1.67

Top trainer/jockey combos by Profit – handicaps

Name of Trainer/Jockey	Qualifiers	Winners	Strike Rate	Profit/Loss to BSP
Nigel Hawke/Tom Scudamore	10	5	50.00%	+£26.42
Dan Skelton/Bridget Andrews	12	5	41.67%	+£23.27
Peter Bowen/James Bowen	25	5	20.00%	+£22.98
Dr Richard Newland/Sam Twiston-Davies	26	9	34.62%	+£17.21
Jonjo O'Neill/Richie McLernon	26	5	19.23%	+£12.63

Profit or Loss backing the unnamed favourite – non-handicaps

Runners	Winners	Strike Rate	Profit/Loss to BSP
232	101	43.53%	-£16.36

Profit or Loss backing the unnamed favourite – handicaps

Runners	Winners	Strike Rate	Profit/Loss to BSP
894	241	26.96%	-£50.97

Profit or loss backing the unnamed second favourite - non-handicaps

Runners	Winners	Strike Rate	Profit/Loss to BSP
220	52	23.64%	-£6.04

Profit or loss backing the unnamed second favourite - handicaps

Runners	Winners	Strike Rate	Profit/Loss to BSP
821	169	20.58%	+£48.00

Profit or Loss backing horses who won last time out - non-handicaps

Runners	Winners	Strike Rate	Profit/Loss to BSP
148	49	33.11%	+£9.74

Profit or Loss backing horses who won last time out - handicaps

Runners	Winners	Strike Rate	Profit/Loss to BSP
838	140	16.71%	+£14.16

Profit or loss backing Top-Weights in handicaps

Runners	Winners	Strike Rate	Profit/Loss to BSP
924	146	15.80%	-£49.20

Most profitable sires – non-handicaps

Sire	Runners	Winners	Strike Rate	Profit/Loss to BSP
Presenting	13	4	30.77%	+£25.42
King's Theatre	10	2	20.00%	+£2.18
Westerner	10	4	40.00%	+£2.08

Most profitable sires – handicaps

Orpen	25	1	4.00%	+£133.95
Network	22	2	9.09%	+£63.25
Oscar	83	12	14.46%	+£42.99
Westerner	76	14	18.42%	+£37.74
Overbury	35	8	22.86%	+£30.49

Market Rasen – Hurdles

Top jockeys by Strike Rate – non-handicaps

Name Of Jockey	Rides	Winners	Strike Rate	Profit/Loss to BSP
James Bowen	11	4	36.36%	+£20.32
Fergus Gregory	14	5	35.71%	+£1.33
Ciaran Gethings	20	7	35.00%	+£10.65
Daryl Jacob	25	8	32.00%	+£32.15
Aidan Coleman	75	23	30.67%	+£4.19

Top jockeys by Strike Rate – handicaps

Name Of Jockey	Rides	Winners	Strike Rate	Profit/Loss to BSP
Danny McMenamin	10	4	40.00%	+£33.10
Bryony Frost	13	5	38.46%	+£29.40
Fergus Gregory	26	9	34.62%	+£21.87
Jonathan England	44	10	22.73%	+£49.58
Charlie Hammond	38	8	21.05%	+£17.42

Top jockeys by Profit – non-handicaps

Name Of Jockey	Rides	Winners	Strike Rate	Profit/Loss to

				BSP
William Kennedy	29	3	10.34%	+£64.74
Daryl Jacob	25	8	32.00%	+£32.15
James Bowen	11	4	36.36%	+£20.32
Conor O'Farrell	15	3	20.00%	+£12.76
Alan Johns	13	2	15.38%	+£12.13

Top jockeys by Profit – handicaps

Name Of Jockey	Rides	Winners	Strike Rate	Profit/Loss to BSP
Lee Edwards	27	5	18.52%	+£67.12
Connor Brace	26	5	19.23%	+£53.25
Jonathan England	44	10	22.73%	+£49.58
Tom Scudamore	73	11	15.07%	+£38.13
Brian Hughes	124	19	15.32%	+£33.64

Top trainers by Strike Rate – non-handicaps

Name Of Trainer	Runners	Winners	Strike Rate	Profit/Loss to BSP
Nicky Henderson	43	18	41.86%	-£4.67
Harry Fry	11	4	36.36%	+£6.21
Stuart Edmunds	18	6	33.33%	+£3.46
David Pipe	13	4	30.77%	-£0.14
Oliver Sherwood	13	4	30.77%	+£28.85

Top trainers by Strike Rate – handicaps

Name Of Trainer	Runners	Winners	Strike Rate	Profit/Loss to BSP
Tom George	14	4	28.57%	+£17.21
Julian Smith	11	3	27.27%	+£25.37
Henry Oliver	27	7	25.93%	+£5.14
Rebecca Menzies	29	7	24.14%	+£18.83
Philip Hobbs	29	7	24.14%	+£36.26

Top trainers by Profit – non-handicaps

Name Of Trainer	Runners	Winners	Strike Rate	Profit/Loss to

				BSP
Brian Ellison	73	15	20.55%	+£71.38
Donald McCain	59	11	18.64%	+£56.21
Philip Kirby	26	3	11.54%	+£33.29
Oliver Sherwood	13	4	30.77%	+£28.85
Nigel Hawke	26	4	15.38%	+£17.49

Top trainers by Profit – handicaps

Name Of Trainer	Runners	Winners	Strike Rate	Profit/Loss to BSP
Dr Richard Newland	63	14	22.22%	+£37.19
Micky Hammond	72	11	15.28%	+£36.39
Philip Hobbs	29	7	24.14%	+£36.26
David O'Meara	11	2	18.18%	+£34.73
Sophie Leech	22	1	4.55%	+£33.47

Top trainer/jockey combos by Strike Rate – non-handicaps

Name of Trainer/Jockey	Qualifiers	Winners	Strike Rate	Profit/Loss to BSP
Stuart Edmunds/Ciaran Gethings	12	6	50.00%	+£9.46
Olly Murphy/Aidan Coleman	23	10	43.48%	+£5.54
David Pipe/Tom Scudamore	10	4	40.00%	+£2.86
Nigel Twiston-Davies/Sam Twiston-Davies	10	4	40.00%	+£3.74
Olly Murphy/Fergus Gregory	13	5	38.46%	+£2.33

Top trainer/jockey combos by Strike Rate – handicaps

Name of Trainer/Jockey	Qualifiers	Winners	Strike Rate	Profit/Loss to BSP
Rebecca	12	4	33.33%	+£5.96

Menzies/Nathan Moscrop				
Olly Murphy/Fergus Gregory	17	5	29.41%	+£3.69
Sam England/Jonathan England	18	5	27.78%	+£32.42
Nigel Twiston-Davies/Sam Twiston-Davies	23	6	26.09%	+£17.29
Peter Bowen/Sean Bowen	20	5	25.00%	+£11.62

Top trainer/jockey combos by Profit – non-handicaps

Name of Trainer/Jockey	Qualifiers	Winners	Strike Rate	Profit/Loss to BSP
Donald McCain/Brian Hughes	12	4	33.33%	+£17.18
Mark Walford/Jamie Hamilton	14	1	7.14%	+£17.03
Stuart Edmunds/Ciaran Gethings	12	6	50.00%	+£9.46
Jonjo O'Neill/Aidan Coleman	12	4	33.33%	+£7.52
Warren Greatrex/Gavin Sheehan	15	5	33.33%	+£6.89

Top trainer/jockey combos by Profit – handicaps

Name of Trainer/Jockey	Qualifiers	Winners	Strike Rate	Profit/Loss to BSP
Sam England/Jonathan England	18	5	27.78%	+£32.42
Nick Kent/Adam	13	3	23.08%	+£20.69

Wedge				
Dan Skelton/Harry Skelton	79	16	20.25%	+£17.75
Nigel Twiston-Davies/Sam Twiston-Davies	23	6	26.09%	+£17.29
Jonjo O'Neill/Aidan Coleman	16	3	18.75%	+£15.11

Profit or Loss backing the unnamed favourite – non-handicaps

Runners	Winners	Strike Rate	Profit/Loss to BSP
685	304	44.38%	-£17.77

Profit or Loss backing the unnamed favourite – handicaps

Runners	Winners	Strike Rate	Profit/Loss to BSP
974	278	28.54%	+£42.71

Profit or loss backing the unnamed second favourite - non-handicaps

Runners	Winners	Strike Rate	Profit/Loss to BSP
659	168	25.49%	+£25.93

Profit or loss backing the unnamed second favourite - handicaps

Runners	Winners	Strike Rate	Profit/Loss to BSP
871	138	15.84%	-£148.52

Profit or Loss backing horses who won last time out- non-handicaps

Runners	Winners	Strike Rate	Profit/Loss to BSP
491	150	30.55%	-£34.46

Profit or Loss backing horses who won last time out - handicaps

Runners	Winners	Strike Rate	Profit/Loss to BSP
998	175	17.54%	+£34.33

Profit or loss backing Top-Weights in handicaps

Runners	Winners	Strike Rate	Profit/Loss to BSP
982	127	12.93%	-£136.64

Most profitable sires – non-handicaps

Sire	Runners	Winners	Strike Rate	Profit/Loss to BSP
Phoenix Reach	11	1	9.09%	+£87.02
Shantou	17	5	29.41%	+£65.92
Haafhd	11	2	18.18%	+£22.00
Multiplex	16	2	12.50%	+£20.26
Rip Van Winkle	11	2	18.18%	+£15.40

Most profitable sires – handicaps

Flemensfirth	57	10	17.54%	+£58.61
Saddler's Hall	13	4	30.77%	+£41.62
Catcher In The Rye	11	2	18.18%	+£31.29
Grape Tree Road	14	4	28.57%	+£29.12
Milan	70	15	21.43%	+£24.25

Musselburgh - Chases

Top jockeys by Strike Rate – non-handicaps

Name Of Jockey	Rides	Winners	Strike Rate	Profit/Loss to BSP
Brian Hughes	10	4	40.00%	+£9.09

Top jockeys by Strike Rate – handicaps

Name Of Jockey	Rides	Winners	Strike Rate	Profit/Loss to BSP
Alan Johns	12	3	25.00%	+£4.01
Danny McMenamin	13	3	23.08%	+£14.79
Aidan Coleman	10	2	20.00%	-£0.35
Craig Nichol	61	12	19.67%	+£5.67
Brian Hughes	135	22	16.30%	-£31.10

Top jockeys by Profit – non-handicaps

Name Of Jockey	Rides	Winners	Strike Rate	Profit/Loss to BSP
Brian Hughes	10	4	40.00%	+£9.09

Top jockeys by Profit – handicaps

Name Of Jockey	Rides	Winners	Strike Rate	Profit/Loss to BSP
Henry Brooke	43	7	16.28%	+£43.33
Callum Bewley	35	5	11.43%	+£36.56
Danny McMenamin	13	3	23.08%	+£14.79
Harry Reed	13	2	15.38%	+£7.13
Craig Nichol	61	12	19.67%	+£5.67

Top trainers by Strike Rate – non-handicaps

Name Of Trainer	Runners	Winners	Strike Rate	Profit/Loss to BSP
Paul Nicholls	13	5	38.46%	-£5.18

Donald McCain	14	5	35.71%	-£2.04

Top trainers by Strike Rate – handicaps

Name Of Trainer	Runners	Winners	Strike Rate	Profit/Loss to BSP
Laura Morgan	10	6	60.00%	+£31.02
Paul Nicholls	12	5	41.67%	+£4.29
Keith Dalgleish	31	10	32.26%	+£14.44
Susan Corbett	10	3	30.00%	+£12.28
N W Alexander	53	12	22.64%	+£13.38

Top trainers by Profit – handicaps

Name Of Trainer	Runners	Winners	Strike Rate	Profit/Loss to BSP
Donald McCain	77	16	20.78%	+£74.67
Laura Morgan	10	6	60.00%	+£31.02
Lisa Harrison	11	1	9.09%	+£23.73
Rebecca Menzies	40	6	15.00%	+£22.39
Barry Murtagh	17	3	17.65%	+£15.92

Top trainer/jockey combos by Strike Rate – handicaps

Name of Trainer/Jockey	Qualifiers	Winners	Strike Rate	Profit/Loss to BSP
Keith Dalgleish/Brian Hughes	14	6	42.86%	+£14.89
Keith Dalgleish/Craig Nichol	11	3	27.27%	+£1.61
Donald McCain/Brian Hughes	19	5	26.32%	-£1.35
Rose Dobbin/Craig Nichol	23	6	26.09%	+£15.07
Tim Vaughan/Alan Johns	12	3	25.00%	+£4.01

Top trainer/jockey combos by Profit – handicaps

Name of Trainer/Jockey	Qualifiers	Winners	Strike Rate	Profit/Loss to BSP
Rose Dobbin/Craig Nichol	23	6	26.09%	+£15.07
Keith Dalgleish/Brian Hughes	14	6	42.86%	+£14.89
Tim Vaughan/Alan Johns	12	3	25.00%	+£4.01
Lucinda Russell/Craig Nichol	14	3	21.43%	+£1.99
Keith Dalgleish/Craig Nichol	11	3	27.27%	+£1.61

Profit or Loss backing the unnamed favourite – non-handicaps

Runners	Winners	Strike Rate	Profit/Loss to BSP
93	38	40.86%	-£10.06

Profit or Loss backing the unnamed favourite – handicaps

Runners	Winners	Strike Rate	Profit/Loss to BSP
344	104	30.23%	-£7.61

Profit or loss backing the unnamed second favourite - non-handicaps

Runners	Winners	Strike Rate	Profit/Loss to BSP
90	28	31.11%	+£34.34

Profit or loss backing the unnamed second favourite - handicaps

Runners	Winners	Strike Rate	Profit/Loss to BSP
349	70	20.06%	-£22.05

Profit or Loss backing horses who won last time out - non-handicaps

Runners	Winners	Strike Rate	Profit/Loss to BSP
76	16	21.05%	-£26.85

Profit or Loss backing horses who won last time out - handicaps

Runners	Winners	Strike Rate	Profit/Loss to BSP
263	40	15.21%	-£112.70

Profit or loss backing Top-Weights in handicaps

Runners	Winners	Strike Rate	Profit/Loss to BSP
376	56	14.89%	+£5.62

Most profitable sires – handicaps

Oscar	48	11	22.92%	+£36.98
Cloudings	16	3	18.75%	+£36.69
Beneficial	95	18	18.95%	+££4.42
Definite Article	16	5	31.25%	+£20.98
Overbury	21	4	19.05%	+£18.83

Musselburgh – Hurdles

Top jockeys by Strike Rate – non-handicaps

Name Of Jockey	Rides	Winners	Strike Rate	Profit/Loss to BSP
Paddy Brennan	10	4	40.00%	+£18.81
A P Heskin	11	3	27.27%	-£4.86
Brian Hughes	113	29	25.66%	-£19.36
William Kennedy	16	4	25.00%	+£8.50
Danny McMenamin	11	2	18.18%	-£14.54

Top jockeys by Strike Rate – handicaps

Name Of Jockey	Rides	Winners	Strike Rate	Profit/Loss to BSP
Aidan Coleman	15	3	20.00%	-£1.33
Alan Johns	11	2	18.18%	+£0.24
Ryan Mania	44	8	18.18%	+£6.49
Theo Gillard	17	3	17.65%	+£8.62
Richie McLernon	12	2	16.67%	+£6.46

Top jockeys by Profit – non-handicaps

Name Of Jockey	Rides	Winners	Strike Rate	Profit/Loss to BSP
Ryan Mania	19	3	15.79%	+£44.95
Paddy Brennan	10	4	40.00%	+£18.81
Henry Brooke	38	4	10.53%	+£13.81
William Kennedy	16	4	25.00%	+£8.50

Top jockeys by Profit – handicaps

Name Of Jockey	Rides	Winners	Strike Rate	Profit/Loss to BSP
Conor O'Farrell	53	8	15.09%	+£66.46
Sean Quinlan	55	5	9.09%	+£40.86
Jamie Hamilton	26	4	15.38%	+£39.41
Derek Fox	58	9	15.52%	+£20.63
Dougie Costello	20	1	5.00%	+£12.55

Top trainers by Strike Rate – non-handicaps

Name Of Trainer	Runners	Winners	Strike Rate	Profit/Loss to BSP
Charlie Longsdon	13	8	61.54%	+£37.51
Nicky Henderson	16	8	50.00%	+£1.80
John Quinn	17	7	41.18%	+£12.78
John C McConnell	10	4	40.00%	+£3.32
Paul Nicholls	19	6	31.58%	-£4.88

Top trainers by Strike Rate – handicaps

Name Of Trainer	Runners	Winners	Strike Rate	Profit/Loss to

				BSP
Paul Nicholls	22	9	40.91%	+£24.90
S R B Crawford	16	4	25.00%	+£24.03
James Ewart	55	11	20.00%	+£83.05
Sandy Thomson	65	13	20.00%	+£10.55
Jennie Candlish	11	2	18.18%	-£2.20

Top trainers by Profit – non-handicaps

Name Of Trainer	Runners	Winners	Strike Rate	Profit/Loss to BSP
Sandy Thomson	14	4	28.57%	+£70.92
Maurice Barnes	17	2	11.76%	+£57.52
Martin Todhunter	11	2	18.18%	+£41.00
Charlie Longsdon	13	8	61.54%	+£37.51
John Quinn	17	7	41.18%	+£12.78

Top trainers by Profit – handicaps

Name Of Trainer	Runners	Winners	Strike Rate	Profit/Loss to BSP
Dianne Sayer	77	10	12.99%	+£125.10
James Ewart	55	11	20.00%	+£83.05
Rose Dobbin	42	4	9.52%	+£28.72
Paul Nicholls	22	9	40.91%	+£24.90
S R B Crawford	16	4	25.00%	+£24.03

Top trainer/jockey combos by Strike Rate – non-handicaps

Name of Trainer/Jockey	Qualifiers	Winners	Strike Rate	Profit/Loss to BSP
Donald McCain/Brian Hughes	25	8	32.00%	-£3.67
Keith Dalgleish/Brian Hughes	14	3	21.43%	-£10.06
James Ewart/Brian Hughes	13	2	15.38%	-£5.23
Iain Jardine/Ross	13	2	15.38%	-£8.90

Chapman				
Rose Dobbin/Craig Nichol	10	1	10.00%	+£8.36

Top trainer/jockey combos by Strike Rate – handicaps

Name of Trainer/Jockey	Qualifiers	Winners	Strike Rate	Profit/Loss to BSP
Sandy Thomson/Ryan Mania	21	6	28.57%	+£10.91
Rebecca Menzies/Nathan Moscrop	11	3	27.27%	+£21.73
Donald McCain/Theo Gillard	13	3	23.08%	+£12.62
Philip Kirby/Adam Nichol	21	4	19.05%	+£8.78
Tim Vaughan/Alan Johns	11	21	18.18%	+£0.24

Top trainer/jockey combos by Profit – non-handicaps

Name of Trainer/Jockey	Qualifiers	Winners	Strike Rate	Profit/Loss to BSP
Rose Dobbin/Craig Nichol	10	1	10.00%	+£8.36

Top trainer/jockey combos by Profit – handicaps

Name of Trainer/Jockey	Qualifiers	Winners	Strike Rate	Profit/Loss to BSP
Lucinda Russell/Derek Fox	53	9	16.98%	+£25.63
Rebecca Menzies/Nathan Moscrop	11	3	27.27%	+£21.73

Donald McCain/Brian Hughes	44	8	18.18%	+£20.12
Donald McCain/Theo Gillard	13	3	23.08%	+£12.62
Sandy Thomson/Ryan Mania	21	6	28.57%	+£10.91

Profit or Loss backing the unnamed favourite – non-handicaps

Runners	Winners	Strike Rate	Profit/Loss to BSP
307	150	48.86%	-£0.90

Profit or Loss backing the unnamed favourite – handicaps

Runners	Winners	Strike Rate	Profit/Loss to BSP
421	119	28.27%	-£2.36

Profit or loss backing the unnamed second favourite - non-handicaps

Runners	Winners	Strike Rate	Profit/Loss to BSP
307	62	20.20%	-£32.30

Profit or loss backing the unnamed second favourite - handicaps

Runners	Winners	Strike Rate	Profit/Loss to BSP
379	77	20.32%	+£32.57

Profit or Loss backing horses who won last time out- non-handicaps

Runners	Winners	Strike Rate	Profit/Loss to BSP
225	63	28.00%	+£58.53

Profit or Loss backing horses who won last time out - handicaps

Runners	Winners	Strike Rate	Profit/Loss to

			BSP
403	74	18.36%	-£13.37

Profit or loss backing Top-Weights in handicaps

Runners	Winners	Strike Rate	Profit/Loss to BSP
429	64	14.92%	-£4.86

Most profitable sires – non-handicaps

Sire	Runners	Winners	Strike Rate	Profit/Loss to BSP
Presenting	19	5	26.32%	+£33.68
Yeats	11	1	9.09%	+£7.36
Authorized	13	4	30.77%	+£4.35
Galileo	10	1	10.00%	+£2.07
Oscar	12	3	25.00%	+£0.95

Most profitable sires – handicaps

Sholokhov	12	2	16.67%	+£46.62
Beat Hollow	26	3	11.54%	+£38.23
Westerner	22	5	22.73%	+£32.12
Arcano	11	1	9.09%	+£20.38
Dansili	15	3	20.00%	+£19.28

Newbury - Chases

Top jockeys by Strike Rate – non-handicaps

Name Of Jockey	Rides	Winners	Strike Rate	Profit/Loss to BSP
Nico de Boinville	14	6	42.86%	-£0.99
Harry Cobden	19	6	31.58%	+£2.15
Daryl Jacob	19	5	26.32%	-£3.50
Tom Scudamore	13	3	23.08%	-£9.25
Aidan Coleman	10	2	20.00%	-£3.29

Top jockeys by Strike Rate – handicaps

Name Of Jockey	Rides	Winners	Strike Rate	Profit/Loss to BSP
Stan Sheppard	14	4	28.57%	+£17.88
Charlie Deutsch	25	7	28.00%	+£50.83
Harry Bannister	11	3	27.27%	+£3.90
Ciaran Gethings	12	3	25.00%	+£2.01
Harry Cobden	54	13	24.07%	+£20.15

Top jockeys by Profit – non-handicaps

Name Of Jockey	Rides	Winners	Strike Rate	Profit/Loss to BSP
Harry Cobden	19	6	31.58%	+£2.15

Top jockeys by Profit – handicaps

Name Of Jockey	Rides	Winners	Strike Rate	Profit/Loss to BSP
Tom Scudamore	79	17	21.52%	+£80.11
Charlie Deutsch	25	7	28.00%	+£50.83
Harry Cobden	54	13	24.07%	+£20.15
Stan Sheppard	14	4	28.57%	+£17.88
Jamie Moore	44	6	13.64%	+£15.96

Top trainers by Strike Rate – non-handicaps

Name Of Trainer	Runners	Winners	Strike Rate	Profit/Loss to BSP
Philip Hobbs	11	4	36.36%	+£8.49
Nicky Henderson	30	10	33.33%	-£8.34
Colin Tizzard	27	7	25.93%	+£4.86
Paul Nicholls	62	16	25.81%	+£0.93
Venetia Williams	10	2	20.00%	-£2.30

Top trainers by Strike Rate – handicaps

Name Of Trainer	Runners	Winners	Strike Rate	Profit/Loss to BSP
David Dennis	12	4	33.33%	+£33.54
Richard Hobson	17	4	23.53%	+£11.46
Tom Lacey	13	3	23.08%	+£3.75
Harry Whittington	18	4	22.22%	-£1.97
Venetia Williams	98	20	20.41%	+£66.86

Top trainers by Profit – non-handicaps

Name Of Trainer	Runners	Winners	Strike Rate	Profit/Loss to BSP
Philip Hobbs	11	4	36.36%	+£8.49
Colin Tizzard	27	7	25.93%	+£4.86
Paul Nicholls	62	16	25.81%	+£0.93

Top trainers by Profit – handicaps

Name Of Trainer	Runners	Winners	Strike Rate	Profit/Loss to BSP
Venetia Williams	98	20	20.41%	+£66.86
Paul Nicholls	127	25	19.69%	+£59.91
David Dennis	12	4	33.33%	+£33.54
Fergal O'Brien	31	6	19.35%	+£23.31
Oliver Sherwood	29	4	13.79%	+£17.64

Top trainer/jockey combos by Strike Rate – non-handicaps

Name Of Trainer/Jockey	Rides	Winners	Strike Rate	Profit/Loss to BSP

| Paul Nicholls/Harry Cobden | 16 | 5 | 31.25% | -£1.92 |

Top trainer/jockey combos by Strike Rate – handicaps

Name of Trainer/Jockey	Qualifiers	Winners	Strike Rate	Profit/Loss to BSP
Venetia Williams/Charlie Deutsch	20	6	30.00%	+£49.73
Colin Tizzard/Harry Cobden	18	5	27.78%	+£2.89
Paul Nicholls/Daryl Jacob	16	4	25.00%	+£6.55
Paul Nicholls/Harry Cobden	32	7	21.88%	+£14.97
David Pipe/Tom Scudamore	34	6	17.65%	+£12.21

Top trainer/jockey combos by Profit – handicaps

Name of Trainer/Jockey	Qualifiers	Winners	Strike Rate	Profit/Loss to BSP
Venetia Williams/Charlie Deutsch	20	6	30.00%	+£49.73
Paul Nicholls/Harry Cobden	32	7	21.88%	+£14.97
David Pipe/Tom Scudamore	34	6	17.65%	+£12.21
Gary Moore/Jamie Moore	23	3	13.04%	+£8.56
Dan Skelton/Harry Skelton	28	4	14.29%	+£7.33

Profit or Loss backing the unnamed favourite – non-handicaps

Runners	Winners	Strike Rate	Profit/Loss to BSP
194	92	47.42%	-£3.70

Profit or Loss backing the unnamed favourite – handicaps

Runners	Winners	Strike Rate	Profit/Loss to BSP
506	136	26.88%	+£11.42

Profit or loss backing the unnamed second favourite - non-handicaps

Runners	Winners	Strike Rate	Profit/Loss to BSP
196	48	24.49%	+£10.73

Profit or loss backing the unnamed second favourite - handicaps

Runners	Winners	Strike Rate	Profit/Loss to BSP
486	89	18.31%	+£14.57

Profit or Loss backing horses who won last time out - non-handicaps

Runners	Winners	Strike Rate	Profit/Loss to BSP
281	77	27.40%	+£19.44

Profit or Loss backing horses who won last time out - handicaps

Runners	Winners	Strike Rate	Profit/Loss to BSP
777	109	14.03%	-£181.43

Profit or loss backing Top-Weights in handicaps

Runners	Winners	Strike Rate	Profit/Loss to BSP
545	71	13.03%	-£100.29

Most profitable sires – non-handicaps

Sire	Runners	Winners	Strike Rate	Profit/Loss to BSP
Oscar	16	4	25.00%	+£16.10
Kayf Tara	10	3	30.00%	+£11.76

Most profitable sires – handicaps

Yeats	24	4	16.67%	+£22.59
Kayf Tara	65	11	16.92%	+£22.40
Brian Boru	32	5	15.63%	+£20.05
Voix Du Nord	11	3	27.27%	+£17.49
Heron Island	13	1	7.69%	+£15.20

Newbury – Hurdles

Top jockeys by Strike Rate – non-handicaps

Name Of Jockey	Rides	Winners	Strike Rate	Profit/Loss to BSP
Nico de Boinville	68	25	36.76%	+£52.50
Harry Cobden	37	12	32.43%	+£.0.50
Harry Skelton	45	8	17.78%	-£8.25
Paddy Brennan	45	8	17.78%	-£4.31
David Bass	19	3	15.79%	-£13.52

Top jockeys by Strike Rate – handicaps

Name Of Jockey	Rides	Winners	Strike Rate	Profit/Loss to BSP
Lorcan Williams	12	3	25.00%	-£1.56
Jonjo O'Neill Jr	26	5	19.23%	+£21.75
Gavin Sheehan	29	5	17.24%	+£32.65
Harry Cobden	35	6	17.14%	+£101.01
Jack Quinlan	12	2	16.67%	+£7.10

Top jockeys by Profit – non-handicaps

Name Of Jockey	Rides	Winners	Strike Rate	Profit/Loss to BSP
Nico de Boinville	68	25	36.76%	+£52.50
Tom O'Brien	30	4	13.33%	+£29.13
Adam Wedge	18	1	5.56%	+£17.30

| Tom Scudamore | 52 | 6 | 11.54% | +£1.04 |
| Harry Cobden | 37 | 12 | 32.43% | +£0.50 |

Top jockeys by Profit – handicaps

Name Of Jockey	Rides	Winners	Strike Rate	Profit/Loss to BSP
Harry Cobden	35	6	17.14%	+£101.01
Gavin Sheehan	29	5	17.24%	+£32.65
Joshua Moore	27	2	7.41%	+£31.26
Sam Twiston-Davies	74	12	16.22%	+£29.33
Harry Bannister	19	3	15.79%	+£22.75

Top trainers by Strike Rate – non-handicaps

Name Of Trainer	Runners	Winners	Strike Rate	Profit/Loss to BSP
Nicky Henderson	166	54	32.53%	+£18.60
Paul Nicholls	60	19	31.67%	+£2.79
Philip Hobbs	47	13	27.66%	+£245.09
Fergal O'Brien	26	7	26.92%	+£76.55
Harry Fry	26	6	23.08%	-£3.34

Top trainers by Strike Rate – handicaps

Name Of Trainer	Runners	Winners	Strike Rate	Profit/Loss to BSP
Nigel Twiston-Davies	59	14	23.73%	+£94.45
Neil Mulholland	23	5	21.74%	+£18.18
Tony Carroll	20	4	20.00%	+£28.48
Alex Hales	10	2	20.00%	+£13.11
Ali Stronge	10	2	20.00%	+£23.03

Top trainers by Profit – non-handicaps

Name Of Trainer	Runners	Winners	Strike Rate	Profit/Loss to BSP
Philip Hobbs	47	13	27.66%	+£245.09
Fergal O'Brien	26	7	26.92%	+£76.55
Seamus Mullins	19	1	5.26%	+£69.22

| Evan Williams | 13 | 2 | 15.38% | +£24.77 |
| Nicky Henderson | 166 | 54 | 32.53% | +£18.60 |

Top trainers by Profit – handicaps

Name Of Trainer	Runners	Winners	Strike Rate	Profit/Loss to BSP
Nigel Twiston-Davies	59	14	23.73%	+£94.45
Paul Nicholls	100	12	12.00%	+£65.99
David Pipe	78	15	19.23%	+£43.15
Philip Hobbs	88	12	13.64%	+£37.79
Lucy Wadham	20	2	10.00%	+£29.88

Top trainer/jockey combos by Strike Rate – non-handicaps

Name of Trainer/Jockey	Qualifiers	Winners	Strike Rate	Profit/Loss to BSP
Paul Nicholls/Harry Cobden	25	12	48.00%	+£12.50
Nicky Henderson/Nico de Boinville	57	23	40.35%	+£30.76
Fergal O'Brien/Paddy Brennan	21	6	28.57%	+£3.11
Dan Skelton/Harry Skelton	42	8	19.05%	-£5.25
Nigel Twiston-Davies/Sam Twiston-Davies	11	2	18.18%	-£0.29

Top trainer/jockey combos by Strike Rate – handicaps

Name of Trainer/Jockey	Qualifiers	Winners	Strike Rate	Profit/Loss to BSP
Warren Greatrex/Gavin Sheehan	10	3	30.00%	+£8.88
Nigel Twiston-	36	10	27.78%	+£58.43

Davies/Sam Twiston-Davies				
Jonjo O'Neill/Jonjo O' Neill Jr	20	5	25.00%	+£27.75
David Pipe/Tom Scudamore	41	7	17.07%	+£13.27
Fergal O'Brien/Paddy Brennan	18	3	16.67%	+£10.07

Top trainer/jockey combos by Profit – non-handicaps

Name of Trainer/Jockey	Qualifiers	Winners	Strike Rate	Profit/Loss to BSP
Nicky Henderson/Nico de Boinville	57	23	40.35%	+£30.76
David Pipe/Tom Scudamore	32	4	12.50%	+£13.55
Paul Nicholls/Harry Cobden	25	12	48.00%	+£12.50
Fergal O'Brien/Paddy Brennan	21	6	28.57%	+£3.11

Top trainer/jockey combos by Profit – handicaps

Name of Trainer/Jockey	Qualifiers	Winners	Strike Rate	Profit/Loss to BSP
Paul Nicholls/Harry Cobden	27	3	11.11%	+£89.93
Nigel Twiston-Davies/Sam Twiston-Davies	36	10	27.78%	+£58.43
Gary Moore/Joshua Moore	22	2	9.09%	+£36.26
Jonjo O'Neill/Jonjo O' Neill Jr	20	5	25.00%	+£27.75

David Pipe/Tom Scudamore	41	7	17.07%	+£13.27

Profit or Loss backing the unnamed favourite – non-handicaps

Runners	Winners	Strike Rate	Profit/Loss to BSP
424	182	42.92%	-£14.57

Profit or Loss backing the unnamed favourite – handicaps

Runners	Winners	Strike Rate	Profit/Loss to BSP
354	96	27.12%	+£25.59

Profit or loss backing the unnamed second favourite - non-handicaps

Runners	Winners	Strike Rate	Profit/Loss to BSP
390	79	20.26%	-£25.88

Profit or loss backing the unnamed second favourite - handicaps

Runners	Winners	Strike Rate	Profit/Loss to BSP
333	49	14.71%	-£41.13

Profit or Loss backing horses who won last time out- non-handicaps

Runners	Winners	Strike Rate	Profit/Loss to BSP
612	123	20.10%	-£159.42

Profit or Loss backing horses who won last time out - handicaps

Runners	Winners	Strike Rate	Profit/Loss to BSP
684	86	12.57%	-£99.94

Profit or loss backing Top-Weights in handicaps

Runners	Winners	Strike Rate	Profit/Loss to BSP

389	45	11.57%	+£2.34

Most profitable sires – non-handicaps

Sire	Runners	Winners	Strike Rate	Profit/Loss to BSP
Oscar	44	6	13.64%	+£77.37
Mahler	22	1	4.55%	+£66.24
Flemensfirth	45	6	13.33%	+£62.04
Getaway	24	6	25.00%	+£18.80
Arcadio	13	1	7.69%	+£16.82

Most profitable sires – handicaps

Martaline	20	5	25.00%	+£46.67
Oscar	43	4	9.30%	+£39.54
Shantou	25	5	20.00%	+£26.11
Fame And Glory	16	3	18.75%	+£25.00
Robin Des Pres	10	2	20.00%	+£20.91

Newcastle - Chases

Top jockeys by Strike Rate – non-handicaps

Name Of Jockey	Rides	Winners	Strike Rate	Profit/Loss to BSP
Brian Hughes	17	8	47.06%	+£2.86

Top jockeys by Strike Rate – handicaps

Name Of Jockey	Rides	Winners	Strike Rate	Profit/Loss to BSP
Tom Scudamore	12	4	33.33%	+£5.70
Brian Hughes	127	30	23.62%	-£4.94
Brendan Powell	10	2	20.00%	+£12.57
Sean Quinlan	53	10	18.87%	+£39.98
Ryan Mania	55	10	18.18%	+£90.56

Top jockeys by Profit – non-handicaps

Name Of Jockey	Rides	Winners	Strike Rate	Profit/Loss to BSP
Brian Hughes	17	8	47.06%	+£2.86

Top jockeys by Profit – handicaps

Name Of Jockey	Rides	Winners	Strike Rate	Profit/Loss to BSP
Ryan Mania	55	10	18.18%	+£90.56
Sam Coltherd	31	3	9.68%	+£64.16
Sean Quinlan	53	10	18.87%	+£39.98
Danny McMenamin	14	2	14.29%	+£17.98
Harry Reed	18	2	11.11%	+£15.15

Top trainers by Strike Rate – handicaps

Name Of Trainer	Runners	Winners	Strike Rate	Profit/Loss to BSP
Jennie Candlish	10	4	40.00%	+£22.99

Michael Scudamore	19	7	36.84%	+£10.88
Iain Jardine	16	5	31.25%	+£17.48
Tom George	10	3	30.00%	-£2.00
Philip Kirby	18	5	27.78%	+£21.49

Top trainers by Profit – handicaps

Name Of Trainer	Runners	Winners	Strike Rate	Profit/Loss to BSP
Sandy Thomson	43	8	18.60%	+£88.69
Ben Haslam	24	6	25.00%	+£87.88
Susan Corbett	17	4	23.53%	+£73.12
Maurice Barnes	23	4	17.39%	+£28.20
Rebecca Menzies	33	7	21.21%	+£26.80

Top trainer/jockey combos by Strike Rate – handicaps

Name of Trainer/Jockey	Qualifiers	Winners	Strike Rate	Profit/Loss to BSP
James Ewart/Brian Hughes	21	8	38.10%	+£16.98
Mark Walford/Jamie Hamilton	10	3	30.00%	+£8.38
Sandy Thomson/Ryan Mania	18	5	27.78%	+£96.50
Sue Smith/Sean Quinlan	12	3	25.00%	+£9.31
Sam England/Jonathan England	11	2	18.18%	+£8.89

Top trainer/jockey combos by Profit – handicaps

Name of Trainer/Jockey	Qualifiers	Winners	Strike Rate	Profit/Loss to BSP
Sandy Thomson/Ryan Mania	18	5	27.78%	+£96.50
James	21	8	38.10%	+£16.98

Ewart/Brian Hughes				
Sue Smith/Sean Quinlan	12	3	25.00%	+£9.31
Sam England/Jonathan England	11	2	18.18%	+£8.89
Mark Walford/Jamie Hamilton	10	3	30.00%	+£8.38

Profit or Loss backing the unnamed favourite – non-handicaps

Runners	Winners	Strike Rate	Profit/Loss to BSP
106	56	52.83%	+£17.86

Profit or Loss backing the unnamed favourite – handicaps

Runners	Winners	Strike Rate	Profit/Loss to BSP
504	148	29.37%	-£16.02

Profit or loss backing the unnamed second favourite - non-handicaps

Runners	Winners	Strike Rate	Profit/Loss to BSP
100	27	27.00%	+£1.89

Profit or loss backing the unnamed second favourite - handicaps

Runners	Winners	Strike Rate	Profit/Loss to BSP
434	79	18.20%	-£67.36

Profit or Loss backing horses who won last time out - non-handicaps

Runners	Winners	Strike Rate	Profit/Loss to BSP
79	21	26.58%	-£17.00

Profit or Loss backing horses who won last time out - handicaps

Runners	Winners	Strike Rate	Profit/Loss to BSP
452	80	17.70%	-£79.90

Profit or loss backing Top-Weights in handicaps

Runners	Winners	Strike Rate	Profit/Loss to BSP
496	98	19.76%	+£192.38

Most profitable sires – handicaps

Fruits Of Love	17	3	17.65%	+£74.16
Presenting	44	8	18.18%	+£66.11
Beneficial	68	8	11.76%	+£31.50
Trans Island	10	2	20.00%	+£30.83
Dushyantor	15	4	26.67%	+£27.78

Newcastle – Hurdles

Top jockeys by Strike Rate – non-handicaps

Name Of Jockey	Rides	Winners	Strike Rate	Profit/Loss to BSP
Danny McMenamin	12	3	25.00%	+£0.49
Harry Skelton	10	2	20.00%	-£4.62
Brian Hughes	91	18	19.78%	-£9.12
Henry Brooke	52	5	9.62%	+£44.56
Conor O'Farrell	42	4	9.52%	-£29.48

Top jockeys by Strike Rate – handicaps

Name Of Jockey	Rides	Winners	Strike Rate	Profit/Loss to BSP
Tom Midgley	12	4	33.33%	+£23.85
Becky Smith	14	3	21.43%	+£13.44
Billy Garritty	15	3	20.00%	-£4.19
Amie Waugh	10	2	20.00%	+£19.66
Dougie Costello	11	2	18.18%	-£3.96

Top jockeys by Profit – non-handicaps

Name Of Jockey	Rides	Winners	Strike Rate	Profit/Loss to BSP
John Kington	11	1	9.09%	+£106.64
Henry Brooke	52	5	9.62%	+£44.56
Jonathon Bewley	11	1	9.09%	+£14.72
Craig Nichol	54	4	7.41%	+£11.77
Ryan Mania	33	3	9.09%	+£9.81

Top jockeys by Profit – handicaps

Name Of Jockey	Rides	Winners	Strike Rate	Profit/Loss to BSP
Sam Coltherd	26	1	3.85%	+£33.38
Tom Midgley	12	4	33.33%	+£23.85
Amie Waugh	10	2	20.00%	+£19.66
Ross Chapman	28	5	17.86%	+£18.59
Thomas Dowson	44	7	15.91%	+£16.94

Top trainers by Strike Rate – non-handicaps

Name Of Trainer	Runners	Winners	Strike Rate	Profit/Loss to BSP
Nicky Henderson	12	10	83.33%	+£5.59
Olly Murphy	13	4	30.77%	-£4.19
Peter Atkinson	10	3	30.00%	+£4.75
Dan Skelton	14	4	28.57%	-£4.85
Donald McCain	68	17	25.00%	+£39.08

Top trainers by Strike Rate – handicaps

Name Of Trainer	Runners	Winners	Strike Rate	Profit/Loss to BSP
Keith Dalgleish	16	8	50.00%	+£32.50
Neil Mulholland	11	4	36.36%	+£4.79
Tim Vaughan	17	5	29.41%	+£22.68
Ann Hamilton	12	3	25.00%	-£3.28
Harriet Graham	18	4	22.22%	+£22.64

Top trainers by Profit – non-handicaps

Name Of Trainer	Runners	Winners	Strike Rate	Profit/Loss to BSP
Keith Dalgleish	14	1	7.14%	+£44.82
Donald McCain	68	17	25.00%	+£39.08
Micky Hammond	33	3	9.09%	+£33.65
Sandy Thomson	34	4	11.76%	+£24.00
James Walton	10	2	20.00%	+£13.94

Top trainers by Profit – handicaps

Name Of Trainer	Runners	Winners	Strike Rate	Profit/Loss to BSP
Susan Corbett	33	5	15.15%	+£65.19
Tim Easterby	23	3	13.04%	+£36.20
Keith Dalgleish	16	8	50.00%	+£32.50
James Moffatt	23	5	21.74%	+£30.84
Mark Walford	13	2	15.38%	+£29.98

Top trainer/jockey combos by Strike Rate – non-handicaps

Name of Trainer/Jockey	Qualifiers	Winners	Strike Rate	Profit/Loss to BSP
Donald McCain/Brian Hughes	12	5	41.67%	+£25.41
Lucinda Russell/Derek Fox	15	2	13.33%	-£7.93
Sandy Thomson/Ryan Mania	15	2	13.33%	+£26.30
Rose Dobbin/Craig Nichol	21	2	9.52%	-£15.61
George Bewley/Jonathon Bewley	11	1	9.09%	+£14.72

Top trainer/jockey combos by Strike Rate – handicaps

Name of Trainer/Jockey	Qualifiers	Winners	Strike Rate	Profit/Loss to BSP

Philip Kirby/Thomas Dowson	12	4	33.33%	+£7.05
Lucinda Russell/Derek Fox	16	3	18.75%	+£3.44
Rebecca Menzies/Nathan Moscrop	11	2	18.18%	+£23.58
Nicky Richards/Brian Hughes	11	2	18.18%	-£4.98
N W Alexander/Bruce Lynn	12	2	16.67%	-£0.84

Top trainer/jockey combos by Profit – non-handicaps

Name of Trainer/Jockey	Qualifiers	Winners	Strike Rate	Profit/Loss to BSP
Sandy Thomson/Ryan Mania	15	2	13.33%	+£26.30
Donald McCain/Brian Hughes	12	5	41.67%	+£25.41
George Bewley/Jonathon Bewley	11	1	9.09%	+£14.72
Philip Kirby/Thomas Dowson	15	1	6.67%	+£9.52

Top trainer/jockey combos by Profit – handicaps

Name of Trainer/Jockey	Qualifiers	Winners	Strike Rate	Profit/Loss to BSP
Rebecca Menzies/Nathan Moscrop	11	2	18.18%	+£23.58
Philip Kirby/Thomas Dowson	12	4	33.33%	+£7.05

| Donald McCain/Brian Hughes | 10 | 1 | 10.00% | +£4.09 |
| Lucinda Russell/Derek Fox | 16 | 3 | 18.75% | +£3.44 |

Profit or Loss backing the unnamed favourite – non-handicaps

Runners	Winners	Strike Rate	Profit/Loss to BSP
346	145	41.91%	-£29.88

Profit or Loss backing the unnamed favourite – handicaps

Runners	Winners	Strike Rate	Profit/Loss to BSP
415	115	27.71%	+£20.17

Profit or loss backing the unnamed second favourite - non-handicaps

Runners	Winners	Strike Rate	Profit/Loss to BSP
342	86	25.15%	+£40.16

Profit or loss backing the unnamed second favourite - handicaps

Runners	Winners	Strike Rate	Profit/Loss to BSP
371	70	18.87%	+£13.13

Profit or Loss backing horses who won last time out- non-handicaps

Runners	Winners	Strike Rate	Profit/Loss to BSP
321	84	26.17%	+£32.32

Profit or Loss backing horses who won last time out - handicaps

Runners	Winners	Strike Rate	Profit/Loss to BSP
344	60	17.44%	-£77.67

Profit or loss backing Top-Weights in handicaps

Runners	Winners	Strike Rate	Profit/Loss to BSP
424	53	12.50%	-£45.25

Most profitable sires – non-handicaps

Sire	Runners	Winners	Strike Rate	Profit/Loss to BSP
Kayf Tara	25	5	20.00%	+£65.87
Mahler	19	1	5.26%	+£26.67
Black Sam Bellamy	13	2	15.38%	+£26.30
Fame And Glory	14	5	35.71%	+£15.81
Cloudings	11	1	9.09%	+£13.82

Most profitable sires – handicaps

Yeats	12	2	16.67%	+£53.28
Tobougg	26	4	15.38%	+£42.97
Flemensfirth	44	9	20.45%	+£33.10
King's Theatre	11	3	27.27%	+£26.95
Dylan Thomas	11	4	36.36%	+£23.87

Newton Abbot - Chases

Top jockeys by Strike Rate – non-handicaps

Name Of Jockey	Rides	Winners	Strike Rate	Profit/Loss to BSP
Sam Twiston-Davies	39	19	48.72%	+£7.50
Daryl Jacob	16	7	43.75%	+£12.33
Aidan Coleman	14	5	35.71%	+£11.98
Harry Cobden	20	5	25.00%	-£8.29
Tom Scudamore	17	3	17.65%	-£7.65

Top jockeys by Strike Rate – handicaps

Name Of Jockey	Rides	Winners	Strike Rate	Profit/Loss to BSP
Jonathan Burke	10	4	40.00%	+£8.95
Daryl Jacob	27	7	25.93%	+£2.11
Lorcan Williams	12	3	25.00%	+£6.99
Charlie Hammond	12	3	25.00%	+£8.78
Brendan Powell	66	15	22.73%	+£23.26

Top jockeys by Profit – non-handicaps

Name Of Jockey	Rides	Winners	Strike Rate	Profit/Loss to BSP
Daryl Jacob	16	7	43.75%	+£12.33
Aidan Coleman	14	5	35.71%	+£11.98
Sam Twiston-Davies	39	19	48.72%	+£7.50

Top jockeys by Profit – handicaps

Name Of Jockey	Rides	Winners	Strike Rate	Profit/Loss to BSP
Tom O'Brien	86	17	19.77%	+£31.73
Paddy Brennan	59	12	20.34%	+£26.69
Tom Cheesman	10	2	20.00%	+£26.30

Gavin Sheehan	34	5	14.71%	+£24.40
Brendan Powell	66	15	2273%	+£23.26

Top trainers by Strike Rate – non-handicaps

Name Of Trainer	Runners	Winners	Strike Rate	Profit/Loss to BSP
Paul Nicholls	74	34	45.95%	-£1.85
Colin Tizzard	25	6	24.00%	+£10.14
Evan Williams	19	4	21.05%	-£4.08
Nigel Twiston-Davies	10	2	20.00%	-£0.18
Philip Hobbs	17	2	11.76%	-£12.87

Top trainers by Strike Rate – handicaps

Name Of Trainer	Runners	Winners	Strike Rate	Profit/Loss to BSP
Joe Tizzard	14	7	50.00%	+£11.84
Oliver Sherwood	10	3	30.00%	+£0.61
Jeremy Scott	51	15	29.41%	+£68.05
Tom George	18	5	27.78%	+£13.64
David Bridgwater	41	11	26.83%	+£14.65

Top trainers by Profit – non-handicaps

Name Of Trainer	Runners	Winners	Strike Rate	Profit/Loss to BSP
Colin Tizzard	25	6	24.00%	+£10.14

Top trainers by Profit – handicaps

Name Of Trainer	Runners	Winners	Strike Rate	Profit/Loss to BSP
Jeremy Scott	51	15	29.41%	+£68.05
Alexandra Dunn	23	4	17.39%	+£41.43
Tim Vaughan	40	8	20.00%	+£29.12
Paul Henderson	65	9	13.85%	+£25.68
Jimmy Frost	73	7	9.59%	+£25.32

Top trainer/jockey combos by Strike Rate – non-handicaps

Name Of Trainer/Jockey	Rides	Winners	Strike Rate	Profit/Loss to BSP
Paul Nicholls/Sam Twiston-Davies	30	16	53.33%	-£0.45
Paul Nicholls/Harry Cobden	16	5	31.25%	-£4.29

Top trainer/jockey combos by Strike Rate – handicaps

Name of Trainer/Jockey	Qualifiers	Winners	Strike Rate	Profit/Loss to BSP
Joe Tizzard/Brendan Powell	11	5	45.45%	+£3.97
Jeremy Scott/Nick Scholfield	19	7	36.84%	+£38.63
Peter Bowen/James Bowen	12	4	33.33%	+£9.87
David Bridgwater/Tom Scudamore	19	6	31.58%	-£0.23
Nigel Twiston-Davies/Sam Twiston-Davies	15	4	26.67%	+£2.42

Top trainer/jockey combos by Profit – handicaps

Name of Trainer/Jockey	Qualifiers	Winners	Strike Rate	Profit/Loss to BSP
Jeremy Scott/Nick Scholfield	19	7	36.84%	+£38.63
Paul Henderson/Tom O'Brien	31	6	19.35%	+£37.03
Colin Tizzard/Brendan Powell	20	5	25.00%	+£29.10
Evan Williams	10	1	10.00%	+£19.23

/Conor Ring				
Jimmy Frost/Bryony Frost	30	4	13.33%	+£10.65

Profit or Loss backing the unnamed favourite – non-handicaps

Runners	Winners	Strike Rate	Profit/Loss to BSP
272	124	45.59%	-£37.37

Profit or Loss backing the unnamed favourite – handicaps

Runners	Winners	Strike Rate	Profit/Loss to BSP
687	203	29.55%	-£18.22

Profit or loss backing the unnamed second favourite - non-handicaps

Runners	Winners	Strike Rate	Profit/Loss to BSP
265	67	25.28%	-£10.23

Profit or loss backing the unnamed second favourite - handicaps

Runners	Winners	Strike Rate	Profit/Loss to BSP
609	120	19.70%	-£30.86

Profit or Loss backing horses who won last time out - non-handicaps

Runners	Winners	Strike Rate	Profit/Loss to BSP
206	70	33.98%	-£7.48

Profit or Loss backing horses who won last time out - handicaps

Runners	Winners	Strike Rate	Profit/Loss to BSP
577	131	22.70%	+£55.22

Profit or loss backing Top-Weights in handicaps

Runners	Winners	Strike Rate	Profit/Loss to BSP
496	98	19.76%	+£192.38

Most profitable sires – non-handicaps

Sire	Runners	Winners	Strike Rate	Profit/Loss to BSP
Anshan	10	2	20.00%	+£8.37
Oscar	12	3	25.00%	+£8.25
King's Theatre	21	10	47.62%	+£5.85

Most profitable sires – handicaps

Ungaro	18	5	27.78%	+£38.85
Luso	22	4	18.18%	+£32.67
Vinnie Roe	14	3	21.43%	+£24.28
King's Theatre	65	10	15.38%	+£21.66
Westerner	18	5	27.78%	+£18,57

Newton Abbot – Hurdles

Top jockeys by Strike Rate – non-handicaps

Name Of Jockey	Rides	Winners	Strike Rate	Profit/Loss to BSP
Nico de Boinville	15	6	40.00%	+£3.13
William Kennedy	13	4	30.77%	+£258.96
Paddy Brennan	27	8	29.63%	+£6.28
Harry Cobden	48	13	27.08%	-£23.88
Daryl Jacob	28	7	25.00%	-£9.33

Top jockeys by Strike Rate – handicaps

Name Of Jockey	Rides	Winners	Strike Rate	Profit/Loss to BSP
Jack Quinlan	10	3	30.00%	+£11.59
Jonathan Burke	11	3	27.27%	+£19.54
Harry Kimber	19	5	26.32%	+£18.10
Patrick Cowley	16	4	25.00%	+£12.67
Charlie Price	12	3	25.00%	+£6.55

Top jockeys by Profit – non-handicaps

Name Of Jockey	Rides	Winners	Strike Rate	Profit/Loss to BSP
William Kennedy	13	4	30.77%	+£258.96
Aidan Coleman	34	8	23.53%	+£97.55
Harry Kimber	12	3	25.00%	+£33.90
Conor O'Farrell	23	2	8.70%	+£32.86
Paddy Brennan	27	8	29.63%	+£6.28

Top jockeys by Profit – handicaps

Name Of Jockey	Rides	Winners	Strike Rate	Profit/Loss to BSP
Ben Poste	25	1	4.00%	+£270.18
Nick Scholfield	105	10	9.52%	+£143.51
Robert Dunne	28	5	17.86%	+£53.01
David Noonan	63	9	14.29%	+£42.28
Harry Cobden	70	15	21.43%	+£39.37

Top trainers by Strike Rate – non-handicaps

Name Of Trainer	Runners	Winners	Strike Rate	Profit/Loss to BSP
Olly Murphy	14	6	42.86%	+£18.37
Paul Nicholls	94	40	42.55%	-£6.39
Nicky Henderson	19	8	42.11%	+£1.32
Ian Williams	12	5	41.67%	+£0.94
Harry Fry	23	9	39.13%	+£0.65

Top trainers by Strike Rate – handicaps

Name Of Trainer	Runners	Winners	Strike Rate	Profit/Loss to BSP
Anthony Honeyball	11	3	27.27%	-£1.93
Jonjo O'Neill	65	16	24.62%	+£1.82
Nicky Henderson	25	6	24.00%	+£18.08
Emma Lavelle	23	5	21.74%	+£38.59
Dr Richard Newland	28	6	21.43%	-£12.10

Top trainers by Profit – non-handicaps

Name Of Trainer	Runners	Winners	Strike Rate	Profit/Loss to BSP
Gail Haywood	27	2	7.41%	+£455.80
Emma Lavelle	17	5	29.41%	+£41.54
Bill Turner	21	3	14.29%	+£22.69
Venetia Williams	14	2	14.29%	+£21.91
Olly Murphy	14	6	42.86%	+£18.37

Top trainers by Profit – handicaps

Name Of Trainer	Runners	Winners	Strike Rate	Profit/Loss to BSP
Gail Haywood	32	3	9.38%	+£284.97
Neil Mulholland	104	9	8.65%	+£115.85
Sue Gardner	90	10	11.11%	+£82.68
Sophie Leech	59	11	18.64%	+£56.61
Bernard Llewellyn	100	10	10.00%	+£56.50

Top trainer/jockey combos by Strike Rate – non-handicaps

Name of Trainer/Jockey	Qualifiers	Winners	Strike Rate	Profit/Loss to BSP
Paul Nicholls/Harry Cobden	26	11	42.31%	-£5.81
Gary Moore/Jamie Moore	13	5	38.46%	+£18.47
Jeremy Scott/Nick Scholfield	12	4	33.33%	+£6.94
Tim Vaughan/Alan Johns	13	4	30.77%	-£0.96
Paul Nicholls/Sam Twiston-Davies	34	10	29.41%	-£8.07

Top trainer/jockey combos by Strike Rate – handicaps

Name of Trainer/Jockey	Qualifiers	Winners	Strike Rate	Profit/Loss to BSP
Colin Tizzard/Harry Cobden	16	6	37.50%	+£24.44
Jonjo O'Neill/Richie McLernon	12	4	33.33%	+£12.39
Nigel Hawke/David Noonan	10	3	30.00%	+£8.09
Peter Bowen/Sean Bowen	12	3	25.00%	+£38.10
Jamie Snowden/Page Fuller	12	3	25.00%	-£1.26

Top trainer/jockey combos by Profit – non-handicaps

Name of Trainer/Jockey	Qualifiers	Winners	Strike Rate	Profit/Loss to BSP
Chris Down/James Davies	18	2	11.11%	+£19.93
Gary Moore/Jamie Moore	13	5	38.46%	+£18.47
Philip Hobbs/Tom O'Brien	22	6	27.27%	+£13.60
Jeremy Scott/Nick Scholfield	12	4	33.33%	+£6.94
Dan Skelton/Harry Skelton	22	6	27.27%	+£1.40

Top trainer/jockey combos by Profit – handicaps

Name of Trainer/Jockey	Qualifiers	Winners	Strike Rate	Profit/Loss to BSP
Peter Bowen/Sean	12	3	25.00%	+£38.10

Bowen				
David Pipe/David Noonan	18	2	11.11%	+£36.28
Tim Vaughan/Alan Johns	25	4	16.00%	+£29.27
Colin Tizzard/Harry Cobden	16	6	37.50%	+£24.44
Colin Tizzard/Brendan Powell	14	2	14.29%	+£18.19

Profit or Loss backing the unnamed favourite – non-handicaps

Runners	Winners	Strike Rate	Profit/Loss to BSP
618	276	44.66%	-£27.55

Profit or Loss backing the unnamed favourite – handicaps

Runners	Winners	Strike Rate	Profit/Loss to BSP
797	228	28.61%	+£7.05

Profit or loss backing the unnamed second favourite - non-handicaps

Runners	Winners	Strike Rate	Profit/Loss to BSP
586	144	24.57%	+£14.72

Profit or loss backing the unnamed second favourite - handicaps

Runners	Winners	Strike Rate	Profit/Loss to BSP
765	129	16.86%	-£66.59

Profit or Loss backing horses who won last time out- non-handicaps

Runners	Winners	Strike Rate	Profit/Loss to BSP
373	140	37.53%	-£4.08

Profit or Loss backing horses who won last time out - handicaps

Runners	Winners	Strike Rate	Profit/Loss to BSP
772	152	19.69%	+£56.36

Profit or loss backing Top-Weights in handicaps

Runners	Winners	Strike Rate	Profit/Loss to BSP
424	53	12.50%	-£45.25

Most profitable sires – non-handicaps

Sire	Runners	Winners	Strike Rate	Profit/Loss to BSP
Mahler	12	3	25.00%	+£266.73
Heron Island	12	3	25.00%	+£47.20
Mountain High	11	2	18.18%	+£37.63
Beneficial	21	4	19.05%	+£9.20
Kalanisi	17	6	35.29%	+£6.29

Most profitable sires – handicaps

Kayf Tara	62	8	12.90%	+£300.92
Saint Des Saints	12	3	25.00%	+£93.06
Arvico	13	2	15.38%	+£89.15
Cape Cross	23	7	30.43%	+£60.11
Zoffany	11	2	18.18%	+£38.76

Perth - Chases

Top jockeys by Strike Rate – non-handicaps

Name Of Jockey	Rides	Winners	Strike Rate	Profit/Loss to BSP
Sam Twiston-Davies	10	6	60.00%	+£0.58
Brian Hughes	18	5	27.78%	-£6.99
Kit Alexander	10	1	10.00%	-£6.10

Top jockeys by Strike Rate – handicaps

Name Of Jockey	Rides	Winners	Strike Rate	Profit/Loss to BSP
James Bowen	19	6	31.58%	+£7.47
Jonjo O'Neill Jr	10	3	30.00%	+£7.61
Sean Bowen	47	13	27.66%	+£22.24
Brian Hughes	198	43	21.72%	+£47.64
Harry Reed	19	4	21.05%	+£7.75

Top jockeys by Profit – non-handicaps

Name Of Jockey	Rides	Winners	Strike Rate	Profit/Loss to BSP
Sam Twiston-Davies	10	6	60.00%	+£0.58

Top jockeys by Profit – handicaps

Name Of Jockey	Rides	Winners	Strike Rate	Profit/Loss to BSP
Brian Hughes	198	43	21.72%	+£47.64
Stephen Mulqueen	66	12	18.18%	+£30.35
Sean Quinlan	62	10	16.13%	+£30.02
Sean Bowen	47	13	27.66%	+£22.24
Dougie Costello	13	2	15.38%	+£19.18

Top trainers by Strike Rate – non-handicaps

Name Of Trainer	Runners	Winners	Strike Rate	Profit/Loss to BSP
Nigel Twiston-Davies	11	6	54.55%	-£1.86
Fergal O'Brien	13	5	38.46%	+£3.35
Donald McCain	10	3	30.00%	-£0.47
Nicky Richards	14	3	21.43%	+£0.41
Gordon Elliott	28	6	21.43%	+£2.00

Top trainers by Strike Rate – handicaps

Name Of Trainer	Runners	Winners	Strike Rate	Profit/Loss to BSP
Paul Nicholls	10	5	50.00%	+£18.42
Tim Reed	11	4	36.36%	+£15.75
David Pipe	15	5	33.33%	+£10.59
Tim Vaughan	18	6	33.33%	+£16.65
Dr Richard Newland	16	5	31.25%	+£3.77

Top trainers by Profit – non-handicaps

Name Of Trainer	Runners	Winners	Strike Rate	Profit/Loss to BSP
N W Alexander	18	1	5.56%	+£35.92
Fergal O'Brien	13	5	38.46%	+£3.35
Gordon Elliott	28	6	21.43%	+£2.00
Nicky Richards	14	3	21.43%	+£0.41

Top trainers by Profit – handicaps

Name Of Trainer	Runners	Winners	Strike Rate	Profit/Loss to BSP
Gordon Elliott	126	32	25.40%	+£53.24
Donald McCain	61	19	31.15%	+£39.57
Sandy Thomson	40	6	15.00%	+£34.87
Jennie Candlish	23	5	21.74%	+£25.21
Fergal O'Brien	55	15	27.27%	+£22.82

Top trainer/jockey combos by Strike Rate – handicaps

Name of Trainer/Jockey	Qualifiers	Winners	Strike Rate	Profit/Loss to BSP

Donald McCain/Brian Hughes	24	10	41.67%	+£9.17
Peter Bowen/James Bowen	13	5	38.46%	+£9.24
David Pipe/Tom Scudamore	13	5	38.46%	+£12.59
Gordon Elliott/Sean Bowen	19	7	36.84%	+£13.34
Tim Reed/Harry Reed	11	4	36.36%	+£15.75

Top trainer/jockey combos by Profit – handicaps

Name of Trainer/Jockey	Qualifiers	Winners	Strike Rate	Profit/Loss to BSP
Lucinda Russell/Stephen Mulqueen	46	10	21.74%	+£35.49
Jennie Candlish/Sean Quinlan	21	5	23.81%	+£27.21
Rose Dobbin/Craig Nichol	25	9	36.00%	+£19.17
Tim Reed/Harry Reed	11	4	36.36%	+£15.75
Gordon Elliott/Sean Bowen	19	7	36.84%	+£13.34

Profit or Loss backing the unnamed favourite – non-handicaps

Runners	Winners	Strike Rate	Profit/Loss to BSP
188	84	44.68%	-£1.77

Profit or Loss backing the unnamed favourite – handicaps

Runners	Winners	Strike Rate	Profit/Loss to BSP

617	153	24.80%	-£102.99

Profit or loss backing the unnamed second favourite - non-handicaps

Runners	Winners	Strike Rate	Profit/Loss to BSP
174	43	24.71%	-£6.13

Profit or loss backing the unnamed second favourite - handicaps

Runners	Winners	Strike Rate	Profit/Loss to BSP
553	126	22.78%	+£75.37

Profit or Loss backing horses who won last time out - non-handicaps

Runners	Winners	Strike Rate	Profit/Loss to BSP
150	49	32.67%	+£1.31

Profit or Loss backing horses who won last time out - handicaps

Runners	Winners	Strike Rate	Profit/Loss to BSP
678	108	15.93%	-£158.03

Profit or loss backing Top-Weights in handicaps

Runners	Winners	Strike Rate	Profit/Loss to BSP
635	108	17.01%	-£36.58

Most profitable sires – handicaps

King's Theatre	24	4	16.67%	+£39.56
Milan	60	14	23.33%	+£38.55
Witness Box	14	5	35.71%	+£29.38
Westerner	25	7	28.00%	+£26.70
Fantastic Light	15	3	20.00%	+£26.61

Perth – Hurdles

Top jockeys by Strike Rate – non-handicaps

Name Of Jockey	Rides	Winners	Strike Rate	Profit/Loss to BSP
Sean Bowen	21	13	61.90%	+£5.15
A P Heskin	11	6	54.55%	+£16.20
Daryl Jacob	17	7	41.18%	+£3.57
Tom O'Brien	14	5	35.71%	+£7.19
Tom Scudamore	27	8	29.63%	-£0.11

Top jockeys by Strike Rate – handicaps

Name Of Jockey	Rides	Winners	Strike Rate	Profit/Loss to BSP
Harry Skelton	10	4	40.00%	+£6.61
Billy Garritty	12	3	25.00%	+£20.09
Sean Bowen	39	8	20.51%	+£2.12
Aidan Coleman	20	4	20.00%	+£13.43
Sam Twiston-Davies	61	12	19.67%	-£0.99

Top jockeys by Profit – non-handicaps

Name Of Jockey	Rides	Winners	Strike Rate	Profit/Loss to BSP
A P Heskin	11	6	54.55%	+£16.20
Callum Bewley	47	2	4.26%	+£15.04
Craig Nichol	58	5	8.62%	+£13.08
Tom O'Brien	14	5	35.71%	+£7.19
Derek Fox	55	3	5.45%	+£5.54

Top jockeys by Profit – handicaps

Name Of Jockey	Rides	Winners	Strike Rate	Profit/Loss to BSP
Sam Coltherd	42	4	9.52%	+£149.32
Stephen Mulqueen	76	2	2.63%	+£37.58
John Dixon	13	1	7.69%	+£36.02
Charlotte Jones	25	4	16.00%	+£26.29
Conor O'Farrell	61	10	16.39%	+£26.09

Top trainers by Strike Rate – non-handicaps

Name Of Trainer	Runners	Winners	Strike Rate	Profit/Loss to BSP
Gordon Elliott	111	51	45.95%	+£10.32
John C McConnell	12	5	41.67%	+£4.80
Tom George	10	4	40.00%	-£0.18
Tim Vaughan	11	4	36.36%	-£1.34
Nigel Twiston-Davies	27	9	33.33%	-£8.29

Top trainers by Strike Rate – handicaps

Name Of Trainer	Runners	Winners	Strike Rate	Profit/Loss to BSP
Dan Skelton	10	5	50.00%	+£11.00
Peter Bowen	22	7	31.82%	+£14.36
Tim Vaughan	22	6	27.27%	+£5.32
Neil Mulholland	29	7	24.14%	+£18.22
Gordon Elliott	150	36	24.00%	+£3.10

Top trainers by Profit – non-handicaps

Name Of Trainer	Runners	Winners	Strike Rate	Profit/Loss to BSP
Maurice Barnes	42	3	7.14%	+£61.09
Jim Goldie	26	1	3.85%	+£31.98
William Young Jnr	11	1	9.09%	+£29.60
Olly Murphy	24	6	25.00%	+£18.06
Lucinda Russell	144	14	9.72%	+£16.84

Top trainers by Profit – handicaps

Name Of Trainer	Runners	Winners	Strike Rate	Profit/Loss to BSP
William Young Jnr	28	2	7.14%	+£98.40
Katie Scott	12	1	8.33%	+£92.35
Sandy Forster	11	2	18.18%	+£55.71
Keith Dalgleish	38	8	21.05%	+£38.92
Susan Corbett	47	8	17.02%	+£36.03

Top trainer/jockey combos by Strike Rate – non-handicaps

Name of Trainer/Jockey	Qualifiers	Winners	Strike Rate	Profit/Loss to BSP
Gordon Elliott/Sean Bowen	12	8	66.67%	+£3.46
Nigel Twiston-Davies/Sam Twiston-Davies	22	6	27.27%	-£8.96
Olly Murphy/Aidan Coleman	10	2	20.00%	-£0.45
Lucinda Russell/Craig Nichol	10	2	20.00%	+£11.05
Iain Jardine/Ross Chapman	10	2	20.00%	-£3.44

Top trainer/jockey combos by Strike Rate – handicaps

Name of Trainer/Jockey	Qualifiers	Winners	Strike Rate	Profit/Loss to BSP
Jim Goldie/Brian Hughes	10	4	40.00%	+£8.15
Gordon Elliott/Sean Bowen	13	4	30.77%	+£10.93
Keith Dalgleish/Brian Hughes	10	3	30.00%	+£14.07
Donald McCain/Brian Hughes	20	6	30.00%	+£24.92
Jim Goldie/Harry Reed	15	4	26.67%	+£12.23

Top trainer/jockey combos by Profit – non-handicaps

Name of Trainer/Jockey	Qualifiers	Winners	Strike Rate	Profit/Loss to BSP
Jim Goldie/Callum Bewley	10	1	10.00%	+£47.98

S R B Crawford/Brian Hughes	17	1	5.88%	+£12.26
Lucinda Russell/Craig Nichol	10	2	20.00%	+£11.05
Gordon Elliott/Sean Bowen	12	8	66.67%	+£3.46

Top trainer/jockey combos by Profit – handicaps

Name of Trainer/Jockey	Qualifiers	Winners	Strike Rate	Profit/Loss to BSP
Stuart Coltherd/Sam Colthered	18	1	5.56%	+£40.82
James Moffatt/Charlotte Jones	18	4	22.22%	+£33.29
Nicky Richards/Craig Nichol	15	3	20.00%	+£28.87
Donald McCain/ Brian Hughes	20	6	30.00%	+£24.92
Lisa Harrison//Callum Bewley	27	3	11.11%	+£21.55

Profit or Loss backing the unnamed favourite – non-handicaps

Runners	Winners	Strike Rate	Profit/Loss to BSP
464	232	50.00%	+£26.42

Profit or Loss backing the unnamed favourite – handicaps

Runners	Winners	Strike Rate	Profit/Loss to BSP
689	198	28.74%	+£25.72

Profit or loss backing the unnamed second favourite - non-handicaps

Runners	Winners	Strike Rate	Profit/Loss to BSP
436	90	20.64%	-£68.69

Profit or loss backing the unnamed second favourite - handicaps

Runners	Winners	Strike Rate	Profit/Loss to BSP
651	143	21.97%	+£111.81

Profit or Loss backing horses who won last time out- non-handicaps

Runners	Winners	Strike Rate	Profit/Loss to BSP
310	116	37.42%	-£6.72

Profit or Loss backing horses who won last time out - handicaps

Runners	Winners	Strike Rate	Profit/Loss to BSP
630	121	19.21%	-£48.89

Profit or loss backing Top-Weights in handicaps

Runners	Winners	Strike Rate	Profit/Loss to BSP
723	79	10.93%	-£233.97

Most profitable sires – non-handicaps

Sire	Runners	Winners	Strike Rate	Profit/Loss to BSP
Flemensfirth	33	3	9.09%	+£38.78
Kalanisi	10	3	30.00%	+£11.67
Sir Percy	12	4	33.33%	+£2.21
Court Cave	15	3	20.00%	+£1.18
Getaway	10	3	30.00%	+£1.01

Most profitable sires – handicaps

Shantou	28	6	21.43%	+£134.03
Dubai	17	2	11.76%	+£53.82

Destination				
Bushranger	31	6	19.35%	+£37.18
Heron Island	15	1	6.67%	+£34.02
Poet's Voice	25	8	32.00%	+£29.18

Plumpton - Chases

Top jockeys by Strike Rate – non-handicaps

Name Of Jockey	Rides	Winners	Strike Rate	Profit/Loss to BSP
Joshua Moore	14	5	35.71%	+£3.62
Jamie Moore	14	4	28.57%	+£2.64

Top jockeys by Strike Rate – handicaps

Name Of Jockey	Rides	Winners	Strike Rate	Profit/Loss to BSP
Harry Bannister	14	6	42.86%	+£26.70
Daryl Jacob	11	4	36.36%	+£3.45
Michael Nolan	11	4	36.36%	+£9.40
Tom Scudamore	52	15	28.85%	+£14.45
Paddy Brennan	30	8	26.67%	+£42.82

Top jockeys by Profit – non-handicaps

Name Of Jockey	Rides	Winners	Strike Rate	Profit/Loss to BSP
Joshua Moore	14	5	35.71%	+£3.62
Jamie Moore	14	4	28.57%	+£2.64

Top jockeys by Profit – handicaps

Name Of Jockey	Rides	Winners	Strike Rate	Profit/Loss to BSP
Tom Cannon	125	23	18.40%	+£67.47
James Best	39	8	20.51%	+£61.36
Paddy Brennan	30	8	26.67%	+£42.82
Richie McLernon	16	4	25.00%	+£36.44
James Davies	24	5	20.83%	+£31.93

Top trainers by Strike Rate – non-handicaps

Name Of Trainer	Runners	Winners	Strike Rate	Profit/Loss to BSP

Nicky Henderson	10	5	50.00%	-£2.56
Alan King	11	5	45.45%	+£0.32
Gary Moore	28	10	35.71%	+£65.13
Paul Nicholls	10	2	20.00%	-£6.84

Top trainers by Strike Rate – handicaps

Name Of Trainer	Runners	Winners	Strike Rate	Profit/Loss to BSP
Oliver Sherwood	20	6	30.00%	+£3.06
Emma Lavelle	20	6	30.00%	+£0.51
Paul Nicholls	14	4	28.57%	+£3.86
Sheena West	22	6	27.27%	+£17.03
Venetia Williams	29	7	24.14%	-£5.42

Top trainers by Profit – non-handicaps

Name Of Trainer	Runners	Winners	Strike Rate	Profit/Loss to BSP
Gary Moore	28	10	35.71%	+£65.13
Alan King	11	5	45.45%	+£0.32

Top trainers by Profit – handicaps

Name Of Trainer	Runners	Winners	Strike Rate	Profit/Loss to BSP
Paul Henderson	71	16	22.54%	+£74.09
David Bridgwater	80	18	22.50%	+£61.10
Seamus Mullins	117	23	19.66%	+£46.40
Chris Gordon	93	20	21.51%	+£26.80
Tony Carroll	10	2	20.00%	+£25.96

Top trainer/jockey combos by Strike Rate – non-handicaps

Name Of Trainer/Jockey	Rides	Winners	Strike Rate	Profit/Loss to BSP
Gary Moore/Joshua Moore	13	5	38.46%	+£4.62
Gary Moore/Jamie	11	4	36.36%	+£5.64

Moore				

Top trainer/jockey combos by Strike Rate – handicaps

Name of Trainer/Jockey	Qualifiers	Winners	Strike Rate	Profit/Loss to BSP
David Pipe/Tom Scudamore	11	4	36.36%	+£6.97
Paul Henderson/Paddy Brennan	11	4	36.36%	+£26.87
Venetia Williams/Aidan Coleman	12	4	33.33%	-£1.40
Sheena West/Marc Goldstein	17	5	29.41%	+£16.52
David Bridgwater/Tom Scudamore	25	7	28.00%	+£0.46

Top trainer/jockey combos by Profit – non-handicaps

Name of Trainer/Jockey	Qualifiers	Winners	Strike Rate	Profit/Loss to BSP
Gary Moore/Jamie Moore	11	4	36.36%	+£5.64
Gary Moore/Joshua Moore	13	5	38.46%	+£4.62

Top trainer/jockey combos by Profit – handicaps

Name of Trainer/Jockey	Qualifiers	Winners	Strike Rate	Profit/Loss to BSP
Chris Gordon/Tom Cannon	58	13	22.41%	+£26.31
Paul Henderson/Nick Scholfield	12	2	16.67%	+£23.95
Sheena	17	5	29.41%	+£16.52

West/Marc Goldstein				
Nick Gifford/Tom Cannon	13	2	15.38%	+£14.34
Paul Henderson/Tom O'Brien	23	5	21.74%	+£11.56

Profit or Loss backing the unnamed favourite – non-handicaps

Runners	Winners	Strike Rate	Profit/Loss to BSP
160	90	56.25%	+£27.15

Profit or Loss backing the unnamed favourite – handicaps

Runners	Winners	Strike Rate	Profit/Loss to BSP
684	213	31.14%	-£15.07

Profit or loss backing the unnamed second favourite - non-handicaps

Runners	Winners	Strike Rate	Profit/Loss to BSP
153	37	24.18%	+£3.89

Profit or loss backing the unnamed second favourite - handicaps

Runners	Winners	Strike Rate	Profit/Loss to BSP
671	143	21.31%	-£20.44

Profit or Loss backing horses who won last time out - non-handicaps

Runners	Winners	Strike Rate	Profit/Loss to BSP
94	32	34.04%	-£10.71

Profit or Loss backing horses who won last time out - handicaps

Runners	Winners	Strike Rate	Profit/Loss to BSP

447	108	24.16%	-£12.98

Profit or loss backing Top-Weights in handicaps

Runners	Winners	Strike Rate	Profit/Loss to BSP
723	128	17.70%	-£132.63

Most profitable sires – handicaps

Robin Des Pres	15	5	33.33%	+£63.37
High Chaparral	12	3	25.00%	+£46.48
Alflora	15	3	20.00%	+£39.98
Jimble	16	4	25.00%	+£39.72
Spadoun	14	2	14.29%	+£30.32

Plumpton – Hurdles

Top jockeys by Strike Rate – non-handicaps

Name Of Jockey	Rides	Winners	Strike Rate	Profit/Loss to BSP
Harry Cobden	21	7	33.33%	+£0.65
Aidan Coleman	49	16	32.65%	+£14.60
Harry Skelton	16	5	31.25%	-£2.52
Nico de Boinville	19	4	21.05%	-£1.04
Gavin Sheehan	55	11	20.00%	+£8.17

Top jockeys by Strike Rate – handicaps

Name Of Jockey	Rides	Winners	Strike Rate	Profit/Loss to BSP
Phillip York	11	3	27.27%	+£45.43
Robert Dunne	15	4	26.67%	+£13.42
Harry Cobden	28	7	25.00%	+£24.91
Harry Bannister	16	4	25.00%	+£1.24
Kieron Edgar	12	3	25.00%	+30.66

Top jockeys by Profit – non-handicaps

Name Of Jockey	Rides	Winners	Strike Rate	Profit/Loss to BSP

Tom O'Brien	45	4	8.89%	+£288.21
Joshua Moore	89	12	13.48%	+£25.70
Trevor Whelan	14	1	7.14%	+£18.09
Aidan Coleman	49	16	32.65%	+£14.60
Kevin Jones	15	2	13.33%	+£8.21

Top jockeys by Profit – handicaps

Name Of Jockey	Rides	Winners	Strike Rate	Profit/Loss to BSP
Tom Cannon	170	24	14.12%	£129.79
Tabitha Worsley	30	2	6.67%	+£62.47
William Featherstone	12	2	16.67%	+£46.52
Phillip York	11	3	27.27%	+£45.43
Sean Houlihan	26	2	7.69%	+£39.29

Top trainers by Strike Rate – non-handicaps

Name Of Trainer	Runners	Winners	Strike Rate	Profit/Loss to BSP
Alan King	61	23	37.70%	-£6.14
Philip Hobbs	14	5	35.71%	-£3.01
Anthony Honeyball	21	7	33.33%	-£7.39
Dan Skelton	18	6	33.33%	-£1.88
Venetia Williams	29	9	31.03%	+£15.26

Top trainers by Strike Rate – handicaps

Name Of Trainer	Runners	Winners	Strike Rate	Profit/Loss to BSP
Paul Nicholls	11	5	45.45%	+£23.98
Nicky Henderson	19	7	36.84%	+£22.64
Ian Williams	12	4	33.33%	+£5.00
Harry Fry	12	4	33.33%	-£1.07
Lydia Richards	10	3	30.00%	+£13.35

Top trainers by Profit – non-handicaps

Name Of Trainer	Runners	Winners	Strike Rate	Profit/Loss to BSP

Suzy Smith	26	3	11.54%	+£64.51
Paul Henderson	17	1	5.88%	+£59.53
Michael Roberts	15	1	6.67%	+£34.06
Chris Gordon	80	20	25.00%	+£16.62
Venetia Williams	29	9	31.03%	+£15.26

Top trainers by Profit – handicaps

Name Of Trainer	Runners	Winners	Strike Rate	Profit/Loss to BSP
Suzy Smith	67	17	25.37%	+£94.79
Chris Gordon	184	27	14.67%	+£63.78
Andy Irvine	33	2	6.06%	+£57.98
Phillip York	11	3	27.27%	+£45.43
Pat Phelan	34	2	5.88%	+£33.90

Top trainer/jockey combos by Strike Rate – non-handicaps

Name of Trainer/Jockey	Qualifiers	Winners	Strike Rate	Profit/Loss to BSP
Paul Nicholls/Harry Cobden	11	5	45.45%	+£0.98
Venetia Williams/Aidan Coleman	18	8	44.44%	+£20.95
Dan Skelton/Harry Skelton	13	5	38.46%	+£0.48
Chris Gordon/Tom Cannon	51	17	33.33%	+£6.62
Nicky Henderson/Nico de Boinville	10	3	30.00%	+£2.98

Top trainer/jockey combos by Strike Rate – handicaps

Name of Trainer/Jockey	Qualifiers	Winners	Strike Rate	Profit/Loss to BSP
Paul Henderson/Tom O'Brien	14	6	42.86%	+£24.32

Chris Gordon/Harry Reed	10	3	30.00%	+£10.37
Suzy Smith/Gavin Sheehan	15	4	26.67%	+£27.03
David Pipe/Tom Scudamore	23	6	26.09%	+£22.19
Gary Moore/Niall Houlihan	21	4	19.05%	-£5.29

Top trainer/jockey combos by Profit – non-handicaps

Name of Trainer/Jockey	Qualifiers	Winners	Strike Rate	Profit/Loss to BSP
Venetia Williams/Aidan Coleman	18	8	44.44%	+£20.95
Warren Greatrex/Gavin Sheehan	24	7	29.17%	+£16.03
Seamus Mullins/Kevin Jones	10	2	20.00%	+£13.21
Sheena West/Marc Goldstein	36	3	8.33%	+£10.42
Chris Gordon/Tom Cannon	51	17	33.33%	+£6.62

Top trainer/jockey combos by Profit – handicaps

Name of Trainer/Jockey	Qualifiers	Winners	Strike Rate	Profit/Loss to BSP
Chris Gordon/Tom Cannon	106	19	17.92%	+£90.56
Pat Phelan/Sean Houlihan	12	1	8.33%	+£51.03
Anna Newton-Smith/Adam	20	2	10.00%	+£32.95

Wedge				
Suzy Smith/Gavin Sheehan	15	4	26.67%	+£27.03
Paul Henderson/Tom O'Brien	14	6	42.86%	+£24.32

Profit or Loss backing the unnamed favourite – non-handicaps

Runners	Winners	Strike Rate	Profit/Loss to BSP
581	248	42.69%	-£65.79

Profit or Loss backing the unnamed favourite – handicaps

Runners	Winners	Strike Rate	Profit/Loss to BSP
705	211	29.93%	+£12.85

Profit or loss backing the unnamed second favourite - non-handicaps

Runners	Winners	Strike Rate	Profit/Loss to BSP
559	128	22.90%	+£4.17

Profit or loss backing the unnamed second favourite - handicaps

Runners	Winners	Strike Rate	Profit/Loss to BSP
650	101	15.54%	-£135.04

Profit or Loss backing horses who won last time out- non-handicaps

Runners	Winners	Strike Rate	Profit/Loss to BSP
288	100	34.72%	+£15.80

Profit or Loss backing horses who won last time out - handicaps

Runners	Winners	Strike Rate	Profit/Loss to BSP
459	115	25.05%	+£52.66

Profit or loss backing Top-Weights in handicaps

Runners	Winners	Strike Rate	Profit/Loss to BSP
735	100	13.61%	-£141.73

Most profitable sires – non-handicaps

Sire	Runners	Winners	Strike Rate	Profit/Loss to BSP
Shirocco	29	7	24.14%	+£255.22
Mahler	21	6	28.57%	+£67.89
Norse Dancer	11	1	9.09%	+£20.38
Hernando	12	6	50.00%	+£9.88
Tikkanen	12	2	16.67%	+£7.97

Most profitable sires – handicaps

Karinga Bay	25	8	32.00%	+£149.52
Gold Well	15	6	40.00%	+£64.75
Montjeu	26	5	19.23%	+£55.51
Winker Watson	40	7	17.50%	+£45.63
Kayf Tara	60	8	13.33%	+£42.70

Sandown - Chases

Top jockeys by Strike Rate – non-handicaps

Name Of Jockey	Rides	Winners	Strike Rate	Profit/Loss to BSP
Jamie Moore	10	5	50.00%	+£20.27
Nico de Boinville	21	10	47.62%	-£4.28
Jody Sole	17	6	35.29%	-£1.44
Daryl Jacob	29	10	34.48%	+£18.86
Harry Cobden	19	4	21.05%	-£3.10

Top jockeys by Strike Rate – handicaps

Name Of Jockey	Rides	Winners	Strike Rate	Profit/Loss to BSP
David Bass	12	3	25.00%	+£10.21
Jamie Moore	75	18	24.00%	+£25.63
Charlie Deutsch	36	8	22.22%	+£4.69
Daryl Jacob	39	8	20.51%	+£24.48
Joshua Moore	26	5	19.23%	+£1.95

Top jockeys by Profit – non-handicaps

Name Of Jockey	Rides	Winners	Strike Rate	Profit/Loss to BSP
Joshua Moore	10	2	20.00%	+£24.61
Jamie Moore	10	5	50.00%	+£20.27
Daryl Jacob	29	10	34.48%	+£18.86

Top jockeys by Profit – handicaps

Name Of Jockey	Rides	Winners	Strike Rate	Profit/Loss to BSP
Sean Bowen	29	4	13.79%	+£47.42
Jamie Moore	75	18	24.00%	+£25.63
Daryl Jacob	39	8	20.51%	+£24.48
Adam Wedge	23	2	8.70%	+£14.92
Harry Bannister	16	2	12.50%	+£13.44

Top trainers by Strike Rate – non-handicaps

Name Of Trainer	Runners	Winners	Strike Rate	Profit/Loss to BSP
Philip Hobbs	17	9	52.94%	+£33.65
Nicky Henderson	51	18	35.29%	-£13.03
Gary Moore	22	7	31.82%	+£42.89
David Pipe	10	3	30.00%	-£0.87
Paul Nicholls	101	25	24.75%	+£2.60

Top trainers by Strike Rate – handicaps

Name Of Trainer	Runners	Winners	Strike Rate	Profit/Loss to BSP
Kerry Lee	16	4	25.00%	+£4.89
Alan King	27	6	22.22%	+£34.54
Henry Daly	10	2	20.00%	+£18.42
Nick Gifford	32	6	18.75%	+£13.55
Oliver Sherwood	22	4	18.18%	-£1.63

Top trainers by Profit – non-handicaps

Name Of Trainer	Runners	Winners	Strike Rate	Profit/Loss to BSP
Gary Moore	22	7	31.82%	+£42.89
Philip Hobbs	17	9	52.94%	+£33.65
Paul Nicholls	101	25	24.75%	+£2.60

Top trainers by Profit – handicaps

Name Of Trainer	Runners	Winners	Strike Rate	Profit/Loss to BSP
Peter Bowen	10	1	10.00%	+£43.55
Alan King	27	6	22.22%	+£34.54
Charlie Longsdon	60	7	11.67%	+£32.71
Henry Daly	10	2	20.00%	+£18.42
Tim Vaughan	13	2	15.38%	+£17.48

Top trainer/jockey combos by Strike Rate – non-handicaps

Name Of	Rides	Winners	Strike Rate	Profit/Loss to

Trainer/Jockey				BSP
Gary Moore/Jamie Moore	10	5	50.00%	+£20.27
Nicky Henderson/Nico de Boinville	19	9	47.37%	-£3.52
Paul Nicholls/Jody Sole	13	5	38.46%	-£2.36
Paul Nicholls/Harry Cobden	19	4	21.05%	-£3.13
Gary Moore/Joshua Moore	10	2	20.00%	+£24.61

Top trainer/jockey combos by Strike Rate – handicaps

Name of Trainer/Jockey	Qualifiers	Winners	Strike Rate	Profit/Loss to BSP
Nick Gifford/Tom Cannon	12	3	25.00%	+£11.75
Venetia Williams/Charlie Deutsch	35	8	22.86%	+£5.69
Paul Nicholls/Harry Cobden	27	6	22.22%	+£15.50
Venetia Williams/Aidan Coleman	41	9	21.95%	+£0.15
Gary Moore/Jamie Moore	50	10	20.00%	+£5.99

Top trainer/jockey combos by Profit – non-handicaps

Name of Trainer/Jockey	Qualifiers	Winners	Strike Rate	Profit/Loss to BSP
Gary Moore/Joshua	10	2	20.00%	+£24.61

Moore				
Gary Moore/Jamie Moore	10	5	50.00%	+£20.27

Top trainer/jockey combos by Profit – handicaps

Name of Trainer/Jockey	Qualifiers	Winners	Strike Rate	Profit/Loss to BSP
Paul Nicholls/Harry Cobden	27	6	22.22%	+£15.50
Nick Gifford/Tom Cannon	12	3	25.00%	+£11.75
Gary Moore/Jamie Moore	50	10	20.00%	+£5.99
Venetia Williams/Charlie Deutsch	35	8	22.86%	+£5.69
Evan Williams/Adam Wedge	16	1	6.25%	+£4.57

Profit or Loss backing the unnamed favourite – non-handicaps

Runners	Winners	Strike Rate	Profit/Loss to BSP
227	115	50.66%	+£31.85

Profit or Loss backing the unnamed favourite – handicaps

Runners	Winners	Strike Rate	Profit/Loss to BSP
393	93	23.66%	-£55.13

Profit or loss backing the unnamed second favourite - non-handicaps

Runners	Winners	Strike Rate	Profit/Loss to BSP
203	45	22.17%	-£7.88

Profit or loss backing the unnamed second favourite - handicaps

Runners	Winners	Strike Rate	Profit/Loss to BSP
354	70	19.77%	+£12.81

Profit or Loss backing horses who won last time out - non-handicaps

Runners	Winners	Strike Rate	Profit/Loss to BSP
314	78	24.84%	-£22.51

Profit or Loss backing horses who won last time out - handicaps

Runners	Winners	Strike Rate	Profit/Loss to BSP
504	71	14.09%	-£86.70

Profit or loss backing Top-Weights in handicaps

Runners	Winners	Strike Rate	Profit/Loss to BSP
398	53	13.32%	-£41.64

Most profitable sires – non-handicaps

Sire	Runners	Winners	Strike Rate	Profit/Loss to BSP
Poliglote	13	6	46.15%	+£13.75
King's Theatre	11	4	36.36%	+£8.55
Voix Du Nord	11	3	27.27%	+£4.75

Most profitable sires – handicaps

King's Theatre	75	7	9.33%	+£75.12
Midnight Legend	55	12	21.82%	+£31.80
Indian River	14	3	21.43%	+£17.40
Kapgarde	26	8	30.77%	+£16.73
Saddler's Hall	10	1	10.00%	+£10.30

Sandown – Hurdles

Top jockeys by Strike Rate – non-handicaps

Name Of Jockey	Rides	Winners	Strike Rate	Profit/Loss to BSP
David Bass	15	7	46.67%	+£27.62
Sean Bowen	10	4	40.00%	+£1.85
Nico de Boinville	30	10	33.33%	-£6.81
Tom O'Brien	14	4	28.57%	+£2.20
Daryl Jacob	31	6	19.35%	-£10.05

Top jockeys by Strike Rate – handicaps

Name Of Jockey	Rides	Winners	Strike Rate	Profit/Loss to BSP
Sean Houlihan	12	3	25.00%	+£34.90
Niall Houlihan	13	3	23.08%	+£5.00
David Noonan	10	2	20.00%	+£1.59
Harry Cobden	39	7	17.95%	+£3.03
Tom Bellamy	23	4	17.39%	+£5.83

Top jockeys by Profit – non-handicaps

Name Of Jockey	Rides	Winners	Strike Rate	Profit/Loss to BSP
David Bass	15	7	46.67%	+£27.62
Joshua Moore	30	4	13.33%	+£17.88
Jamie Moore	46	10	21.74%	+£5.28
Tom O'Brien	14	4	28.57%	+£2.20
Sean Bowen	10	4	40.00%	+£1.85

Top jockeys by Profit – handicaps

Name Of Jockey	Rides	Winners	Strike Rate	Profit/Loss to BSP
William Kennedy	12	2	16.67%	+£70.83
Joshua Moore	43	7	16.28%	+£69.54
Sam Twiston-Davies	53	7	13.21%	+£48.69
Sean Houlihan	12	3	25.00%	+£34.90
Tom O'Brien	35	5	14.29%	+£28.17

Top trainers by Strike Rate – non-handicaps

Name Of Trainer	Runners	Winners	Strike Rate	Profit/Loss to BSP
Harry Fry	18	8	44.44%	+£18.01
Nicky Henderson	87	32	36.78%	+£33.87
Alan King	24	7	29.17%	+£7.50
Colin Tizzard	25	7	28.00%	+£13.17
Philip Hobbs	23	6	26.09%	-£4.26

Top trainers by Strike Rate – handicaps

Name Of Trainer	Runners	Winners	Strike Rate	Profit/Loss to BSP
Phil Middleton	11	3	27.27%	+£9.30
Nigel Twiston-Davies	39	8	20.51%	+£105.15
Neil King	10	2	20.00%	+£6.94
Suzy Smith	10	2	20.00%	+£31.54
Fergal O'Brien	35	6	17.14%	+£19.65

Top trainers by Profit – non-handicaps

Name Of Trainer	Runners	Winners	Strike Rate	Profit/Loss to BSP
Nicky Henderson	87	32	36.78%	+£33.87
Harry Fry	18	8	44.44%	+£18.01
Gary Moore	73	13	17.81%	+£13.89
Colin Tizzard	25	7	28.00%	+£13.17
Jonjo O'Neill	21	3	14.29%	+£8.29

Top trainers by Profit – handicaps

Name Of Trainer	Runners	Winners	Strike Rate	Profit/Loss to BSP
Nigel Twiston-Davies	39	8	20.51%	+£105.15
Dr Richard Newland	36	4	11.11%	+£58.65
Tim Vaughan	24	3	12.50%	+£47.12

Gary Moore	108	14	12.96%	+£39.91
Nicky Henderson	118	20	16.95%	+£36.32

Top trainer/jockey combos by Strike Rate – non-handicaps

Name of Trainer/Jockey	Qualifiers	Winners	Strike Rate	Profit/Loss to BSP
Paul Nicholls/Sam Twiston-Davies	11	5	45.45%	+£11.66
Nicky Henderson/Nico de Boinville	24	9	37.50%	-£3.22
Gary Moore/Jamie Moore	41	10	24.39%	+£10.28
Paul Nicholls/Harry Cobden	20	3	15.00%	+£1.58
Gary Moore/Joshua Moore	23	3	13.04%	+£12.61

Top trainer/jockey combos by Strike Rate – handicaps

Name of Trainer/Jockey	Qualifiers	Winners	Strike Rate	Profit/Loss to BSP
Gary Moore/Niall Houlihan	10	3	30.00%	+£8.00
Nigel Twiston-Davies/Sam Twiston-Davies	14	3	21.43%	+£46.64
Paul Nicholls/Harry Cobden	27	5	18.52%	+£7.27
Gary Moore/Joshua Moore	34	6	17.65%	+£70.49
Nicky Henderson/Nico de Boinville	35	6	17.14%	+£20.43

Top trainer/jockey combos by Profit – non-handicaps

Name of Trainer/Jockey	Qualifiers	Winners	Strike Rate	Profit/Loss to BSP
Gary Moore/Joshua Moore	23	3	13.04%	+£12.61
Paul Nicholls/Sam Twiston-Davies	11	5	45.45%	+£11.66
Gary Moore/Jamie Moore	41	10	24.39%	+£10.28
Paul Nicholls/Harry Cobden	20	3	15.00%	+£1.58

Top trainer/jockey combos by Profit – handicaps

Name of Trainer/Jockey	Qualifiers	Winners	Strike Rate	Profit/Loss to BSP
Gary Moore/Joshua Moore	34	6	17.65%	+£70.49
Nigel Twiston-Davies/Sam Twiston-Davies	14	3	21.43%	+£46.64
Nicky Henderson/Nico de Boinville	35	6	17.14%	+£20.43
Paul Nicholls/Sam Twiston-Davies	19	3	15.79%	+£15.95
Gary Moore/Niall Houlihan	10	3	30.00%	+£8.00

Profit or Loss backing the unnamed favourite – non-handicaps

Runners	Winners	Strike Rate	Profit/Loss to BSP
266	124	46.62%	+£7.86

Profit or Loss backing the unnamed favourite – handicaps

Runners	Winners	Strike Rate	Profit/Loss to BSP
359	85	23.68%	+£0.94

Profit or loss backing the unnamed second favourite - non-handicaps

Runners	Winners	Strike Rate	Profit/Loss to BSP
256	57	22.27%	-£16.67

Profit or loss backing the unnamed second favourite - handicaps

Runners	Winners	Strike Rate	Profit/Loss to BSP
341	54	15.84%	-£24.51

Profit or Loss backing horses who won last time out- non-handicaps

Runners	Winners	Strike Rate	Profit/Loss to BSP
389	93	23.91%	-£59.16

Profit or Loss backing horses who won last time out - handicaps

Runners	Winners	Strike Rate	Profit/Loss to BSP
782	86	11.00%	-£156.18

Profit or loss backing Top-Weights in handicaps

Runners	Winners	Strike Rate	Profit/Loss to BSP
371	48	12.94%	+£72.34

Most profitable sires – non-handicaps

Sire	Runners	Winners	Strike Rate	Profit/Loss to BSP
Kapgarde	10	2	20.00%	+£0.93
Milan	17	4	23.53%	+£0.39

Most profitable sires – handicaps

Beneficial	24	5	20.83%	+£59.73
Kapgarde	23	3	13.04%	+£39.98
Black Sam Bellamy	14	3	21.43%	+£34.77
Montjeu	24	3	12.50%	+£29.50
Old Vic	10	1	10.00%	+£27.26

Sedgefield - Chases

Top jockeys by Strike Rate – non-handicaps

Name Of Jockey	Rides	Winners	Strike Rate	Profit/Loss to BSP
Brian Hughes	15	6	40.00%	+£5.46

Top jockeys by Strike Rate – handicaps

Name Of Jockey	Rides	Winners	Strike Rate	Profit/Loss to BSP
James Bowen	12	5	41.67%	+£4.51
Sean Bowen	27	10	37.04%	+£41.83
Theo Gillard	11	4	36.36%	+£2.44
David England	10	3	30.00%	+£35.02
Brendan Powell	10	3	30.00%	+£35.02

Top jockeys by Profit – non-handicaps

Name Of Jockey	Rides	Winners	Strike Rate	Profit/Loss to BSP
Brian Hughes	15	6	40.00%	+£5.46

Top jockeys by Profit – handicaps

Name Of Jockey	Rides	Winners	Strike Rate	Profit/Loss to BSP
Shane Quinlan	11	2	18.18%	+£149.75
Henry Brooke	126	30	23.81%	+£76.75
Ryan Mania	53	12	22.64%	+£70.89
Philip Armson	10	2	20.00%	+£49.33
Sean Bowen	27	10	37.04%	+£41.83

Top trainers by Strike Rate – non-handicaps

Name Of Trainer	Runners	Winners	Strike Rate	Profit/Loss to BSP
Donald McCain	12	3	25.00%	-£5.20
Brian Ellison	10	2	20.00%	+£6.42
Victor	21	1	4.76%	-£13.98

| Thompson | | | | |

Top trainers by Strike Rate – handicaps

Name Of Trainer	Runners	Winners	Strike Rate	Profit/Loss to BSP
Christian Williams	14	7	50.00%	+£4.18
Neil Mulholland	19	9	47.37%	+£7.23
Ann Hamilton	23	7	30.43%	+£12.88
Nicky Richards	10	3	30.00%	+£12.98
Fergal O'Brien	18	5	27.78%	+£0.26

Top trainers by Profit – handicaps

Name Of Trainer	Runners	Winners	Strike Rate	Profit/Loss to BSP
Victor Thompson	109	9	8.26%	+£180.41
Sue Smith	171	31	18.13%	+£48.64
Mike Sowersby	38	6	15.79%	+£39.39
Andrew Crook	32	5	15.63%	+£33.57
David Thompson	18	4	22.22%	+£32.49

Top trainer/jockey combos by Strike Rate – handicaps

Name of Trainer/Jockey	Qualifiers	Winners	Strike Rate	Profit/Loss to BSP
Brian Ellison/Henry Brooke	15	6	40.00%	+£4.77
Donald McCain/Brian Hughes	25	9	36.00%	+£13.74
Peter Bowen/Sean Bowen	18	6	33.33%	+£26.84
Evan Williams/Adam Wedge	21	7	33.33%	+£29.00
Donald McCain/Henry Brooke	12	4	33.33%	+£9.23

Top trainer/jockey combos by Profit – handicaps

Name of Trainer/Jockey	Qualifiers	Winners	Strike Rate	Profit/Loss to BSP
Ben Haslam/Richie McLernon	39	5	12.82%	+£36.32
Sam England/Jonathan England	57	13	22.81%	+£31.68
Evan Williams/Adam Wedge	21	7	33.33%	+£29.00
Peter Bowen/Sean Bowen	18	6	33.33%	+£26.84
Sue Smith/Ryan Mania	41	9	21.95%	+£25.82

Profit or Loss backing the unnamed favourite – non-handicaps

Runners	Winners	Strike Rate	Profit/Loss to BSP
255	110	43.14%	+£15.72

Profit or Loss backing the unnamed favourite – handicaps

Runners	Winners	Strike Rate	Profit/Loss to BSP
754	229	30.37%	-£22.24

Profit or loss backing the unnamed second favourite - non-handicaps

Runners	Winners	Strike Rate	Profit/Loss to BSP
246	50	20.33%	-£22.06

Profit or loss backing the unnamed second favourite - handicaps

Runners	Winners	Strike Rate	Profit/Loss to BSP
704	138	19.60%	-£66.06

Profit or Loss backing horses who won last time out - non-handicaps

Runners	Winners	Strike Rate	Profit/Loss to BSP
104	31	29.81%	-£9.43

Profit or Loss backing horses who won last time out - handicaps

Runners	Winners	Strike Rate	Profit/Loss to BSP
527	131	24.86%	-£32.58

Profit or loss backing Top-Weights in handicaps

Runners	Winners	Strike Rate	Profit/Loss to BSP
767	109	14.21%	-£131.45

Most profitable sires – handicaps

Nayef	19	3	15.79%	+£145.45
Arcadio	14	7	50.00%	+£42.79
Alflora	43	9	20.93%	+£34.11
Fruits Of Love	39	13	33.33%	+£33.30
Scorpion	28	2	7.14%	+£31.33

Sedgefield – Hurdles

Top jockeys by Strike Rate – non-handicaps

Name Of Jockey	Rides	Winners	Strike Rate	Profit/Loss to BSP
Alan Johns	12	6	50.00%	+£15.99
Harry Skelton	11	5	45.45%	+£1.19
Gavin Sheehan	12	4	33.33%	-£2.96
Sam Twiston-Davies	10	3	30.00%	-£4.74
Adam Wedge	10	3	30.00%	+£0.18

Top jockeys by Strike Rate – handicaps

Name Of Jockey	Rides	Winners	Strike Rate	Profit/Loss to BSP
Adam Wedge	14	4	28.57%	+£15.47
Paddy Brennan	19	5	26.32%	+£5.68
Danny McMenamin	50	12	24.00%	+£34.34
Amie Waugh	17	4	23.53%	+£17.13
Theo Gillard	27	6	22.22%	+£26.81

Top jockeys by Profit – non-handicaps

Name Of Jockey	Rides	Winners	Strike Rate	Profit/Loss to BSP
Ross Chapman	23	1	4.35%	+£192.62
Lorcan Murtagh	11	2	18.18%	+£191.14
Ryan Mania	24	2	8.33%	+£33.83
Alan Johns	12	6	50.00%	+£15.99
Craig Nichol	48	4	8.33%	+£13.59

Top jockeys by Profit – handicaps

Name Of Jockey	Rides	Winners	Strike Rate	Profit/Loss to BSP
Charlotte Jones	10	1	10.00%	+£213.31
Stephen Mulqueen	41	5	12.20%	+£149.72
Richie McLernon	61	10	16.39%	+£74.78
Sean Quinlan	138	25	18.12%	+£56.39
Thomas Dowson	79	12	15.19%	+£41.41

Top trainers by Strike Rate – non-handicaps

Name Of Trainer	Runners	Winners	Strike Rate	Profit/Loss to BSP
Kevin Ryan	10	4	40.00%	+£3.67
Gordon Elliott	15	6	40.00%	-£3.00
Harry Whittington	10	4	40.00%	-£2.87
Dan Skelton	24	9	37.50%	+£0.08
David Pipe	14	5	35.71%	-£5.09

Top trainers by Strike Rate – handicaps

Name Of Trainer	Runners	Winners	Strike Rate	Profit/Loss to BSP
Neil Mulholland	27	8	29.63%	+£10.10
Henry Oliver	11	3	27.27%	-£0.24
Jonjo O'Neill	15	4	26.67%	+£10.06
Tristan Davidson	12	3	25.00%	+£4.68
Nicky Richards	21	5	23.81%	+£65.86

Top trainers by Profit – non-handicaps

Name Of Trainer	Runners	Winners	Strike Rate	Profit/Loss to BSP
Maurice Barnes	59	3	5.08%	+£221.21
Micky Hammond	77	15	19.48%	+£156.50
Ann Hamilton	14	4	28.57%	£44.04
Oliver Greenall	21	5	23.81%	+£24.22
Jamie Snowden	16	5	31.25%	+£18.77

Top trainers by Profit – handicaps

Name Of Trainer	Runners	Winners	Strike Rate	Profit/Loss to BSP
James Moffatt	39	5	12.82%	+£208.74
Tina Jackson	20	4	20.00%	+£161.31
Dianne Sayer	102	24	23.53%	+£78.25
Rebecca Menzies	69	10	14.49%	+£72.28
Nicky Richards	21	5	23.81%	+£65.86

Top trainer/jockey combos by Strike Rate – non-handicaps

Name of Trainer/Jockey	Qualifiers	Winners	Strike Rate	Profit/Loss to BSP
Tim Vaughan/Alan Johns	12	6	50.00%	+£15.99
Dan Skelton/Harry Skelton	11	5	45.45%	+£1.19
Brian Ellison/Henry Brooke	12	5	41.67%	+£9.91

Donald McCain/Brian Hughes	49	16	32.65%	-£8.38
Donald McCain/Henry Brooke	17	5	29.41%	+£27.53

Top trainer/jockey combos by Strike Rate – handicaps

Name of Trainer/Jockey	Qualifiers	Winners	Strike Rate	Profit/Loss to BSP
Dianne Sayer/Danny McMenamin	18	8	44.44%	+£22.73
Dianne Sayer/Sean Quinlan	13	5	38.46%	+£18.71
Dianne Sayer/Brian Hughes	17	6	35.29%	+£28.48
Sue Smith/Sean Quinlan	12	4	33.33%	+£12.24
Sue Smith/Jonathan England	15	4	26.67%	+£0.10

Top trainer/jockey combos by Profit – non-handicaps

Name of Trainer/Jockey	Qualifiers	Winners	Strike Rate	Profit/Loss to BSP
Sue Smith/Ryan Mania	16	1	6.25%	+£37.92
Donald McCain/Henry Brooke	17	5	29.41%	+£27.53
Tim Vaughan/Alan Johns	12	6	50.00%	+£15.99
Brian Ellison/Henry Brooke	12	5	41.67%	+£9.91
Dan Skelton/Harry	11	5	45.45%	+£1.19

Skelton				

Top trainer/jockey combos by Profit – handicaps

Name of Trainer/Jockey	Qualifiers	Winners	Strike Rate	Profit/Loss to BSP
James Moffatt/Charlotte Jones	10	1	10.00%	+£213.31
Ben Haslam/Richie McLernon	49	8	16.33%	+£72.35
Donald McCain/Abbie McCain	14	3	21.43%	+£38.72
Dianne Sayer/Brian Hughes	17	6	35.29%	+£28.48
Donald McCain/Theo Gillard	20	5	25.00%	+£26.88

Profit or Loss backing the unnamed favourite – non-handicaps

Runners	Winners	Strike Rate	Profit/Loss to BSP
607	301	49.59%	+£12.56

Profit or Loss backing the unnamed favourite – handicaps

Runners	Winners	Strike Rate	Profit/Loss to BSP
858	256	29.84%	+£41.86

Profit or loss backing the unnamed second favourite - non-handicaps

Runners	Winners	Strike Rate	Profit/Loss to BSP
598	131	21.91%	-£52.34

Profit or loss backing the unnamed second favourite – handicaps

Runners	Winners	Strike Rate	Profit/Loss to

			BSP
789	143	18.12%	-£59.35

Profit or Loss backing horses who won last time out- non-handicaps

Runners	Winners	Strike Rate	Profit/Loss to BSP
359	141	39.28%	+£30.81

Profit or Loss backing horses who won last time out - handicaps

Runners	Winners	Strike Rate	Profit/Loss to BSP
622	142	22.83%	-£49.49

Profit or loss backing Top-Weights in handicaps

Runners	Winners	Strike Rate	Profit/Loss to BSP
888	131	14.75%	+£59.20

Most profitable sires – non-handicaps

Sire	Runners	Winners	Strike Rate	Profit/Loss to BSP
Fruits Of Love	11	3	27.27%	+£28.03
Fame And Glory	20	6	30.00%	+£18.22
Yeats	23	4	17.39%	+£12.64
Arcadio	17	3	17.65%	+£10.15
Westerner	29	6	20.69%	+£7.28

Most profitable sires – handicaps

Fantastic Light	12	3	25.00%	+£38.46
Overbury	25	5	20.00%	+£34.81
Kayf Tara	37	9	24.32%	+£33.69
Luso	13	1	7.69%	+£33.37
Rock Of Gibraltar	30	6	20.00%	+£30.44

Southwell - Chases

Top jockeys by Strike Rate – non-handicaps

Name Of Jockey	Rides	Winners	Strike Rate	Profit/Loss to BSP
Aidan Coleman	11	5	45.45%	+£4.69

Top jockeys by Strike Rate – handicaps

Name Of Jockey	Rides	Winners	Strike Rate	Profit/Loss to BSP
Charlie Deutsch	10	5	50.00%	+£7.50
Harry Cobden	10	4	40.00%	+£6.00
Richard Patrick	10	4	40.00%	+£8.23
Bryony Frost	15	5	33.33%	+£14.55
Harry Skelton	68	22	32.35%	+£3.33

Top jockeys by Profit – non-handicaps

Name Of Jockey	Rides	Winners	Strike Rate	Profit/Loss to BSP
Aidan Coleman	11	5	45.45%	+£4.69

Top jockeys by Profit – handicaps

Name Of Jockey	Rides	Winners	Strike Rate	Profit/Loss to BSP
Sean Bowen	67	17	25.37%	+£69.66
Tom Scudamore	54	14	25.93%	+£61.74
A P Heskin	17	4	23.53%	+£52.68
James Best	25	7	28.00%	+£42.51
Brian Hughes	61	12	19.67%	+£27.23

Top trainers by Strike Rate – non-handicaps

Name Of Trainer	Runners	Winners	Strike Rate	Profit/Loss to BSP
Dan Skelton	10	4	40.00%	+£1.47

Top trainers by Strike Rate – handicaps

Name Of Trainer	Runners	Winners	Strike Rate	Profit/Loss to BSP
Laura Morgan	37	14	37.84%	+£23.99
Lucy Wadham	14	5	35.71%	+£3.43
Dan Skelton	59	20	33.90%	+£10.84
Dr Richard Newland	21	7	33.33%	+£2.82
Martin Keighley	40	13	32.50%	+£81.60

Top trainers by Profit – non-handicaps

Name Of Trainer	Runners	Winners	Strike Rate	Profit/Loss to BSP
Dan Skelton	10	4	40.00%	+£1.47

Top trainers by Profit – handicaps

Name Of Trainer	Runners	Winners	Strike Rate	Profit/Loss to BSP
Martin Keighley	40	13	32.50%	+£81.60
Ben Pauling	15	3	20.00%	+£46.70
Peter Winks	15	2	13.33%	+£34.19
Peter Bowen	39	10	25.64%	+£32.73
Sarah Humphrey	10	1	10.00%	+£26.30

Top trainer/jockey combos by Strike Rate – handicaps

Name of Trainer/Jockey	Qualifiers	Winners	Strike Rate	Profit/Loss to BSP
Martin Keighley/James Best	13	7	53.85%	+£54.51
Laura Morgan/Adam Wedge	21	9	42.86%	+£16.08
Tom George/Paddy Brennan	14	5	35.71%	+£13.41
Dan Skelton/Harry Skelton	46	16	34.78%	+£1.54
Michael	15	5	33.33%	+£5.79

Scudamore/Tom Scudamore				

Top trainer/jockey combos by Profit – handicaps

Name of Trainer/Jockey	Qualifiers	Winners	Strike Rate	Profit/Loss to BSP
Martin Keighley/James Best	13	7	53.85%	+£54.51
David Pipe/Tom Scudamore	10	3	30.00%	+£22.66
Peter Bowen/Sean Bowen	20	6	30.00%	+£18.05
Laura Morgan/Adam Wedge	21	9	42.86%	+£16.08
Tom George/Paddy Brennan	14	5	35.71%	+£13.41

Profit or Loss backing the unnamed favourite – non-handicaps

Runners	Winners	Strike Rate	Profit/Loss to BSP
170	86	50.59%	+£2.30

Profit or Loss backing the unnamed favourite – handicaps

Runners	Winners	Strike Rate	Profit/Loss to BSP
677	201	29.69%	-£13.11

Profit or loss backing the unnamed second favourite - non-handicaps

Runners	Winners	Strike Rate	Profit/Loss to BSP
164	46	28.05%	+£23.62

Profit or loss backing the unnamed second favourite - handicaps

Runners	Winners	Strike Rate	Profit/Loss to

			BSP
588	123	20.92%	-£13.32

Profit or Loss backing horses who won last time out - non-handicaps

Runners	Winners	Strike Rate	Profit/Loss to BSP
103	40	38.83%	-£7.88

Profit or Loss backing horses who won last time out - handicaps

Runners	Winners	Strike Rate	Profit/Loss to BSP
454	115	25.33%	+£16.77

Profit or loss backing Top-Weights in handicaps

Runners	Winners	Strike Rate	Profit/Loss to BSP
700	134	19.14%	+£118.88

Most profitable sires – handicaps

Stowaway	37	5	13.51%	+£45.48
Vinnie Roe	11	5	45.45%	+£43.51
King's Theatre	49	16	32.65%	+£43.20
Midnight Legend	64	14	21.88%	+£40.55
Trans Island	21	3	14.29%	+£34.97

Southwell – Hurdles

Top jockeys by Strike Rate – non-handicaps

Name Of Jockey	Rides	Winners	Strike Rate	Profit/Loss to BSP
A P Heskin	21	7	33.33%	+£1.24
Nico de Boinville	37	11	29.73%	-£1.35
Paddy Brennan	54	16	29.63%	+£52.18
Gavin Sheehan	46	11	23.91%	+£71.06
Harry Skelton	96	22	22.92%	-£16.70

Top jockeys by Strike Rate – handicaps

Name Of Jockey	Rides	Winners	Strike Rate	Profit/Loss to BSP
Tommy M O'Brien	11	4	36.36%	+£23.33
Sean Bowen	54	16	29.63%	+£31.94
Stan Sheppard	20	5	25.00%	+£7.19
Harry Skelton	110	26	23.64%	+£37.92
Bryony Frost	13	3	23.08%	+£13.28

Top jockeys by Profit – non-handicaps

Name Of Jockey	Rides	Winners	Strike Rate	Profit/Loss to BSP
Charlie Hammond	19	3	15.79%	+£269.55
Trevor Whelan	27	4	14.81%	+£100.11
Gavin Sheehan	46	11	23.91%	+£71.06
Paddy Brennan	54	16	29.63%	+£52.18
Tom Scudamore	42	9	21.43%	+£28.29

Top jockeys by Profit – handicaps

Name Of Jockey	Rides	Winners	Strike Rate	Profit/Loss to BSP
Charlie Hammond	34	4	11.76%	+£58.23
Brian Hughes	83	13	15.66%	+£56.12
Tom Bellamy	22	3	13.64%	+£46.07
Nick Scolfield	39	5	12.82%	+£42.04
Tom Cannon	26	5	19.23%	+£41.60

Top trainers by Strike Rate – non-handicaps

Name Of Trainer	Runners	Winners	Strike Rate	Profit/Loss to BSP
Harry Whittington	23	11	47.83%	+£89.86
David Pipe	17	7	41.18%	+£47.38
Paul Nicholls	15	6	40.00%	+£2.03
Dr Richard Newland	33	11	33.33%	-£6.67
Nicky	45	14	31.11%	-£7.43

Henderson				

Top trainers by Strike Rate – handicaps

Name Of Trainer	Runners	Winners	Strike Rate	Profit/Loss to BSP
John Mackie	10	4	40.00%	+£9.09
Justin Landy	10	4	40.00%	+£6.63
Caroline Bailey	51	217	33.33%	+£74.06
Gary Hanmer	14	4	28.57%	+£7.47
Tom Lacey	25	7	28.00%	+£20.06

Top trainers by Profit – non-handicaps

Name Of Trainer	Runners	Winners	Strike Rate	Profit/Loss to BSP
Harry Whittington	23	11	47.83%	+£89.86
David Pipe	17	7	41.18%	+£47.38
Fergal O'Brien	43	8	18.60%	+£35.21
Tom Lacey	23	4	17.39%	+£28.41
Tom Symonds	17	3	17.65%	+£24.32

Top trainers by Profit – handicaps

Name Of Trainer	Runners	Winners	Strike Rate	Profit/Loss to BSP
Caroline Bailey	51	217	33.33%	+£74.06
Alex Hales	65	7	10.77%	+£69.82
Sarah Humphrey	24	2	8.33%	+£64.71
Mike Sowersby	55	7	12.73%	+£58.55
Charlie Pogson	45	7	15.56%	+£49.83

Top trainer/jockey combos by Strike Rate – non-handicaps

Name of Trainer/Jockey	Qualifiers	Winners	Strike Rate	Profit/Loss to BSP
David Pipe/Tom Scudamore	14	6	42.86%	+£46.93
Nicky Henderson/Nico de Boinville	22	8	36.36%	-£5.32
Tom George/ A	12	4	33.33%	+£2.86

P Heskin				
Dr Richard Newland/Sam Twiston-Davies	21	7	33.33%	-£4.23
Tom George/Paddy Brennan	20	6	30.00%	+£1.28

Top trainer/jockey combos by Strike Rate – handicaps

Name of Trainer/Jockey	Qualifiers	Winners	Strike Rate	Profit/Loss to BSP
Martin Keighley/Sean Bowen	11	5	45.45%	+£6.50
Richard Phillips/Daniel Hiskett	11	3	27.27%	+£13.35
Nigel Twiston-Davies/Sam Twiston-Davies	22	6	27.27%	+£24.58
Dan Skelton/Harry Skelton	84	18	21.43%	+£7.00
Fergal O'Brien/Paddy Brennan	33	7	21.21%	+£18.49

Top trainer/jockey combos by Profit – non-handicaps

Name of Trainer/Jockey	Qualifiers	Winners	Strike Rate	Profit/Loss to BSP
David Pipe/Tom Scudamore	14	6	42.86%	+£46.93
Fergal O'Brien/Paddy Brennan	23	5	21.74%	+£40.32
Tom George/A P Heskin	12	4	33.33%	+£2.86
Tom George/Paddy Brennan	20	6	30.00%	+£1.28

Top trainer/jockey combos by Profit – handicaps

Name of Trainer/Jockey	Qualifiers	Winners	Strike Rate	Profit/Loss to BSP
Alex Hales/Kielan Woods	26	4	15.38%	+£82.18
Nigel Twiston-Davies/Sam Twiston-Davies	22	6	27.27%	+£24.58
Philip Kirby/Thomas Dowson	16	1	6.25%	+£23.58
Mike Sowersby/Brian Hughes	10	2	20.00%	+£22.97
Jonjo O'Neill/Richie McLernon	28	4	14.29%	+£20.60

Profit or Loss backing the unnamed favourite – non-handicaps

Runners	Winners	Strike Rate	Profit/Loss to BSP
505	241	47.72%	+£19.85

Profit or Loss backing the unnamed favourite – handicaps

Runners	Winners	Strike Rate	Profit/Loss to BSP
682	221	32.40%	+£53.28

Profit or loss backing the unnamed second favourite - non-handicaps

Runners	Winners	Strike Rate	Profit/Loss to BSP
496	104	20.97%	-£57.91

Profit or loss backing the unnamed second favourite - handicaps

Runners	Winners	Strike Rate	Profit/Loss to BSP
633	82	12.95%	-£177.40

Profit or Loss backing horses who won last time out- non-handicaps

Runners	Winners	Strike Rate	Profit/Loss to BSP
232	77	33.19%	-£20.23

Profit or Loss backing horses who won last time out - handicaps

Runners	Winners	Strike Rate	Profit/Loss to BSP
611	136	22.26%	+£16.94

Profit or loss backing Top-Weights in handicaps

Runners	Winners	Strike Rate	Profit/Loss to BSP
765	106	13.86%	+£123.00

Most profitable sires – non-handicaps

Sire	Runners	Winners	Strike Rate	Profit/Loss to BSP
Authorized	15	4	26.67%	+£278.19
Yeats	18	3	16.67%	+£69.66
Mastercraftsman	12	3	25.00%	+£65.50
Kayf Tara	76	12	15.79%	+£33.16
Getaway	29	8	27.59%	+£26.00

Most profitable sires – handicaps

Galileo	28	4	14.29%	+£79.76
Flemensfirth	62	11	17.74%	+£73.80
Cloudings	34	5	14.71%	+£55.57
Brian Boru	32	7	21.88%	+£45.24
Oscar	87	11	12.64%	+£43.25

Stratford - Chases

Top jockeys by Strike Rate – non-handicaps

Name Of Jockey	Rides	Winners	Strike Rate	Profit/Loss to BSP
Dale Peters	10	5	50.00%	+£27.10
Tom Scudamore	10	3	30.00%	+£44.37
Aidan Coleman	10	3	30.00%	-£0.88
Gina Andrews	19	3	15.79%	+£12.00
James King	10	1	10.00%	-£4.64

Top jockeys by Strike Rate – handicaps

Name Of Jockey	Rides	Winners	Strike Rate	Profit/Loss to BSP
Kielan Woods	23	7	30.43%	+£3.13
Kevin Jones	10	3	30.00%	+£23.69
A P Heskin	24	7	29.17%	+£27.13
Harry Skelton	56	15	26.79%	+£2.40
Paul O'Brien	19	5	26.32%	+£8.17

Top jockeys by Profit – non-handicaps

Name Of Jockey	Rides	Winners	Strike Rate	Profit/Loss to BSP
Tom Scudamore	10	3	30.00%	+£44.37
Dale Peters	10	5	50.00%	+£27.10
Gina Andrews	19	3	15.79%	+£12.00
William Biddick	16	1	6.25%	+£7.54

Top jockeys by Profit – handicaps

Name Of Jockey	Rides	Winners	Strike Rate	Profit/Loss to BSP
James Best	56	7	12.50%	+£43.67
Charlie Poste	30	4	13.33%	+£37.19
Tom Cannon	38	8	21.05%	+£34.43
Stan Sheppard	24	6	25.00%	+£34.24

Brian Hughes	34	8	23.53%	+£33.45

Top trainers by Strike Rate – non-handicaps

Name Of Trainer	Runners	Winners	Strike Rate	Profit/Loss to BSP
Dan Skelton	12	4	33.33%	+£0.08
Paul Nicholls	20	4	20.00%	-£1.28
Philip Hobbs	11	2	18.18%	-£6.25

Top trainers by Strike Rate – handicaps

Name Of Trainer	Runners	Winners	Strike Rate	Profit/Loss to BSP
Peter Winks	10	3	30.00%	+£5.92
Chris Gordon	21	6	28.57%	+£34.33
John Flint	11	3	27.27%	+£11.33
Dr Richard Newland	43	11	25.58%	+£14.32
Phil Middleton	16	4	25.00%	+£6.37

Top trainers by Profit – non-handicaps

Name Of Trainer	Runners	Winners	Strike Rate	Profit/Loss to BSP
Dan Skelton	12	4	33.33%	+£0.08

Top trainers by Profit – handicaps

Name Of Trainer	Runners	Winners	Strike Rate	Profit/Loss to BSP
Matt Sheppard	52	10	19.53%	+£58.32
Chris Gordon	21	6	28.57%	+£34.33
Neil King	28	7	25.00%	+£30.71
Nigel Twiston-Davies	84	18	21.43%	+£30.53
Seamus Mullins	31	4	12.90%	+£29.33

Top trainer/jockey combos by Strike Rate – handicaps

Name of Trainer/Jockey	Qualifiers	Winners	Strike Rate	Profit/Loss to BSP
Tom George/A P	11	4	36.36%	+£14.58

Heskin				
Dr Richard Newland/Sam Twiston-Davies	17	6	35.29%	+£8.85
Philip Hobbs/Tom O'Brien	19	6	31.58%	+£24.16
Dr Richard Newland/Charlie Hammon	10	3	30.00%	+£0.17
Rob Summers/James Best	10	3	30.00%	+£14.27

Top trainer/jockey combos by Profit – handicaps

Name of Trainer/Jockey	Qualifiers	Winners	Strike Rate	Profit/Loss to BSP
Matt Sheppard/Sam Sheppard	22	6	27.27%	+£36.24
Chris Gordon/Tom Cannon	17	4	23.53%	+£28.65
Seamus Mullins/Daniel Sansom	12	2	16.67%	+£28.41
Philip Hobbs/Tom O'Brien	19	6	31.58%	+£24.16
Tom George/Paddy Brennan	21	4	19.05%	+£23.92

Profit or Loss backing the unnamed favourite – non-handicaps

Runners	Winners	Strike Rate	Profit/Loss to BSP
287	105	36.59%	-£47.36

Profit or Loss backing the unnamed favourite – handicaps

Runners	Winners	Strike Rate	Profit/Loss to

			BSP
725	200	27.59%	-£12.35

Profit or loss backing the unnamed second favourite - non-handicaps

Runners	Winners	Strike Rate	Profit/Loss to BSP
285	63	22.11%	-£8.94

Profit or loss backing the unnamed second favourite - handicaps

Runners	Winners	Strike Rate	Profit/Loss to BSP
683	112	16.40%	-£100.48

Profit or Loss backing horses who won last time out - non-handicaps

Runners	Winners	Strike Rate	Profit/Loss to BSP
392	83	21.17%	+£25.74

Profit or Loss backing horses who won last time out - handicaps

Runners	Winners	Strike Rate	Profit/Loss to BSP
706	132	18.70%	+£4.80

Profit or loss backing Top-Weights in handicaps

Runners	Winners	Strike Rate	Profit/Loss to BSP
753	113	15.01%	-£104.58

Most profitable sires – non-handicaps

Sire	Runners	Winners	Strike Rate	Profit/Loss to BSP
Karinga Bay	10	2	20.00%	+£117.01
Gold Well	11	2	18.18%	+£8.34
Kapgarde	10	2	20.00%	+£6.50
Presenting	38	8	21.05%	+£5.30
Kayf Tara	17	1	5.88%	+£3.60

Most profitable sires – handicaps

Video Rock	10	4	40.00%	+£46.47
Beneficial	101	17	16.83%	+£46.04
Presenting	100	18	18.00%	+£42.41
Dr Massini	37	8	21.62%	+£41.52
Tamayaz	10	3	30.00%	+£33.31

Stratford – Hurdles

Top jockeys by Strike Rate – non-handicaps

Name Of Jockey	Rides	Winners	Strike Rate	Profit/Loss to BSP
Aidan Coleman	59	19	32.20%	+£41.41
A P Heskin	13	4	30.77%	-£6.78
Daryl Jacob	20	6	30.00%	+£0.90
Marc Goldstein	18	5	27.78%	-£1.16
Sean Bowen	15	4	26.67%	+£0.45

Top jockeys by Strike Rate – handicaps

Name Of Jockey	Rides	Winners	Strike Rate	Profit/Loss to BSP
Paul O'Brien	10	4	40.00%	+£27.01
Harry Bannister	32	11	34.38%	+£62.66
Bryony Frost	17	5	29.41%	+£16.63
Jonjo O'Neill Jr	11	3	27.27%	+£6.73
Daryl Jacob	19	5	26.32%	+£3.64

Top jockeys by Profit – non-handicaps

Name Of Jockey	Rides	Winners	Strike Rate	Profit/Loss to BSP
Sam Twiston-Davies	81	14	17.28%	+£176.69
Chris Ward	10	1	10.00%	+£62.20
Aidan Coleman	59	19	32.20%	+£41.41
James Davies	37	2	5.41%	+£40.95
Brendan Powell	36	5	13.89%	+£26.55

Top jockeys by Profit – handicaps

Name Of Jockey	Rides	Winners	Strike Rate	Profit/Loss to BSP
Ben Poste	31	1	3.23%	+£118.39
Tom Scudamore	61	10	16.39%	+£70.06
Harry Bannister	32	11	34.38%	+£62.66
Aidan Coleman	55	10	18.18%	+£43.73
Paul O'Brien	10	4	40.00%	+£27.01

Top trainers by Strike Rate – non-handicaps

Name Of Trainer	Runners	Winners	Strike Rate	Profit/Loss to BSP
Warren Greatrex	35	12	34.29%	+£19.73
Rebecca Curtis	21	7	33.33%	+£3.32
Milton Harris	10	3	30.00%	+£7.98
Sheena West	17	5	29.41%	-£0.14
Paul Nicholls	15	7	28.00%	-£9.29

Top trainers by Strike Rate – handicaps

Name Of Trainer	Runners	Winners	Strike Rate	Profit/Loss to BSP
Ben Pauling	14	5	35.71%	+£39.68
Gary Hanmer	14	5	35.71%	-£1.24
Henry Daly	28	9	32.14%	+£79.27
Charlie Longsdon	43	11	25.58%	+£29.27
Nicky Henderson	40	10	25.00%	+£0.17

Top trainers by Profit – non-handicaps

Name Of Trainer	Runners	Winners	Strike Rate	Profit/Loss to BSP
Neil Mulholland	40	5	12.50%	+£184.58
Henry Oliver	20	2	10.00%	+£57.95
Tim Vaughan	62	12	19.35%	+£49.29
Michael Appleby	14	3	21.43%	+£42.69
Donald McCain	26	6	23.08%	+£41.55

Top trainers by Profit – handicaps

Name Of Trainer	Runners	Winners	Strike Rate	Profit/Loss to BSP
Adrian Wintle	22	4	18.18%	+£158.03
Henry Daly	28	9	32.14%	+£79.87
Ben Pauling	14	5	35.71%	+£39.68
Neil Mulholland	55	9	16.36%	+£38.37
Jonjo O'Neill	64	13	20.31%	+£37.71

Top trainer/jockey combos by Strike Rate – non-handicaps

Name of Trainer/Jockey	Qualifiers	Winners	Strike Rate	Profit/Loss to BSP
Kim Bailey/David Bass	10	4	40.00%	+£7.03
Sheena West/Marc Goldstein	16	5	31.25%	+£0.84
Jamie Snowden/Gavin Sheehan	14	4	28.57%	-£6.19
Dan Skelton/Harry Skelton	55	15	27.27%	-£10.80
Warren Greatrex/Gavin Sheehan	12	3	25.00%	-£4.10

Top trainer/jockey combos by Strike Rate – handicaps

Name of Trainer/Jockey	Qualifiers	Winners	Strike Rate	Profit/Loss to BSP
Dr Richard Newland/Charlie Hammond	10	4	40.00%	+£0.61
Donald McCain/Brian Hughes	12	4	33.33%	+£2.22
Kim Bailey/ David Bass	10	3	30.00%	+£8.69
Neil King/Trevor Whelan	17	4	23.53%	+£27.99

Nicky Henderson/Nico de Boinvlle	13	3	23.08%	-£1.90

Top trainer/jockey combos by Profit – non-handicaps

Name of Trainer/Jockey	Qualifiers	Winners	Strike Rate	Profit/Loss to BSP
Kim Bailey/David Bass	10	4	40.00%	+£7.03
Dan Skelton/Bridget Andrews	14	3	21.43%	+£2.87
Sheena West/Marc Goldstein	16	5	31.25%	+£0.84
Nigel Twiston-Davies/Sam Twiston-Davies	20	3	15.00%	+£0.64

Top trainer/jockey combos by Profit – handicaps

Name of Trainer/Jockey	Qualifiers	Winners	Strike Rate	Profit/Loss to BSP
Neil King/Trevor Whelan	17	4	23.53%	+£27.99
David Pipe/Tom Scudamore	22	5	22.73%	+£13.24
Warren Greatrex/Gavin Sheehan	11	2	18.18%	+£9.33
Kim Bailey/David Bass	10	3	30.00%	+£8.69
Jonjo O'Neill/Richie McLernon	13	1	7.69%	+£3.39

Profit or Loss backing the unnamed favourite – non-handicaps

Favourite	Runners	Winners	Strike Rate	Profit/Loss to BSP
	594	256	43.10%	-£18.21

Profit or Loss backing the unnamed favourite – handicaps

Favourite	Runners	Winners	Strike Rate	Profit/Loss to BSP
	641	177	27.61%	-£6.79

Profit or loss backing the unnamed second favourite - non-handicaps

Second Favourite	Runners	Winners	Strike Rate	Profit/Loss to BSP
	583	139	23.84%	+£52.89

Profit or loss backing the unnamed second favourite - handicaps

Second Favourite	Runners	Winners	Strike Rate	Profit/Loss to BSP
	621	112	18.04%	+£18.68

Profit or Loss backing horses who won last time out- non-handicaps

Won Last Time out	Runners	Winners	Strike Rate	Profit/Loss to BSP
	403	131	32.51%	+£53.16

Profit or Loss backing horses who won last time out - handicaps

Won Last Time Out	Runners	Winners	Strike Rate	Profit/Loss to BSP
	683	116	16.98%	+£1.17

Profit or loss backing Top-Weights in handicaps

Top Weight	Runners	Winners	Strike Rate	Profit/Loss to BSP
	668	107	15.67%	+£101.81

Most profitable sires – non-handicaps

Sire	Runners	Winners	Strike Rate	Profit/Loss to BSP
Mastercraftsman	13	2	15.38%	+£26.99
Shantou	16	4	25.00%	+£16.92

Milan	26	7	26.92%	+£15.51
Galileo	14	4	28.57%	+£7.92
Alflora	10	1	10.00%	+£7.77

Most profitable sires – handicaps

Kayf Tara	54	9	16.67%	+£150.851
Sakhee	11	5	45.45%	+£59.50
Royal Applause	28	9	32.14%	+£41.61
Nayef	15	3	20.00%	+£35.87
Beneficial	42	6	14.29%	+£33.79

Taunton - Chases

Top jockeys by Strike Rate – handicaps

Name Of Jockey	Rides	Winners	Strike Rate	Profit/Loss to BSP
William Kennedy	14	5	35.71%	+£23.92
Sam Twiston-Davies	45	12	26.67%	+£18.19
Daryl Jacob	19	5	26.32%	-£3.17
Matt Griffiths	16	4	25.00%	+£14.73
Alan Johns	29	6	20.69%	+£32.94

Top jockeys by Profit – handicaps

Name Of Jockey	Rides	Winners	Strike Rate	Profit/Loss to BSP
Alan Johns	29	6	20.69%	+£32.94
James Davies	24	4	16.67%	+£26.95
William Kennedy	14	5	35.71%	+£23.92
David Noonan	29	4	13.79%	+£22.13
Sam Twiston-Davies	45	12	26.67%	+£18.19

Top trainers by Strike Rate – non-handicaps

Name Of Trainer	Runners	Winners	Strike Rate	Profit/Loss to BSP
Paul Nicholls	17	7	41.18%	-£3.25
Colin Tizzard	11	2	18.18%	+£1.37
David Pipe	10	1	10.00%	-£1.90

Top trainers by Strike Rate – handicaps

Name Of Trainer	Runners	Winners	Strike Rate	Profit/Loss to BSP
Emma-Jane Bishop	11	4	36.36%	+£48.07
Keiran Burke	13	4	39.77%	+£9.85
Sarah-Jaybe	20	6	30.00%	+£18.80

Davies				
Harry Fry	14	4	28.57%	+£2.72
Robert Walford	23	6	26.09%	+£6.12

Top trainers by Profit – non-handicaps

Name Of Trainer	Runners	Winners	Strike Rate	Profit/Loss to BSP
Colin Tizzard	11	2	18.18%	+£1.37

Top trainers by Profit – handicaps

Name Of Trainer	Runners	Winners	Strike Rate	Profit/Loss to BSP
Emma-Jane Bishop	11	4	36.36%	+£48.07
Polly Gundry	16	3	18.75%	+£29.73
Tim Vaughan	43	7	16.28%	+£29.25
Neil Mulholland	33	7	21.21%	+£24.70
Jeremy Scott	27	6	22.22%	+£20.42

Top trainer/jockey combos by Strike Rate – handicaps

Name of Trainer/Jockey	Qualifiers	Winners	Strike Rate	Profit/Loss to BSP
Paul Nicholls/Sam Twiston-Davies	17	6	35.29%	+£5.14
Philip Hobbs/Tom O'Brien	18	5	27.78%	+£1.26
Tim Vaughan/Alan Johns	23	6	26.09%	+£38.94
Evan Williams/Adam Wedge	38	8	21.05%	+£6.99
Philip Hobbs/Michael Nolan	10	2	20.00%	-£0.31

Top trainer/jockey combos by Profit – handicaps

Name of Trainer/Jockey	Qualifiers	Winners	Strike Rate	Profit/Loss to BSP
Tim Vaughan/Alan Johns	23	6	26.09%	+£38.94
Jackie Du Plessis/James Best	13	1	7.69%	+£7.60
Evan Williams/Adam Wedge	38	8	21.05%	+£6.99
Colin Tizzard/Brendan Powell	21	3	14.29%	+£6.06
Paul Nicholls/Sam Twiston-Davies	17	6	35.29%	+£5.14

Profit or Loss backing the unnamed favourite – non-handicaps

Runners	Winners	Strike Rate	Profit/Loss to BSP
170	75	44.12%	-£10.73

Profit or Loss backing the unnamed favourite – handicaps

Runners	Winners	Strike Rate	Profit/Loss to BSP
440	128	29.09%	-£4.91

Profit or loss backing the unnamed second favourite - non-handicaps

Runners	Winners	Strike Rate	Profit/Loss to BSP
166	34	20.48%	-£39.31

Profit or loss backing the unnamed second favourite - handicaps

Runners	Winners	Strike Rate	Profit/Loss to BSP
413	88	21.31%	+£35.86

Profit or Loss backing horses who won last time out - non-handicaps

Runners	Winners	Strike Rate	Profit/Loss to BSP
74	17	22.97%	-£11.83

Profit or Loss backing horses who won last time out - handicaps

Runners	Winners	Strike Rate	Profit/Loss to BSP
309	72	23.30%	-£21.10

Profit or loss backing Top-Weights in handicaps

Runners	Winners	Strike Rate	Profit/Loss to BSP
462	79	17.10%	-£19.28

Most profitable sires – handicaps

King's Theatre	65	13	20.00%	+£82.55
Dr Massini	16	5	31.25%	+£24.79
Tikkanen	18	5	27.78%	+£23.93
Heron Island	10	2	20.00%	+£19.43
Fair Mix	10	2	20.00%	+£18.85

Taunton – Hurdles

Top jockeys by Strike Rate – non-handicaps

Name Of Jockey	Rides	Winners	Strike Rate	Profit/Loss to BSP
Lorcan Williams	12	5	41.67%	-£2.27
Harry Cobden	61	25	40.98%	+£13.61
Sam Twiston-Davies	66	21	31.82%	+£14.42
Harry Skelton	33	9	27.27%	-£7.60
Sean Bowen	21	5	23.81%	-£7.04

Top jockeys by Strike Rate – handicaps

Name Of Jockey	Rides	Winners	Strike Rate	Profit/Loss to BSP

Gavin Sheehan	19	5	26.32%	+£11.77
Stan Sheppard	21	5	23.81%	+£22.40
Nico de Boinvlle	17	4	23.53%	+£125.46
Aidan Coleman	57	13	22.81%	+£15.91
Daryl Jacob	28	6	21.43%	+£13.51

Top jockeys by Profit – non-handicaps

Name Of Jockey	Rides	Winners	Strike Rate	Profit/Loss to BSP
Michael Nolan	53	9	16.98%	+£265.17
Nick Scholfield	75	10	13.33%	+£100.81
Sam Twiston-Davies	66	21	31.82%	+£14.42
Harry Cobden	61	25	40.98%	+£13.61
Tom Scudamore	75	9	12.00%	+£2.07

Top jockeys by Profit – handicaps

Name Of Jockey	Rides	Winners	Strike Rate	Profit/Loss to BSP
Nico de Boinville	17	4	23.53%	+£125.46
Kieron Edgar	41	6	14.63%	+£95.39
James Davies	64	8	12.50%	+£53.51
Mitchell Bastyan	27	2	7.41%	+£35.47
James Best	106	9	8.49%	+£24.91

Top trainers by Strike Rate – non-handicaps

Name Of Trainer	Runners	Winners	Strike Rate	Profit/Loss to BSP
Nicky Henderson	35	13	37.14%	-£0.66
Paul Nicholls	168	62	36.90%	+£13.85
Dan Skelton	38	11	28.95%	-£7.11
Harry Fry	63	16	25.40%	-£25.28
Venetia Williams	20	4	20.00%	+£1.08

Top trainers by Strike Rate – handicaps

Name Of Trainer	Runners	Winners	Strike Rate	Profit/Loss to BSP
Tom Lacey	21	8	38.10%	+£24.13

Anthony Honeyball	32	12	37.50%	+£78.82
Emma Lavelle	24	7	29.17%	+£11.58
Stuart Kittow	14	4	28.57%	+£20.27
Warren Greatrex	22	5	22.73%	+£9.70

Top trainers by Profit – non-handicaps

Name Of Trainer	Runners	Winners	Strike Rate	Profit/Loss to BSP
Jeremy Scott	43	5	11.63%	+£88.66
Paul Nicholls	168	62	36.90%	+£13.85
Gary Moore	17	3	17.65%	+£9.28
Alan King	53	5	9.43%	+£9.09
Carroll Gray	13	1	7.69%	+£2.21

Top trainers by Profit – handicaps

Name Of Trainer	Runners	Winners	Strike Rate	Profit/Loss to BSP
Ben Pauling	16	1	6.25%	+£111.42
Chris Down	108	15	13.89%	+£81.11
Anthony Honeyball	32	12	37.50%	+£78.82
Chris Gordon	25	4	16.00%	+£45.61
Paul Nicholls	98	22	22.45%	+£44.37

Top trainer/jockey combos by Strike Rate – non-handicaps

Name of Trainer/Jockey	Qualifiers	Winners	Strike Rate	Profit/Loss to BSP
Jeremy Scott/Nick Scholfield	15	3	20.00%	+£111.36
Paul Nicholls/Harry Cobden	52	23	44.23%	+£16.69
David Pipe/Tom Scudamore	44	5	11.36%	+£12.03
Paul Nicholls/Sam Twiston-Davies	39	17	43.59%	+£5.19
Venetia	11	2	18.18%	+£2.36

Williams/Aidan Coleman				

Top trainer/jockey combos by Strike Rate – handicaps

Name of Trainer/Jockey	Qualifiers	Winners	Strike Rate	Profit/Loss to BSP
Anthony Honeyball/David Noonan	10	4	40.00%	£12.28
Venetia Williams/Aidan Coleman	16	5	31.25%	+£20.00
Jeremy Scott/Rex Dingle	13	4	30.77%	+£0.25
Colin Tizzard/Harry Cobden	18	4	22.22%	+£22.70
Jonjo O'Neill/Jonjo O'Neill Jr	10	2	20.00%	+£3.35

Top trainer/jockey combos by Profit – non-handicaps

Name of Trainer/Jockey	Qualifiers	Winners	Strike Rate	Profit/Loss to BSP
Jeremy Scott/Nick Scholfield	15	3	20.00%	+£111.36
Paul Nicholls/Harry Cobden	52	23	44.23%	+£16.69
David Pipe/Tom Scudamore	44	5	11.36%	+£12.03
Paul Nicholls/Sam Twiston-Davies	39	17	43.59%	+£5.19
Venetia Williams/Aidan Coleman	11	2	18.18%	+£2.36

Top trainer/jockey combos by Profit – handicaps

Name of Trainer/Jockey	Qualifiers	Winners	Strike Rate	Profit/Loss to BSP
Chris Down/James Davies	41	6	14.63%	+£55.27
Colin Tizzard/Harry Cobden	18	4	22.22%	+£22.70
Venetia Williams/Aidan Coleman	16	5	31.25%	+£20.00
Anthony Honeyball/David Noonan	10	4	40.00%	+£12.28
Evan Williams/Conor Ring	13	2	15.38%	+£8.50

Profit or Loss backing the unnamed favourite – non-handicaps

Runners	Winners	Strike Rate	Profit/Loss to BSP
514	256	49.81%	+£17.86

Profit or Loss backing the unnamed favourite – handicaps

Runners	Winners	Strike Rate	Profit/Loss to BSP
655	189	28.85%	+£10.76

Profit or loss backing the unnamed second favourite - non-handicaps

Runners	Winners	Strike Rate	Profit/Loss to BSP
526	121	23.00%	+£18.03

Profit or loss backing the unnamed second favourite - handicaps

Runners	Winners	Strike Rate	Profit/Loss to BSP
623	107	17.17%	-£36.84

Profit or Loss backing horses who won last time out- non-handicaps

Runners	Winners	Strike Rate	Profit/Loss to BSP
294	93	31.63%	-£4.98

Profit or Loss backing horses who won last time out - handicaps

Runners	Winners	Strike Rate	Profit/Loss to BSP
512	102	19.92%	-£17.18

Profit or loss backing Top-Weights in handicaps

Runners	Winners	Strike Rate	Profit/Loss to BSP
704	90	12.78%	-£67.82

Most profitable sires – non-handicaps

Sire	Runners	Winners	Strike Rate	Profit/Loss to BSP
Scorpion	22	2	9.09%	+£11.04
Turgeon	10	4	40.00%	+£10.67
Shantou	20	3	15.00%	+£3.72
Black Sam Bellamy	14	1	7.14%	+£2.31

Most profitable sires – handicaps

Brian Boru	18	3	16.67%	+£121.23
Milan	87	16	18.39%	+£78.36
Tikkanen	15	3	20.00%	+£56.25
Sir Percy	16	1	6.25%	+£47.72
Flemensfirth	37	6	16.22%	+£42.17

Uttoxeter - Chases

Top jockeys by Strike Rate – non-handicaps

Name Of Jockey	Rides	Winners	Strike Rate	Profit/Loss to BSP
Harry Skelton	17	9	52.94%	+£22.47
Tom Scudamore	13	4	30.77%	-£6.96
Aidan Coleman	18	5	27.78%	+£11.30
Sam Twiston-Davies	13	3	23.08%	+£4.71
David Bass	13	1	7.69%	-£7.95

Top jockeys by Strike Rate – handicaps

Name Of Jockey	Rides	Winners	Strike Rate	Profit/Loss to BSP
Bryan Carver	13	4	30.77%	+£3.79
Matt Griffiths	20	6	30.00%	+£22.32
Harry Skelton	96	25	26.04%	-£12.56
Ben Jones	13	3	23.08%	-£1.56
Harry Cobden	27	6	22.22%	+£12.40

Top jockeys by Profit – non-handicaps

Name Of Jockey	Rides	Winners	Strike Rate	Profit/Loss to BSP
Harry Skelton	17	9	52.94%	+£22.47
Aidan Coleman	18	5	27.78%	+£11.30
Sam Twiston-Davies	13	3	23.08%	+£4.71

Top jockeys by Profit – handicaps

Name Of Jockey	Rides	Winners	Strike Rate	Profit/Loss to BSP
Robert Dunne	57	10	17.54%	+£334.29
James Bowen	34	4	11.76%	+£93.22
Adam Wedge	72	8	11.11%	+£65.55
Richie McLernon	74	8	10.81%	+£60.42

| Brendan Powell | 44 | 7 | 15.91% | +£43.79 |

Top trainers by Strike Rate – non-handicaps

Name Of Trainer	Runners	Winners	Strike Rate	Profit/Loss to BSP
Dan Skelton	20	10	50.00%	+£23.33
Charlie Longsdon	11	4	36.36%	-£1.51
Nicky Henderson	18	6	33.33%	-£5.75
Philip Hobbs	15	5	33.33%	-£0.13
Nigel Twiston-Davies	13	4	30.77%	-£0.26

Top trainers by Strike Rate – handicaps

Name Of Trainer	Runners	Winners	Strike Rate	Profit/Loss to BSP
Harry Fry	33	11	33.33%	+£40.30
James Evans	18	5	27.78%	+£11.05
Mark Walford	18	5	27.78%	+£11.02
Alan Jones	11	3	27.27%	+£21.65
Jackie Du Plessis	11	3	27.27%	-£0.05

Top trainers by Profit – non-handicaps

Name Of Trainer	Runners	Winners	Strike Rate	Profit/Loss to BSP
Dan Skelton	20	10	50.00%	+£23.33
Tim Vaughan	10	2	20.00%	+£6.55
Jonjo O'Neill	21	4	19.05%	+£3.14

Top trainers by Profit – handicaps

Name Of Trainer	Runners	Winners	Strike Rate	Profit/Loss to BSP
Peter Bowen	91	13	14.29%	+£60.32
Fergal O'Brien	72	18	25.00%	+£47.53
Katy Price	27	7	25.93%	+£46.25
Colin Tizzard	46	9	19.57%	+£42.80
Nigel Twiston-Davies	102	16	15.69%	+£42.03

Top trainer/jockey combos by Strike Rate – non-handicaps

Name Of Trainer/Jockey	Rides	Winners	Strike Rate	Profit/Loss to BSP
Dan Skelton/Harry Skelton	17	9	52.94%	+£22.47
Kim Bailey/David Bass	11	1	9.09%	-£5.95

Top trainer/jockey combos by Strike Rate – handicaps

Name of Trainer/Jockey	Qualifiers	Winners	Strike Rate	Profit/Loss to BSP
Jeremy Scott/Matt Griffiths	16	6	37.50%	+£26.32
Katy Price/Ben Poste	22	7	31.82%	+£51.25
Jonjo O'Neill/Aidan Coleman	29	8	27.59%	+£32.67
Oliver Greenall/Henry Brooke	11	3	27.27%	+£9.17
Nicky Henderson/Nico de Boinville	11	3	27.27%	+£13.21

Top trainer/jockey combos by Profit – non-handicaps

Name of Trainer/Jockey	Qualifiers	Winners	Strike Rate	Profit/Loss to BSP
Dan Skelton/Harry Skelton	17	9	52.94%	+£22.47

Top trainer/jockey combos by Profit – handicaps

Name of Trainer/Jockey	Qualifiers	Winners	Strike Rate	Profit/Loss to BSP

Peter Bowen/James Bowen	18	2	11.11%	+£52.73
Katy Price/Ben Poste	22	7	31.82%	+£51.25
Nigel Twiston-Davies/Sam Twiston-Davies	46	9	19.57%	+£50.95
Ben Haslam/Richie McLernon	11	1	9.09%	+£34.68
Jonjo O'Neill/Aidan Coleman	29	8	27.59%	+£32.67

Profit or Loss backing the unnamed favourite – non-handicaps

Runners	Winners	Strike Rate	Profit/Loss to BSP
255	108	42.35%	-£17.37

Profit or Loss backing the unnamed favourite – handicaps

Runners	Winners	Strike Rate	Profit/Loss to BSP
939	259	27.58%	-£15.95

Profit or loss backing the unnamed second favourite - non-handicaps

Runners	Winners	Strike Rate	Profit/Loss to BSP
237	68	28.69%	+£40.93

Profit or loss backing the unnamed second favourite - handicaps

Runners	Winners	Strike Rate	Profit/Loss to BSP
891	177	19.87%	+£33.42

Profit or Loss backing horses who won last time out - non-handicaps

Runners	Winners	Strike Rate	Profit/Loss to BSP

152	51	33.55%	+£10.94

Profit or Loss backing horses who won last time out - handicaps

Runners	Winners	Strike Rate	Profit/Loss to BSP
1006	182	18.09%	+£25.03

Profit or loss backing Top-Weights in handicaps

Runners	Winners	Strike Rate	Profit/Loss to BSP
997	150	15.05%	-£54.88

Most profitable sires – non-handicaps

Sire	Runners	Winners	Strike Rate	Profit/Loss to BSP
Milan	11	5	45.45%	+£28.37
Flemensfirth	14	5	35.71%	+£7.55
Midnight Legend	11	4	36.36%	+£5.34
Presenting	10	3	30.00%	+£21.6

Most profitable sires – handicaps

Whitmore's Conn	11	2	18.18%	+£326.90
Tobougg	22	5	22.73%	+£75.97
Trade Fair	15	1	6.67%	+£38.16
Indian Danehill	16	2	12.50%	+£35.84
King's Theatre	88	16	18.18%	+£34.18

Uttoxeter – Hurdles

Top jockeys by Strike Rate – non-handicaps

Name Of Jockey	Rides	Winners	Strike Rate	Profit/Loss to BSP
Harry Skelton	72	26	36.11%	+£2.48
A P Heskin	11	3	27.27%	+£19.02
Gavin Sheehan	54	14	25.93%	+£41.00
Brian Hughes	47	12	25.53%	+£3.39

| Joshua Moore | 12 | 3 | 25.00% | +£3.52 |

Top jockeys by Strike Rate – handicaps

Name Of Jockey	Rides	Winners	Strike Rate	Profit/Loss to BSP
Harry Skelton	117	38	32.48%	+£126.38
Ben Godfrey	17	5	29.41%	+£12.32
Rex Dingle	24	7	29.17%	+£24.33
Kevin Brogan	11	3	27.27%	+£12.69
Archie Bellamy	13	3	23.08%	+£21.57

Top jockeys by Profit – non-handicaps

Name Of Jockey	Rides	Winners	Strike Rate	Profit/Loss to BSP
Paddy Brennan	63	11	17.46%	+£83.22
Ben Poste	57	1	1.75%	+£68.42
Henry Brooke	43	4	9.30%	+£42.29
Gavin Sheehan	54	14	25.93%	+£41.00
Nick Scholfield	48	8	16.67%	+£35.96

Top jockeys by Profit – handicaps

Name Of Jockey	Rides	Winners	Strike Rate	Profit/Loss to BSP
Cillin Leonard	11	2	18.18%	+£312.53
Conor Ring	46	5	10.87%	+£207.05
Joshua Moore	18	3	16.67%	+£138.26
Harry Skelton	117	38	32.48%	+£126.38
Stan Sheppard	50	10	20.00%	+£78.90

Top trainers by Strike Rate – non-handicaps

Name Of Trainer	Runners	Winners	Strike Rate	Profit/Loss to BSP
Dr Richard Newland	56	21	37.50%	+£6.36
Alastair Ralph	18	6	33.33%	+£17.99
Nicky Henderson	54	17	31.48%	-£13.63
Kerry Lee	10	3	30.00%	+£17.09
Rebecca Curtis	20	6	30.00%	+£23.02

Top trainers by Strike Rate – handicaps

Name Of Trainer	Runners	Winners	Strike Rate	Profit/Loss to BSP
Noel C Kelly	13	5	38.46%	+£36.83
Phil Middleton	20	6	30.00%	+£39.17
Dan Skelton	136	36	26.47%	+£77.84
Harry Whittington	19	5	26.32%	+£15.99
Dr Richard Newland	65	17	26.15%	+£9.28

Top trainers by Profit – non-handicaps

Name Of Trainer	Runners	Winners	Strike Rate	Profit/Loss to BSP
Michael Mullineaux	22	1	4.55%	+£103.42
Sue Smith	24	3	12.50%	+£84.08
Fergal O'Brien	76	8	10.53%	+£63.44
Donald McCain	120	23	19.17%	+£43.58
Harry Whittington	20	3	15.00%	+£31.89

Top trainers by Profit – handicaps

Name Of Trainer	Runners	Winners	Strike Rate	Profit/Loss to BSP
Jake Coulson	16	1	6.25%	+£231.41
Clare Hobson	13	1	7.69%	+£181.62
Claire Dyson	65	3	4.62%	+£97.28
Dan Skelton	136	36	26.47%	+£77.84
Tom Symonds	47	8	17.02%	+£68.07

Top trainer/jockey combos by Strike Rate – non-handicaps

Name of Trainer/Jockey	Qualifiers	Winners	Strike Rate	Profit/Loss to BSP
Donald McCain/Brian Hughes	14	7	50.00%	+£24.09
Olly	12	5	41.67%	+£4.52

Murphy/Aidan Coleman				
Dr Richard Newland/Sam Twiston-Davies	30	12	40.00%	+£1.50
Dan Skelton/Harry Skelton	69	26	37.68%	+£5.48
Jamie Snowden/Gavin Sheehan	13	4	30.77%	+£5.49

Top trainer/jockey combos by Strike Rate – handicaps

Name of Trainer/Jockey	Qualifiers	Winners	Strike Rate	Profit/Loss to BSP
Dr Richard Newland/Sam Twiston-Davies	28	11	39.29%	+£22.24
Tom Lacey/Stan Sheppard	13	5	38.46%	+£71.06
Dan Skelton/Harry Skelton	98	35	35.71%	+£112.93
Harry Fry/Sean Bowen	12	4	33.33%	+£6.67
Kerry Lee/Richard Patrick	13	4	30.77%	+£13.83

Top trainer/jockey combos by Profit – non-handicaps

Name of Trainer/Jockey	Qualifiers	Winners	Strike Rate	Profit/Loss to BSP
Fergal O'Brien/Paddy Brennan	36	5	13.89%	+£88.49
Oliver Greenall/Henry Brooke	12	1	8.33%	+£33.33
Tom George/Jonathan Burke	14	4	28.57%	+£26.08

Donald McCain/Brian Hughes	14	7	50.00%	+£24.09
Olly Murphy/Fergus Gregory	15	4	26.67%	+£12.53

Top trainer/jockey combos by Profit – handicaps

Name of Trainer/Jockey	Qualifiers	Winners	Strike Rate	Profit/Loss to BSP
Dan Skelton/Harry Skelton	98	35	35.71%	+£112.93
Tom Lacey/Stan Sheppard	13	5	38.46%	+£71.06
Tony Carroll/Lee Edwards	47	6	12.77%	+£47.20
David Pipe/Conor O'Farrell	13	2	15.38%	+£31.19
Neil Mulholland/Sam Twiston-Davies	10	2	20.00%	+£24.92

Profit or Loss backing the unnamed favourite – non-handicaps

Runners	Winners	Strike Rate	Profit/Loss to BSP
912	396	43.42%	+£25.34

Profit or Loss backing the unnamed favourite – handicaps

Runners	Winners	Strike Rate	Profit/Loss to BSP
1187	335	28.22%	+£35.37

Profit or loss backing the unnamed second favourite - non-handicaps

Runners	Winners	Strike Rate	Profit/Loss to BSP
875	188	21.49%	-£66.29

Profit or loss backing the unnamed second favourite - handicaps

Runners	Winners	Strike Rate	Profit/Loss to BSP
1116	187	16.76%	-£58.81

Profit or Loss backing horses who won last time out- non-handicaps

Runners	Winners	Strike Rate	Profit/Loss to BSP
538	164	30.48%	+£5.89

Profit or Loss backing horses who won last time out - handicaps

Runners	Winners	Strike Rate	Profit/Loss to BSP
1122	223	19.88%	+£6.81

Profit or loss backing Top-Weights in handicaps

Runners	Winners	Strike Rate	Profit/Loss to BSP
1296	171	13.19%	-£10.08

Most profitable sires – non-handicaps

Sire	Runners	Winners	Strike Rate	Profit/Loss to BSP
Shirocco	36	2	5.56%	+£173.28
Mastercraftsman	11	3	27.27%	+£89.05
Robin Des Pres	12	2	16.67%	+£79.20
Darsi	14	1	7.14%	+£22.34
Tiger Hill	10	2	20.00%	+£21.52

Most profitable sires – handicaps

Court Cave	66	8	12.12%	+£244.16
Morozov	40	7	17.50%	+£239.82
Antarctique	11	2	18.18%	+£164.66
Scorpion	42	5	11.90%	+£123.74
Teofilo	20	3	15.00%	+£79.71

Warwick - Chases

Top jockeys by Strike Rate – non-handicaps

Name Of Jockey	Rides	Winners	Strike Rate	Profit/Loss to BSP
Harry Skelton	20	8	40.00%	+£5.42
Sam Twiston-Davies	21	8	38.10%	-£0.53
Daryl Jacob	21	7	33.33%	-£6.99
Aidan Coleman	19	6	31.58%	-£7.01
David Maxwell	11	2	18.18%	-£7.03

Top jockeys by Strike Rate – handicaps

Name Of Jockey	Rides	Winners	Strike Rate	Profit/Loss to BSP
Ben Jones	13	4	30.77%	+£12.17
Harry Skelton	79	20	25.32%	-£3.42
Jonathan Burke	30	7	23.33%	+£54.15
Jonjo O'Neill Jr	23	5	21.74%	+£15.66
Max Kendrick	14	3	21.43%	+£9.44

Top jockeys by Profit – non-handicaps

Name Of Jockey	Rides	Winners	Strike Rate	Profit/Loss to BSP
Harry Skelton	20	8	40.00%	+£5.42
Sam Twiston-Davies	21	8	38.10%	-£0.53

Top jockeys by Profit – handicaps

Name Of Jockey	Rides	Winners	Strike Rate	Profit/Loss to BSP
Jonathan Burke	30	7	23.33%	+£54.15
Daryl Jacob	27	4	14.81%	+£30.92
Jamie Moore	37	5	13.51%	+£24.67
Aidan Coleman	61	13	21.31%	+£23.48
Adam Wedge	28	4	14.29%	+£21.51

Top trainers by Strike Rate – non-handicaps

Name Of Trainer	Runners	Winners	Strike Rate	Profit/Loss to BSP
Alan King	20	10	50.00%	+£3.45
Paul Nicholls	29	13	44.83%	+£2.09
Philip Hobbs	14	5	35.71%	+£3.62
Dan Skelton	29	10	34.48%	+£1.12
Henry Daly	12	3	25.00%	+£1.12

Top trainers by Strike Rate – handicaps

Name Of Trainer	Runners	Winners	Strike Rate	Profit/Loss to BSP
Nicky Henderson	16	7	43.75%	+£26.16
Gary Hanmer	13	5	38.46%	+£12.34
Dan Skelton	81	22	27.16%	+£4.69
Anthony Honeyball	12	3	25.00%	+£3.11
Jonjo O'Neill	87	20	22.99%	+£63.89

Top trainers by Profit – non-handicaps

Name Of Trainer	Runners	Winners	Strike Rate	Profit/Loss to BSP
Philip Hobbs	14	5	35.71%	+£3.62
Alan King	20	10	50.00%	+£3.45
Paul Nicholls	29	13	44.83%	+£2.09
Henry Daly	12	3	25.00%	+£1.12
Dan Skelton	29	10	34.48%	+£1.12

Top trainers by Profit – handicaps

Name Of Trainer	Runners	Winners	Strike Rate	Profit/Loss to BSP
Tom George	41	9	21.95%	+£76.26
Jonjo O'Neill	87	20	22.99%	+£63.89
Caroline Bailey	38	5	13.16%	+£42.34
Ben Case	22	3	13.64%	+£30.91
Nicky Henderson	16	7	43.75%	+£26.16

Top trainer/jockey combos by Strike Rate – non-handicaps

Name Of Trainer/Jockey	Rides	Winners	Strike Rate	Profit/Loss to BSP
Dan Skelton/Harry Skelton	20	8	40.00%	+£5.42

Top trainer/jockey combos by Strike Rate – handicaps

Name of Trainer/Jockey	Qualifiers	Winners	Strike Rate	Profit/Loss to BSP
Tom George/Jonathan Burke	11	5	45.45%	+£66.51
Philip Hobbs/Tom O'Brien	16	5	31.25%	+£11.39
Dan Skelton/Harry Skelton	67	19	28.36%	+£5.64
Jonjo O'Neill/Jonjo O'Neill Jr	18	5	27.78%	+£20.66
Ian Williams/Charlie Todd	11	3	27.27%	+£7.62

Top trainer/jockey combos by Profit – non-handicaps

Name of Trainer/Jockey	Qualifiers	Winners	Strike Rate	Profit/Loss to BSP
Dan Skelton/Harry Skelton	20	8	40.00%	+£5.42

Top trainer/jockey combos by Profit – handicaps

Name of Trainer/Jockey	Qualifiers	Winners	Strike Rate	Profit/Loss to BSP
Tom George/Jonathan Burke	11	5	45.45%	+£66.51

Evan Williams/Adam Wedge	17	3	17.65%	+£22.74
Jonjo O'Neill/Jonjo O'Neill Jr	18	5	27.78%	+£20.66
Jonjo O'Neill'Aidan Coleman	13	3	23.08%	+£16.00
Venetia Williams/Aidan Coleman	19	5	26.32	+£13.17

Profit or Loss backing the unnamed favourite – non-handicaps

Runners	Winners	Strike Rate	Profit/Loss to BSP
230	124	53.91%	+£20.98

Profit or Loss backing the unnamed favourite – handicaps

Runners	Winners	Strike Rate	Profit/Loss to BSP
532	167	31.39%	+£51.86

Profit or loss backing the unnamed second favourite - non-handicaps

Runners	Winners	Strike Rate	Profit/Loss to BSP
229	46	20.09%	-£41.09

Profit or loss backing the unnamed second favourite - handicaps

Runners	Winners	Strike Rate	Profit/Loss to BSP
469	93	19.83%	-£14.14

Profit or Loss backing horses who won last time out - non-handicaps

Runners	Winners	Strike Rate	Profit/Loss to BSP
210	72	34.29%	+£107.23

Profit or Loss backing horses who won last time out - handicaps

Runners	Winners	Strike Rate	Profit/Loss to BSP
447	78	17.45%	-£39.40

Profit or loss backing Top-Weights in handicaps

Runners	Winners	Strike Rate	Profit/Loss to BSP
537	90	16.76%	+£125.02

Most profitable sires – non-handicaps

Sire	Runners	Winners	Strike Rate	Profit/Loss to BSP
Milan	16	6	37.50%	+£48.14

Most profitable sires – handicaps

Milan	71	17	23.94%	+£94.47
Martaline	26	8	30.77%	+£47.48
Network	15	6	40.00%	+£38.34
Witness Box	18	1	5.56%	+£36.74
Westerner	48	11	22.92%	+£30.53

Warwick – Hurdles

Top jockeys by Strike Rate – non-handicaps

Name Of Jockey	Rides	Winners	Strike Rate	Profit/Loss to BSP
Chester Williams	12	4	33.33%	+£6.30
Harry Skelton	123	36	29.27%	+£1.45
Nico de Boinville	47	13	27.66%	-£7.46
Tom Scudamore	35	7	20.00%	+£179.27
Trevor Whelan	11	2	18.18%	-£1.44

Top jockeys by Strike Rate – handicaps

Name Of Jockey	Rides	Winners	Strike Rate	Profit/Loss to BSP

Bryony Frost	12	4	33.33%	+£26.83
Chester Williams	14	4	28.57%	+£9.27
Nico de Boinville	36	8	22.22%	+£36.03
Ben Jones	14	3	21.43%	+£8.21
Conor Ring	14	3	21.43%	+£21.05

Top jockeys by Profit – non-handicaps

Name Of Jockey	Rides	Winners	Strike Rate	Profit/Loss to BSP
Jamie Moore	28	4	14.29%	+£304.22
Tom Scudamore	35	7	20.00%	+£179.27
Jonjo O'Neill Jr	18	1	5.56%	+£70.22
Jonathan Burke	36	6	16.67%	+£37.53
Brendan Powell	27	3	11.11%	+£36.01

Top jockeys by Profit – handicaps

Name Of Jockey	Rides	Winners	Strike Rate	Profit/Loss to BSP
James Davies	39	4	10.26%	+£135.43
Jack Quinlan	33	7	21.21%	+£84.15
Ciaran Gethings	26	4	15.38%	+£44.10
Nico de Boinville	36	8	22.22%	+£36.03
Bryony Frost	12	4	33.33%	+£26.83

Top trainers by Strike Rate – non-handicaps

Name Of Trainer	Runners	Winners	Strike Rate	Profit/Loss to BSP
Nicky Henderson	80	23	28.75%	-£22.27
Alan King	108	30	27.78%	-£10.71
Dan Skelton	147	37	25.17%	-£31.07
Neil King	17	4	23.53%	-£2.70
Stuart Edmunds	20	4	20.00%	+£51.28

Top trainers by Strike Rate – handicaps

Name Of Trainer	Runners	Winners	Strike Rate	Profit/Loss to BSP
Mrs Jane Williams	10	4	40.00%	+£13.27

Paul Nicholls	12	4	33.33%	+£7.40
Nicky Henderson	40	10	25.00%	+£40.64
Caroline Bailey	13	3	23.08%	+£7.56
Stuart Edmunds	14	3	21.43%	+£1.38

Top trainers by Profit – non-handicaps

Name Of Trainer	Runners	Winners	Strike Rate	Profit/Loss to BSP
Ian Williams	60	2	3.33%	+£201.55
Jonjo O'Neill	81	5	6.17%	+£57.86
Stuart Edmunds	20	4	20.00%	+£51.28
Olly Murphy	46	4	8.70%	+£38.97
Tom George	24	1	4.17%	+£31.41

Top trainers by Profit – handicaps

Name Of Trainer	Runners	Winners	Strike Rate	Profit/Loss to BSP
Jonjo O'Neill	111	21	18.92%	+£103.13
Nikki Evans	13	2	15.38%	+£101.11
Lucy Wadham	30	5	16.67%	+£75.45
Nicky Henderson	40	10	25.00%	+£40.64
Fergal O'Brien	42	6	14.29%	+£34.59

Top trainer/jockey combos by Strike Rate – non-handicaps

Name of Trainer/Jockey	Qualifiers	Winners	Strike Rate	Profit/Loss to BSP
Nicky Henderson/Nico de Boinville	32	11	34.38%	-£1.04
David Pipe/Tom Scudamore	12	4	33.33%	+£1.81
Dan Skelton/Harry Skelton	118	35	29.66%	-£6.31
Charlie Longsdon/Aidan Coleman	12	3	25.00%	-£6.47
Alan King/Tom	21	5	23.81%	+£11.68

Bellamy				

Top trainer/jockey combos by Strike Rate – handicaps

Name of Trainer/Jockey	Qualifiers	Winners	Strike Rate	Profit/Loss to BSP
Nicky Henderson/Nico de Boinville	21	6	28.57%	+£32.57
Philip Hobbs/Tom O'Brien	12	3	25.00%	+£19.46
Jonjo O'Neill/Jonjo O'Neill Jr	27	6	22.22%	+£5.21
Fergal O'Brien/Paddy Brennan	14	3	21.43%	+£5.22
Jonjo O'Neill/Aidan Coleman	10	2	20.00%	+£6.80

Top trainer/jockey combos by Profit – non-handicaps

Name of Trainer/Jockey	Qualifiers	Winners	Strike Rate	Profit/Loss to BSP
Jonjo O'Neill/Jonjo O'Neill Jr	16	1	6.25%	+£72.22
Tom George/Jonathan Burke	10	1	10.00%	+£45.41
Fergal O'Brien/Paddy Brennan	30	6	20.00%	+£17.47
Jonjo O'Neill/Richie McLernon	24	3	12.50%	+£12.36
Alan King/Tom Bellamy	21	5	23.81%	+£11.68

Top trainer/jockey combos by Profit – handicaps

Name of Trainer/Jockey	Qualifiers	Winners	Strike Rate	Profit/Loss to BSP
Nicky Henderson/Nico de Boinville	21	6	28.57%	+£32.57
Philip Hobbs/Tom O'Brien	12	3	25.00%	+£19.46
Jonjo O'Neill/Richie McLernon	27	2	7.41%	+£15.49
Dan Skelton/Bridget Andrews	12	1	8.33%	+£11.54
Henry Oliver/James Davies	14	1	7.14%	+£11.50

Profit or Loss backing the unnamed favourite – non-handicaps

Runners	Winners	Strike Rate	Profit/Loss to BSP
425	198	46.59%	+£14.92

Profit or Loss backing the unnamed favourite – handicaps

Runners	Winners	Strike Rate	Profit/Loss to BSP
475	121	25.47%	-£21.99

Profit or loss backing the unnamed second favourite - non-handicaps

Runners	Winners	Strike Rate	Profit/Loss to BSP
418	101	24.16%	+£33.36

Profit or loss backing the unnamed second favourite - handicaps

Runners	Winners	Strike Rate	Profit/Loss to BSP
451	76	16.85%	-£28.83

Profit or Loss backing horses who won last time out- non-handicaps

Runners	Winners	Strike Rate	Profit/Loss to BSP
368	102	27.72%	-£17.52

Profit or Loss backing horses who won last time out - handicaps

Runners	Winners	Strike Rate	Profit/Loss to BSP
504	95	18.85%	+£79.99

Profit or loss backing Top-Weights in handicaps

Runners	Winners	Strike Rate	Profit/Loss to BSP
518	59	11.39%	+£22.00

Most profitable sires – non-handicaps

Sire	Runners	Winners	Strike Rate	Profit/Loss to BSP
Yeats	35	10	28.57%	+£366.32
Milan	75	8	10.67%	+£41.27
Black Sam Bellamy	35	7	20.00%	+£40.49
Doyen	20	5	25.00%	+£28.40
Shirocco	42	5	11.90%	+£8.38

Most profitable sires – handicaps

Midnight Legend	71	9	12.68%	+£81.74
Shantou	42	13	30.95%	+£62.24
Dansili	10	3	30.00%	+£48.13
Winged Love	12	4	33.33%	+£41.25
Karinga Bay	20	3	15.00%	+£35.50

Wetherby - Chases

Top jockeys by Strike Rate – non-handicaps

Name Of Jockey	Rides	Winners	Strike Rate	Profit/Loss to BSP
Tom Scudamore	10	4	40.00%	-£0.36
Harry Skelton	19	6	31.58%	-£6.87
Brian Hughes	31	5	16.13%	-£16.78
Paddy Brennan	12	1	8.33%	-£8.12
Ryan Mania	14	1	7.14%	-£9.32

Top jockeys by Strike Rate – handicaps

Name Of Jockey	Rides	Winners	Strike Rate	Profit/Loss to BSP
Tom Scudamore	23	8	34.78%	+£6.15
Robert Dunne	10	3	30.00%	+£10.28
Harry Skelton	43	12	27.91%	+£10.29
James Davies	11	3	27.27%	+£8.32
Charlie Deutsch	13	3	23.08%	-£0.83

Top jockeys by Profit – handicaps

Name Of Jockey	Rides	Winners	Strike Rate	Profit/Loss to BSP
Dougie Costello	24	2	8.33%	+£18.51
Adam Wedge	16	3	18.75%	+£17.84
Conor O'Farrell	38	7	18.42%	+£14.34
Sean Quinlan	71	12	16.90%	+£12.67
John Kington	11	1	9.09%	+£12.45

Top trainers by Strike Rate – non-handicaps

Name Of Trainer	Runners	Winners	Strike Rate	Profit/Loss to BSP
Kim Bailey	10	7	70.00%	+£16.33
Nicky Henderson	10	6	60.00%	+£3.98

Nigel Twiston-Davies	16	6	37.50%	+£9.23
David Pipe	11	4	36.36%	-£1.36
Dan Skelton	22	7	31.82%	-£5.96

Top trainers by Strike Rate – handicaps

Name Of Trainer	Runners	Winners	Strike Rate	Profit/Loss to BSP
Dr Richard Newland	24	9	37.50%	+£15.87
Michael Scudamore	16	5	31.25%	+£24.60
Warren Greatrex	11	3	27.27%	+£25.88
Fergal O'Brien	12	3	25.00%	+£11.82
Dan Skelton	54	13	24.07%	+£9.01

Top trainers by Profit – non-handicaps

Name Of Trainer	Runners	Winners	Strike Rate	Profit/Loss to BSP
Kim Bailey	10	7	70.00%	+£16.33
Nigel Twiston-Davies	16	6	37.50%	+£9.23
Nicky Henderson	10	6	60.00%	+£3.98

Top trainers by Profit – handicaps

Name Of Trainer	Runners	Winners	Strike Rate	Profit/Loss to BSP
Micky Hammond	143	14	9.79%	+£34.77
Warren Greatrex	11	3	27.27%	+£25.88
Michael Scudamore	16	5	31.25%	+£24.60
Maurice Barnes	28	6	21.43%	+£24.50
Michael Easterby	20	3	15.00%	+£16.21

Top trainer/jockey combos by Strike Rate – non-handicaps

Name Of	Rides	Winners	Strike Rate	Profit/Loss to

Trainer/Jockey				BSP
Dan Skelton/Harry Skelton	18	6	33.33%	-£5.87
Sue Smith/Ryan Mania	10	1	10.00%	-£5.32

Top trainer/jockey combos by Strike Rate – handicaps

Name of Trainer/Jockey	Qualifiers	Winners	Strike Rate	Profit/Loss to BSP
Micky Hammond/Connor O'Farrell	10	4	40.00%	+£26.98
David Pipe/Tom Scudamore	10	4	40.00%	+£6.42
Dan Skelton/Harry Skelton	38	11	28.95%	+£12.27
Stuart Coltherd/Sam Coltherd	16	4	25.00%	+£6.55
Dr Richard Newland/Charlie Hammond	12	3	25.00%	+£1.39

Top trainer/jockey combos by Profit – handicaps

Name of Trainer/Jockey	Qualifiers	Winners	Strike Rate	Profit/Loss to BSP
Micky Hammond/Connor O'Farrell	10	4	40.00%	+£26.98
Dan Skelton/Harry Skelton	38	11	28.95%	+£12.27
Rose Dobbin/Craig Nichol	16	3	18.75%	+£6.90
Stuart Coltherd/Sam Coltherd	16	4	25.00%	+£6.55
David Pipe/Tom Scudamore	10	4	40.00%	+£6.42

Profit or Loss backing the unnamed favourite – non-handicaps

Runners	Winners	Strike Rate	Profit/Loss to BSP
281	141	50.18%	+£14.32

Profit or Loss backing the unnamed favourite – handicaps

Runners	Winners	Strike Rate	Profit/Loss to BSP
625	166	26.56%	-£59.91

Profit or loss backing the unnamed second favourite - non-handicaps

Runners	Winners	Strike Rate	Profit/Loss to BSP
269	64	23.79%	-£19.08

Profit or loss backing the unnamed second favourite - handicaps

Runners	Winners	Strike Rate	Profit/Loss to BSP
573	111	19.37%	-£42.19

Profit or Loss backing horses who won last time out - non-handicaps

Runners	Winners	Strike Rate	Profit/Loss to BSP
234	70	29.91%	-£25.66

Profit or Loss backing horses who won last time out - handicaps

Runners	Winners	Strike Rate	Profit/Loss to BSP
563	108	19.18%	-£35.96

Profit or loss backing Top-Weights in handicaps

Runners	Winners	Strike Rate	Profit/Loss to BSP
639	107	16.74%	-£37.46

Most profitable sires – non-handicaps

Sire	Runners	Winners	Strike Rate	Profit/Loss to BSP
King's Theatre	21	7	33.33%	+£4.08

Most profitable sires – handicaps

Flemensfith	52	7	13.46%	+£56.69
Sholokhov	11	4	36.36%	+£26.85
Kayf Tara	89	15	16.85%	+£23.35
Mahler	14	4	28.57%	+£21.89
Dansili	10	1	10.00%	+£19.60

Wetherby – Hurdles

Top jockeys by Strike Rate – non-handicaps

Name Of Jockey	Rides	Winners	Strike Rate	Profit/Loss to BSP
Harry Skelton	69	26	37.68%	+£6.00
Daryl Jacob	16	5	31.25%	+£6.88
Sam Twiston-Davies	28	8	28.57%	+£14.02
Jonathan Burke	11	3	27.27%	+£3.89
A P Heskin	15	4	26.67%	-£1.56

Top jockeys by Strike Rate – handicaps

Name Of Jockey	Rides	Winners	Strike Rate	Profit/Loss to BSP
Paddy Brennan	12	4	33.33%	+£22.04
Harry Skelton	47	12	25.53%	+£8.75
Fergus Gregory	12	3	25.00%	+£28.99
Dougie Costello	36	9	25.00%	+£55.40
Charlie Hammond	17	4	23.53%	+£10.27

Top jockeys by Profit – non-handicaps

Name Of Jockey	Rides	Winners	Strike Rate	Profit/Loss to BSP
William Kennedy	20	4	20.00%	+£36.30
Billy Garritty	10	2	20.00%	+£22.03

Paddy Brennan	27	7	25.93%	+£14.75
Sam Twiston-Davies	28	8	28.57%	+£14.02
Conor O'Farrell	23	1	4.35%	+£12.30

Top jockeys by Profit – handicaps

Name Of Jockey	Rides	Winners	Strike Rate	Profit/Loss to BSP
Dougie Costello	36	9	25.00%	+£55.40
Jamie Hamilton	50	7	14.00%	+£46.39
Fergus Gregory	12	3	25.00%	+£28.99
Paddy Brennan	12	4	33.33%	+£22.04
John Dixon	12	2	16.67%	+£18.42

Top trainers by Strike Rate – non-handicaps

Name Of Trainer	Runners	Winners	Strike Rate	Profit/Loss to BSP
Nicky Henderson	12	7	58.33%	+£7.26
Paul Nicholls	17	7	41.18%	+£10.59
Philip Hobbs	18	7	38.89%	+£1.22
Dan Skelton	84	30	35.71%	+£8.69
Tom George	17	5	29.41%	+£11.28

Top trainers by Strike Rate – handicaps

Name Of Trainer	Runners	Winners	Strike Rate	Profit/Loss to BSP
Neil Mulholland	23	6	26.09%	+£25.38
Jonjo O'Neill	48	12	25.00%	+£13.67
Warren Greatrex	20	5	25.00%	+£10.02
Samuel Drinkwater	13	3	23.08%	+£18.13
Dan Skelton	53	12	22.64%	+£22.85

Top trainers by Profit – non-handicaps

Name Of Trainer	Runners	Winners	Strike Rate	Profit/Loss to BSP
Nick Kent	16	1	6.25%	+£157.41
Andrew Crook	21	1	4.76%	+£120.44

Rebecca Menzies	26	3	11.54%	+£57.30
Tom George	17	5	29.41%	+£11.28
Fergal O'Brien	21	6	28.57%	+£11.08

Top trainers by Profit – handicaps

Name Of Trainer	Runners	Winners	Strike Rate	Profit/Loss to BSP
Philip Kirby	143	20	13.99%	+£50.14
Alan Brown	12	1	8.33%	+£36.22
Chris Grant	43	7	16.28%	+£29.99
Simon Waugh	12	2	16.67%	+£27.63
Neil Mulholland	23	6	26.09%	+£25.38

Top trainer/jockey combos by Strike Rate – non-handicaps

Name of Trainer/Jockey	Qualifiers	Winners	Strike Rate	Profit/Loss to BSP
Dan Skelton/Harry Skelton	67	26	38.81%	+£8.00
Fergal O'Brien/Paddy Brennan	13	5	38.46%	+£17.44
Warren Greatrex/Gavin Sheehan	11	4	36.36%	+£3.52
Maurice Barnes/Stephen Mulqueen	11	3	27.27%	+£13.47
Nigel Twiston-Davies/Sam Twiston Davies	16	4	25.00%	-£4.05

Top trainer/jockey combos by Strike Rate – handicaps

Name of Trainer/Jockey	Qualifiers	Winners	Strike Rate	Profit/Loss to BSP
Dan Skelton/Harry Skelton	39	10	25.64%	+£10.10
Michael	12	3	25.00%	+£7.63

Easterby/Harry Bannister				
Rose Dobbin/Craig Nichol	11	2	18.18%	+£3.84
Jonjo O'Neill/Jonjo O'Neill Jr	11	2	18.18%	-£4.62
John Dixon/John Dixon	12	2	16.67%	+£18.42

Top trainer/jockey combos by Profit – non-handicaps

Name of Trainer/Jockey	Qualifiers	Winners	Strike Rate	Profit/Loss to BSP
Fergal O'Brien/Paddy Brennan	13	5	38.46%	+£17.44
Maurice Barnes/Stephen Mulqueen	11	3	27.27%	+£13.47
Dan Skelton/Harry Skelton	67	26	38.81%	+£8.00
Warren Greatrex/Gavin Sheehan	11	4	36.36%	+£3.52

Top trainer/jockey combos by Profit – handicaps

Name of Trainer/Jockey	Qualifiers	Winners	Strike Rate	Profit/Loss to BSP
John Dixon/John Dixon	12	2	16.67%	+£18.42
Dan Skelton/Harry Skelton	39	10	25.64%	+£10.10
Michael Easterby/Harry Bannister	12	3	25.00%	+£7.63
Tim Easterby/Jamie Hamilton	10	1	10.00%	+£6.72

Rose Dobbin/Craig Nichol	11	2	18.18%	+£3.84

Profit or Loss backing the unnamed favourite – non-handicaps

Runners	Winners	Strike Rate	Profit/Loss to BSP
625	264	42.24%	-£36.85

Profit or Loss backing the unnamed favourite – handicaps

Runners	Winners	Strike Rate	Profit/Loss to BSP
633	188	29.70%	+£76.80

Profit or loss backing the unnamed second favourite - non-handicaps

Runners	Winners	Strike Rate	Profit/Loss to BSP
617	149	24.15%	+£68.72

Profit or loss backing the unnamed second favourite - handicaps

Runners	Winners	Strike Rate	Profit/Loss to BSP
587	94	16.01%	-£58.35

Profit or Loss backing horses who won last time out- non-handicaps

Runners	Winners	Strike Rate	Profit/Loss to BSP
536	132	24.63%	-£84.08

Profit or Loss backing horses who won last time out - handicaps

Runners	Winners	Strike Rate	Profit/Loss to BSP
596	105	17.62%	-£97.18

Profit or loss backing Top-Weights in handicaps

Runners	Winners	Strike Rate	Profit/Loss to

			BSP
668	78	11.68%	-£103.85

Most profitable sires – non-handicaps

Sire	Runners	Winners	Strike Rate	Profit/Loss to BSP
Fame And Glory	15	3	20.00%	+£164.23
Sir Harry Lewis	11	2	18.18%	+£81.18
Kalanisi	19	4	21.05%	+£42.64
Westerner	40	10	25.00%	+£36.86
Grape Tree Road	13	1	7.69%	+£26.33

Most profitable sires – handicaps

Milan	80	16	20.00%	+£78.82
Zagreb	10	1	10.00%	+£45.34
Saddler's Hall	16	2	12.50%	+£35.03
Mastercraftsman	14	1	7.14%	+£35.02
Flemensfirth	47	9	19.15%	+£28.78

Wincanton - Chases

Top jockeys by Strike Rate – non-handicaps

Name Of Jockey	Rides	Winners	Strike Rate	Profit/Loss to BSP
Daryl Jacob	14	7	50.00%	+£8.85
Harry Cobden	13	4	30.77%	-£3.29

Top jockeys by Strike Rate – handicaps

Name Of Jockey	Rides	Winners	Strike Rate	Profit/Loss to BSP
Paul O'Brien	16	6	37.50%	+£26.33
Jordan Nailor	13	4	30.77%	+£63.37
Tom Bellamy	30	9	30.00%	+£20.79
Conor O'Farrell	17	5	29.41%	+£17.62
A P Heskin	18	5	27.78%	+£6.16

Top jockeys by Profit – non-handicaps

Name Of Jockey	Rides	Winners	Strike Rate	Profit/Loss to BSP
Daryl Jacob	14	7	50.00%	+£8.85

Top jockeys by Profit – handicaps

Name Of Jockey	Rides	Winners	Strike Rate	Profit/Loss to BSP
Mitchell Bastyan	19	3	15.79%	+£67.87
Jordan Nailor	13	4	30.77%	+£63.37
Rex Dingle	24	5	20.83%	+£35.92
Jamie Moore	32	7	21.88%	+£31.20
Ben Poste	15	3	20.00%	+£29.33

Top trainers by Strike Rate – non-handicaps

Name Of Trainer	Runners	Winners	Strike Rate	Profit/Loss to BSP
Paul Nicholls	44	17	38.64%	-£3.57
Philip Hobbs	12	3	25.00%	-£3.61

| Colin Tizzard | 16 | 3 | 18.75% | -£10.22 |

Top trainers by Strike Rate – handicaps

Name Of Trainer	Runners	Winners	Strike Rate	Profit/Loss to BSP
Mrs Jane Williams	10	3	30.00%	+£3.54
David Pipe	58	16	27.59%	+£55.03
Anna Newton-Smith	11	3	27.27%	+£31.50
Nigel Twiston-Davies	43	10	23.26%	+£76.22
Michael Scudamore	13	3	23.08%	+£1.20

Top trainers by Profit – handicaps

Name Of Trainer	Runners	Winners	Strike Rate	Profit/Loss to BSP
Nigel Twiston-Davies	43	10	23.26%	+£76.22
David Pipe	58	16	27.59%	+£55.03
Jeremy Scott	70	10	14.29%	+£33.79
Anna Newton-Smith	11	3	27.27%	+£31.50
Christian Williams	28	4	14.29%	+£23.30

Top trainer/jockey combos by Strike Rate – non-handicaps

Name Of Trainer/Jockey	Rides	Winners	Strike Rate	Profit/Loss to BSP
Paul Nicholls/Harry Cobden	11	4	36.36%	-£1.29

Top trainer/jockey combos by Strike Rate – handicaps

Name of Trainer/Jockey	Qualifiers	Winners	Strike Rate	Profit/Loss to BSP
Nigel Twiston-Davies/Sam	15	5	33.33%	+£26.35

Twiston-Davies				
Paul Nicholls/Harry Cobden	33	10	30.30%	+£1.79
Jeremy Scott/Rex Dingle	10	3	30.00%	+£28.34
Tom George/Paddy Brennan	35	10	28.57%	+£6.09
Colin Tizzard/Harry Cobden	36	10	27.78%	+£11.28

Top trainer/jockey combos by Profit – handicaps

Name of Trainer/Jockey	Qualifiers	Winners	Strike Rate	Profit/Loss to BSP
Jeremy Scott/Rex Dingle	10	3	30.00%	+£28.34
Nigel Twiston-Davies/Sam Twiston-Davies	15	5	33.33%	+£26.35
David Pipe/Tom Scudamore	23	6	26.09%	+£21.59
Kim Bailey/David Bass	12	2	16.67%	+£17.25
Paul Nicholls/Bryony Frost	17	4	23.53%	+£14.74

Profit or Loss backing the unnamed favourite – non-handicaps

Runners	Winners	Strike Rate	Profit/Loss to BSP
211	94	44.55%	-£15.98

Profit or Loss backing the unnamed favourite – handicaps

Runners	Winners	Strike Rate	Profit/Loss to BSP
727	222	30.54%	+£23.20

410

Profit or loss backing the unnamed second favourite - non-handicaps

Runners	Winners	Strike Rate	Profit/Loss to BSP
197	54	27.41%	+£14.22

Profit or loss backing the unnamed second favourite - handicaps

Runners	Winners	Strike Rate	Profit/Loss to BSP
652	136	20.86%	-£4.65

Profit or Loss backing horses who won last time out - non-handicaps

Runners	Winners	Strike Rate	Profit/Loss to BSP
172	53	30.81%	+£0.65

Profit or Loss backing horses who won last time out - handicaps

Runners	Winners	Strike Rate	Profit/Loss to BSP
667	138	20.69%	+£44.01

Profit or loss backing Top-Weights in handicaps

Runners	Winners	Strike Rate	Profit/Loss to BSP
740	132	17.84%	+£64.29

Most profitable sires – handicaps

Shantou	12	2	16.67%	+£33.41
Broadway Flyer	13	3	23.08%	+£29.50
Beat All	12	5	41.67%	+£28.26
Old Vic	24	5	20.83%	+£21.56
Robin Des Pres	33	5	15.15%	+£19.99

Wincanton – Hurdles

Top jockeys by Strike Rate – non-handicaps

Name Of Jockey	Rides	Winners	Strike Rate	Profit/Loss to BSP
Lorcan Williams	11	6	54.55%	+£10.46
Harry Cobden	85	41	48.24%	+£27.59
Daryl Jacob	70	21	30.00%	-£10.42
Sam Twiston-Davies	54	16	29.63%	-£18.36
Harry Skelton	28	8	28.57%	+£8.84

Top jockeys by Strike Rate – handicaps

Name Of Jockey	Rides	Winners	Strike Rate	Profit/Loss to BSP
Bryan Carver	18	6	33.33%	+£73.80
Adam Wedge	27	7	25.93%	+£99.20
Harry Cobden	71	15	21.13%	+£61.00
Mitchell Bastyan	24	5	20.83%	+£13.41
Aidan Coleman	37	7	18.92%	-£1.07

Top jockeys by Profit – non-handicaps

Name Of Jockey	Rides	Winners	Strike Rate	Profit/Loss to BSP
James Davies	43	3	6.98%	+£99.93
James Best	64	2	3.13%	+£90.21
Kevin Jones	24	1	4.17%	+£80.76
Michael Nolan	64	5	7.81%	+£47.00
Harry Cobden	85	41	48.24%	+£27.59

Top jockeys by Profit – handicaps

Name Of Jockey	Rides	Winners	Strike Rate	Profit/Loss to BSP
Adam Wedge	27	7	25.93%	+£99.20
Charlie Deutsch	19	1	5.26%	+£92.98
Rex Dingle	24	4	16.67%	+£77.67
Bryan Carver	18	6	33.33%	+£73.80
Gavin Sheehan	39	6	15.38%	+£68.13

Top trainers by Strike Rate – non-handicaps

Name Of Trainer	Runners	Winners	Strike Rate	Profit/Loss to BSP

Paul Nicholls	203	88	43.35%	+£24.95
Oliver Sherwood	18	6	33.33%	-£1.59
Dan Skelton	32	9	28.13%	+£33.28
Nicky Henderson	38	7	18.42%	-£21.17
Olly Murphy	22	4	18.18%	-£3.74

Top trainers by Strike Rate – handicaps

Name Of Trainer	Runners	Winners	Strike Rate	Profit/Loss to BSP
Tom Lacey	13	4	30.77%	+£15.91
Chris Gordon	39	9	23.08%	+£44.97
Emma Lavelle	40	9	22.50%	+£10.06
Paul Nicholls	149	32	21.48%	+£5.80
Harry Fry	53	10	18.87%	+£19.54

Top trainers by Profit – non-handicaps

Name Of Trainer	Runners	Winners	Strike Rate	Profit/Loss to BSP
Carroll Gray	16	1	6.25%	+£166.96
Chris Down	29	3	10.34%	+£113.93
Milton Harris	18	2	11.11%	+£89.06
Neil Mulholland	100	4	4.00%	+£49.03
Dan Skelton	32	9	28.13%	+£33.28

Top trainers by Profit – handicaps

Name Of Trainer	Runners	Winners	Strike Rate	Profit/Loss to BSP
Alexandra Dunn	39	4	10.26%	+£171.31
Jeremy Scott	88	14	15.91%	+£80.15
Laura Young	19	2	10.53%	+£56.33
Susan Gardner	43	4	9.30%	+£49.43
Chris Gordon	39	9	23.08%	+£44.97

Top trainer/jockey combos by Strike Rate – non-handicaps

Name of Trainer/Jockey	Qualifiers	Winners	Strike Rate	Profit/Loss to BSP
Paul Nicholls/Daryl	30	16	53.33%	+£14.04

Jacob				
Paul Nicholls/Harry Cobden	67	35	52.24%	+£17.63
Paul Nicholls/Sam Twiston-Davies	38	16	42.11%	-£2.36
Dan Skelton/Harry Skelton	19	6	31.58%	+£9.23
Kim Bailey/David Bass	16	5	31.25%	+£20.13

Top trainer/jockey combos by Strike Rate – handicaps

Name of Trainer/Jockey	Qualifiers	Winners	Strike Rate	Profit/Loss to BSP
Paul Nicholls/Harry Cobden	36	11	30.56%	+£11.94
Harry Fry/Sean Bowen	12	3	25.00%	+£24.25
David Pipe/Tom Scudamore	40	9	22.50%	+£4.16
Warren Greatrex/Gavin Sheehan	14	3	21.43%	+£13.07
Jeremy Scott/Nick Scholfield	25	5	20.00%	+£7.00

Top trainer/jockey combos by Profit – non-handicaps

Name of Trainer/Jockey	Qualifiers	Winners	Strike Rate	Profit/Loss to BSP
Chris Down/James Davies	17	3	17.65%	+£125.93
Philip Hobbs/Michael Nolan	24	4	16.67%	+£23.28
Kim Bailey/David	16	5	31.25%	+£20.13

Bass				
Paul Nicholls/Harry Cobden	67	35	52.24%	+£17.63
Paul Nicholls/Daryl Jacob	30	16	53.33%	+£14.04

Top trainer/jockey combos by Profit – handicaps

Name of Trainer/Jockey	Qualifiers	Winners	Strike Rate	Profit/Loss to BSP
Jeremy Scott/Rex Dingle	11	2	18.18%	+£72.99
Susan Gardner/Lucy Gardner	29	4	13.79%	+£63.43
Colin Tizzard/Harry Cobden	24	1	4.17%	+£44.06
Colin Tizzard/Brendan Powell	33	6	18.18%	+£40.00
Tim Vaughan/Alan Johns	16	3	18.75%	+£25.28

Profit or Loss backing the unnamed favourite – non-handicaps

Runners	Winners	Strike Rate	Profit/Loss to BSP
535	270	50.47%	+£14.06

Profit or Loss backing the unnamed favourite – handicaps

Runners	Winners	Strike Rate	Profit/Loss to BSP
658	173	26.29%	-£53.89

Profit or loss backing the unnamed second favourite - non-handicaps

Runners	Winners	Strike Rate	Profit/Loss to BSP

530	117	22.08%	+£30.20

Profit or loss backing the unnamed second favourite - handicaps

Runners	Winners	Strike Rate	Profit/Loss to BSP
622	123	19.77%	+£50.83

Profit or Loss backing horses who won last time out- non-handicaps

Runners	Winners	Strike Rate	Profit/Loss to BSP
349	117	33.52%	+£46.67

Profit or Loss backing horses who won last time out - handicaps

Runners	Winners	Strike Rate	Profit/Loss to BSP
606	110	18.15%	-£56.78

Profit or loss backing Top-Weights in handicaps

Runners	Winners	Strike Rate	Profit/Loss to BSP
716	94	13.13%	-£6.70

Most profitable sires – non-handicaps

Sire	Runners	Winners	Strike Rate	Profit/Loss to BSP
Saint Des Saints	13	7	53.85%	+£189.41
Fair Mix	20	2	10.00%	+£127.47
Kalanisi	21	3	14.29%	+£50.97
Shirocco	31	5	16.13%	+£29.54
Kayf Tara	62	15	24.19%	+£9.48

Most profitable sires – handicaps

Brian Boru	29	5	17.24%	+£58.98
Polish Precedent	12	1	8.33%	+£53.47
Tobougg	18	1	5.56%	+£50.06
Midnight Legend	72	7	9.72%	+£39.01
Definite Article	18	3	16.67%	+£37.95

Worcester - Chases

Top jockeys by Strike Rate – non-handicaps

Name Of Jockey	Rides	Winners	Strike Rate	Profit/Loss to BSP
Daryl Jacob	12	5	41.67%	+£30.47
Sam Twiston-Davies	38	13	34.21%	-£4.84
Aidan Coleman	22	7	31.82%	+£9.25
Sean Bowen	11	3	27.27%	+£35.50
Harry Skelton	14	3	21.43%	+£18.82

Top jockeys by Strike Rate – handicaps

Name Of Jockey	Rides	Winners	Strike Rate	Profit/Loss to BSP
Gavin Sheehan	39	10	25.64%	+£51.16
Liam Harrison	12	3	25.00%	-£2.48
David Bass	23	5	21.74%	+£20.21
Aidan Coleman	72	15	20.83%	+£8.36
Sean Bowen	64	13	20.32%	+£6.05

Top jockeys by Profit – non-handicaps

Name Of Jockey	Rides	Winners	Strike Rate	Profit/Loss to BSP
Sean Bowen	11	3	27.27%	+£35.50
Daryl Jacob	12	5	41.67%	+£30.47
Harry Skelton	14	3	21.43%	+£18.82
Aidan Coleman	22	7	31.82%	+£9.25
Tom Scudamore	15	2	13.33%	+£4.98

Top jockeys by Profit – handicaps

Name Of Jockey	Rides	Winners	Strike Rate	Profit/Loss to BSP
Brendan Powell	65	11	16.92%	+£114.62
Gavin Sheehan	39	10	25.64%	+£51.16
Sean Houlihan	17	2	11.76%	+£44.78

Tom O'Brien	74	12	16.22%	+£40.61
Alan Johns	27	4	14.81%	+£40.43

Top trainers by Strike Rate – non-handicaps

Name Of Trainer	Runners	Winners	Strike Rate	Profit/Loss to BSP
Paul Nicholls	29	12	41.38%	+£4.65
Nigel Hawke	11	4	36.36%	+£41.84
Neil Mulholland	12	4	33.33%	-£2.51
Dr Richard Newland	15	5	33.33%	-£1.29
Nigel Twiston-Davies	12	4	33.33%	£1.26

Top trainers by Strike Rate – handicaps

Name Of Trainer	Runners	Winners	Strike Rate	Profit/Loss to BSP
Rebecca Curtis	18	6	33.33%	+£21.78
Robert Walford	10	3	30.00%	+£0.23
Kerry Lee	17	5	29.41%	+£21.75
Neil King	14	4	28.57%	+£30.72
Caroline Bailey	14	4	28.57%	+£7.80

Top trainers by Profit – non-handicaps

Name Of Trainer	Runners	Winners	Strike Rate	Profit/Loss to BSP
Nigel Hawke	11	4	36.36%	+£41.84
Dan Skelton	16	4	25.00%	+£19.85
Jonjo O'Neill	26	7	26.92%	+£9.59
Paul Nicholls	29	12	41.38%	+£4.65

Top trainers by Profit – handicaps

Name Of Trainer	Runners	Winners	Strike Rate	Profit/Loss to BSP
Philip Hobbs	68	15	22.06%	+£56.45
Sheila Lewis	10	2	20.00%	+£51.78
Emma Lavelle	37	9	24.32%	+£47.16
Ben Pauling	30	8	26.67%	+£43.82
Donald McCain	39	10	25.64%	+£40.73

Top trainer/jockey combos by Strike Rate – non-handicaps

Name Of Trainer/Jockey	Rides	Winners	Strike Rate	Profit/Loss to BSP
Nigel Twiston-Davies/Sam Twiston-Davies	10	4	40.00%	+£0.74
Dr Richard Newland/Sam Twiston-Davies	11	4	36.36%	+£0.83
Paul Nicholls/Sam Twiston-Davies	11	4	36.36%	-£1.72
Dan Skelton/Harry Skelton	12	3	25.00%	+£20.82

Top trainer/jockey combos by Strike Rate – handicaps

Name of Trainer/Jockey	Qualifiers	Winners	Strike Rate	Profit/Loss to BSP
Charlie Longsdon/Aidan Coleman	10	3	30.00%	+£14.23
Kim Bailey/David Bass	10	3	30.00%	+£1.76
Peter Bowen/Sean Bowen	38	11	28.95%	+£16.20
Jeremy Scott/Nick Scholfield	16	4	25.00%	+£2.61
Philip Hobbs/Tom O'Brien	26	6	23.08%	+£31.84

Top trainer/jockey combos by Profit – non-handicaps

Name of Trainer/Jockey	Qualifiers	Winners	Strike Rate	Profit/Loss to BSP
Dan	12	3	25.00%	+£20.82

Skelton/Harry Skelton				
Dr Richard Newland/Sam Twiston-Davies	11	4	36.36%	+£0.83
Nigel Twiston-Davies/Sam Twiston-Davies	10	4	40.00%	+£0.74

Top trainer/jockey combos by Profit – handicaps

Name of Trainer/Jockey	Qualifiers	Winners	Strike Rate	Profit/Loss to BSP
Tim Vaughan/Alan Johns	22	4	18.18%	+£45.43
Rosemary Gasson/Ben Poste	15	3	20.00%	+£40.24
Philip Hobbs/Tom O'Brien	26	6	23.08%	+£31.84
Charlie Longsdon/Jonathan Burke	14	1	7.14%	+£23.18
Peter Bowen/Sean Bowen	38	11	28.95%	+£16.20

Profit or Loss backing the unnamed favourite – non-handicaps

Runners	Winners	Strike Rate	Profit/Loss to BSP
239	96	40.17%	-£15.95

Profit or Loss backing the unnamed favourite – handicaps

Runners	Winners	Strike Rate	Profit/Loss to BSP
709	181	25.53%	-£60.01

Profit or loss backing the unnamed second favourite - non-handicaps

Runners	Winners	Strike Rate	Profit/Loss to BSP
222	64	28.83%	+£15.06

Profit or loss backing the unnamed second favourite - handicaps

Runners	Winners	Strike Rate	Profit/Loss to BSP
633	106	16.75%	-£57.28

Profit or Loss backing horses who won last time out - non-handicaps

Runners	Winners	Strike Rate	Profit/Loss to BSP
144	37	25.69%	-£38.59

Profit or Loss backing horses who won last time out - handicaps

Runners	Winners	Strike Rate	Profit/Loss to BSP
599	96	16.03%	-£46.31

Profit or loss backing Top-Weights in handicaps

Runners	Winners	Strike Rate	Profit/Loss to BSP
738	96	13.01%	+£27.59

Most profitable sires – non-handicaps

Sire	Runners	Winners	Strike Rate	Profit/Loss to BSP
Presenting	22	3	13.64%	+£14.02
Winged Love	11	2	18.18%	+£4.24
Oscar	17	6	35.29%	+£1.16

Most profitable sires – handicaps

Dr Massini	42	8	19.05%	+£69.32
Robin Des Pres	26	5	19.23%	+£67.82
Sulamani	13	2	15.38%	+£38.02
Anshan	21	3	14.29%	+£37.86
Network	18	4	22.22%	+£36.86

Worcester – Hurdles

Top jockeys by Strike Rate – non-handicaps

Name Of Jockey	Rides	Winners	Strike Rate	Profit/Loss to BSP
James Bowen	21	7	33.33%	+£51.50
Harry Cobden	13	4	30.77%	+£3.13
Tom Bellamy	21	5	23.81%	+£12.91
Harry Skelton	59	14	23.73%	+£6.59
Paddy Brennan	63	14	22.22%	-£16.49

Top jockeys by Strike Rate – handicaps

Name Of Jockey	Rides	Winners	Strike Rate	Profit/Loss to BSP
Marc Goldstein	14	5	35.71%	+£25.97
Kevin Brogan	12	3	25.00%	+£24.64
Liam Harrison	18	4	22.22%	+£67.39
Jack Quinlan	26	5	19.23%	+£10.54
Richard Patrick	26	5	19.23%	+£19.89

Top jockeys by Profit – non-handicaps

Name Of Jockey	Rides	Winners	Strike Rate	Profit/Loss to BSP
Michael Nolan	28	3	10.71%	+£238.41
Sean Bowen	27	4	14.81%	+£208.09
William Kennedy	28	4	14.29%	+£65.16
James Bowen	21	7	33.33%	+£51.50
Kielan Woods	30	6	20.00%	+£42.57

Top jockeys by Profit – handicaps

Name Of Jockey	Rides	Winners	Strike Rate	Profit/Loss to BSP
Jamie Moore	58	7	12.07%	+£84.55
Liam Harrison	18	4	22.22%	+£67.39
Charlie Price	12	2	16.67%	+£66.89
Tom Cannon	50	6	12.00%	+£56.73
Adam Wedge	56	9	16.07%	+£52.34

Top trainers by Strike Rate – non-handicaps

Name Of Trainer	Runners	Winners	Strike Rate	Profit/Loss to

				BSP
Nicky Henderson	49	20	40.82%	+£38.28
Alan King	29	10	34.48%	+£2.12
Kim Bailey	27	9	33.33%	+£11.52
Paul Nicholls	34	11	32.35%	+£1.08
Olly Murphy	13	4	30.77%	+£5.28

Top trainers by Strike Rate – handicaps

Name Of Trainer	Runners	Winners	Strike Rate	Profit/Loss to BSP
Amy Murphy	11	5	45.45%	+£25.54
D J Jeffreys	10	3	30.00%	+£15.53
Bernard Llewellyn	11	3	27.27%	+£20.98
Harry Whittington	16	4	25.00%	+£10.47
Debra Hamer	46	11	23.91%	+£41.63

Top trainers by Profit – non-handicaps

Name Of Trainer	Runners	Winners	Strike Rate	Profit/Loss to BSP
Peter Bowen	20	5	25.00%	+£227.64
Philip Hobbs	58	16	27.59%	+£201.00
Rebecca Curtis	30	8	26.67%	+£150.49
Martin Keighley	41	3	7.32%	+£79.16
Fergal O'Brien	73	16	21.92%	+£60.22

Top trainers by Profit – handicaps

Name Of Trainer	Runners	Winners	Strike Rate	Profit/Loss to BSP
Michael Scudamore	33	4	12.12%	+£77.89
Neil Mulholland	150	23	15.33%	+£67.89
Laura Young	36	8	22.22%	+£66.08
Laura Mongan	20	3	15.00%	+£61.41
Alexandra Dunn	39	3	7.69%	+£55.79

Top trainer/jockey combos by Strike Rate – non-handicaps

Name of Trainer/Jockey	Qualifiers	Winners	Strike Rate	Profit/Loss to BSP
Nicky Henderson/Nico de Boinville	20	7	35.00%	-£2.73
Dr Richard Newland/Charlie Hammond	10	3	30.00%	-£3.08
Philip Hobbs/Tom O'Brien	10	3	30.00%	-£2.00
Fergal O'Brien/Paddy Brennan	42	12	28.57%	-£3.57
Dan Skelton/Harry Skelton	53	13	24.53%	-£9.43

Top trainer/jockey combos by Strike Rate – handicaps

Name of Trainer/Jockey	Qualifiers	Winners	Strike Rate	Profit/Loss to BSP
Shaun Lycett/Marc Goldstein	10	5	50.00%	+£29.97
Amy Murphy/Jack Quinlan	11	5	45.45%	+£25.54
Jeremy Scott/Nick Scholfield	11	4	36.36%	+£13.96
Robert Stephens/Tom O'Brien	22	7	31.82%	+£15.92
John Spearing/Jamie Moore	12	3	25.00%	+£14.23

Top trainer/jockey combos by Profit – non-handicaps

Name of Trainer/Jockey	Qualifiers	Winners	Strike Rate	Profit/Loss to BSP
David	19	4	21.05%	+£23.44

Bridgwater/Tom Scudamore				
David Pipe/Tom Scudamore	37	7	18.92%	+£22.14
Robert Stephens/Tom O'Brien	11	2	18.18%	+£4.50
Kim Bailey/David Bass	14	3	21.43%	+£2.15

Top trainer/jockey combos by Profit – handicaps

Name of Trainer/Jockey	Qualifiers	Winners	Strike Rate	Profit/Loss to BSP
Laura Mongan/Tom Cannon	12	3	25.00%	+£69.41
David Pipe/Tom Scudamore	81	16	19.75%	+£36.42
Shaun Lycett/Marc Goldstein	10	5	50.00%	+£29.97
Amy Murphy/Jack Quinlan	11	5	45.45%	+£25.54
Sarah-Jayne Davies/William Kennedy	14	1	7.14%	+£17.38

Profit or Loss backing the unnamed favourite – non-handicaps

Runners	Winners	Strike Rate	Profit/Loss to BSP
685	312	45.55%	+£37.26

Profit or Loss backing the unnamed favourite – handicaps

Runners	Winners	Strike Rate	Profit/Loss to BSP
814	214	26.29%	-£29.30

Profit or loss backing the unnamed second favourite - non-handicaps

Runners	Winners	Strike Rate	Profit/Loss to BSP
622	149	23.95%	+£38.57

Profit or loss backing the unnamed second favourite - handicaps

Runners	Winners	Strike Rate	Profit/Loss to BSP
774	127	16.41%	-£40.98

Profit or Loss backing horses who won last time out- non-handicaps

Runners	Winners	Strike Rate	Profit/Loss to BSP
383	126	32.90%	-£39.77

Profit or Loss backing horses who won last time out - handicaps

Runners	Winners	Strike Rate	Profit/Loss to BSP
806	154	19.11%	-£2.55

Profit or loss backing Top-Weights in handicaps

Runners	Winners	Strike Rate	Profit/Loss to BSP
901	96	10.65%	-£120.37

Most profitable sires – non-handicaps

Sire	Runners	Winners	Strike Rate	Profit/Loss to BSP
Scorpion	31	7	22.58%	+£192.40
Robin Des Champs	14	2	14.29%	+£149.54
Multiplex	23	3	13.04%	+£94.26
Dr Massini	24	3	13.04%	+£66.78
Passing Glance	18	6	33.33%	+£22.45

Most profitable sires – handicaps

Sir Harry Lewis	19	2	10.53%	+£157.82
Court Cave	46	12	26.09%	+£133.20

Montjeu	15	2	13.33%	+£53.64
Fame And Glory	24	3	12.50%	+£50.77
Halling	41	10	24.39%	+£43.55

Testimonials:

"Sean and I have worked together for many years now, and his knowledge of racing is well known and respected throughout the industry. If the articles and opinion shared with readers of News - The World of Sport are any indication as to just how valuable this book will be to punters, then it's a "must have" weapon in your punting arsenal. If you do not bet using stats, you will lose more often than you win and, whether you bet for profit or fun, you need this on your side"

Ron Robinson – Owner, The World of Sport

"Sean Trivass is better known as the 'Statman' to my readers and has contributed excellent comprehensive articles on horse racing for my monthly newsletter What really Wins Money. His stats angles are totally unique and a real deep dive into the world of horse racing stats based betting angles.

He's looked at jockeys, trainers, race courses, sires and dams (breeding), the draw, the all weather, favourites, 2nd and 3rd favourites , ground conditions, race distance, handicaps versus non-handicap and many other angles, for both the horse racing backer and layer.

There have been some real eye-catching finds from Sean's work, some of which I use myself. This guy knows his onions! "

Clive Keeling – What Really Wins Money

"Statistics can be presented in many a varied manner for varied reasons and we are right to retain a sceptical mind of them and how and why they are revealed. However, with horse racing they are a vital component and my colleague Sean Trivass is an equally vital component in collating and interpreting them for our use.

Watching, listening, reading Sean's dissection of a field using his calibrated statistics is a racing marvel. He professes to not liking full-sized handicap fields, but in reality he is in his element pouring over the variables using his statistics as he slices and dices the field into a logical order for the likes of you and I to understand.

Group 1 elite contests to the full field handicaps are all part of Sean's vision and depth of years of experience. From watching the world's best on the track to a humble maiden, he approaches each contest with the same enthusiasm to find the outcome

I have watched and enjoyed Sean's work for twenty years as we have travelled to race meetings in many parts of the globe and when back home in Australia he is my guide for UK racing. Racing is international, broadcasting 24 hours a day somewhere in the world, and Sean's delving into the statistics give us all a steady platform to participate".

Rob Burnet
Editor
Thoroughbrednews.com.au

Finally, should you have any questions (no abuse thank you, all of this has been written in good faith) or just want to know a little bit more about my upcoming projects and books, feel free to contact me via www.writesports.net

Printed in Great Britain
by Amazon

46748655R00242